Structural Conflict

STUDIES IN INTERNATIONAL POLITICAL ECONOMY

Edited by Stephen D. Krasner
Department of Political Science
Stanford University

Albert O. Hirschman, *National Power and the Structure of Foreign Trade*

Robert A. Pastor, *Congress and the Politics of U.S. Foreign Economic Policy 1929–1976*

Oran R. Young, *Natural Resources and the State: The Political Economy of Resource Management*

Oran R. Young, *Resource Regimes: Natural Resources and Social Institutions*

Stephen J. Kobrin, *Managing Political Risk Assessment: Strategic Response to Environmental Change*

Charles Lipson, *Standing Guard: Protecting Foreign Capital in the Nineteenth and Twentieth Centuries*

Stephen D. Krasner, *Structural Conflict: The Third World Against Global Liberalism*

STRUCTURAL CONFLICT

The Third World Against Global Liberalism

Stephen D. Krasner

University of California Press / Berkeley, Los Angeles, London

University of California Press
Berkeley and Los Angeles, California

University of California Press, Ltd.
London, England

Copyright © 1985 by The Regents of the University of California

Library of Congress Cataloging in Publication Data

Krasner, Stephen D., 1942–
   Structural conflict

   (Studies in international political economy)
   Bibliography
   Includes index.
   1. Developing countries—Foreign economic relations.   2. International
economic relations.   I. Title.   II. Series.
   HF1413.K68   1985   337'.09172'4   84–16332
   ISBN 0–520–05400–8
        0–520–05478–4 (pbk.)

Printed in the United States of America

          5   6   7   8   9

For Joan

Contents

Acknowledgments

In writing, rewriting, and revising this manuscript I have accumulated more debts than I can remember, perhaps more than I care to remember. The critical observations of my colleagues and friends at many professional meetings forced me to reconsider a number of arguments that in the final analysis were untenable. Several individuals were particularly generous. Roger Hansen and Abraham Lowenthal provided comments on an earlier version of the manuscript and Peter Katzenstein and Charles Lipson suggested many ways in which the penultimate draft could be improved. The recommendations of Alan Cafruny, Ann Hollick, and M. J. Peterson prevented me from making a number of errors in chapters 8 and 9. Katherine Elwood, David Lumsdaine, and Mark Woodward provided very helpful research assistance. John Kroll very ably carried out the statistical analysis for some of the findings presented in chapter 4. Wilma Fuller and especially Willa Leonard met my many requests for typing with a level of efficiency that cannot simply be attributed to the availability of a word processing system. Financial support was provided by the Faculty Senate of the University of California, Los Angeles, and the Committee on Research in International Studies at Stanford. Sections of this manuscript earlier appeared in *International Organization, International Studies Quarterly,* and the *Review of International Studies.*

Part One

Argument

I

Introduction: The Argument

What do Third World countries want? More wealth. How can they get it? By adopting more economically rational policies. What should the North do? Facilitate these policies. How should the North approach global negotiations? With cautious optimism. What is the long-term prognosis for North-South relations? Hopeful, at least if economic development occurs. This is the common wisdom about relations between industrialized and developing areas in the United States and in much of the rest of the North. Within this fold there are intense debates among adherents of conventional liberal, basic human needs, and interdependence viewpoints. But the emphasis on economics at the expense of politics, on material well-being as opposed to power and control, pervades all of these orientations.

In this book, I set forth an alternative perspective. I assume that Third World states, like all states in the international system, are concerned about vulnerability and threat; and I note that national political regimes in almost all Third World countries are profoundly weak both internationally and domestically. This book offers a very different set of answers to the questions posed in the preceding paragraph. Third World states want power and control as much as wealth. One strategy for achieving this objective is to change the rules of the game in various international issue areas. In general, these efforts will be incompatible with long-term Northern interests. Relations between industrialized and developing areas are bound to be conflictual because most Southern countries cannot hope to cope with their international vulnerability except by challenging principles, norms, and rules preferred by industrialized countries.

Political weakness and vulnerability are fundamental sources of Third World behavior. This weakness is a product of both external and internal factors. Externally, the national power capabilities of most Third World states are extremely limited. The national economic and military resources at the disposal of their leaders are unlikely to alter the behavior of Northern actors or the nature of international regimes. Southern states are subject to external pressures that they cannot influence through unilateral action. The international weakness of almost all less developed countries (LDCs) is compounded by the internal underdevelopment of their political and social systems. The social structures of most LDCs are rigid, and their central political institutions lack the power to make societal adjustments that could cushion external shocks. They are exposed to vacillations of an international system from which they cannot extricate themselves but over which they have only limited control.[1] The gap between Northern and Southern capabilities is already so great that even if the countries of the South grew very quickly and those of the North stagnated (an unlikely pair of assumptions in any event), only a handful of developing countries would significantly close the power gap within the next one hundred years. The physical conditions of individuals in developing areas may improve dramatically without altering the political vulnerabilities that confront their political leaders.

Third World states have adopted a range of strategies to cope with their poverty and vulnerability. Strategies directed primarily toward alleviating vulnerability are most frequently played out in international forums concerned with the establishment or maintenance of international regimes. Regimes are principles, norms, rules, and decision-making procedures around which actor expectations converge. Principles are a coherent set of theoretical statements about how the world works. Norms specify general standards of behavior. Rules and decision-making procedures refer to specific prescriptions for behavior in clearly defined areas. For instance, a liberal international regime for trade is based on a set of neoclassical economic principles that demonstrate that global utility is maximized by the free flow of goods. The basic norm of a liberal trading regime is that tariff and nontariff barriers should be reduced and ultimately eliminated. Specific rules and decision-making procedures are spelled out in the General Agreement on Tariffs and Trade. Principles and norms define the basic character of any regime. Although rules and

---

[1]The two major exceptions to this generalization are the small number of developing countries that are so large that they can limit external interactions, notably China and India, and a few smaller developing states that have flexible and effective sociopolitical and economic structures that allow them to adjust to international conditions, such as the newly industrializing countries (NICs) in Southeast Asia—South Korea, Taiwan, Singapore, and Hong Kong.

decision-making procedures can be changed without altering the fundamental nature of a regime, principles and norms cannot. Regimes define basic property rights. They establish acceptable patterns of behavior. They coordinate decision making. They can enhance global well-being by allowing actors to escape from situations in which individual decision making leads to Pareto-suboptimal outcomes. Changes in regimes can alter the control and allocation of resources among actors in the international system. Every state wants more control over international regimes in order to make its own basic values and interests more secure.[2]

The Third World has supported international regimes that would ameliorate its weakness. As a group, the developing countries have consistently endorsed principles and norms that would legitimate more authoritative as opposed to more market-oriented modes of allocation. Authoritative allocation involves either the direct allocation of resources by political authorities, or indirect allocation by limiting the property rights of nonstate actors, including private corporations. A market-oriented regime is one in which the allocation of resources is determined by the endowments and preferences of individual actors who have the right to alienate their property according to their own estimations of their own best interests.

For developing countries, authoritative international regimes are attractive because they can provide more stable and predictable transaction flows. External shocks and pressures are threatening to developing countries because their slack resources and adjustment capabilities are so limited. Shocks are particularly troubling for political leaders because they are the likely targets of unrest generated by sudden declines in material well-being. Authoritative regimes may also provide a level of resource transfer that developing countries could not secure through market-oriented exchange. Given equal levels of resource transfer, developing states prefer authoritative to market-oriented regimes. Even when market-oriented regimes are accompanied by substantial increases in wealth, as has been the case in the post–World War II period, developing states have still sought authoritative regimes that would provide more security. I do not claim in this study that developing countries prefer control to wealth; rather I argue that authoritative regimes can provide them with both, whereas market-oriented ones cannot. I do not claim that LDCs are uninterested in wealth for its own sake. Purely wealth-

[2]Gilpin, *War and Change*, p. 50; Krasner, *International Regimes*, esp. pts. 1 and 2.

oriented activities can be pursued within existing international regimes at the same time that developing states seek basic changes in principles and norms. But I do claim that the South has fundamentally challenged the extant liberal order, most visibly in the call for a New International Economic Order.

The general goal of moving toward more authoritative international regimes has been pursued using two, more specific strategies. First, the Third World has sought to alter existing international institutions, or create new ones that would be more congruent with its preferred principles and norms. Second, developing countries have pressed for regimes that would legitimate the unilateral assertion of sovereign authority by individual states. With regard to international institutions, Third World states have demanded greater participation in global forums. They have supported universal organizations with one-nation, one-vote decision-making procedures. They have pressed for the creation of new bureaucracies that would be more sympathetic to regimes based on authoritative allocation. For instance, in the area of trade, UNCTAD (the United Nations Conference on Trade and Development) was created to offer a counterweight to the General Agreement on Tariffs and Trade (GATT), which was perceived by developing countries as an institution dedicated to a market-oriented approach. International organizations based on authoritative rather than market-oriented principles can limit the discretionary behavior of Northern actors by redefining property rights including, in the most extreme case, compelling additional resource transfers from the North to the South. For instance, the Law of the Sea Convention provides for the compulsory transfer of technology from multinational corporations to an international entity called the Enterprise, the operating instrument of the International Sea-Bed Authority. The UNCTAD Liner Code states that liners from developing countries (ocean freighters plying regular routes on regular schedules) ought to have 40 percent of the cargo originating in their own home ports.

The second strategy pursued by the Third World has been to support international regimes that legitimate the right of individual states to exercise sovereign control over a wider range of activities than previously. The Third World has sought to enhance the scope of activities that are universally accepted as subject to the unilateral control of the state. For instance, Latin American countries led the fight for extended economic zones in the ocean. By securing international acceptance of this right at the United Nations Conference on the Law of the Sea, developing coastal countries were able to secure both greater economic returns and more control than would have been the case if narrower limits had been recognized. By accepting property-right claims that were being unilaterally asserted by developing countries, the international community greatly reduced the costs of enforcement. Similarly, in dealing with multinational corporations, the Third World has sought international legitimation of national controls. Such legitimation limits competition among developing countries and makes it more difficult for multinational corporations and their home governments to challenge host-country policies either legally or diplomatically. The South has also resisted Northern efforts to create new international regimes that would delimit existing sovereign powers. For instance, the Third World has rejected Northern efforts to legitimate new international norms regarding population control and individual human rights. The regime objectives pursued by the Third World are designed to limit the market power of the North by enhancing the sovereign prerogatives of the South, either through universal international organizations in which each nation has a single vote, or by widening the scope of activities exclusively subject to the unilateral sovereign will of individual developing states.

The demands associated with proposals for the New International Economic Order (NIEO), which assumed their greatest saliency in the mid-1970s, are the clearest manifestation of Third World efforts to restructure market-oriented international regimes. The NIEO and related proposals covered a wide range of issue areas, including trade, primary commodities, aid, debt, space, multinational corporations, journalism, and shipping. The NIEO was the culmination of Third World efforts that had begun in the 1940s.

The degree to which developing countries have succeeded in altering international regimes has been a function of three variables: the nature of existing institutional structures; the ability to formulate a coherent system of ideas, which set the agenda for international negotiations and cemented Third World unity; and the attitude and power of the North, especially the United States, toward both the demands of the South and the forums in which they have been made.

The nature of existing regime structures, including existing international organizations, has influenced the ability of Third World states to secure an environment governed by authoritative, as opposed to market, allocation. The most important general institutional advantage enjoyed by the Third World has been the acceptance of the principle of the sovereign equality of states. There have always been weak states in the international system, although in recent years disparities in per capita income have magnified distinctions in size and population. Before the twentieth century, however, the great powers were accepted as the dominant actors in the system, possessing rights of unilateral action that were denied to smaller states: the principle of great-power primacy dominated that of sovereign equality. At best, small states could maintain a precarious neutrality, relying on the balance of power to provide them with some freedom of action. In the present system the principle of sovereign equality dominates that of great-power primacy, and states with the most exiguous national power capabilities deny that others have special prerogatives.

The most important organizational manifestation of the principle of sovereign equality has been the United Nations. The U.N. system provided the major forums at which developing countries could present their demands. Developing states have had automatic access to United Nations agencies. With the exception of international financial institutions and the Security Council, states have had equal voting power. New agencies such as UNCTAD and UNIDO (U.N. Industrial Development Organization) have been created. The standard operating procedures of agencies have been changed. In areas where existing institutions limited access, such as with the Antarctic, developing states have had little success. If the United Nations had not existed, it would have been impossible for the Third World to articulate a general program for altering international regimes.

Aside from nonspecialized universal institutions, the principles, norms, rules, and decision-making procedures confronting Third World countries in a number of specific issue areas conditioned their ability to secure their objectives. For developing states the most attractive situations have been ones in which existing international regimes, supported by the North, already embodied norms of authoritative, rather than market, allocation. If developing countries could secure access to these regimes, they could make claims on resources that would have been barred to them in a market-oriented world. For instance, the regime governing civil aviation has, since its inception after World War I, been governed by principles emphasizing state security, and norms that call for an equal allocation of traffic between foreign and domestic carriers in any given national market. Furthermore, fares have been influenced by agreements among airline companies, which are subject to state approval. This regime gave any Third World country that wanted to begin its own national airline a presumptive right to passengers, a reciprocal right to landing privileges, and some guarantee against competitive rate-cutting. Many Third World states took advantage of this situation. In contrast, critical aspects of ocean shipping have been governed by norms and rules (some of whose antecedents stretch back to the late Middle Ages) which are predominantly based on commercial principles emphasizing market allocation. Some rate structures have been negotiated by cartels, to which developing country shipping lines have limited access. The legitimation of flags of convenience has offset some of the competitive advantage that developing countries might have had from cheap labor. Developing countries have been less successful in establishing their own shipping lines than in establishing their own commercial airlines, in part because of the nature of existing international regimes.

The second variable affecting the ability of developing countries to secure their preferred international regimes has been the coherence of the ideological arguments used to rationalize and justify their demands. The degree of coherence has increased over time. Developing states were never entranced with the liberal market-oriented regimes established at the conclusion of the Second World War. But their initial forays were limited to sniping at bits and pieces of this order and calling attention to areas where developed states had violated their own liberal principles. However, beginning with the work of Raul Prebisch at the Economic Commission for Latin America in the late 1940s, spokesmen for Third World countries developed a set of arguments that placed the major responsibility for underdevelopment on the workings of the international system rather than on the specific characteristics of developing countries and the policies adopted by their leaders. This line of argument was developed and propagated over time, drawing on Marxist as well as conventional economic analyses. The ability of the Third World to present a coherent world view—one which depicted the exploitation of the Third World as an inherent feature of the global economy—provided a rationale for making demands on the North, helped the Group of 77 (formed at the first UNCTAD meeting by seventy-seven LDCs) to coordinate its programs across several issue areas, and reduced negotiating costs among developing countries by suggesting specific policy proposals. By the early 1970s the industrialized world was on the defensive in major international forums. The agenda was being set by the Third World. The Gramscian hegemony enjoyed by liberal doctrines in the immediate postwar period had been totally undermined. It was rejected by almost all Third World leaders and questioned by many specific groups, including some policymakers, in the North.

The final variable influencing the degree of success realized by the Third World in securing international regimes based upon authoritative allocation has been the power of the North, especially that of the United States. This too changed over time. The United States emerged from the Second World War in an extraordinarily dominant position. Its physical plant had not been damaged by the fighting. Its gross national product was three times as large as that of its main rival, the Soviet Union. It had a monopoly on nuclear weapons. It enjoyed a technological advantage over its major competitors in most industrial sectors. Over time this domination has eroded. The Europeans and the Japanese recovered. The Soviet Union and several other countries secured nuclear weapons. The Japanese challenged the United States even in the most technologically advanced industries. Dependence on imported energy supplies increased dramatically. Vietnam undermined the domestic consensus that had supported U.S. foreign policy.[3]

The early 1970s proved to be the most propitious moment for the developing world to launch a major attack on the liberal international order that had been so assiduously cultivated by U.S. policymakers. The United States had been the moving force behind the international organizations created at the conclusion of the Second World War. For a hegemonic power, the purpose of such organizations is to legitimate its preferences, and values. Legitimation requires that the organizations be given autonomy. If they are seen merely as handmaidens of the hegemon, they will be ineffective. Despite formal autonomy, the United States had great influence over specific decisions and general policies in all major international organizations through the 1950s.

Decolonization eroded American influence. In the United Nations, and in other international organizations, voting majorities changed. Third World states questioned both the underlying values and specific policy preferences of the United States. This did not immediately lead to an American renunciation of existing institutions, however, or even to a decline in American commitments. In the absence of alternatives, such a radical shift was unattractive because Third World behavior could be

[3]Holsti and Rosenau, "Vietnam, Consensus, and the Belief Systems of American Leaders."

interpreted as a temporary aberration, and the reaction of other countries to a dramatic change could not be easily gauged. At least some American policymakers were committed to the strategy, deeply rooted in basic American attitudes toward international affairs, of resolving conflicts through negotiations and international agreements. Thus, despite a growing inability to influence decisions in the United Nations and other international forums, the United States did not simply walk out. Had it done so the developing world would have been reduced to vacuous rhetoric in chambers devoid of influence, if not of individuals.

The early 1970s offered a unique window of opportunity for the Third World because it was a period characterized by Third World control of major international forums but continued Northern commitment. Through the 1960s the South had not wielded itself into a disciplined voting block or presented a coherent program across many issue areas. By the late 1970s, Northern commitments had begun to erode, especially those of the United States. Financial contributions declined. The United States temporarily withdrew from the International Labor Organization in the late 1970s, and in January 1985 formally withdrew from UNESCO. Other industrialized market-economy states, notably Great Britain, also indicated their deep dissatisfaction with UNESCO. In 1982, several Northern states, including the United States, rejected the United Nations Law of the Sea Convention. Without American participation the Convention is of limited utility. In January 1985 the United States, for the first time, refused to take part in a World Court case, an action in defiance of the Court's rules.

In sum, the desire to secure international regimes embodying authoritative rather than market allocation of resources has been an enduring aspect of Third World policy in the postwar period. It reflects the profound national weakness of most developing countries. This weakness stems from the inability to influence unilaterally or to adjust internally to the pressures of global markets. Larger industrialized states are able to influence the international environment and can adjust internally. Smaller industrialized states have little influence over the global pattern of transactions, but their domestic political economies allow them to adjust. Small size and inflexible domestic structures make Third World states vulnerable: severe domestic political and economic dislocation can occur as a result of shocks and fluctuations emanating from the international system. Such dislocation can be especially painful for political leaders who become the targets of a counter-elite or of popular discontent.

By changing the nature of international regimes, Third World leaders hope not only to increase the flow of material resources but also to create a more predictable and stable environment. The success of developing countries in pursuing their regime objectives has depended on the nature of extant institutional arrangements, their ability to articulate a coherent viewpoint, and the willingness of the North, particularly the United States, to tolerate international forums that produced undesired results. These last two factors explain why the North-South conflict reached such intensity during the mid-1970s. At that moment, the South had developed an effective ideological position, the international forums were available, and the United States was still committed to global negotiations. Ironically, it was the last years of the American hegemonic apogee that provided weak states with their greatest opportunity to attack the prevailing order.

This interpretation of Southern behavior draws upon a structural, or third-image, approach to international politics which maintains that the behavior of states is determined by their relative power capabilities.[4] The countries of the South are not purveyors of some new and superior morality, nor are their policies any less reasonable than those of the industrialized world. They are behaving the way states have always behaved; they are trying to maximize their power—their ability to control their own destinies. The claims of the Group of 77 have been based on the equality of sovereign states and have been made for the state and the state alone, not for individual citizens.[5] For developing countries, restructuring regimes was an attractive strategy, particularly in the early 1970s, because of their lack of national power capabilities, their ability to break the ideological hegemony of the North, and the access provided by international organizations.

The implications of this analysis for maintaining universal principles and norms are not sanguine. Effective international regime construction, as opposed to regime maintenance, is difficult. Historically, new regimes are most easily created by hegemonic states possessing overwhelming military, economic, and ideological power. Once regimes are created, narrow calculations of interests, uncertainty about alternatives, and habit may provide support even if the power of the hegemonic state fades and its policy preferences change. The countries of the developing world

[4]Waltz, *Man, the State, and War,* and *Theory of International Relations.*
[5]Tucker, "A New International Order?" and *The Inequality of Nations.*

are, however, interested in altering liberal international regimes, not in maintaining them. They want new principles, norms, rules, and decision-making procedures. They can bring to bear powerful ideological arguments to legitimate their preferences, but they lack national economic and military capabilities.

Existing international regimes are likely to continue to weaken, not only because of attacks from the South but also because of disaffection in the North. Especially for the United States, declining power will make policymakers less willing to tolerate free riders or to bear a disproportionate share of the costs of maintaining international regimes. Although the South will not abandon calls for a New International Economic Order, it will give less emphasis to this program because the prospects for success are dim. The behavior of both the North and the South will be increasingly motivated by short-term calculations of interest rather than by long-term goals that require efficacious regimes. When mutual interests are high, such calculations can lead to cooperative relations. Where specific interests are not present, interaction will decline. For both developing and industrialized states this is not such a daunting prospect. Given fundamental conflicts stemming from outlandish disparities in power, there would be more security in a world with lower levels of transnational interactions. Self-reliance and collective self-reliance rather than interdependence may serve the interests of the North as well as those of the South.

THE VARIETY OF THIRD WORLD GOALS

By emphasizing weakness, vulnerability, and the quest for control in this study, I do not mean to imply that LDCs are uninterested in purely economic objectives. Third World states have pursued a wide variety of goals. These include economic growth, international political equality, influence in international decision-making arenas, autonomy and independence, the preservation of territorial integrity from external invasion or internal fragmentation, the dissemination of new world views at the global level, and the maintenance of domestic regime stability.[6] They have used a wide variety of tactics to promote these objectives, includ-

[6]For a particularly helpful discussion, see Wriggins, "Third World Strategies for Change," pp. 37–39. See also Rothstein, *Global Bargaining*, p. 3, and *The Third World and U.S. Foreign Policy*, pp. 11, 24–25; Hansen, "North-South Policy," pp. 1105–1106.

ing international commodity organizations such as OPEC and CIPEC (*Conseil Intergouvernment des Pays Exportateurs Cuivre*), regional organizations such as the Organization of African Unity (OAU) and the Association of Southeast Asian Nations (ASEAN), universal coalitions such as the Group of 77 (G-77) at UNCTAD and the United Nations, alliances with major powers, local wars to manipulate major powers, irregular violence such as national liberation movements, bilateral economic arrangements, national regulation of multinational corporations, nationalization of foreign holdings, foreign exchange manipulation, and international loans.

In this study I do not address all aspects of Third World behavior or North-South relations. Rather, I investigate Third World efforts to secure control and wealth through the establishment of international regimes that legitimate authoritative, rather than market, allocation. The first analytic task of this study is to demonstrate that Third World proposals can be comprehended and described in this way. The second is to explain variation in Third World success as a function of the access provided by existing regimes, Northern attitudes and capabilities, and ideological coherence.

The boundaries of this work can be more clearly delineated by distinguishing between two categories of political behavior. Relational power behavior refers to efforts to maximize values within a given set of institutional structures; meta-power behavior refers to efforts to change the institutions themselves. Relational power refers to the ability to change outcomes or affect the behavior of others within a given regime. Meta-power refers to the ability to change the rules of the game.[7]

Outcomes can be changed both by altering the resources available to individual actors and by changing the regimes that condition action. Changing the outcome of struggles fought with relational power requires changing actor capability. But such changes do not necessarily imply an alteration in meta-power. An individual may win more money by learning to become a better poker player without being able to change the rules of poker. A political party may win more offices by attracting more voters without altering the laws governing elections. A state may prevail

---

[7]The terms are from Baumgartner et al., "Unequal Exchange and Uneven Development." See also Bachrach and Baratz, "The Two Faces of Power"; Lukes, *Power: A Radical View*; Baumgartner and Burns, "International Economic Relations"; Baumgartner et al., "Meta-Power."

more frequently in disputes with other international actors by enhancing its national power capabilities without altering the principles, norms, and rules that condition such disputes.

Outcomes can also be changed by changing regimes. Meta-power behavior is designed to do this. When successfully implemented, it usually means a change in relational power as well. Individuals who win at poker may lose at bridge; political parties that secure seats under a proportional representation system might be excluded by single-seat districts; states that secure greater revenue from cartelized exports would be poorer if the price of their product were dictated by those with the greatest military capability. An actor capable of changing the game from poker to bridge, from proportional representation to single-seat, from economic to military capability, possesses meta-power. Actors may seek to enhance their relational power by enhancing their own national capabilities, or they may attempt to secure more favorable outcomes by pursuing a meta-power strategy designed to change regimes.

Max Weber's distinction between formal economic rationality and substantive economic rationality is relevant to an understanding of the distinction between relational power and meta-power. By formal rationality Weber means the "extent of quantitative calculation or accounting which is technically possible and which is actually applied."[8] It involves the most efficient use of resources given a specific decision environment and set of objectives. Substantive rationality refers to the extent to which economic activity is guided by "some criterion (past, present, or potential) of ultimate values, regardless of the nature of these ends."[9] Action determined by substantive rationality involves ultimate ends, not just the efficient use of resources.

The exercise of relational power involves only questions of formal rationality. Relational power behavior accepts existing goals and institutional structures. The challenge is to achieve these goals most efficiently. Meta-power rejects existing goals and institutional structures. It employs formal, rational calculations to promote new goals and institutions. Behavior that is formally rational given one set of substantive objectives may be formally irrational given another.

Third World states are interested in employing both relational power and meta-power. Proposals for international regime change, voiced by

[8]*Economy and Society*, p. 85.
[9]Ibid.

the less developed countries, are an effort to exercise meta-power. The objective of these proposals, of which the program associated with the New International Economic Order is the most salient, is to alter the principles, norms, rules, and decision-making procedures that condition international transactions. Such transformation is attractive because in a market-oriented regime the ability of Third World states to achieve their objectives solely through the exercise of relational power is limited by the exiguousness of their national capabilities. These capabilities alone could not resolve the vulnerability problems of poorer states. For the Third World, altering international regimes is a relatively attractive way to secure some control over the environment.

Third World efforts to change regimes have been most clearly manifest in international organizations. Debates within these organizations have concerned principles, norms, rules, and decision-making procedures, not just the transfer of resources. LDCs have also used national legislation to try to alter international rules of the game. However, the NIEO and other proposals for regime change have been but one of many kinds of interactions between the North and the South. With regard to actual resource movements, the most important settings have been national and bilateral. In such settings, developing states have used relational power to enhance specific economic interests. When, for instance, a developing country borrows on the Eurodollar market, it attempts to get the best possible terms; it does not, however, challenge the right of private financial institutions to base their decisions on maximizing private economic returns. When a developing country accepts foreign assistance, it tries to alter both the amounts and the terms on which it is dispensed; it does not, however, usually challenge the prerogative of donor countries to base aid allocations on self-determined principles or interests. When a state negotiates a standby agreement with the International Monetary Fund (IMF) it attempts to use relational power to adjust the terms and conditions of the arrangement; it does not, however, challenge the authority of the IMF to sign such an agreement. The modal form of interaction between industrialized and developing areas has involved the transfer of resources and the exercise of relational power, and has taken place in bilateral arenas.

Some examples of relational power and meta-power policies in national and bilateral, as opposed to multilateral, settings are shown in the following table. Multilateral settings are further broken down into North-South and South-South arrangements.

TABLE 1.1

Negotiating forum	Behavior type	
	Relational power behavior (formal rationality)	Meta-power behavior (substantive rationality)
National and bilateral	Eurodollar loans Tax treaties Bilateral aid	Some regulation of MNCs (1960s) Control of oil production (1970s) Expansive national claims to ocean resources (1945–1970) Unilateral alteration of loan terms (early 1980s)
South-South	Existing trade arrangements among LDCs	OPEC Andean Pact Collective self-reliance
Multilateral Universal, including North-South	Civil aviation Nuclear nonproliferation	New International Information Order (NIIO) NIEO Generalized systems of preferences Commodity agreements Aspects of Lome Convention Integrated Program for Commodities UNCLOS

Behavior that falls within one of the cells is not incompatible with behavior that falls in another. It is not inconsistent for developing countries to pursue different goals in various arenas at the same time. During the 1970s the Group of 77 pressed for generalized debt relief for the least developed states at universal international forums such as UNCTAD and the United Nations General Assembly, while downplaying this issue at multilateral financial institutions such as the World Bank and the IMF.[10] In the area of raw materials, the less developed countries sought both compensatory finance, which would enhance their economic well-being without altering basic regime characteristics, as well as the formation of the Integrated Program for Commodities, which would fundamentally change the principles and norms governing the international movement of primary products. Under the *sexenio* Luis Echeverría, Mexico played a prominent role in the Third World movement. At the same time, the Mexican finance and development ministries were engaged in extensive pragmatic discussions with multinational corporations about conditions for their entry into Mexico.[11] Similarly, Algeria pursued purely economic policies with respect to liquefied natural gas exports while Boumedienne acted as the leader of the Non-Aligned Movement. The pursuit of different goals in various forums is not inconsistent or incoherent.[12] It does not reflect disagreement between politically oriented foreign affairs officials, who do not understand economics, and finance ministry officials, who recognize the "realities" of global interdependence. Rather, the variety of Third World strategies is a manifestation of a variety of objectives.

This study is concerned with what is shown in the right-hand column of table 1.1, especially the lower right-hand cell. My objective is to analyze and describe Third World efforts to exercise meta-power, particularly in multilateral forums. Developing countries have sought to alter regimes in a variety of issue areas. They have attempted to create new institutions, or to change patterns of influence in existing ones. They have sought to establish new international norms. And they have tried to change rules. Many of these quests have been at least partially successful.

[10] *Wall Street Journal,* October 4, 1976, 8:3; Rothstein, *Global Bargaining,* p. 161.

[11] Purcell and Purcell, "State and Society in Mexico."

[12] For a similar conclusion, see Gosovic and Ruggie, "On the Creation of a New International Economic Order," p. 312.

ALTERNATIVE APPROACHES TO
NORTH-SOUTH RELATIONS

The interpretation presented in this study both complements and challenges a number of prominent alternatives: basic human needs, conventional liberalism, and global interdependence. Analysts concerned with basic human needs emphasize the material well-being of individuals rather than the political concerns of states. Advocates of free enterprise and liberal economics focus on problems of economic growth. Those who see interdependence as the defining characteristic of the present international system emphasize the ties that bind the North to the fate of the South. Both those of interdependence orientation and those embracing some variants of the liberal approach are sensitive to the political demands made by developing countries. However, basic human needs, conventional liberal, and interdependence arguments all include the implication that accelerated economic growth accompanied by equitable distribution would eliminate the basic source of North-South conflict. Demands for the restructuring of international regimes are understood as instrumental tactics whose ultimate purpose is to enhance economic well-being. Economic well-being for either individuals or the collectivity, rather than state concerns with vulnerability and control, is (tacitly or explicitly) seen as the fundamental motivation for Southern behavior.

As president of the World Bank, Robert McNamara was a prominent exponent of the basic human needs orientation. Under his leadership the bank emphasized the alleviation of absolute poverty. The bank's allocation of funds shifted away from infrastructure and industry toward projects that had a direct effect on the poor, especially small-scale agriculture. In his 1979 address to the board of governors of the bank McNamara averred:

If we focus on the ultimate objectives of development, it is obvious that an essential one must be the liberation of the 800 million individuals in the developing world who are trapped in absolute poverty—a condition of life so limited by malnutrition, illiteracy, disease, high infant-mortality, and low life expectancy as to be below any rational definition of human decency.[13]

In the same speech, he maintained that income gaps between rich and poor are "largely irrelevant for determining the long-term objectives of

[13]McNamara, *Address to the Board of Governors*, p. 19.

the developing countries themselves."[14] In a 1977 talk he argued that it would quickly become apparent that "it is relatively unimportant whether the assistance is to take the form of commodity agreements, debt relief, trade concessions, bilateral or multilateral financing—or any particular combination of these—provided the overall total is adequate.[15]

The alleviation of absolute poverty has also been a major theme of American foreign aid doctrines. It has been embodied in legislation and instructions to American executive directors at international financial institutions. Secretary of State Vance maintained in a 1979 speech that "Programs such as those I have mentioned today are not a cure-all. But they come to grips with the most pressing problems of the developing countries, and they will make a difference where it counts most—in the daily lives of people. They will insure that more people in the developing countries will have enough food to eat, that fewer children will die in infancy, that there is sufficient energy to power more irrigation pumps and to bring more heat and light to distant villages."[16]

The emphasis on basic needs exemplifies a wider trend explicated by Robert W. Tucker. Tucker argues that some Western elites are advocates of what he terms the "politics of sensibility." These elites have come to assume that the Third World is primarily concerned with improving the well-being of individuals. They maintain that justice cannot tolerate existing inequalities. They argue that men should no longer distinguish between fellow citizens and the rest of mankind in the provision of basic needs. The countries of the South are seen by such elites, Tucker argues, as expositors of a new international morality that extends across national boundaries.[17]

General economic performance in the South has been a second focus of attention for Northern policymakers and analysts. Discussion of Third World growth has been deeply influenced by the precepts of liberal neoclassical economics. Within this general approach orthodox liberals have emphasized domestic factors in the Third World, while reformist liberals have also taken global systemic factors into account.

For orthodox liberals the problems of developing countries must be resolved internally. Low per capita incomes are the result of inadequate

---

[14]Ibid., p. 6.

[15]*New York Times.* January 15, 1977, 33:6.

[16]U.S. State Department *Bulletin*, May 1979, p. 37.

[17]Tucker, *Inequality of Nations*, esp. pp. 138 ff. Tucker thoroughly rejects the "politics of sensibility."

factor endowments. The rate of capital formation is low; infrastructures are underdeveloped; soil conditions are poor; education is limited. To some extent these conditions, and the consequent unsatisfactory economic performance of many developing countries, are blamed on inappropriate economic policies. Underdeveloped countries have authored their own failures. Orthodox liberals are especially perturbed by the Third World's rejection of market mechanisms. Trade barriers promote inefficient domestic industries. Investment regulations discourage multinational corporations. Low payments to farmers reduce food production. Artificial exchange rates distort production and consumption. Taxes on primary exports encourage smuggling. Enforced collectivization destroys individual incentives. P. T. Bauer and B. S. Yamey, probably the best-known exponents of this orientation, conclude that such policies "have brought about prompt and readily observable reverses or even collapse in large sectors of the economy in many countries, including reversion to subsistence production following the destructions of the trading system."[18]

The policy implications for the North of orthodox liberal views are readily apparent. The New International Economic Order (NIEO) program should be rejected in its entirety. There is no need to change the international economic system. Third World policies are responsible for Third World poverty. Indeed, such change would be counterproductive because it would substitute state activity for the market. The NIEO is seen as a cockeyed set of proposals inspired by erroneous dependency arguments at best, and economic stupidity at worst.

Orthodox liberals have not paid much attention to Northern policies that impede the functioning of the market. Such policies are unfortunate, even reprehensible. But the fate of the South will not be determined by anything that the North does; while the present system may be flawed in modest ways, it still offers enormous opportunities to those developing countries, such as Taiwan, South Korea, Hong Kong, and Singapore, which are prepared to seize them.

Reformist liberals start with the same basic presuppositions as orthodox liberals, but place more emphasis on the need for more forthcoming Northern policies. Such policies, they say, should recognize the peculiar circumstances of LDCs as well as making markets work more effectively. Reformist liberals strongly condemn import restrictions imposed by

[18]Bauer and Yamey, "Against the New Economic Order."

developed countries, which not only discourage adjustment in the North but impede exports from the South. They support criticisms of the system which point to imperfections in existing markets. For instance, the transfer of technology is carried out largely by multinational corporations that often have oligopoly if not monopoly power. International agreements concerning technology-transfer and restrictive business practices are needed because, like American antitrust legislation, they facilitate the functioning of the market.

Reformist liberals are also more tolerant than their orthodox colleagues of domestic policies in developing countries which do not strictly accord with market principles. They more readily accept the infant-industry argument. Given market imperfections, developing countries' domestic subsidies may be the second-best solution. When basic human needs are at stake, the state may have to allocate. But reformist liberals are as unhappy about inefficient domestic policies in developing countries as their orthodox brethren.

This analysis leads reformist liberals to a more sympathetic view of the New International Economic Order. The demands of the Third World are seen as reformist, not revolutionary. The Third World is understood to believe that the world economy can provide benefits for all. Rhetoric that condemns the system as a whole is just rhetoric. Compromise is possible at the international level. Moreover, the North needs to reform its own policies. Northern restrictions on imports from the South can seriously impede economic development. Present structures do not necessarily provide the price signals needed to maximize global efficiency. A more efficient system would provide benefits for both industrialized and developing areas.

Albert Fishlow has written one of the most persuasive expositions of the position that LDCs should be incorporated into an improved version of the present order. Fishlow states:

The New International Economic Order, despite occasional rhetorical excesses, does not as formulated hinge upon a fundamentally different conception of international economic relationships. It inherently accepts the mutuality of benefits from trade and foreign investment and rejects the Marxist contentions of inevitable exploitation. What it proposes are structural reforms to underwrite a more favorable division of the gains to the Third World than the marketplace presently affords.[19]

[19]Fishlow, "A New International Economic Order: What Kind?" p. 14.

He argues that North-South relations should be restructured according to two principles: "One is a joint commitment to extending and making markets more effective; the other is greater participation of developing nations in policing such markets and in making specific rules."[20] The special situation confronting developing countries must be appreciated. Industrialized nations should lower trade barriers and accept some temporary LDC export subsidization. Compensatory finance schemes should be encouraged for primary commodity exporters. Financial flows should be increased by providing more resources for international financial institutions and by creating international tax funds for the poorest countries. There should be more disclosure of information regarding technology to lessen the imperfections resulting from oligopolistic control. To reduce the divisiveness of expropriation disputes, Fishlow advocates international agreement on book value as a basis for compensation.[21]

Liberal orientations of one cast or another have dominated American attitudes toward the Third World during the postwar period. Democratic administrations have tended to accept reformist liberal arguments. Such arguments were particularly prevalent under Jimmy Carter. Republicans have been more sympathetic to orthodox liberal perspectives, a viewpoint strongly reflected in the positions taken by the Reagan administration. Undergirding both these approaches is a set of beliefs about the relationship between economic well-being and political behavior which incorporates a reductionist, or second-image, understanding of international politics.[22] Louis Hartz has argued that American views of foreign affairs are dominated by the prevailing liberal approach to politics within the United States. Because America's historical experience isolated it from the mainstream of both conservative and socialist developments in Europe, Lockean liberalism with its emphasis on individualism, free enterprise, and political democracy has set the boundaries of political discourse.[23] The leitmotif of American foreign policy has been to reconstruct the American experience in other parts of the world. The external behavior of states has been understood as a manifestation of their domestic sociopolitical characteristics rather than their international power capabilities.

In a study written before the demands for a New International

[20]Ibid., p. 54.
[21]Ibid., pp. 56–76.
[22]Waltz, *Man, the State, and War* and *Theory of International Relations.*
[23]Hartz, *The Liberal Tradition in America.*

Economic Order came to dominate North-South relations, Robert Packenham used Hartz's insights to analyze American foreign aid doctrines.
He argued that the liberal roots of American attitudes led to four basic
precepts. First, change and development are easy. Second, all good things
go together. Third, radicalism and revolution are bad. Fourth, distribut-
ing power is more important than accumulating power. American leaders
saw the poorer countries of the world moving along the same path that
had been followed by the United States. Economic development would
promote political development. Political development meant democracy.
Democratic regimes would follow international policies that coincided
with the interests of the United States.[24]

In 1963 David Bell, the administrator of the Agency for International
Development (AID), argued before the House Foreign Affairs Committee that:

In virtually all of the 24 countries in the first two groups of economically
successful aid programs, democratic institutions have been strengthened or less
democratic regimes liberalized. At the other extreme, unsatisfactory economic
conditions have clearly contributed to political instability.[25]

In 1980 Thomas Ehrlich, the director of the U.S. International Development and Cooperation Agency (as AID was then called) made the following statement before the same committee:

We have learned that dictatorships which consistently fail to meet the economic
and political aspirations of their people raise the risk of internal strife. Frustrated
and enraged people, mired in poverty and oppressed by a few, breed terror,
revolution, and chaos. They do not produce nations that can resist subversion.
Nor can such nations strengthen their national independence. They are prey to
destabilizing influences from within and without. They raise the temptations of
intervention for their neighbors and more distant major powers. Often those
temptations threaten the peace we seek.[26]

Ehrlich was only reflecting the sentiments of his superior. In his 1980
State of the Union Message, President Carter said:

[24]Packenham, *Liberal America and the Third World*, esp. chap. 3; see also Rothstein,
The Third World and U.S. Foreign Policy, p. 199.
[25]Quoted in Packenham, p. 64.
[26]U.S. State Department *Bulletin*, March 1980, p. 53.

In repressive regimes, popular frustrations often have no outlet except through violence. But when peoples and their governments can approach their problems together—through open democratic methods—the basis for stability and peace is far more solid and far more enduring.[27]

The world view of American policymakers has not changed much in the postwar period, and the American response to the New International Economic Order was not very different from the response to earlier Third World demands. Economic development within the countries of the Third World has been seen as the key to their domestic evolution, and domestic political evolution as the key to their international behavior.

For reformist liberals the analogies used to clarify Third World behavior are drawn from domestic politics rather than from international relations. John Sewell of the Overseas Development Council writes that the demands of LDCs bear "some similarity to the emergence of organized labor in this country in the late 1920s and 1930s."[28] Robert Rothstein states that UNCTAD should be viewed as a "trade union movement."[29] Gerald Helleiner suggests that in the area of technology transfer less developed countries are engaging in "consumerism."[30]

Few Northern commentators have perceived the NIEO as a challenge to the basic nature of the liberal regime. Rather, the Third World has been understood to be calling for adjustments within an existing set of principles and norms. Radical transformation was not necessary because a reformed version of the extant liberal order could meet many Third World economic needs. And it was these needs, not the desire to compensate for vulnerability by regime control, which were understood to be the gravamen of LDC dissatisfaction.[31]

While the focus of various liberal and basic human needs perspectives

---

[27]Ibid., p. 54.

[28]Sewell, *The United States and World Development, Agenda 1977*, p. 8.

[29]Rothstein, *The Weak in the World of the Strong*, p. 145.

[30]Helleiner, "International Technology Issues," p. 298.

[31]This is not to say that all commentators utilizing a reformist liberal perspective think that marginal changes would be adequate. Roger Hansen, in particular, maintains that the basic nature of international politics has changed. The realist world of force and hierarchy is eroding, and is being replaced by a world of complex interdependence: the efficacy of force has declined, transnational interactions have increased, international organizations are more important, issue hierarchy is disappearing. In such a world, Hansen believes that fundamental changes, especially in the area of basic needs, are necessary (Hansen, *Beyond the North-South Stalemate*).

is on the well-being of the South, the emphasis in interdependence approaches is on the links between the North and the South. The fate of all countries is intertwined. The basic assumptions of the realist approach, which underlies this study, are rejected. Viewing states as the only constitutive element of the international system obscures the inability of ostensibly sovereign political institutions to control many transnational flows. The formal imprimatur of sovereignty may remain, but revolutionary changes in the technology of communication and transportation have transformed the global system into a web of interdependence from which states can extricate themselves only at extremely high cost, if at all. Various private and subnational actors have developed their own transnational relations. Multinational corporations orchestrate subsidiaries in various parts of the world. Billions of dollars can be transferred electronically from one financial center to another in a matter of seconds. Domestic economic policies can be undermined or reinforced by choices made by other countries for purely domestic reasons. Partisans of an interdependence perspective maintain that this is a world that cannot be adequately understood by focusing on states and power. Economic failure for the South would have dire consequences for the North.[32]

The first report of the Independent Commission for International Economic Cooperation offers elegant testimony for this approach.[33] The commission was chaired by Willy Brandt, and included notables from the industrialized and developing worlds. The report includes the statement that "the world is now a fragile and interlocking system, whether for its people, its ecology or its resources" (p. 33). Brandt avers that "this Report deals with peace. War is often thought of in terms of military conflict, or even annihilation. But there is a growing awareness that an equal danger might be chaos—as a result of mass hunger, economic disaster, environmental catastrophes, and terrorism" (p. 13). The report contains a number of specific arguments about the way in which developments in the South affect the North. For instance, a surging demand for grain in the South, a result of local crop failures, would contribute to

[32]See Keohane and Nye, *Power and Interdependence*, for a discussion of complex interdependence. For classic statements on interdependence in the North, see Cooper, *The Economics of Interdependence*, and "Economic Interdependence and Foreign Policy in the Seventies."

[33]Independent Commission on International Development Issues (Brandt Commission), *North South: A Program for Survival*.

inflation in the North. Rapid population growth could have a deleterious impact on the earth's ecosystem. Developing countries are increasingly important trading partners for the North. Economic collapse in the South could spawn international terrorism and even nuclear blackmail.

The commission's analysis led it to policy conclusions that were more sympathetic to the Third World than those arrived at by analysts with liberal or basic human needs perspectives. While recognizing that the developing countries themselves must carry "the major share of the burden" for effectively attacking poverty, substantial changes in the global economic system were called for in the report (p. 29). Economic forces cannot be left entirely to themselves because they "tend to produce growing inequality" (p. 33). Aid levels should be increased, and the international provision of capital should be more automatic. Levies on armaments and luxury goods trade, taxes on the use of the global commons, or the sale of more gold by the IMF could provide the resources for such transfers. Commodity prices, it is argued in the report, should be stabilized through international agreement. Northern barriers to exports from the South should be eliminated.

The approach taken by the Brandt Commission, and by other analysts who see interdependence as the basic characteristic of the current world system, are closer in some ways to the perspective I have taken in this study than to other interpretations of the North-South situation. Like this study, interdependence arguments have a strong systemic orientation. They address not only the domestic poverty of the South but also the consequences of conditions in the South for the North. While those with basic human needs and liberal orientations focus on the relational power behavior of developing countries, those using interdependence arguments do address meta-power concerns as well. However, while economic growth and prosperity as the center of Third World concerns is stressed in interdependence arguments, I seek to demonstrate in this study that questions of vulnerability and control are more important, at least for some aspects of Third World behavior. Enhancing economic utility will not resolve conflicts between the North and the South. Vulnerability, not simply poverty, is the motivating force for the Third World's meta-power program for transforming international regimes. Those following basic human needs, liberal, and interdependence approaches have failed to comprehend the fundamentally political character of many Third World demands.

CONCLUSION

This study is based on a realist, or structural, approach to international relations. I regard states as the basic actors in the international system. The behavior of other actors, including multinational corporations and international organizations, is conditioned and delimited by state decisions and state power. All states share the same minimalist objectives of preserving territorial and political integrity. States may pursue a more diverse range of nonminimalist objectives. The particular strategies adopted by a given state will be constrained by structural considerations—the distribution of power in the international system as a whole, and the place of a given state in that distribution. Within these structural constraints, strategies will also be affected by domestic attributes such as ideology, interest groups, and state-society relations.

The meta-political goals of Third World states, and many of their relational goals as well, can be understood in reference to the minimalist objective of preserving political integrity. Most developing countries have very weak domestic political institutions. Nonconstitutional regime changes occur frequently. Domestic violence is common. Slack resources are limited. The material resources controlled by Third World states are typically heavily dependent on international economic transactions, which can be taxed relatively easily compared with domestic transactions. Declines in the value of trade can deprive state officials of revenues that are critical for maintaining domestic political control. Hence, the positions of Third World political leaders are very vulnerable to changes in the international economic environment. Making that environment more predictable and stable would contribute to domestic political stability. Regimes legitimating authoritative, rather than market, allocation can provide more stability as well as greater transfers of wealth.

In this study, however, unlike those presenting conventional structural arguments, I have taken seriously not only international power but also international regimes. Those using conventional structural arguments view international politics as a zero-sum conflict among states. Regimes have little autonomy. They are regarded as being only one small step removed from the underlying power configurations that support them. When national power capabilities change, regimes will change as well. For conventional realists, regimes are purely epiphenomenal. The direct clash of interests among states is the basic characteristic of international life.

Because I have adopted the modified structural, or modified realist, orientation in this study I accept the critical importance of political power for regime creation. It is impossible to establish *de novo* durable principles, norms, rules, and decision-making procedures unless they are supported by the more powerful states in the system. Once regimes are actually in place, however, the relationship between power and regimes can become more attenuated. Established regimes generate inertia if only because of sunk costs and the absence of alternatives.[34] Bureaucrats in international organizations actively cultivate supportive clientele. The distribution of influence within organizations may not reflect underlying national power capabilities, one-nation, one-vote procedures being the most obvious example. Regimes with norms and rules giving open access can be altered by new members. Agendas within established regimes can be influenced not only by voting power but also by the persuasiveness and coherence of intellectual arguments. Hence, regimes do not move in lockstep with changes in underlying national power capabilities. Third World states cannot establish new regimes from scratch, but they have been able to change existing regimes, sometimes in very significant ways.

From a modified structuralist perspective, the normative implications of regime autonomy depend on the degree of disparity between underlying national power capabilities and regime characteristics. Some moderate degree of disparity is acceptable, even desirable. It makes it possible for regimes to have enough longevity and stability to produce mutually beneficial outcomes. The greater the disparity, however, the greater the probability of a sudden rupture. Powerful states can destroy regimes that are antithetical to their interests. By disrupting existing patterns of behavior and introducing high levels of uncertainty, such ruptures can be particularly damaging to global well-being and can exacerbate international tensions.

From a modified structural perspective, therefore, the Third World's quest for regimes based more on authoritative allocation is not quixotic, but it is normatively suspect. Developing states do not have the power to create completely new international regimes that involve the North. A minimum condition for Southern initiatives has been access to existing international organizations. Given access, the Third World has consistently attempted to move regimes away from market-oriented principles, norms, and rules. Ideological coherence and declining Northern

[34]Keohane, "The Demand for International Regimes," and *After Hegemony.*

capabilities have made possible some genuine success despite the lack of national power resources in the South. However, Third World accomplishments only rarely contribute to a stable international environment. The greater the success of the Third World in changing regimes against Northern preferences, the more likely the North is to rupture existing practices by withdrawing support.

The tensions between the South and the North, between weak and vulnerable states on the one hand and strong and resilient ones on the other, cannot be resolved through either economic growth or regime change. Even if very optimistic projections of economic performance for the South were realized, national vulnerabilities would not be significantly reduced even with substantial improvements in individual well-being. In only a limited number of cases will the South's support for regimes based on authoritative allocation coincide with the desires of the North. For industrialized states, market-oriented regimes in which resource allocation is determined by present endowments and preferences are more economically attractive and, given developed domestic political and economic structures, disruptions and dislocations can be managed so that political integrity is not put in jeopardy. The international system would be more stable and less conflictual if the North and the South had less to do with each other. From a Northern as well as a Southern perspective collective self-reliance is preferable to greater interdependence.

In sum, this book focuses on one aspect of North-South relations: Third World support for international regimes based on authoritative, rather than market, principles and norms. This strategy has been motivated by Third World weakness and vulnerability stemming from a paucity of resources that can be used externally, and from fragile domestic political and social institutions that cannot adjust to shocks. Third World demands were most strident during the mid-1970s because it was a particularly favorable historical moment to make such demands. The power of the United States had begun to decline, but American policymakers were still committed to international organizations that provided forums for developing countries. The crystallization of a coherent ideological position by 1970 made it easier to coordinate behavior among developing countries and to put the North on the defensive. Before the 1970s the North dominated international organizations, and the South did not have a shared, coherent world view. By the 1980s the North, especially the United States, took universal international organizations less seriously, depriving the Third World of its most telling point of access. The call for a New International Economic Order became muted even though it did not disappear. Although the basic structural condition of power asymmetry remains, the possibility of Third World victories has faded. Both Northern and Southern states have increasingly based their behavior on short-term calculations of interest rather than on principles and norms embedded in existing or proposed international regimes.

II

The Structural Causes of
Third World Strategy

The prominence accorded to efforts to alter international regimes reflects the weakness of Third World states. This weakness exists at both the international and domestic levels. International asymmetries of aggregate and issue-specific power resources are very high. Because the domestic political and social structures of developing countries are weak, they have difficulty adjusting to externally generated disturbances. Third World states are buffeted by international flows, a manifestation of their small size; they are unable to absorb shocks by altering domestic social configurations, a manifestation of their weak and fragile political and economic systems. It is authoritative regimes, not market regimes, that can mitigate international and domestic weakness by basing allocation on inalienable rights conferred by sovereign states rather than on the resources and preferences of individual actors exchanging alienable goods.

In this analysis I do not mean to imply that exchange relations within existing institutional arrangements are unimportant for developing countries. On the contrary, their poverty makes the increase of material well-being a pressing need. Most intercourse between actors from the North and the South involves such straightforward exchanges. Such relational power behavior, however, has been carried on alongside meta-power behavior designed to change international regimes in ways that would not only ensure greater transfers of wealth but also mitigate shocks emanating from the international system by increasing state control.

INTERNATIONAL STRUCTURES

There have always been small states in the modern state system. Before the industrial revolution, however, there was little variation in levels of economic development. In terms of per capita income the richest country was only about twice as well off as the poorest at the beginning of the nineteenth century. Now the richest countries are eighty to one hundred times better off than the poorest. The combination of small size and underdevelopment has left many a Third World state in an unprecedentedly weak position.

Measuring relative power resources is a perennial problem for students of international relations. There is no simple statistic that adequately summarizes all aspects of national power capabilities. Resources and, conversely, vulnerabilities vary from one issue area to another.[1] The best single indicator is a measure of aggregate economic output. Aggregate national account statistics incorporate a wide range of activities that can be tapped by the state to one extent or another. They reflect both wealth and population size.

Before the Napoleonic Wars there was a general propensity for the number of independent political actors in the international system to decline. Since the beginning of the nineteenth century, however, the number, particularly of small states, has expanded.[2] This tendency increased dramatically with decolonization after World War II. Table 2.1 shows the distribution of the ratios of the GNP of the largest state in the system to other states for the years 1830, 1938, and 1970.

In 1830 the ratio of the GNP of the largest European state, Russia, to the smallest state for which figures are available, Denmark, was 41 : 1. Four countries out of twenty-six, or 15 percent, had GNPs equal to at least one-fifth of Russia's. In 1970 the ratio of national incomes (NIs) of the largest state, the United States, to the smallest, the Maldives, was 97,627 : 1. In 1970, 34 percent of the states in the international system had national incomes that were less than 1/1000 that of the United States, and 72 percent had NIs less than 1/100. Only one other country, the Soviet Union, had a national income equal to at least one-fifth that of the United States. These are staggering disparities. In 1970 the Third World as a whole accounted for only 11 percent of the world's GNP.[3]

There is not an absolute discontinuity between the aggregate power capabilities of individual Northern and Southern states. The largest Third World countries have GNPs that are greater than those of the smallest

[1]See Keohane and Nye, *Power and Interdependence*, pp. 49–54; David Baldwin, "Power Analysis and World Politics."
[2]Stein and Russett, "Evaluating War," pp. 31–32.
[3]Leontief et al., *The Future of the World Economy*, p. 8.

TABLE 2.1

RATIO OF GNP[1] OF LARGEST STATE TO GNPs OF
OTHER STATES (NUMBER OF COUNTRIES)

Largest state	Less than 5	5–25	25–100	100–1,000	Greater than 1,000	Missing values[2]
1830 Russia	4	5	1			16
1938 U.S.	4	9	18	10	4	14
1970 U.S.	1	10	23	51	47	0

Sources: Derived from figures in Bairoch, "Europe's Gross National Product," table 4; Woytinsky and Woytinsky, *World Population*, table 185; U.N. *Statistical Yearbook*, 1975, pp. 694–696; IBRD, *World Development Report*, 1978, table 1 for Eastern Bloc; Singer and Small, *Wages of War*, table 2–2.

[1]Figures for 1970 based on national income.

[2]Missing values based on the difference between the number of states for which figures were available and Singer and Small's listing of states in the international system. For 1830, missing states are primarily German and Italian principalities.

industrialized states. The degree of overlap is strikingly small, however. Figure 2.1 shows the GNPs of all countries for which figures are available from the *1979 World Bank Atlas* for 1977. If the two smallest INs (industrialized nations)—Iceland and Luxembourg—are excluded, 67 percent of all developing states had GNPs smaller than those of any industrialized country. In 1977 the gross national product of Luxembourg was greater than that of more than fifty LDCs. China, with aggregate economic power about equal to that of France, was the largest nonindustrialized country. The GNPs of Brazil and India (the two largest in the Third World after China) were about the same as those of Spain and Poland; Iran's (before Khomeini) rivaled Belgium's; Saudi Arabia and Nigeria had GNPs about equal to those of Denmark and Finland. These figures suggest that, although there are substantial differences among the aggregate power capabilities of developing states, very few can hope to exercise wide-ranging influence over the international environment based on national power capabilities.

Such influence would be difficult even for the very largest of the nonindustrialized states. Their great structural advantage is not so much that they can change the international rules of the game as that they can withdraw. During the 1970s the ratio of exports plus imports to GNP for China was about 5 percent, for India, it was 12 percent—both extremely low figures. Other relatively large developing countries are

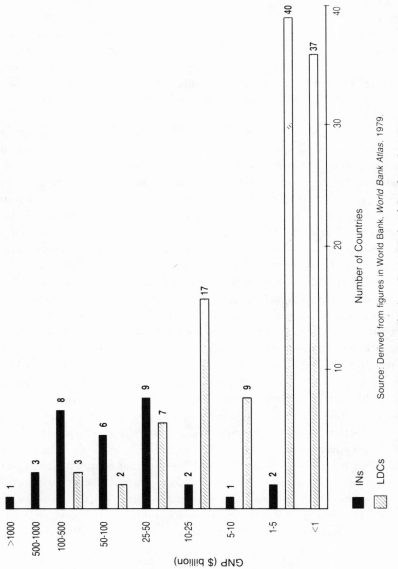

Source: Derived from figures in World Bank. *World Bank Atlas.* 1979.

FIGURE 2.1 Distribution Gross National Products in 1977

more heavily involved in the world trading system: Brazil's trade ratio was 17 percent; Argentina's, 18; Mexico's, 20; Indonesia's, 42; South Korea's, 43; Nigeria's, 57; Venezuela's, 59; and Saudi Arabia's, 103. Figures for smaller LDCs are generally in the 30 to 50 percent range.[4] These smaller countries do not have the national power capabilities necessary to influence the international environment, and they can extricate themselves from the system only at very great material cost. In this sense of being small and involved, nonindustrialized states, with the clear exception of China and India, and the possible exception of one or two other LDCs, are analytically similar.

It is necessary, however, to distinguish between overall power capabilities and capabilities relevant to specific issue areas. Limited general capability does not preclude influence in specific issue areas. The oil-exporting states created a new international regime after bargaining power shifted radically in their favor in the early 1970s as a result of the depletion of excess capacity in the United States, and the existence of surplus revenues in Libya and the Arab Gulf states. Occasionally, LDCs have intervened in other raw-material areas, but their success has been limited.[5] Countries with large foreign debts do have some hold over their creditors. To paraphrase a comment made by a Brazilian official in the late 1970s: If you owe the bank a million dollars, it is your problem, but if you owe 40 billion dollars, it's the bank's problem. But these examples are the exceptions, not the rule. Even in specific issue areas, developing countries rarely have the national power capabilities to bargain effectively with the more industrialized states, much less change international regimes. The relative opportunity costs of change are almost always significantly greater for the developing country than for the industrialized one. Developing states usually have less information and technical expertise.

At the present time, the position of the Third World is weak, and there is little prospect for fundamental change in the foreseeable future. In a study for the United Nations, Wassily Leontief made estimates of aggregate and per capita income in the year 2000 for various areas of the world under various assumptions. To meet his optimistic target for LDC growth, Leontief argued that "two general conditions are necessary: first, far-reaching internal changes of a social, political and institutional charac-

[4]Figures for the period 1970–1977 from World Bank, *World Tables*, 1980. Pages pertaining to individual countries.

[5]Krasner, "Oil Is the Exception"; Varon and Takeuchi, "Developing Countries and Non-Fuel Minerals."

ter in the developing countries, and second, significant changes in the world economic order. Accelerated development leading to a substantial reduction of the income gap between the developing and the developed countries can only be achieved through a combination of both these conditions."[6] It would also be necessary to increase investment from the mid-1970's level of 20 percent to 41 percent in African and Middle Eastern oil-exporting countries; from 17–20 percent to 31–33 percent in Latin America, and from 15 percent to 23–25 percent in non-oil Asia and Africa. Trade would have to increase at the rate of 6 percent per annum until the year 2000, and manufacturing trade at the rate of 7 percent. Balance of payments equilibrium for the Third World could only be achieved by increasing the level of processing of their exports.[7] Even if these stringent conditions were met, the gap in power capabilities, as indicated by GNP, between the North and the South would still be enormous. Based upon Leontief's figures for rapid growth in developing areas, table 2.2 shows index numbers for GNP with the index for North

TABLE 2.2

INDEX NUMBERS FOR GNP IN THE YEAR 2000

North America	100
Latin America	32
West Europe	79
Soviet Union	73
East Europe	25
Socialist Asia	31
Japan	31
Asia	28
Middle Asia	36
Arid Africa	3
Tropical Africa	3
Southern Africa	5
Oceania	6

Source: Derived from figures in Leontief et al., *The Future*, Annex VI. Even under the most favorable conditions Leontief estimates that the share of global aggregate output accounted for by the less developed countries would rise to only 22 percent in the year 2000 (Leontief, p. 8).

[6]Leontief et al., *Future of the World Economy*, p. 11.
[7]Ibid., pp. 7–10.

America set at 100. (The U.S. now accounts for about 90% of North American GNP.)

If attention is focused on the cross-national GNP gap between the North and the South, as opposed to changes over time in social and economic indicators, the situation of Third World countries is certainly bleak. Few can hope to challenge medium-sized or even small industrialized countries with regard to aggregate economic activity. And, even with rapid rates of economic growth, the absolute gap is now so large that it cannot be closed in the foreseeable future.[8] The relative GNP gap is likely to close but, even with rapid growth, less than one-third of all LDCs would have a GNP greater than 5 percent that of the United States.

Intertemporal changes are a good indicator of economic progress; but cross-national comparisons are needed to assess relative power capabilities. Given the existing gap between the North and the South, progress in the former does not necessarily mean much change in the latter. That is why Northern statesmen focusing on economic objectives can argue that the postwar system has been a dramatic success, while leaders of the Third World can argue that it has failed. It is not the numbers that are in dispute but whether a nation's current condition should be compared with its own past or with the present attributes of industrialized areas.

The extraordinary international weakness of virtually all developing countries is the first condition that has driven them to attempt to alter international regimes fundamentally. There have never been so many small states in the international system which could claim sovereign equality; there have never been such large disparities in power capabilities among juridically equal actors. Such weak actors cannot hope to influence the international environment solely by the exercise of their national power capabilities. They must find some alternative or supplement to conventional statecraft, based on national material attributes. A meta-political strategy that takes advantage of access to existing institutions is a viable option.

DOMESTIC STRUCTURES

The second condition that has driven Third World states to attempts to alter international regimes fundamentally is the weakness of their domes-

---

[8] The condition for *beginning* to close the absolute gap is that the ratio of the growth rate of the smaller country to the growth rate of the larger exceeds the ratio of the GNP

tic societies and political systems. The international weakness of most developing states, as indicated by their small aggregate output in comparison with that of industrialized states, suggests that they cannot directly influence the international system. It also suggests that they will be subject to external forces that they cannot change. Small states are usually more heavily involved in the world economy. For instance, in 1973, trade (exports plus imports) was equal to 37 percent of GNP for developing countries, and 29 percent for industrialized countries. In the same year, forty-eight out of eighty-seven LDCs had trade proportions greater than 50 percent.[9]

The size of a state, however, does not determine its internal capacity to modulate and adjust to the pressures emanating from an uncertain international environment. A small state with a flexible political-economic structure can cope more easily with external shocks. Such a state could accept its lack of influence at the international level but remain confident of its ability to cope with environmental disturbances over a wide range of international rules, norms, and institutions.

The ability to cope with environmental disturbances depends on the mobility, flexibility, and diversity of a country's resources. A country with highly mobile, flexible, and diverse factors can absorb shocks emanating from the international system. It can reallocate its factors of production when environmental conditions change. Such adjustments might be achieved by coordinated political action, or through private markets. Small states, like perfectly competitive firms, cannot change international market conditions, but they can adjust to changes in opportunities with differing degrees of success.

SOCIAL RIGIDITY

Social, political, and economic analyses of developing areas indicate that most LDCs cannot absorb and adjust to external shocks. At the social and economic levels, this rigidity is captured by the distinction between traditional and modern societies. Kenneth Jowitt has elaborated on six

---

of the larger country to the GNP of the smaller. In the mid-1970s even the fastest growing LDCs, such as Korea and Brazil (which were growing four times as fast as most industrialized countries), did not meet this condition for the United States, although they did for most European countries.

[9]Derived from World Bank, *World Tables*, 1976, table 3.

characteristics of a traditional, or status, society. First, a status society is based on exclusive corporate groups; individuals are locked within a rigid structure. Second, social action is determined by personal rather than impersonal norms; various individuals are treated in different ways because of ascriptive characteristics. Third, the division of labor in the society is based on assignment to specific ascriptive groups; an individual's economic activity is permanently established by his group membership. Fourth, the ontology of the society stresses the concrete and discrete; general principles that can be applied in a wide range of situations are eschewed. Fifth, the world is seen composed of "concrete and discrete elements—that is, indivisible units—economic, social, cultural, and political resources are seen as being finite and immobile rather than expanding and flexible."[10] In contrast, modern societies are market-based rather than status-based. Interactions are governed by impersonal norms of action. The individual and the nuclear family rather than the corporate group are the building blocks of the society.[11] The transition from traditional to modern society is taking place in the Third World, but it is a slow and difficult process, one that is not unidirectional or irreversible, as events in Iran and Cambodia demonstrate.

Modern societies are less vulnerable to external changes because their factors of production are more mobile. Better-trained workers are able to perform a wider variety of tasks. Developed capital markets can deploy resources more efficiently. Dense information networks disseminate technological innovations more quickly. In his seminal study of the power aspects of international trade, Albert Hirschman argues that "the inherent advantage with respect to all these aspects of the mobility of resources lies overwhelmingly with the great manufacturing and trade countries as opposed to countries in which agriculture or mining predominates."[12] Although adjustment can often be very painful for Northern actors, it is even more difficult for most Southern ones.

POLITICAL WEAKNESS

The rigidity of the social and economic structures in developing countries is reflected in the political system. The state is often treated as but one

[10]Jowitt, *The Leninist Response to National Dependency*, p. 8.
[11]Ibid., pp. 7–10.
[12]Hirschman, *National Power and the Structure of Foreign Trade*, p. 28.

more compartmentalized unit. Its ability to extract resources from the society is limited. Efforts to combine diverse social and material units are likely to be frustrated by the rigid nature of the society. Economic activity that takes place outside the market cannot be effectively tapped by the state.[13] Administrative capacity is limited. Relative to industrialized countries, LDCs have few policy instruments, making it more difficult for them to adjust to cyclical swings generated by either external or internal factors.[14]

Developing states are subject to demands generated not only by internal social mobilization but also by global values. Most Third World states are not a product of autochthonous political, economic, and social forces. Not only were specific boundaries in many areas of the world set by foreign powers, but the basic form of political organization, the sovereign state, was externally imposed as well. The agenda of the contemporary state is strongly influenced by transnational factors. Having entered the world system at a late date, states in the Third World have been compelled to adopt simultaneously a whole panoply of tasks which states in industrialized areas had the luxury of handling sequentially. Third World regimes endemically promise more than they can deliver not only because they are beleaguered by the consequences of rapid domestic social mobilization but also because their images of desirable behavior are influenced by the values of the global system (which primarily reflect the values of the most-developed areas). Thomas and Meyer have argued that the "gap is not only a social psychological creation of the modern system (a revolution of rising expectations, relative deprivation, or discontent created by high aspirations), but is also a structural fact that the peripheral state—with the same world-culturally defined obligations as an advanced one, but with fewer social and organizational resources—legitimates social claims that cannot be met, makes national plans that cannot be implemented, and defines forms of national and international justice that cannot be sustained. The gap is not only between expectations and reality but also between the state organization and its legitimating environment."[15]

[13]See Ardant, "Financial Policy and Economic Infrastructure" for a discussion of European fiscal development.

[14]Lewis, *The Evolution of the International Economic Order*, pp. 47–55.

[15]Thomas and Meyer, "Regime Changes and State Power," p. 145. See also Gilpin, *War and Change in World Politics*, p. 122; Grindle, "Policy Content and Context in Implementation," pp. 22–23.

Social mobilization and unrealizable externally generated demands, coupled with limited institutional capacity, produce political decay rather than political development.[16] Authority and legitimacy are limited. The leader's need to rely on direct subventions results in perverse economic policies that constrain national productivity.[17] Political unrest is high. Coups are frequent.[18] Leaders in many developing countries thus live close to the edge. Externally generated shocks are more threatening because they cannot be absorbed, given limited domestic resources, or adjusted to, given the rigidities of traditional society.[19]

Inherent in the preceding arguments is the presumption that Third World states and their political leaders are autonomous, if constrained, actors. This approach is fundamentally incompatible with those dependency orientations that deny substantial autonomy to the central political institutions of Third World countries. The position taken here also raises empirical questions about any theory that views Third World states as mere puppets of advanced capitalist actors, whether public or private. The Third World has vigorously, and with some success, challenged the postwar international economic order. This challenge has involved the denial of basic capitalist principles, such as nondiscriminatory treatment of international trade and investment. Even where the challenge has failed with regard to specific issues, it has undermined the liberal ethos that enhanced the legitimacy of the postwar order. Dependency arguments have been oriented to domestic political and economic developments in Third World countries. They have not included the international policies of these states, especially those meta-political activities designed to alter international regimes.

The meta-political demands of Third World states cannot be easily incorporated within dependency arguments. Dependency is seen as a pervasive set of transactions that condition all aspects of a society's

[16]Huntington, *Political Order in Changing Societies.*

[17]For an illuminating discussion of the political motivations for such perverse policies in African agriculture see Bates, *Markets and States in Tropical Africa.*

[18]Between 1958 and the summer of 1981 there were forty-one successful coups in the twenty-three black African states. (Jackson and Rosberg, "Why Africa's Weak States Persist," pp. 7–12.)

[19]This is a sweeping set of generalizations. There are important exceptions. The Southeast Asian NICs—South Korea, Taiwan, Hong Kong, and Singapore—have effective state or market systems that have guided economic development. These countries are discussed later in this chapter. Mexico, also discussed later in this chapter, has a highly developed and articulated political system. Brazil's military government directed an exceptionally effective burst of economic growth during the late 1960s and the 1970s. India and China, two other very large developing states, are examined in the conclusion of this volume.

character and behavior. It must be distinguished from dependence, which refers to the state's bargaining power with regard to external actors. Dependence reflects only a state's position in the international system. Dependence does not necessarily mean dependency; that is, all small states suffer from dependence but only those whose societies and political institutions are penetrated by external actors are in a situation of dependency.[20] The modal dependency perspective shows the dependency relationship as self-reinforcing. The country may develop, but its development will be perverted by the forces of world capitalism, which penetrate and shape its social, political, and economic institutions. There are no dialectic tendencies, or exogenous variables that could undermine these processes.

How can the dependency-oriented deal with the meta-political demands of Third World states? There are two possibilities, neither of which is analytically comforting. The first is to accord a high degree of autonomy to the state. Peter Evans's notion of a triple alliance between the domestic bourgeoisie, the transnational corporation, and the Third World state does, for instance, accept a high level of state autonomy.[21] This position, however, obscures lines of causation. How independent can the Third World state become? How much can it play various forces off against one another? Why is the state attacking at the international level those same forces that it allies with at the domestic level? The answers to these questions are not obvious.

A second tack would be for dependency theorists to argue that international behavior is designed as a substitute for domestic social and economic reform. International radicalism is coupled with domestic repression. Third World-ism may enhance the domestic political legitimacy of weak exploitative regimes. These are fair arguments, providing that the actual impact of Third World activity on the international system is not ignored. The Third World has altered international regimes. The one case of effective Third World use of national power, OPEC, weakened the world capitalist system. It may be possible to claim a dialectic process in which Third World political elites ally themselves with private and public Northern elites; this alliance undermines the legitimacy of Southern elites; they try to recover through radical international activities; however, these radical international activities undermine the capitalist system on which their positions depend. This is neat enough, but it denies

[20]Caporaso, "Dependence, Dependency, and Power in the Global System."
[21]Evans, *Dependent Development*.

the self-reinforcing, positive-feedback orientation of some dependency literature. It is much closer in spirit to the arguments of Lenin and Hobson, which see world capitalism leading to social and economic transformation (and dialectic progress) in backward areas. Analytically, it is difficult to fit the international radicalism of the Third World into a dependency framework.

To return to the main theme of this section, however—the domestic weakness of Third World states—this discussion of dependency theory is not meant to deny its utility. A dependency orientation can be used to supplement, rather than supplant, arguments that have been put forth by conventional analysts, provided that the state is treated as an autonomous actor. What dependency theorists then suggest is that the difficulties faced by Third World states can be aggravated by external penetration of their domestic social and economic structures. It may be more difficult, for instance, to control a multinational corporation operating in many countries than a national corporation operating in one. Northern states may support dissident political factions, or provide assistance for domestic groups, particularly the military. The Northern media can create expectations, especially among members of the elite, which can increase domestic disaffection. The penetration of domestic structures emphasized by dependency theory thus aggravates the difficulties of adjustment already imposed on central political institutions in developing countries by the rigidity of their own domestic social structures.

The situations of most Third World states can be illuminated by contrasting them with those of small industrialized countries. The small developed countries have not rejected the existing international economic order. Although they have generally accepted international norms more readily than larger industrialized countries have, and placed more emphasis on international organizations, they have not made international regime transformation a major aspect of their foreign policy.

Peter Katzenstein made a study of foreign economic policymaking in seven small European states—Belgium, Switzerland, the Netherlands, Austria, Norway, Denmark, and Sweden. All of these states are heavily committed to a liberal and open international economic system. Their tariffs have been lower than those of large states. They have been more reluctant to protect declining industries. They have welcomed foreign capital. Yet they are all subject to external perturbations because of their heavy involvement in the world economy. These small European states have been able to cope with this dilemma through effective domestic stabilization policies. Switzerland, the Netherlands, and Belgium have been more aggressive, following an "offensive strategy" based on extremely low tariffs, high export intensities, specialization in industries and services with inelastic demand, and high rates of investment. Austria, Norway, and Denmark have pursued a more "defensive strategy," oriented toward innovations in traditional industries, somewhat higher tariffs, and lower research and development expenditures. Sweden's strategy has been mixed. Despite these variations the political systems of all seven small European states are characterized by dense policy networks that fuse the public and the private sectors, a situation that Katzenstein refers to as democratic corporatism. These networks integrate all groups within the society; they facilitate communication and prevent stalemate. The political organizations of the small industrialized states have made it possible for them to enjoy the economic benefits of full participation in the international economy, while insulating their domestic social structures from the disruptive consequences that would ensue from uncontrolled external perturbations.[22]

TAX STRUCTURES

One variable that illustrates differences between the political capabilities of industrialized and developing countries is tax structure. Tax collection is generally a good indicator of the ability of a state to extract resources from its own society.[23] Developing countries collect a smaller proportion

[22]Katzenstein, "Capitalism in One Country?" pp. 113–119, and *Between Power and Plenty.* David Cameron, in an analysis of increases in government expenditures for eighteen industrialized countries comes to a similar, if somewhat narrower, conclusion. Cameron finds that the best explanation for increases in government expenditures for the period 1960 to 1975 is the degree of their openness to the world economy in 1960. Openness is closely related to size: the ratio of trade to aggregate economic activity is higher for small countries. He argues that small states with open economies are usually dominated by a few economic sectors. This promotes strong peak associations and, more importantly, high unionization and strong labor confederations. Strong labor organizations press the state for higher levels of social expenditure. They also provide a base of support for leftist parties, which favor relatively high levels of social expenditure. This leads to a relatively high rate of increase in the share of government expenditure. (See Cameron, "The Expansion of the Public Economy.") Although Cameron does not emphasize the point, higher rates of expenditure can help to cushion labor from the vicissitudes of the world economy.

[23]The most glaring exceptions to this generalization are levies imposed by oil-exporting and some other resource-producing countries on multinational corporations. The centralized structure of resource-extraction industries makes them easy targets even for weak states.

of their GNPs than do industrialized states; their methods of collection are based more heavily on trade taxes; the level of state revenue is, therefore, more subject to international economic vicissitudes.

Third World countries are poor and their governments cannot tax much of what there is. In 1973 total government revenue was equal to 33.5 percent of gross domestic product (GDP) for industrialized countries and 19.9 percent for developing countries. Mali was able to collect only 1.5 percent of its GDP, Nepal only 5.6 percent. The lowest figure for industrialized countries was 21.6 percent for Japan; the highest, 51.7 percent for Sweden.[24] There is a strong curvilinear relationship between per capita GNP and government revenue as a percentage of GNP, with revenue rising sharply, up to a per capita income in the neighborhood of $2,000, and then leveling off.[25]

There is also a strong relationship between economic development and the nature of the tax structure. In particular, developing countries are far more dependent on trade taxes than are industrialized countries. Trade taxes are relatively easy to collect because imports and exports are channeled through centralized port facilities. Even with smuggling and corruption (often very serious problems) tariffs and export taxes are easier to obtain than direct taxes, which require high levels of bureaucratic skill and voluntary compliance.[26] The pattern is again curvilinear. A cross-national comparison for the mid-1970s indicates that trade revenue as a proportion of total revenue declines sharply for countries with per capita incomes of up to $2,000 and levels off for countries with higher per capita incomes. Some of the poorest developing countries derive up to 60 percent of their revenue from taxes on trade, whereas the range for industrialized countries is 2 to 10 percent. The following equation is based on figures for sixty-six countries in 1974.

$$\frac{\text{Trade Revenue}}{\text{Total Revenue}} = 66.6 - 15.9 \text{ GNP per capita.}$$

$$r^2 = 0.38$$

[24]The figures are from the World Bank, *World Tables*, 1976, Comparative Economic Data, table 7.

[25]Hinrichs, *A General Theory of Tax Structure Change*, pp. 15–16; Hinrich's figures were updated for fifty-six countries for 1974 and 1975 and show the same pattern. The sharp decline in the slope at $2,000/capita is based on the mid-1970s figures.

[26]Conybeare, "International Organization and the Theory of Property Rights," pp. 36–40.

Significance > 0.00

Given this pattern, it is not surprising that developing-country revenues are more seriously affected by fluctuations in international economic flows than the revenues of industrialized countries. Cross-national analyses were conducted on the relationship between changes in total trade and changes in government revenue for the period 1974 to 1975. This was one of the rare episodes in which world trade declined from one year to the next. Based on constant-dollar figures, equations were estimated for developing and industrialized countries. For sixty-one developing countries:

$$\% \text{ Change in Revenue 1974 to 1975} = 0.25 + 0.61\% \text{ Change in Trade 1974 to 1975}$$

$$r^2 = 0.28$$

Significance > 0.00

(If one outlier, Indonesia, is dropped from the calculation, the slope changes to 0.64 and the r^2 increases to 0.36.)

For industrialized countries as a whole there is no relationship between changes in trade and changes in government revenue. For the period 1974 to 1975 the following equation was estimated for twenty industrialized countries:

$$\% \text{ Change in Revenue 1974 to 1975} = 4.81 - 0.11\% \text{ Change in Trade 1974 to 1975}$$

$$r^2 = 0.008$$

Significance < 0.10

A comparison between *small* industrial countries and developing countries suggests a more subtle set of distinctions. For the small developing countries there is a strong positive relationship between changes in trade and changes in government revenue. For nine small developed countries for which data are available (Austria, Denmark, Finland, Netherlands, Norway, Sweden, Switzerland, Australia, and New Zealand) the following equation expresses the relationship between percentage changes in trade and percentage changes in government for the period 1974 to 1975.

% Change in Revenue 1974 to 1975 =
    11.2 + 0.80% Change in Trade

$$r^2 = 0.39$$

These are strong relationships suggesting that even though small industrialized countries do not rely on trade revenues, as opposed to other forms of taxation, their economies are so integrated into the world economy that a decline in trade has substantial indirect effects on government revenue.

Despite a decline in trade from 1974 to 1975 for all nine countries, however, which ranged from 2.8 percent for Norway to 18.9 percent for Switzerland, eight out of the nine countries (Switzerland being the exception) were able to increase government revenue in real terms. In contrast, out of the sixty-five LDCs for which data were available, thirty-eight experienced a decline in trade between 1974 and 1975. Out of these thirty-eight, nineteen were able to raise their revenue but seventeen experienced a fall in revenue. Thus, the revenues of small industrialized countries are susceptible to changes in their trade, but these countries appear at least able to resist an absolute decline in real income, whereas almost half of the developing countries that experienced a decline in trade also suffered a decline in government revenues.[27]

Government revenues are but one indicator of the impact of the world economy on particular states. The experience of the developing countries in the 1974–1975 recession does, however, suggest a source for their concern about trade vacillations, which has been largely ignored. One of the persistent complaints of Third World countries has been that they suffer from substantial trade fluctuations. The Third World has argued that these vacillations inhibit their economic growth. However, no empirical substantiation has been found for this claim. One study even reveals a positive relationship between export instability and economic growth.

[27]The preceding calculations are based on data from the following sources: United Nations, *Statistical Yearbook*, Public Finance Tables for total government revenue, total government expenditures, and trade revenues; National Accounts and Gross Domestic Tables for gross domestic product; International Monetary Fund, *International Financial Statistics* for consumer price indices, imports and exports; and World Bank, *World Bank Atlas*, 1977, for per capita GNP.

This relationship is explained by the argument that higher levels of instability lead to greater savings (to smooth out fluctuations in disposable resources), which lead to higher levels of growth.[28]

Although vacillations in trade may not be related to economic growth, they are related to the state's ability to extract revenue. Political leaders can be more sensitive to threats to their command over resources that can be used for immediate political purposes than to threats to the long-term economic growth prospects of their countries. Third World disaffection with the trading regime reflects the weak domestic political structures of LDCs, which necessitate reliance on trade taxes.

THE NICS VS. OPEC

There is one major exception that must be made to these generalizations about weak political and rigid social structures in Third World countries. The newly industrializing countries (NICs) of Asia have been able to adjust effectively to the international environment. Singapore, Hong Kong, Taiwan, and South Korea have adopted aggressive export-oriented strategies. This required effective government capability or the possession of developed flexible markets. Explicit state decisions were taken to move toward export-oriented growth and away from protectionism based on quantitative restrictions, which insulated domestic industries from the world market. Resources secured from world capital markets were used to bolster the role of national entrepreneurs.

For instance, in the early 1960s Korea adopted a set of policies that led to very rapid economic growth. The exchange rate was devalued. Tariffs replaced quantitative limits on imports. Specific industries were encouraged. Implementation of these measures required a strong state that could resist domestic pressures. South Korea was able to develop such a state in part because the Korean War had shattered existing relations in the agrarian sector and because the military coup of 1961 concentrated power in the office of the president. Taiwan and Singapore also have strong states. Hong Kong has relied more on the flexibility and responsiveness of the private market: its industrial structure, characterized by many small firms, has been able to adjust rapidly to changing international demand.[29]

---

[28]Knudsen and Parnes, *Trade Instability and Economic Development*, pp. 7–15.

[29]For a discussion of Korea's implementation of more liberal international economic policies, see Krueger, *Foreign Trade Regimes and Economic Development*, chap. 2. For the

During the 1970s the NICs were able to cope with restrictions imposed by INs by moving into new product lines and diversifying their exports. For the period 1970–1976 Korea's exports grew at an annual average rate of 31.7 percent, Taiwan's at 16.2, Hong Kong's at 8.6, and Singapore's at 14.1. The average rate of export growth for low-income countries for the same period was − 0.4 percent; for all middle-income LDCs (the category into which the NICs fall), 3.8 percent; and for industrialized countries, 7.8 percent. During the same period, the GDP growth rate of these four countries ranged from 7.5 percent for Hong Kong to 10.3 percent for Korea, compared with an average of 2.9 percent for low-income LDCs, 6.0 percent for middle-income LDCs, and 3.2 percent for industrialized countries.[30]

The NICs are one of the two groups providing dramatic success stories with regard to economic growth, or at least resource transfers, in the postwar period. The other is oil-exporting states. During the early 1970s most of the oil-exporting states enjoyed quite spectacular levels of economic growth. For the period 1970–1976 the GDP of Saudi Arabia rose at an average annual rate of 14.4 percent, that of Nigeria at 7.4 percent, of Iraq at 9.5 percent, of Algeria at 6.2 percent, of Iran at 8.9 percent, of Ecuador at 10.7 percent, of Indonesia at 8.3 percent, of Venezuela at 5.3 percent, and of Libya (which had experienced growth rates of 23.3 percent from 1960–1970) at 3.8 percent.[31]

The foreign policy orientations of many oil-exporting states and the NICs have been very different, however. A number of oil-exporting countries have been leaders of the Third World's call for a New International Economic Order. During the early 1970s Algeria and Venezuela were particularly active. Under Echeverría's presidency (1970–1976) Mexico (an oil-exporting state although not a member of OPEC) played

---

underlying political developments, see Haggard and Moon, "The South Korean State in the International Economy"; Benjamin, "The Political Economy of Korea." Cumings, in his "Origins of the Northeast Asian Political Economy," offers an extremely illuminating and historically rich discussion of the political economy of Taiwan, South Korea, and Japan. For a description of Hong Kong, see *World Business Weekly*, August 25, 1980, pp. 29–37. Yoffie, in *Power and Protectionism*, describes how the NICs adjusted to trade restrictions imposed by industrialized states. Frieden, in "Third World Indebted Industrialization," analyzes the ability of Third World states, especially the NICs, to use world capital markets to promote indigeneous industrialization.

[30]Figures from the World Bank, *World Development Report*, 1978, tables 2 and 6.
[31]Ibid., table 2.

the major role in formulating the general principles of the NIEO. Libya rejected existing regime arrangements as sinful, not merely exploitative, a position adopted by Iran after Khomeini came to power. Iraq has also taken a generally radical posture. The OPEC countries insisted on bringing other Third World states into the Conference on International Economic Cooperation (CIEC), which met during 1976 and 1977, making CIEC a forum for discussing North-South issues rather than one that would focus on cooperation in the energy area. Although the NICs have not explicitly broken with the Third World, they have never taken a leading role in presenting any of its demands.

This variation cannot be explained by economic performance: both the NICs and the oil-exporting states did well in the 1970s. It can be explained, however, by variations in vulnerability to external shocks. The NICs have moved toward flexible economic structures and strong domestic political regimes, which have facilitated adjustment. They did well during the 1970s, even though higher oil prices, slower growth in the North, and more protectionism created a less hospitable international environment. Although the NICs are hardly immune to shocks from the global system, they have demonstrated that they can reallocate their factors of production in response to changing opportunities.

The oil-exporting countries cannot be characterized in the same way. Although some of the oil-exporting states have moved to more diversified economic activity based on a more skilled labor force, most are still highly dependent on one product. They do not have the economic or political capacities needed to adjust. The global system showered them with riches in the 1970s but they still remained hostage to external events over which they had little control. When increasing production from non-OPEC sources, economic recession in the North, and conservation measures led to a decline in oil prices in the early 1980s, some oil-exporting states experienced severe economic difficulties.

With regard to vulnerability, the OPEC countries remain a part of the Third World. The contemporary NICs, and other developing countries that become more capable of adjustment, may eventually find it more attractive to throw in their lot with the North. They may come to resemble the smaller industrialized states in their structural characteristics (externally weak but internally strong) and in their positive attitudes toward liberal international regimes. OPEC countries, regardless of their level of wealth, will continue to identify themselves with the Third World.

IDEOLOGY AND PERSONALISTIC LEADERSHIP

Ideology and personalistic leadership are two other domestic attributes of many LDCs which make an international strategy oriented toward fundamentally changing regimes attractive. Most Third World states have adopted an ideological orientation that lets them attribute their underdevelopment to the workings of the international system. Leaving aside questions about the correctness of this approach (although much in this volume suggests that explaining the economic situation of the Third World with a dependency theory is not correct), this ideological formulation can be used to serve important domestic legitimation functions. In many LDCs, sources of legitimacy are limited. Democratic institutions rarely exist. Legal bureaucratic modes of behavior are not widely practiced. Legitimacy then often inheres in the individual ruler. However, charismatic legitimacy based on individual leaders is contingent on the appearance, if not the reality, of success. Given the severe limitations on effective domestic action, the NIEO program was an attractive alternative, especially for states advocating nonliberal principles at home as well as abroad. More left-leaning regimes were more active supporters of the NIEO during the mid-1970s.[32] Prominence in universal coalitions can enhance a leader's domestic position. Castigating the North can rally bureaucratic, military, and popular support. The structure of international organizations affords Third World statesmen an opportunity to play on the world stage, a platform that they could not mount if they had to rely solely on the domestic power capabilities of their countries. Even if their role is perceived as a minor walk-on by more powerful countries, an effective leader may transform it into a major part for domestic political consumption.[33]

Third World leaders who follow such a course must use ideological arguments that resonate with their domestic populations. One accessible theme for many LDCs is the rejection of existing international regimes. For most countries in Asia and Africa, if not Latin America, the central historical event was decolonization. Anticolonialism and nationalism are widely accepted values endorsed by virtually all groups in the Third

---

[32]Hart, *The New International Economic Order*, p. 100.
[33]Wriggins, "Third World Strategies for Change," p. 40; Korany, *Social Change, Charisma and International Behaviour*, p. 86; Good, "State-building," p. 7. See James N. Rosenau, "Pre-Theories and Theories," for idiosyncratic factors.

World.[34] Dependency arguments are widely diffused. A Third World leader who tries to enhance domestic support through international rhetoric will reject liberal principles, norms, rules, and decision-making procedures.[35]

In sum, domestic structural weakness, a manifestation of traditional social norms and political underdevelopment, is a second factor that makes international regime transformation attractive for almost all Third World countries. These countries cannot easily adjust to external changes because their domestic social structures are rigid and immobile and their political institutions do not have the capabilities needed to alter these conditions. The external environment is inherently threatening, even in the absence of any direct effort by more powerful states to exercise leverage. International regimes controlled by developing countries could lessen exposure to systemically generated shocks. They could offer some stability in a situation where the lack of adjustment capacity precludes effective domestic cushioning.

MEXICO: AN ILLUSTRATIVE CASE

Perhaps no country better illustrates the dilemmas of the Third World and their consequences for foreign policy than Mexico. Mexico experienced rapid growth through the 1970s. This was true even before the discovery of large new oil reserves. Between 1960 and 1965 the average annual rate of growth of GDP was 7.4 percent; between 1965 and 1970, 7.9 percent, between 1970 and 1981, 6.5 percent. Manufacturing paced this increase, growing at annual rates of 9.0 percent, 8.7 percent, and 6.0 percent for the same periods. The share of manufactured products in Mexico's merchandise exports increased from 15.6 percent in 1962, to 32.5 percent in 1970, to 39.6 in 1981. Despite an exceptionally high rate

---

[34]Packenham, *Liberal America and the Third World*, p. 41; Good, "State-building," p. 5; Rothstein, *The Weak in the World of the Strong*, pp. 75–76, 110; Nettl, "The State as a Conceptual Variable," p. 591.

[35]It is not necessary to maintain that this pattern of behavior occurs in all Third World countries at all times. Clearly it does not. Many LDC leaders have not adopted foreign policies based on vocal advocacy of Third World positions, but none has strongly allied with the North in defending the existing order. For the sake of the argument presented here it is merely necessary to note that personalistic leadership and the widespread acceptance of dependency formulations are structural incentives that encourage attacks on the liberal international order.

of population growth, per capita GDP increased at 4.0 percent annually for the period 1960 to 1965, 4.4 percent for the period 1965 to 1970, and 3.4 percent for the period 1970 to 1981.[36]

This impressive economic performance, however, did not dissuade Mexican leaders from acting as major critics of the existing order. Under the presidency of Luis Echeverría (1970–1976) Mexico took a leading position in formulating the New International Economic Order. This was a break with past policy in which Mexico had generally taken a low profile on North-South issues. Echeverría first proposed what later became the Charter of Economic Rights and Duties of States at the 1972 UNCTAD meeting. During the initial years of his presidency he traveled extensively, and these trips were greeted with enthusiasm within Mexico.[37]

Echeverría's behavior was deeply rooted in Mexico's international and domestic structural problems. Mexico's impressive economic development did little to lessen her dependence on the United States. In 1976 more than 56 percent of Mexico's exports went to the United States, while Mexico accounted for only 4 percent of American exports. Conversely, 63 percent of Mexico's imports came from the United States, while Mexico accounted for only 3 percent of U.S. imports. Multinational corporations, mostly American, are strongly represented in many of the most dynamic export sectors. By the late 1970s the United States accounted for more than two-thirds of direct foreign investment in Mexico. The ratio of U.S. to Mexican GNP was about 25 : 1.[38]

Even in the area of petroleum, some Mexican policymakers see their country as potentially subject to overwhelming American pressure. If there are further supply disruptions from the Middle East, the United States may look to Mexico to make up the gap. If Mexico were unable to do this using her own resources, America might press for greater involvement by the international oil companies. Mexican resistance to such pressures could precipitate a major crisis between the two countries. In such an eventuality the economic, if not the political, leverage of the United States would be substantial. Such a scenario may be unlikely, but

[36]World Bank. *World Tables,* 1983, Comparative Economic Data, tables 1 and 5.

[37]Grant, "Domestic Determinants of Mexican Foreign Policy"; Gwin, "The Seventh Special Session," p. 100.

[38]See Sepulveda, "Structural Constraints on Recent Mexican Foreign Economic Policy," passim, for a discussion of structural problems. Trade figures are from the International Monetary Fund, *Direction of Trade* annual, 1970–1976.

it is not one that Mexican policymakers can ignore, given existing asymmetries of power.[39]

Domestic conditions, however, are a more proximate explanation for Echeverría's Third World-ism. Although Mexico's colonial experience is far in the past, the country's political culture is still influenced by its struggles with Spain and the United States, and the revolutionary egalitarian ideology that emerged from the Mexican Revolution. At the same time, there are deep cleavages between the elite and the masses. Income is maldistributed and the benefits of Mexican economic development have gone disproportionately to the middle class. Revolutionary ideology offers a link between the masses and the regime, but it also generates pressures for social reform.

Foreign policy has long offered Mexican political leaders opportunities to resolve some of the tensions inherent in their political situation. During the 1960s Mexico adopted a positive attitude toward Castro's Cuba and pursued traditional nationalist postures designed to maintain independence from American policy. By the 1970s, however, this stance was too conventional to lend much prestige to the Mexican regime. A new policy was needed which would reinvigorate the official ideology and consolidate ties between the presidency and the intellectuals. Echeverría's Third World-ism served these purposes. His sponsorship of the Charter of the Economic Rights and Duties of States gave elements in the Mexican political system an opportunity to pledge their loyalty to the executive. Such pledges form a critical support for the stability of the Mexican political system.[40]

Echeverría's relationship with Mexican intellectuals and the left was particularly strained because of developments during the late 1960s. As minister of state security he had been involved in the events leading to the shooting of 200 students before the 1968 Olympic games. Díaz Ordaz, the conservative president who governed from 1964–1970, had handpicked Echeverría as his successor. There was a high rate of abstention in the 1970 election, and in the Federal District (Mexico City) the opposition PAN received 32.9 percent of the vote, compared with a national total of 13.8 percent.[41] All of these factors inclined Echeverría

[39]Based on discussions with Mexican officials, October 1980.

[40]Pellicer, "*Tercermundismo del Capitalismo Mexicano*," esp. pp. 52–53, 58–59; Sepulveda, "Structural Constraints on Recent Mexican Foreign Economic Policy," pp. 13 ff; Purcell and Purcell, "State and Society in Mexico."

[41]Grant, "Domestic Determinants of Mexican Foreign Policy," pp. 7–8; Fagan, "The Realities of U.S.-Mexican Relations," pp. 692–694.

toward a policy that would establish his ties with the left. Prominent advocacy of Third World demands was a way to enhance domestic legitimacy because it resounded with traditional Mexican ideology.

President Echeverría did not set Mexico along a permanent path of Third World leadership, however. While he was making a highly visible attack on the existing global order, other institutions, particularly the Ministry of Foreign Affairs, were encouraging discrete bilateral ties with the United States and maintaining Mexico's traditional role as an intermediary between the United States and the rest of Latin America. The Ministry of Industry and Commerce favored nationalization in principle but was very sensitive to the need for foreign investment.[42]

Echeverría's successor, López Portillo, pursued a more restrained policy. While reaffirming support for Cuba and keeping some distance from the United States, Mexico projected a more positive image toward direct foreign investment. The government took care not to jeopardize the flow of loans from foreign banks. Domestically, López Portillo strengthened the regime's ties with the business community, which had been strained by Echeverría's policies.[43] However, in one of the most difficult decisions of his first four years in office, he rejected Mexican membership in GATT. The announcement was made in March 1980 at a ceremony marking the anniversary of the 1938 nationalization of the petroleum industry, the seminal event in the history of Mexican economic nationalism. López Portillo was subject to a wide range of domestic pressures, some of which reflected purely economic interests, but he was also responding to a desire to maintain Mexico's freedom of movement at the international level and to the nationalistic and egalitarian arguments of the Mexican intelligentsia. He justified his decisions by arguing that trade liberalization would not promote a more just international economic order.[44]

The vacillation and inconsistency in Mexican policy in the 1970s was not rooted in any failings of its bureaucratic structure or in the contrasting personalities or belief systems of its political leaders. Rather, it reflected the profound countervailing pressures that emerge from a desire by LDCs to secure both independence and development. Mexican development has been closely tied to relations with the United States, her major trading

[42]Pellicer, "*Tercermundismo del Capitalismo Mexicano*," p. 55; Purcell and Purcell, "State and Society in Mexico," pp. 215–217.

[43]Hart, *The New International Economic Order*, pp. 17–20; Grant, "Domestic Determinants of Mexican Foreign Policy," p. 27.

[44]Story, "Trade Politics in the Third World."

partner and source of capital. Development does provide Mexico with additional power capabilities. But these capabilities, even if they were to increase at a very rapid rate, would do little to alter the relative vulnerabilities inherent in Mexican-American relations. The absolute gap is already too large. If the United States were to grow at 2.5 percent annually until 2005, and Mexico at 5 percent for the same period, the absolute gap would double, and the United States would still be thirteen times as large as Mexico. This structural situation, which inclines Mexican leaders to seek international mechanisms for securing greater control of the external environment including the United States, is reinforced by domestic political ideology. Especially in times of stress, foreign elements are blamed for Mexico's difficulties.[45] A radical foreign policy can enhance the legitimacy of a particular ruler.

Mexico is not an isolated example of the relationship between domestic conditions and foreign policy. Populist movements such as Perónism in Argentina are prone to scapegoating. Speculators are blamed for inflation, foreign forces for economic stagnation. Condemning the external world helps to transcend domestic class conflicts. Heightened internal tension in China has been related to a more aggressive foreign policy. Mass antiforeign rallies were important for Mao during the Cultural Revolution because they provided a forum for denouncing domestic opponents. Nationalism unified factions within the Cultural Revolution. Nigeria's obsession with the problem of South Africa can be attributed in part to the leadership's desire to diffuse and deflect pressure from the Nigerian left. Foreign policy has always been central for the Castro regime. Involvement in the Non-Aligned Movement was initially part of Castro's effort to establish independence from the United States. Ties with the Group of 77 helped to legitimate Cuba's presence in Africa, which gave Castro some leverage with the Soviet Union. Jamaican prime minister Michael Manley made a conscious decision to break with the United States and Great Britain in the mid-1970s. After the 1968 seizure of power, Peru's new leaders not only nationalized the International Petroleum Company (a subsidiary of Exxon) but also took a leading role in Third World affairs. These measures helped to increase the military government's domestic political legitimacy.[46]

[45]Purcell and Purcell, "State and Society in Mexico," pp. 214–220.

[46]Ayres, "The 'Social Pact' as Anti-inflationary Policy," p. 491. Liao, "Linkage Politics in China," esp. pp. 598–599; Ungar, "Dateline West Africa," pp. 187–188; O'Flaherty, "Finding Jamaica's Way," pp. 137–147; Bell and Gibson, "Independent Jamaica Faces the Outside World"; and Lowenthal, "Dateline Peru," p. 183.

CONCLUSION

In summary, the international and domestic weaknesses of Third World states make them vulnerable to systemic shocks, which they cannot control. The extent of this vulnerability does vary across states. A few nonindustrialized countries, notably China and India, are so large they can pursue relatively isolationist foreign economic policies without prohibitive economic cost. Some developing states are moving towards, or have already developed, flexible and adaptive domestic political economic structures. Such structures facilitate adjustment to external pressures and make it easier to take advantages of opportunities in the world market. Factor mobility enhances the gains achieved from engaging solely in relational power behavior. A country that can take advantage of economic opportunities and absorb shocks without political disruption, within the existing rules of the game, has fewer incentives to pursue meta-power activity designed to promote authoritatively based regimes. The higher the level of factor mobility, the more attractive market-oriented regimes become.

The East Asian NICs offer the clearest example of Third World political economies characterized by flexible domestic structures. Although these states have not rejected Third World proposals, they have not taken an active role in formulating or defending them in international forums. In contrast, some oil-exporting states, which have done extremely well economically but remain vulnerable to external shocks because their factor endowments are concentrated and their mobility is limited, have taken leadership roles in demanding a New International Economic Order.

The vast majority of developing states is weak internationally and domestically. Market-oriented regimes can provide them with economic benefits, but fluctuations in global economic conditions threaten their domestic political stability. Trade-related taxes are a major source of state revenue. Leaders use public expenditures to bolster their political support. In the absence of more-enduring sources of legitimacy, fluctuations in external performance can have devastating internal political consequences. It is much easier for a Third World state to manage in a stable global environment than in a vacillating and unpredictable one.[47]

---

[47]For a deductive analysis of the difficulties of maintaining state support in an unstable global environment, see Duvall and Freeman, "The Techno-Bureaucratic Elite."

III

Third World Goals and Determinants of Success

Developing countries have attempted to sustain or create international regimes based on authoritative, rather than market, allocation. They have enunciated a coherent set of programs that challenge liberal rules of the game. Their success in implementing their objectives has varied over time and across issue areas. Three variables have influenced the extent to which the Third World has been able to secure its preferred regimes: existing institutions, American power, and ideological coherence.

The Third World states have not had the national power to create international institutions *de novo*. They have been dependent on existing institutional structures. The most important general institutional structure for the Third World has been the acceptance of the claim that all sovereign states are equal. By 1960 the rival norm of great-power primacy had been rejected, and developing countries could claim a presumptive right to participate in decision-making procedures with more powerful states on an equal footing. In specific issue areas the degree of access provided by existing international organizations has been critically important for the Third World. Where membership has been limited, as in the Antarctic Treaty, it has been very difficult for developing countries to launch an effective program. Where membership has been open, developing states have been more successful in promoting their preferred regimes.

Third World success has also been influenced by the relative power position of the United States. American power has declined, particularly since 1960, across a range of issue areas. Through the 1950s American material and ideological resources precluded an effective challenge of international liberal regimes. After 1960 such challenges could not be so easily turned aside. However, declining American power has not had a unidirectional impact. For the Third World, continued American commitment to international organizations has been critical because these organizations not only offered forums for the expression of ideas and bureaucratic resources for their implementation but also provided the base on which regimes oriented more toward authoritative allocation could be constructed. U.S. commitment began to wane in the late 1970s as policymakers became increasingly frustrated over their inability to control outcomes, particularly in organizations with universal membership. The early 1970s were thus a particularly propitious moment for the Third World because the North, especially the United States, continued to support universal international organizations but had lost the ability to control their agendas or programs.

The degree of ideological coherence generated by the Third World has been the third determinant of success. From the late 1940s through the early 1970s the Third World developed a cognitive alternative to the reigning set of liberal ideas. This movement of thought provided a rationale for attacking existing regimes. It facilitated the formulation of a coherent Third World position on a number of different issues. It weakened opposition from the North because some groups in industrialized countries accepted the arguments made by the Third World. Most importantly, it provided a subjective identity that welded the Third World into an effective political bloc. This subjective self-identity was a critical complement to the objective international and domestic weaknesses that provided the basic motivation for Third World demands. Without a common world view, which explained why all countries of the South were alike despite their diverse national attributes, it would have been impossible to act as a unified force in international organizations.

THE POSTWAR REGIME

International transactions are influenced by regimes. Regimes are principles, norms, rules, and decision-making procedures around which actor expectations converge. Regimes coordinate behavior. They overcome problems concerning the provision of collective goods. They can make it possible to reach a Pareto-optimal frontier when purely egoistic calculations would not yield so desirable an outcome. In some issue areas, such as zero-sum conflicts involving relative power capabilities, regimes make little difference. Actors are rarely constrained by international principles, norms, rules, or decision-making procedures. But under variable-sum or purely cooperative conditions the rules of the game can matter. Changing international regimes can alter national behavior as well as the allocation of control and material resources among states.[1]

After the Second World War, the United States used its power to establish a new set of regimes. American central decision-makers moved to create a liberal global order characterized by multilateralism, nondiscrimination, the minimization of impediments to the movement of goods and factors (with the exception of labor) and the control of such movements by privately owned rather than publicly owned entities. These objectives were a reflection of American interests and American values. America is a liberal society and one key attribute of American foreign policy has been the desire to project its domestic values on to the rest of the world. The experience of the 1930s gave greater impetus to these inclinations by apparently demonstrating that a closed, often state-run, international economic system was destructive of both peace and prosperity. Although American efforts to create an overarching regime failed after the First World War because of a lack of domestic political support, they succeeded after the Second World War when domestic opinion was more favorable, and America's international position was stronger.[2]

Less developed states were not treated in any fundamentally different way within this liberal order. They were expected to adopt open economic policies, to treat foreign investors in a nondiscriminatory way, and to provide prompt and adequate compensation for nationalized property. Such policies were thought to benefit the South as well as the North. Poorer areas of the world were expected to follow the developmental course charted by the advanced areas. Free trade would raise incomes and promote technological innovation. Growth would be stimulated by foreign investment. Multinational corporations would provide capital

[1] Krasner, "Structural Causes and Regime Consequences"; Stein, "Coordination and Collaboration"; Jervis, "Security Regimes."

[2] John Gerard Ruggie maintains that the postwar regime ought to be characterized as one of embedded, rather than orthodox, liberalism. Ruggie argues that the regime legitimated domestic social stability as well as a freer flow of international transactions. This is a provocative and original thesis. It does not entirely conform with underlying American values nor with behavior at Bretton Woods where U.S. policymakers insisted on a relatively limited International Monetary Fund with conditional access. Ruggie's view is consistent with the orientation of social democratic parties in Europe, and some aspects of American experience with the New Deal. However, even if Ruggie's formulation is accepted, his embedded liberalism still stands in sharp contrast to the authoritative allocation advocated by the Third World. (See Ruggie, "International Regimes, Transactions and Change.") See also Maier, "The Politics of Productivity," for the impact of the 1930s.

and new skills and open backward areas to the stimulus of the world market. American decision makers saw economic growth contributing to political stability, and political stability to democracy. Democratic regimes would adopt foreign policies that were coincident with America's vision of the global order.[3]

An important aspect of the postwar international system was the role played by international organizations, a role that reflected America's power, peculiar history and style, and economic interests. With regard to power, international organizations are a useful instrument for a hegemonic state because they can help to veil domination. It is difficult and costly for a state to impose its preferences by brute force or economic coercion; voluntary compliance is greatly preferable. Because the endorsement of international organizations can enhance legitimacy, they can be a useful instrument of policy for a hegemonic state that enjoys de facto but not de jure control. Thus, from a purely power-oriented structural perspective, it is not surprising that the United States, whose resource capabilities were far greater than those of any other state in the years immediately after World War II, should have found international organizations attractive.

A second factor that contributed to U.S. support for international organizations was America's style and historical experience. While Franklin Roosevelt was hardly naive about the exercise of power, there was still a strong desire among American leaders of the 1940s to alter fundamentally the way in which the international system had functioned. The balance of power approach, which had been the mainstay of European thinking about international relations, had been discredited by the First World War. The isolationism and economic nationalism of the interwar years had failed to preserve peace for America. Policymakers were determined that the United States would never again cut itself off from an active role on the global scene. For some, international organizations were even seen as an alternative to power politics.

The United States was thus prepared to establish and support a number of international economic institutions after the Second World War. Articles of Agreement for the International Bank for Reconstruction and Development (IBRD, or World Bank) and the International Monetary

---

[3]Packenham, *Liberal America*. The Havana Charter for the proposed International Trade Organization, which was never approved by the Senate, did offer more special provisions for developing areas than the GATT.

Fund (IMF) were concluded at Bretton Woods in 1944. The charter for an International Trade Organization (ITO) was concluded at Havana in 1948, but it was never endorsed by the American Congress. Instead the General Agreement on Tariffs and Trade (GATT), originally envisioned as an interim arrangement, became the primary organization embodying the international regime for trade. Economic organizations were understood to be particularly important because they would help to prevent a recurrence of the economic nationalism of the 1930s. For Secretary of State Hull, the administration's most ardent votary of free trade, a liberal world order was a crucial precondition for world peace. Finally, the New Deal, with its greatly enhanced level of government activity, made it easier for American leaders to claim a greater role for public organizations in the international system.[4]

U.S. policymakers also supported the creation of the United Nations; British and Russian leaders were unenthusiastic. The structure of this organization, which reserved considerable power to the Security Council where the major powers held veto rights and permanent seats, was sensitive to realist considerations. However, the United Nations also reflected an American effort to surmount balance of power politics. Realpolitik had, many American leaders believed, dragged the United States into two global confrontations. The failure of the United States to participate in the League of Nations left moot the question of its efficacy. The United Nations would be a more efficacious institution. Involvement would also prevent American popular sentiment from once again turning to isolationism.[5]

In the political sphere, U.S. leaders did not foresee the potential for conflict between U.N. preferences and U.S. decisions except for problems generated by the Communist Bloc. After the Cold War began, the United Nations was used as an instrument of American policy. The original members of the U.N. were, with the exception of the Communist Bloc, not hostile to the United States. Communist countries commanded only six votes out of fifty-eight in 1949. American leaders believed they could depend on the rest. The Uniting for Peace resolution, which gave the General Assembly a greater role in security matters as well as

---

[4]Gardner, *Sterling-Dollar Diplomacy*, pp. 8–11; Eckes, *A Search for Solvency*, pp. 11 ff; LaFeber, *America, Russia and the Cold War*, p. 7; Halle, *The Cold War as History*, pp. 38–39, 50–54; Feis, *Europe: The World's Banker*, p. 428.

[5]Dallek, *Franklin D. Roosevelt and American Foreign Policy*, pp. 434–435, 508.

legitimating U.S. action in Korea, was a manifestation of U.S. policy-makers' confidence that they could secure desired results from the United Nations.

The regimes established at the conclusion of the Second World War reflected American economic interests as well as American norms. The open international economic order that the World Bank, IMF, and the GATT were designed to reinforce would be beneficial for the largest and most economically advanced state in the international system. A hegemonic state can compete effectively in an open system. The social disruption that is generated by such arrangements is mitigated by its size and the mobility of its factors. An open regime for capital provides opportunities for portfolio and direct investment. Elaborate economic ties open possibilities for exercising political influence.[6]

The instruments of power at the disposal of American central decision-makers, and the resources that they could use to change the behavior of other actors and to structure the regime as a whole, were critical in the creation of liberal norms and practices. First, and perhaps least important, American military capabilities were far greater than those of any other noncommunist state. Although links between the protection of Western Europe and Japan, and the acceptance of American views on the world economy were rarely made explicit, the fear of alienating the United States did impose some tacit constraints on the range of policies that other states could pursue.

Second, and most important, the economic resources possessed by American actors, both public and private, were very large. Marshall Plan funds helped to reconstruct Europe after the Second World War. Reconstruction was a prerequisite for establishing a more open international economic regime; states whose indigenous industrial structures had been ravaged could not be expected to permit the unrestricted entry of foreign commodities. American leaders were, until the late 1960s, willing to tolerate an asymmetric set of relations with Europe and Japan. European economic unification was supported despite the inevitable trade-diverting effects for the United States. Although American barriers to Japanese goods were reduced, formal and informal restrictions imposed by the Japanese on foreign goods and investments were tolerated. Only a very large and economically secure state could have accepted this situation. The American dollar was a critical component of the international mone-

[6]Krasner, "State Power and the Structure of International Trade"; Gilpin, *U.S. Power and the Multinational Corporation.*

tary system that emerged during the 1950s; the American balance of payments deficit became the principal source of liquidity for the international system. American multinational corporations provided, at least initially, new capital, technology, and market knowledge to other countries. The IMF, World Bank, and other international organizations received most of their usable resources from the United States. Five out of the seven largest international oil companies were American. These corporations met rapidly increasing international energy demand at virtually stable nominal prices and falling real prices until 1970.

Finally, American leaders deployed less tangible power resources. A stable international economic regime cannot be built with brute force alone, or even with force in combination with economic incentives and sanctions. Stability is more likely when a regime can be rationalized by an effective ideology. In the years after World War II, American leaders expounded such a set of ideas—liberalism. They argued that the minimization of barriers to trade, nondiscrimination, and private control would provide benefits for all actors in the system. These benefits were not limited to economic growth; they extended into the political sphere. Economic nationalism would lead to conflict, whereas economic intercourse would lead to interdependence and cooperation. These doctrines had all been articulated a century earlier by the Manchester liberals in Great Britain. What made them so potent in the early postwar period was not only that they were backed by a very large and powerful state but also that that state appeared to embody the future. Colonial empires were under attack. Fascism had been discredited. Communism was too threatening for the elites of the West. Liberalism was the most compelling alternative. In sum, the United States used its military, economic, and ideological resources to create and nourish liberal principles and norms.

THE THIRD WORLD CHALLENGE

Developing countries have rejected liberal regimes. Across a wide variety of issue areas they have offered alternative arrangements for organizing transnational behavior. The Third World's program was most fully enunciated in the Program for a New International Economic Order and the Charter of Economic Rights and Duties of States adopted by the United Nations General Assembly in the mid-1970s. The proposals presented by LDCs have not simply been a product of logrolling and compromise.

They have been guided by a coherent set of underlying principles and norms that are antithetical to those that inform liberal regimes.

Developing countries have supported authoritative, rather than market, allocation. With market allocation the distribution of resources is determined by the endowments and preferences of individual actors. These actors are usually private firms but they may also be publicly owned firms, or even states. The defining characteristic of the market is that the actors have the right to alienate property. Under authoritative allocation the distribution of resources is dictated by the rules set by authoritative political institutions. This may be done directly through taxation and public expenditures; indirectly by limiting the right of economic actors to alienate property.

The two dimensions of ownership and allocation suggest four ideal types. In the free enterprise system, ownership is private and allocation is determined by the endowments and preferences of actors who have full rights to alienate their property. Under state capitalism, ownership is formally public but the managers of firms are authorized to allocate the resources under their control to maximize the profits of the firm. Under a redistributive system, the state owns all property and dictates its use. A system of authoritative allocation and private ownership (here labeled paternalism) is one in which property is formally owned by private actors but cannot be alienated. (For instance, laws of primogeniture limited patterns of inheritance.) Any actual economic system will be a mix of these types with different transactions falling into different categories.

With regard to international regimes, major struggles have focused on the principle of allocation. The dichotomous presentation in table 3.1 clarifies basic distinctions. However, the actual disputes between the North and the South have ranged over a continuum that stretches between pure market and pure authoritative allocation. At the market end of that continuum all property can be alienated in any way. The only role for the state is to prevent the use of force. Even contracts can be treated as self-enforcing, since the trustworthiness of individuals and the likelihood of future dealings are reflected in the terms of specific transactions.[7] At the opposite end of the continuum all property is allocated by the state, and other actors cannot engage in exchange relationships.

Both domestically and internationally all extant sets of property rights

[7]See Axelrod, "The Emergence of Cooperation."

TABLE 3.1

ECONOMIC ORDERS

Principle of allocation	Type of ownership	
	Private	Public
Market	Free enterprise	State capitalism
Authoritative	Paternalism	Redistribution

occupy some intermediate position. The liberal regimes of the postwar period accepted the need for some forms of state intervention. In the international trading regime, escape clause provisions legitimated temporary restrictions to mitigate import-generated social dislocation. The International Monetary Fund and the World Bank were both premised on Keynesian assumptions that purely private capital allocation could be suboptimal. When national security was at stake, authoritative allocation always took precedence over the private market. Liberal norms were never applied to transactions with the Communist Bloc.

Moreover, the actual practices of the industrialized state have not always been faithful to the liberal principles which they espoused. The most glaring departures have come in the trading area. Transnational flows of agriculture products have been heavily influenced by domestic and international subsidies and non-tariff barriers. Manufactures, especially from developing countries, have been subject to restrictions imposed by the North. Although some of the newly industrializing countries have been able to circumvent these barriers, at times with the tacit acceptance of executive officials in industrialized states committed to free trade, such practices have created uncertainty, which impedes development planning in the South.[8]

Various restrictive practices, however, do not indicate that the North has abandoned its commitment to liberal rules of the game. Trade barriers have been regarded as unfortunate concessions to interest-group pressure. The proper role of the state is to promote the efficient functioning of markets, not to allocate resources directly by authoritative fiat. Especially in the United States, market allocation is viewed as the normal state of affairs. Discourse, even by groups advocating protectionism, must be

[8]Yoffie, *Power and Protectionism*; Goldstein, *A Re-Examination of American Trade Policy*.

conducted using a liberal vocabulary.[9] The North continues to advocate extending the scope of liberal norms and rules, a policy reflected in the non–tariff-barrier codes negotiated during the Tokyo Round of multilateral trade negotiations and American support for a new round of negotiations dealing with services.

The Third World has adopted a very different orientation toward the international system. Developing countries have offered a set of proposals that would move international regimes toward the authoritative end of the continuum. They are more receptive to direct state intervention. More importantly, they want to constrain the right of private actors to alienate property by either international agreements or national regulation. Developing countries do not necessarily want to eliminate markets but they do want to truncate them, to limit the range of outcomes that can be determined by the endowments and preferences of private actors.

The principles, norms, rules, and decision-making procedures supported by the Third World are in conflict with those defended by the North. The principles informing the Third World's program, its underlying intellectual rationales, have come from dependency analysts who link underdevelopment to the workings of the world capitalist system. The rationale for the liberal order is provided by neoclassical economic theory, which can be used to demonstrate the efficiency of the market. The norms informing the Third World's program legitimate both direct and indirect state intervention; the norms informing the liberal order lead policymakers to be skeptical of state intervention. The rules proposed by developing countries support differential treatment for various classes of states; the rules supported by the North emphasize nondiscrimination. The decision-making procedures included in the Third World's program emphasize either one-nation, one-vote arrangements in international organizations, or legitimate unilateral action by individual Third World states. The North has favored some weighted voting and sought to limit the unilateral right of states to intervene in the market.

The Third World's effort to move toward more authoritative forms of allocation through either direct state redistribution or restrictions on rights of property alienation are manifest in proposals covering a wide

---

[9]The American labor movement can invoke fair trade as a slogan arguing that foreign countries have not adhered to liberal precepts. Public officials can call for "a level playing field." However, principled appeals for trade restriction based, for instance, on national autarky or increased social stability have been outside the accepted range of political discourse, at least in the United States.

range of issues. With regard to international trade, the Third World has supported special and differential treatment, such as generalized systems of preferences for exports to industrialized countries. The Integrated Program for Commodities, the centerpiece of Third World efforts to alter existing regimes during the mid-1970s, called for international commodity agreements and a Common Fund that would stabilize the prices of raw materials through export restrictions, publicly held buffer stocks, or other forms of market intervention. Developing countries have backed international codes for multinational corporations which proscribe some behavior, and legitimate national restrictions on corporate rights such as mandating joint ownership, the employment of nationals, specific export levels, and the reinvestment of local earnings. Developing countries have argued that the allocation of radio spectrum frequencies and geosynchronous orbits (for communications satellites) should be based on long-term developmental needs rather than on current demand. They have endorsed the principle that the deep seabed and space are both part of the common heritage of mankind, whose resources cannot simply be appropriated by those actors, public or private, with the requisite factor endowments. They have supported an extensive territorial sea enhancing the scope of sovereign control of littoral states. They have challenged the open rights of access, and freedom of reporting of international news agencies and foreign correspondents. The Third World has backed new rules of the game for shipping, which would give developing states a presumptive right to 40 percent of liner cargoes generated from their ports. Developing states have argued that technology is part of the common heritage of mankind rather than the private property of the innovating agency. They have endorsed the norm that industrialized countries have an obligation to provide 0.7 percent of their aggregate income in the form of foreign assistance. All of these programs would either enhance the direct sovereign control of individual developing states or establish international norms that would limit the ability of Northern actors to engage in exchange relationships.

DETERMINANTS OF THIRD WORLD SUCCESS

The ability of the Third World to implement its regime preferences has varied over time and across issue areas. Over time the decline of American power and the increase of Third World ideological coherence made the 1970s a particularly propitious moment for altering international regimes. The most important determinant of variation across various issue areas has been the degree of access provided by existing international organizations.

THE DECLINE OF AMERICAN POWER

American capabilities have declined across a wide range of power resources. Force can no longer be cheaply employed in the Third World. The USSR's military capability is equal or superior in many areas. In 1950 the gross national product of the United States was more than four times greater than that of Great Britain, the next largest noncommunist state; by 1981 it was only one and a half times greater than that of Japan, its closest challenger.[10] During the same period, American petroleum output fell from 51 percent of world output to 16 percent; crude steel production from 45 percent to 20 percent; iron ore from 42 percent to 11 percent; wheat from 17 to 12 percent.[11] Furthermore, by the early 1970s a number of major American industrial sectors including steel and textiles were encountering significant foreign competition. This change in competitive position, which was a natural outcome of the success of the postwar economic regime, reflected a decline in the unchallenged technological superiority enjoyed by most sectors of the American economy in the immediate postwar years. (The decline of ideological hegemony is discussed at the end of this chapter.)

The overall and issue-specific decline in power made it more difficult for American political leaders to provide unstinting support to liberal international economic regimes. With increasing frequency, specific American economic interests were given priority over regime maintenance. In August 1971 the United States violated some of the central norms and rules of the postwar monetary system by abruptly and unilaterally suspending the sale of gold to official agencies, and by imposing a 10 percent surcharge on imports. Central decision-makers continued to espouse liberal values, but they were forced to make more compromises with domestic firms threatened by foreign competition. Trade in major industrial sectors, most notably steel and textiles, was subject to various forms of restriction. The 1974 and 1979 Trade Acts made it easier for

[10]World Bank, *World Tables*, 1983 ed., pp. 254–257.
[11]Krasner, "U.S. Commercial and Monetary Policy," pp. 542–543.

industries to secure protection. Voluntary export restraint and orderly marketing agreements were signed for a variety of products.

The decline of American power and changes in a postwar economic regime are nowhere more dramatically evident than in the area of crude petroleum. Through the 1960s, basic choices regarding exploration, exploitation, production, processing, pricing, and marketing were made by seven giant multinational corporations, five of which were based in the United States. These corporations held concessions in Third World countries which gave them broad rights to make economic decisions regarding petroleum in exchange for royalty payments (later disguised as taxes) to host-country governments. However, the bargaining power of the major corporations declined as a result of increased host-country knowledge of technology and the market, and the growth of independent oil companies. The power of host countries increased vis-à-vis consuming countries because of the exhaustion of surplus capacity in non-OPEC producing countries, particularly the United States. Although the United States had been able to abort an Arab oil embargo after the 1967 Middle East war, the embargo and production cutbacks following the 1973 Middle East war led to a quadrupling of prices. The postwar oil regime characterized by private corporate control (although hardly a free market) was shattered in the early 1970s.

Examples of the relationship between the decline in American power capabilities and changes or erosion of international regimes could be multiplied. In some areas, such as oil, the United States no longer had the issue-relevant power to maintain the existing regime. In others, such as trade, declining capabilities made it more difficult for American leaders to sacrifice specific, narrow interests for regime stability. Exceptions to existing norms increased. Rules were bent. As a consequence of the decline in American power there was thus a weakening of regimes in many international issue areas: rules and decision-making procedures, as well as actual behavior, violated liberal norms and principles more frequently.

Weaker regimes were more vulnerable to attack from the Third World. OPEC demonstrated to the South that it was possible to challenge successfully principles, norms, rules, and decision-making procedures supported by multinational corporations and their home-country governments. Growing disagreements on economic issues undermined the unity of the North. Clear violations of liberal principles, such as restrictions on textile exports from the South, exposed the North to charges of hypocrisy and suggested that wealthier countries would bend or violate liberal rules of the game when it suited their purposes.

EXISTING INSTITUTIONS

Developing states have rarely had the national power capabilities necessary to dismantle existing regimes or to establish alternative global institutions on their own. The creation of new regimes is closely linked to national power capabilities. Once regimes are in place, however, their evolution can be influenced by a wide range of variables. National power capabilities are only one of a number of factors that can affect regime change as opposed to regime creation. The ability of the Third World to move regimes toward authoritative, rather than market-oriented, principles and norms was a function of the nature of existing institutions and the intellectual coherence of the Third World's program. Without access to, and the leverage provided by, existing institutional arrangements, the Third World would not have been able to launch a sustained attack on prevailing liberal practices. Two institutional arrangements—the norm of the sovereign equality of states, and the rules governing access to formal international organizations—have been major determinants of Third World success. Sovereign equality legitimated Third World claims to an equal voice in discussions of international rules of the game regardless of disparities in national power capabilities. Open access provided forums where Third World opinions could be expressed and votes counted; in issue areas where access to decision-making institutions has been closed, LDCs have not been able to alter prevailing principles, norms, and rules.

The Sovereign Equality of States

Hedley Bull has referred to sovereignty as the constitutive principle of the present international system.[12] Without the triumph of sovereignty, the North-South debate would not exist in its present form. Weaker areas would be subject to formal or informal domination by more powerful actors in the system. After the Second World War, the sovereign national state emerged as the only legitimate constitutive form of political organization in the international system. Colonialism was rejected. Tributary

[12]Bull, *The Anarchical Society.*

status was unacceptable. One political entity could not share political functions (such as foreign policy) with another without making its status suspect. Areas with very limited territory and population were accorded formal statehood.[13]

The triumph of sovereignty, of the principle that political life is organized within a defined territorial unit in which there is only one legitimate hierarchy of authority, does not, however, mean that all states will be recognized as having the same kinds of responsibilities in the international system. There has been an enduring struggle between the norms of great-power primacy and the sovereign equality of states. Great-power primacy implies that the major powers in the system have international rights and prerogatives that are denied to lesser powers. They can act unilaterally in certain areas even if their actions affect smaller powers. Sovereign equality implies that all states have the same rights. Lesser powers do not have to recognize as legitimate unilateral assertions by the great powers, although they might be compelled to accept such actions by superior force.

Until the last part of the twentieth century, great-power primacy dominated sovereign equality. The concept of an international system composed of great powers emerged during the eighteenth century. Writers who developed the theory of the balance of power "made a sharp distinction between the Great Powers and the smaller states, which could not have an independent policy."[14] In the first part of the nineteenth century the notion of a hierarchy of states, with special obligations falling on great powers, was embodied in the various treaties associated with the end of the Napoleonic wars and the Concert of Europe. In the Western Hemisphere the United States asserted great power status in the Monroe Doctrine and subsequent declarations. At the Paris Peace Conference following the First World War small states had two delegates on each commission, large ones five. The rights accorded to the major powers in the Council of the League of Nations and the Security Council of the United Nations were formal organizational manifestations of the norm of great-power primacy.[15]

Over time, however, sovereign equality became an increasingly impor-

[13]For an interesting discussion of failed British efforts to find some intermediate status for Caribbean mini-states, see Gilmore, "Requiem for Associated Statehood?" pp. 9 ff.

[14]Hinsley, *Power and the Pursuit of Peace,* p. 161.

[15]Klein, *Sovereign Equality Among States,* pp. 8, 46–49, 58–62, 108–111; Hinsley, *Power and the Pursuit of Peace,* pp. 153–161, 180–181; Bull, *The Anarchical Society,* p. 38; Craig and George, *Force and Statecraft,* p. 3.

tant counterpoint; by the 1960s it had become the dominant theme. At the first and second Hague Conferences for international peace held in 1899 and 1907 the major powers tacitly accepted the juridical equality of some weak states. The Latin American states, which sent eighteen out of the forty-four delegations to the 1907 conference, pressed strongly for sovereign equality. The Covenant of the League of Nations reflected sovereign equality (in providing for equal voting in the assembly) as well as great-power primacy. Over time the importance of the assembly increased relative to that of the council because of the American decision not to join, the initial exclusion of the Soviet Union and Germany, and disputes among the major powers. In the Western Hemisphere the United States formally relinquished the right to unilateral intervention in the "Good Neighbor Policy." The Inter-American Mutual Assistance Treaty of 1947 (one of the Rio treaties) provided that the signatories would abide by a two-thirds' majority vote; there was no veto. The Charter of the United Nations, like the Covenant of the League, enshrined both great-power primacy and sovereign equality, but over time the latter became more important. The Security Council was trammeled by divisions between the Soviet Union and the United States. The 1950 Uniting for Peace Resolution adopted the principle of sovereign equality expressed in the Rio treaties and made the General Assembly, with its one-nation, one-vote decision-making procedure, the central focus of United Nations' activities.[16]

Sovereign equality triumphed because of pressure from specific states, analogies made to domestic politics, and particular great-power calculations of interest. The Latin American states were leading advocates of sovereign equality. They were not constrained by the historical experience and endemic insecurity that had conditioned the leaders of small European states to accept great-power primacy. Demands for greater equality at the international level were also bolstered by analogies to domestic norms. If individual citizens were regarded as juridically equal, why not states as well? The success of democratic principles in the domestic sphere provided a constant source of inspiration for those states which advocated the same principles in the international system. Finally, specific political calculations by large states sometimes undermined claims to great-power primacy. The United States endorsed sovereign equality in the Western Hemisphere in the 1930s to improve relations with Latin American states, some of which were seen as toying with fascism and fascist alliances. The

[16]Klein, *Sovereign Equality Among States*, passim; Handel, *Weak States*, app. B.

Uniting for Peace Resolution was designed to legitimate American intervention in Korea.[17]

It is the conjuncture of small size and sovereign equality that makes the postwar international system unique. There were many small states in Europe before the nineteenth century.[18] These states, however, accepted the primacy of the great powers. They did not challenge the rules of the game, which were established by actors with weightier national power capabilities. In the postwar period the number of weak states has increased dramatically as a result of decolonization, and these states have entered an international system in which sovereign equality is an accepted principle. Weak states have been able to attack, persistently and systematically, the principles, norms, rules, and decision-making procedures supported by actors with much more substantial national power capabilities.

International Organizations

The second institutional arrangement influencing the Third World's ability to alter international regimes has been the access provided to decision-making arenas by existing international organizations. The degree of access is the most important factor in explaining the variations in Third World success across issue areas. In some cases existing international organizations afforded developing states very little opportunity to influence policy. Under such conditions Third World states were stymied because they lacked the national power capabilities to act on their own. In general, however, the existing structure of international organizations did provide access, usually equal access, for all states. The distribution of votes and power in most international organizations was not congruent with the underlying distribution of power among states.

It is possible to specify four relationships between the power and preferences of states on the one hand, and the nature of international regimes including international organizations on the other. First, there may be congruence between structure and regime: the characteristics of the regime reflect the preferences of individual states (weighted by their national power capabilities) and do not affect capabilities. Second, there

---

[17]Klein, *Sovereign Equality Among States*, pp. 36–37, 65–66, 67; Handel, *Weak States*, p. 266.

[18]The number of political units in Europe fell from 500 in 1500 to 25 in 1900. (Hechter and Brustein, "Regional Modes of Production.")

may be incongruence: the characteristics of the regime do not correspond to the preferences of individual states weighted by their national power capabilities, but the regime does not alter relative capabilities. Third, there may be dynamic stability between the structure and the regime. The characteristics of the regime conform with the preferences of the strong and reinforce the existing power distribution: the regime makes the strong stronger and the weak weaker.[19] The claim of dependency theorists is that the present set of international economic regimes serves the same function making the rich richer and the poor poorer. This occurs through a series of unequal exchanges. Political institutions on the periphery are weak and unable to defend their national economies from foreign encroachments. Political leaders identify themselves more with elites in the center than with their own populations. Multinational corporations can manipulate transfer prices. Raw-material operations have few links with the rest of the economy. Capital flows are pernicious. The capitalist world economy thus serves to reinforce the dependent position of peripheral areas.[20] Fourth, there may be dynamic instability between the regime and the international structure: transactions facilitated by the international regime tend to undermine the position of the more powerful states. These four possibilities are summarized in table 3.2.

During periods of hegemonic decline there is a propensity to move from congruence to incongruence or even to dynamic instability. For hegemonic powers there is a paradox, perhaps an inevitable dialectic, involved in the creation of international regimes that include formal international organizations. Regimes that the hegemon initially creates to serve its own interests can be seized and restructured by other actors in the system.

Hegemonic powers are likely to establish regimes that are congruent rather than dynamically stable. Their national material dominance is so complete that they can downplay narrow national interests in favor of broader milieu goals. This propensity became apparent in American foreign policy after 1946 when political leaders realized that within the Western alliance Britain could not pose a serious challenge. During the

[19]One example is the Anglo-Portuguese Treaty of 1703. Britain was the more powerful actor at the outset. In return for British military and political support the Portuguese agreed to restrict their trade with Britain, concentrating their exports on port wine and abandoning the export of wool while giving British manufacturers preferred access to Portugal. This reinforced the decline in Portuguese power. (Baumgartner et al., "Unequal Exchange and Uneven Development.")

[20]See, for example, the work of Wallerstein; Chase-Dunn and Rubinson, "Toward a Structural Perspective on the World-System"; Emmanuel, *Unequal Exchange*.

TABLE 3.2

REGIMES AND NATIONAL POWER

State preferences weighted by national power capabilities and regime characteristics	Impact of Regime on Underlying National Power Capabilities		
	Neutral	Reinforces existing power distribution	Undermines existing power distribution
Identical	Congruence	Dynamic stability	
Divergent	Incongruence		Dynamic instability

1950s and 1960s the United States accepted many departures from strict rules of economic liberalism by allowing Europe, and especially Japan, to discriminate against American products while offering ready access to the American market. These actions damaged specific economic interests but were consistent with the long-term political goals of strengthening the Western alliance and combating communism.

There are several factors that tend to move a regime from congruence to incongruence or to dynamic instability during periods of hegemonic decline. First, from the outset the hegemonic power is compelled to endow institutional structures with some autonomy. The purpose of the regime is to legitimate hegemonic preferences. Legitimacy cannot be promoted if the regime is perceived as merely an appendage of the hegemonic state. In the modern international system, legitimacy has required recognizing the sovereign equality of all states, implying an equal distribution of votes in international organizations despite radical differences in size or power. An equal division of votes, however, gives weaker states an opportunity to enhance their influence and control within these institutions.

A second dialectic element in the relationship between regimes and power is the independent inertia that can develop within international organizations. One of the conclusions of an exceptionally rigorous analysis of the behavior of international organizations is that "once established, organizations take on a life of their own and develop their own inner dynamics."[21] This process of independent growth is again facilitated by the behavior of a hegemon during periods of regime creation. One aspect of the autonomy that must be provided if organizations are to legitimate the rules and norms preferred by the dominant power is the establishment of objective criteria for the selection of staff. The hegemon cannot simply dictate appointments. Furthermore, goals must be stated in general terms. But once this is done the organization can fend for itself. It may autochthonously generate its own ethos. It can respond to new opportunities in ways that do not conform with the preference of its most powerful members. It can welcome new clients. Like individuals, organizational maturation is influenced by both genetic characteristics and environmental pressures. Over time the preferences of the organization and those of the hegemon may drift apart.[22]

A third dialectic element in the evolution of regimes from congruence to incongruence is the specific consequences for international organizations of the decline of a hegemonic power. At the pinnacle of its power the hegemonic state is prone to supply collective goods for the system disproportionately.[23] For instance, it will shoulder a large share of international organization budgets. But as its power declines, it will become more reluctant to do this. America's share of contributions to the budgets of various international organizations has fallen. The declining hegemon will become more reluctant to forgo specific national advantages to preserve international principles and norms. The organization's staff then has a strong incentive to move on its own to generate additional support. Furthermore, the influence of the hegemon on other states will decline, making them less likely to support its initiatives within international organizations.[24]

[21]Cox and Jacobsen, *Anatomy of Influence*, p. 7.

[22]John Ruggie has described an interesting example of the independent functioning of international organizations. In 1974 the United Nations Environmental Program (UNEP) and UNCTAD sponsored a conference on the global environment. The participants were experts serving in their individual capacities. The Cocoyoc Declaration that emerged from this meeting emphasized the link between waste and environmental degradation, and economic growth. It criticized the industrialized countries directly and the developing countries obliquely. The declaration itself was then faulted by both INs and LDCs. In this case the organization set the agenda for national states and offered the opportunity for expressing views that were rejected by all major blocs of countries. (Ruggie, "On the Problem of the 'Global Problematique.'")

[23]Olson and Zeckhauser, "An Economic Theory of Alliances."

[24]One study of U.N. voting and various economic measures of dependence on the United States concludes that "great U.S. economic advantage can no longer be used to generate

As international organizations drift out of the control of the hegemonic power, smaller and weaker states can become more influential. Most organizations offer these states formal equality. Constitutional documents endorse nonaggression, a doctrine particularly attractive to states with limited military capabilities. Small states can articulate ethical norms and standards as substitutes for material power. They can deploy their limited resources relatively efficiently in global forums. Disaffected weak states are likely to account for much of the incongruence that is apt to develop between the preferences of more powerful states and the characteristics of international regimes during periods of hegemonic decline.[25]

In the postwar period the Third World has made international organizations the primary venue for demands for regime change. The South has succeeded in dominating the agendas of all major multifunctional universal organizations. The North has been compelled to respond rather than initiate. Convening an international conference places an issue on the agendas of Northern states. Position papers have to be prepared. Voting positions must be determined.[26] The South has used international forums to initiate tactical and fragmented linkage strategies.[27] International organizations are used as vehicles for introducing new norms into the system. Without such forums weak states would have much less opportunity to present their positions. International organizations make it possible to address attentive elites as well as policymakers in the North. The audience for conventional bilateral diplomatic encounters is more limited.

There has been variation, however, in the degree of access afforded by the existing structure of international institutions. The modal category has been the universal organization that provides each state with a single vote. This is true for the United Nations as well as for most specialized agencies. In such forums developing countries could present their cases. But there are a number of exceptions. International financial institutions

voting support in the General Assembly" (Richardson, *Foreign Policy and Economic Dependence*, p. 177). The United States lost several votes on major IMF loans in the late 1970s, although in the 1950s it had been able to dictate policy.

[25]Hoadley, "Small States as Aid Donors," p. 124; Vital, *The Inequality of States*, pp. 33–34; Rothstein, *Alliances and Small Powers*, p. 39.

[26]Wriggins, "Third World Strategies for Change," p. 113; Krishnamuti, "UNCTAD," pp. 16–20.

[27]Tactical linkage is used to enhance the bargaining power of the weaker party by joining together issues that had previously been treated independently. Fragmented linkage is used to maintain the cohesion of a coalition. (Haas, "Why Collaborate?" pp. 370–375.)

have weighted voting systems.[28] There is no public international regime for certain services, most notably for insurance. Behavior in Antarctica has been governed by a treaty that has severely limited membership to functionally relevant states. In these issue areas the South has had great difficulty placing its program on the agenda, much less securing significant changes in existing principles, norms, rules, and decision-making procedures.

Furthermore, there are constraints on how far weak states can push, even when they have access, without undermining the efficaciousness of a regime. There can be incongruities between regime characteristics and underlying national power capabilities, but regimes become empty shells if they are ignored by the most powerful states in the system. By the late 1970s the disparity between U.S. preferences and some regime-related behavior threatened the institutions on which Third World states depended to voice their program for a new order. Even in the 1960s the relative size of American contributions to international organizations had begun to decline. Under the Carter administration the United States temporarily withdrew from the International Labor Organization because of differences over the membership's treatment of certain social issues. In early 1984 the United States announced its intention to withdraw from UNESCO, arguing that the organization had adopted positions "systematically hostile to Western values."[29] In 1982 American policymakers rejected the Law of the Sea Convention. This agreement had been concluded after negotiations lasting more than a decade. However, the Reagan administration refused to endorse the treaty because its provisions for the exploitation of deep-seabed nodules (rocks containing valuable elements) mandated the creation of an international entity called the Enterprise, which had a presumptive right to share technology and harvesting sites with private corporations. Moreover, modest limits on nodule exploitation were seen as a potential threat to national security because of the strategic significance of cobalt, nickel, and manganese. Some other industrialized nations also refused to sign. When the most powerful states in the system cannot get the rules they want from a given institutional arrangement, they can reject that arrangement even though they may not be able to build a new one.

[28]These systems are not as weighted as they appear. This issue is discussed in detail in chap. 6.

[29]*New York Times*, Feb. 16, 1984, p. 10. In January 1985 the United States withdrew from UNESCO.

The 1970s were the optimal moment for the Third World to press its demands for a new international order. The United States was still committed to the existing structure of institutions and willing to engage in global negotiations. It had accepted, for instance, a universal conference to decide on a new Law of the Sea treaty. But, at the same time, effective American control over international organizations had dissipated. By the late 1970s American commitment to existing institutions had waned. In several cases, Third World actions had led to American withdrawal, an extremely unattractive outcome for developing states because it forces them to rely more on their own exiguous national power capabilities.

MOVEMENTS OF THOUGHT

The third factor that has influenced the ability of the Third World to alter international regimes has been the development of a coherent system, or movement, of thought concerning the functioning of the postwar international economic system.[30] This system of thought has been endorsed by virtually all Third World states and has found many unofficial, and even some official, adherents in the First World as well. The South's ability to present an effective analysis of the global economy enhanced the unity of developing countries, weakened the capacity of the North to defend the liberal order, and facilitated the formulation of specific policy proposals.

Those responsible for the Third World's meta-political programs have drawn upon a theoretical analysis which concludes that the existing order is fundamentally flawed. Marginal changes cannot alter the liberal regime's basically exploitative character. The Third World cannot reach its full potential unless a new set of norms and rules comes to govern the international movement of goods, factors, and services.

Many analysts interested in world poverty, especially those from the Third World, never entirely accepted liberal arguments, but over time their criticisms have become more fundamental and more widely, albeit selectively, accepted by LDC policymakers. The early critics of the system, who were associated with both international organizations, such as the Economic Commission for Latin America (ECLA), and Western universities, argued that the assumptions needed to conclude that freer trade was mutually beneficial were inappropriate for less developed coun-

[30]Shils, "Ideology," provides the terminology.

tries. They pointed out that poor areas often had high levels of disguised unemployment. They argued that the terms of trade for primary commodities were declining over time: improvements in technique in manufacturing industries were appropriated in the form of higher profits and wages, while in raw-material industries they led to lower prices. The development of synthetics and the low-income elasticity of demand for agricultural commodities also contributed to declining terms of trade. Raw-material industries were isolated from the rest of the society; rather than creating a series of links that might promote economic development, such industries remained appendages of the economies of the more highly industrialized countries.[31]

The implication contained in these arguments was that the state would have to intervene in the economy to promote development. During the 1950s emphasis was placed on domestic policies, although international regimes were not ignored. The most widespread prescription, which carried over into the 1960s, called for a strategy of import substitution encouraged by restricting manufactured imports.

An import substitution strategy violated important liberal norms. It sanctioned state intervention and restrictive trade policies. However, the leading early critics of the postwar order used the vocabulary and analytic apparatus of neoclassical economic theory. LDCs were seen to be in a peculiar position, trapped by commodities whose long-term prospects were not promising. The assumption of perfect internal factor mobility, needed to demonstrate that openness led to Pareto-optimal outcomes, did not hold in developing countries. Individuals like Raul Prebisch of ECLA and Hans Singer of the United Nations appealed to the North, using readily understood terminology and reasoning.[32]

In the 1960s, however, a number of analysts from the Third World began to challenge American ideological hegemony in a much more fundamental way. *Dependencia*, or dependency, theorists maintain that the under- or perverted development of the Third World and the development of the industrialized nations are intimately related. The poverty of the one is a consequence of the wealth of the other. Whereas conventional economic growth theorists explain underdevelopment primarily by the

[31]Prebisch, "Commercial Policy in the Underdeveloped Countries"; Hans W. Singer, "The Distribution of Gains Between Investing and Borrowing Countries"; Murphy, *New International Economic Order Ideology*; Hart, *The New International Economic Order*, pp. 7–12.

[32]Presbisch; Singer (see n. 31, above).

national characteristics of backward countries, dependency theorists see underdevelopment as a product of the workings of the international system. It is not the absence of education, infrastructure, capital, or foreign exchange per se that account for poverty; rather, these lacunae are a manisfestation of a pernicious set of transnational interactions. The international order corrupts the economic, political, and cultural development of dependent areas. Rather than whittling away at the edge of liberal orthodoxy, dependency theorists have sought to pulverize the intellectual structure altogether.

There are some important distinctions among dependency theorists. They can be broken into two general classes: unorthodox and orthodox.[33] Unorthodox dependency theorists view domination by industrialized countries, particularly the United States, as being loose and uncoordinated. There is some discretion for the dependent state. International economic ties are compatible with economic growth, but the pattern of development itself is perverted.

For instance, multinational corporations can make a positive contribution to economic change in peripheral areas. Producers of manufactures with a large stake in the markets of developing countries do support measures that would enhance domestic demand. Through these corporations, elements of the middle class, the army, the state bureaucracy, and even the working class become integrated into the world capitalist system. The prospects for peripheral areas, however, are truncated.[34] The generation of technology and capital goods remains concentrated at the center. Demand is skewed to middle-class products produced by the multinationals, which reflect consumer tastes in the North. The majority of the working class must be suppressed. The masses are marginalized: they cannot be integrated into political activity, nor can their quality of life be significantly improved. Income distribution becomes more inequitable and foreign debts increase.

Other writers associated with the notion of dependency have taken an even dimmer view of the workings of the world economy. Orthodox dependency theorists see very few benefits accruing to the weaker partner. By concentrating on the production of raw materials, the developing nations have drained their own natural endowments. Cash crops drive out food crops, lowering the nutritional level of the population. Foreign

[33]Dominguez, "Consensus and Divergence," pp. 106–107.
[34]Evans, *Dependent Development*; Cardoso and Faletto, *Dependency and Development*.

investment has weakened indigenous technology and skills. Foreign investors use heavily capital-intensive production processes that are transferred from advanced areas, and fail to utilize fully under- or unemployed labor. The large initial capital outlays of foreign investors create barriers to entry for domestic entrepreneurs. Multinational corporations (MNCs) can secure monopoly profits, which are often remitted to their home countries. Foreign investors have kept part of the production process physically located in the industrial center, making it difficult for host-country nationals to learn the skills necessary to establish full control.[35]

Foreign investors, orthodox dependency theorists maintain, have failed to increase the capital endowments of host countries. Most capital investments are made from profits generated in developing areas rather than from new capital inputs from the center. Foreign investors borrow from banks of the host country. Interest and dividend payments transfer large amounts of capital out of the developing nation. Foreign investment, rather than increasing the capital endowment of the host country, may actually deplete it.[36]

Both orthodox and unorthodox *dependencia* theorists also argue that the existing order distorts cultural and social development in backward areas. Demand does not reflect autonomously arrived at tastes but, rather, the pattern of incomes and values associated with international capitalism. The elite in backward areas mimic the consumption patterns of their counterparts in nations with much higher per capita incomes. The medical, educational, and social practices of advanced states are indiscriminately copied, even though they are inappropriate for poorer countries.

From a dependency perspective, existing international economic structures are also understood to pervert political development in the Third World. A reactionary alliance develops between elite groups in the backward area and foreign investors. Paul Baran was one of the first to etch out this possibility. In an article written in 1952, he argued that the workings of the international system stifled economic, social and, therefore, political evolution in less developed states. The domestic entreprenurial class was absorbed by multinational corporations. The local merchant class allied itself with foreign elements against the dangers presented by radical domestic groups.[37] For Osvaldo Sunkel, the national

[35]Gunder Frank's writings contain the best-known orthodox dependency formulations.
[36]Baran and Sweezy, *Monopoly Capitalism*, p. 193; Baran, *The Political Economy of Growth*, p. 180.
[37]Baran, *The Political Economy of Growth*.

bourgeoisie in Latin America is being transformed into a "private, trans-national, technocracy."[38] Samir Amin has argued that in the African Islamic savannah the breakup of feudal estates, and the more efficient production and democratic political base this should have fostered, was frustrated by ties between the local ruling class and foreign capital.[39] Peter Evans avers that the local political elite is forced into an alliance with local capital and MNCs, which precludes an equitable distribution of the benefits of industrialization.[40] Furthermore, international corporations will appeal to their own governments to support conservative groups in backward areas. Military assistance, economic coercion, and even covert military intervention can all be used to prevent the emergence of "pro-gressive" forces in the Third World. At worst, from an orthodox depen-dency perspective, the governments of Third World countries become merely puppets of the North; at best, from an unorthodox dependency perspective, the state in developing areas is confronted with a truncated set of options that preclude effective national integration of the masses.

Dependency theorists thus view the liberal international economy as a self-reinforcing mechanism of exploitation. The Third World is per-meated by external forces; there is no dialectic. Bargains are inherently unjust because power disparities are so great. So long as the present patterns of behavior, institutional arrangements, rules, and norms persist, there is no possibility for autochthonous growth in developing areas.

Third World leaders have increasingly based their proposals for change on selective aspects of dependency theory. Dependency theory is useful because it offers a much broader range of criticisms of the postwar economy than did Prebisch and other early writers. It explains many phenomena within a single overarching framework: terms of trade, capital flows, technology transfers, consumer tastes, political oppression can all be systematically linked with the workings of the world capitalist system. Those political arguments associated with dependency theory, however, which depict elites as pawns of world imperialism or multinational corpo-rations, cannot be accepted easily by Third World leaders. Rather, depen-dency theory has been treated as a policy critique, not as basic social analysis: its economic arguments have been placed in the conventional political framework used by earlier critics of the liberal order. The state is accepted as an autonomous entity striving to enhance the well-being

[38]Sunkel, "Big Business and *Dependencia*," p. 527.
[39]Amin, *The Maghreb*, p. 214.
[40]Evans, *Dependent Development*, chap. 5.

of its own population. But its efforts are hamstrung by a set of self-reinforcing, exploitative mechanisms linking the economies of the South with those of the North. For Third World leaders, unequal exchange is the key to understanding the deleterious consequences of the world capitalist system.

The development of a coherent intellectual position has provided a basis for Third World meta-political demands, enhanced Third World cooperation, and weakened the unity of the North. The major documents associated with Third World meta-political demands, such as the Economic Declaration and the Action Programme for Economic Cooperation adopted at the 1973 Algiers Non-Aligned Summit, and the Declaration on the Establishment of a New International Economic Order passed at the Sixth Special Session of the U.N. General Assembly, call for fundamental changes in the present international economic structure. Mahbub ul Haq, a vice-president of the World Bank in the 1970s, who emerged as an important expositor of Third World views, has written that "the Third World has to make it quite clear in its future negotiations that what is at stake is not a few marginal adjustments in the international system; it is its complete overhaul."[41] In analyzing the basic problems afflicting the world economy before a 1978 meeting of the Trade and Development Board, UNCTAD's secretary general, Gamani Corea, argued:

There is better recognition that these [basic problems] would not be solved by a mere recovery of the industrialized countries and a return to past patterns of growth with benefits to the developing countries emerging as a mere byproduct of this process. On the contrary, there is a growing understanding that the problems also call for more basic structural changes in the world economy, growing recognition that the framework of rules and principles that have hitherto governed trade and international economic relations need to evolve and be adapted to meet changing requirements.[42]

Calls for extensive change have been justified by arguments drawn from the system of thought adopted by the Third World. Major aspects of the international economic system are flawed because the underlying mechanisms of exchange are unequal. Market-oriented regimes are inherently problematic because they provide unfair advantages for larger and

[41]Haq, *The Poverty Curtain*, p. 168.
[42]UNCTAD, *Monthly Bulletin*, no. 144.

more knowledgeable economic actors. Multinational corporations can manipulate transfer prices to evade taxation. Shipping liner conferences can freeze out competitors from the Third World. International news agencies can monopolize the flow of information and issue distorted reports about developing areas. Labor unions and firms in the North can appropriate the benefits of technological progress. Sophisticated corporations can plunder the global commons with no concern for the rights or well-being of poorer areas. International lending agencies can impose politically embarrassing, even fatal, conditions on loans. Import competing sectors in the North can often force their governments to impose trade restrictions on products from LDCs.

The concept of unequal exchange suggests that far-reaching changes are needed in many areas. These changes involve moving away from market-oriented regimes toward regimes based on authoritative allocation. The extent of desired change varies across issue areas as a function of existing principles and norms. In cases where market-oriented regimes have prevailed, the South has pushed hard for basic change. In issue areas where authoritative regimes were already in place, the Third World has not presented meta-political challenges.

My argument here is not meant to imply that all efforts by Third World countries involve regime change. On the contrary, many specific discussions have been carried out within the context of exisiting liberal principles, norms, and rules. The NICs have been especially vigorous in pressing the industrialized countries to honor their commitments to liberal trading principles. Heavy borrowers have tried to secure the best terms for rescheduling their loans. However, these efforts are analytically distinct from the call for a New International Economic Order and related programs. They involve relational, rather than meta-power, behavior. They do not challenge prevailing liberal principles and norms. They are justified in terms of the self-interest of single states rather than the well-being of the Third World as a whole.

Moreover, the argument made here is not meant to imply that all of the proposals embodied in the New International Economic Order and related efforts were endoised by all LDCs with equal enthusiasm, or that there was no debate within the Third World. Many specific packages were a product of logrolling among some countries. There have been instances in which individual countries broke rank on specific substantive issues. Liberia has not supported calls for an end to flags of convenience. Argentina opposed the Integrated Program for Commodities. Countries that were heavy borrowers distanced themselves from proposals for general debt cancellation in the late 1970s. The amount of support that various countries gave to specific parts of the NIEO program varied with their specific economic interests.[43]

These exceptions, however, should not obscure the striking overall unity and coherence of the Third World's program and behavior in global negotiations. Although the Group of 77 includes more than a hundred countries, it has still been able to offer proposals on an exceptionally wide range of issues that have, at the very least, the voting support of all of its members. Moreover, these programs have not been an intellectual hodgepodge; they all share the common characteristic of endorsing principles, norms, rules, and decision-making procedures that are more oriented toward authoritative allocation than those presently in place. Only certain kinds of logs have been rolled. All of the central planks of the NIEO program and associated proposals are consistent with an intellectual analysis in which unequal exchange is seen as the defining characteristic of the world economic system, and authoritative, rather than market, modes of allocation are seen as the prescription for rectifying this inequity.

The development of a coherent set of ideas has contributed to the NIEO program in an even more fundamental way—it has provided the basis not simply for unity among Third World states but for the very idea of the Third World itself. Although almost all developing countries share the common structural characteristics of international and domestic weakness, they vary in their specific economic concerns, religious commitments, political organizations, and historical experiences. For the Third World to wield itself into a coherent political force it was necessary to have a set of ideas that provided a common, intersubjective understanding of the global order. Domestic and international weaknesses made Southern unity an immanent tendency in the post–World War II global order; but the actualization of that unity was dependent on the development of a common world view.

In the period immediately after the Second World War there was no clear distinction between the North and the South. Major Latin American countries granted aid to the United Nations Relief and Rehabilitation Agency and to war-devastated European states.[44] The Non-Aligned

[43]For a discussion of Latin America, see Hart, *The New International Economic Order*, chap. 4.

[44]Murphy, *New International Economic Order Ideology*, p. 77.

Movement, organized in the mid-1950s, represented the first effort by developing states to formulate a position that was separate and distinct from that of wealthier areas. However, it was defined by the East-West conflict, not the North-South one. It was an effort by LDCs to legitimate a neutral position between the Soviet Union and the United States, not to open an entirely new dimension of discourse. In the main, the Latin American states stayed aloof from the Non-Aligned Movement. The francophone African states were also initially unenthusiastic. At the beginning of the 1960s there was only a limited similarity between the United Nations votes of the Afro-Asian states, which were members of the Non-Aligned Movement, and the Latin American states, which were not. Only in the late 1960s did the U.N. voting patterns of the two groups begin to converge.[45] The official groupings established at the first UNCTAD meeting were basically regional—Afro-Asian, Latin American, advanced market-economy, and socialist—not North-South. The Group of 77, which was organized to coordinate the behavior of the Afro-Asian and Latin American groups, represented the first major effort at Third World unity in the economic area. It was distinct from the Non-Aligned Movement. At its 1970 meeting in Lusaka the Non-Aligned Movement began to incorporate both economic and political concerns. This orientation was reinforced by the 1973 Algiers Non-Aligned summit, which completed the de facto coalescence of the Group of 77 and the Non-Aligned Movement. At this meeting, where Algeria played a leading role, economic issues were given primary attention. A series of resolutions was passed, which became the basis of the South's position at the Sixth U.N. Special Assembly in 1974.[46]

The formulation of a coherent intellectual position provided an image of a shared history of Northern domination and of a common future for states with very different domestic characteristics, an identity obscured by alternative analyses, in which the world was divided into communist and noncommunist, or aligned and nonaligned, or Asian, African, Latin American, socialist, and market-oriented. This shared image linked proposals as disparate as those concerned with commodity agreements, debt relief, territorial seas, geosynchronous orbits, and multinational corporations. It showed that the states of Latin America, whose direct experiences with colonialism had ended in the nineteenth century, were in the same structural situation as African states that had received their independence

[45]Willetts, *The Non-Aligned Movement*, p. 990.
[46]Hansen, *Beyond the North-South Stalemate*, p. 21.

in the 1960s. It implied that the nature of domestic political regimes was secondary to the pattern of international transactions so that states with very different domestic institutions and ideologies could put these distinctions aside. It showed how the fate of extremely poor countries, primarily concerned with the terms for official capital flows, was related to the prospects for more prosperous, resource-exporting developing countries, which were worried about declining terms of trade. A common world view made it possible to preserve unity in the face of diverse and shifting interests.[47]

In sum, the movement of thought embraced by developing countries was not merely a rationalization. It was the subjective complement to the objective condition of domestic and international weakness.[48] It allowed the political leaders of developing countries, and many of their subjects, to find a common identity that moved beyond seeing themselves as Moslems or Christians, Latins or Asians, neutrals or allies. Without this shared intellectual position, it is unlikely that the countries of the South would have become a coherent political force. The social-choice problems of maintaining an alliance among more than one hundred and twenty countries across a wide range of issues would have been overwhelming had their behavior simply been based on calculations of their own narrow economic self-interest. Even if fully implemented, the benefits of many of the programs of the NIEO, including the Integrated Program for Commodities, the centerpiece of Third World efforts at the height of NIEO demands in the 1970s, would be limited to a relatively small number of countries. Third World unity is more difficult to understand from a perspective that emphasizes logrolling on purely economic issues than from one that sees the development of a common ideology, which rejected liberal principles and norms, as a necessary adjunct to the objective structural conditions confronting almost all Third World states.

A final consequence of the effective articulation of an explanation for

[47]See Hansen, *North-South Policy*, p. 1106, and Rothstein, *The Third World and U.S. Foreign Policy*, p. 30, for similar conclusions. One study based on interviews with diplomats involved in NIEO negotiations in the 1970s found that 46 percent of the representatives from LDCs had consulted with other LDCs in determining their countries' policies. No delegate from an industrialized nation mentioned consultation with other countries. (Jacobsen et al., "Revolutionaries or Bargainers," p. 340.) Another study based on interview data argues that "the solidarity of the developing countries was the product of the spread of terms of trade theories as a widely accepted view among officials of Third World countries of how the world economy works" (Hart, *The New International Economic Order*, p. 144).

[48]See Sabel, *Work and Politics*, for a discussion of the relationship between objective conditions and subjective self-assessment.

Third World weakness and poverty based on an exploitative international capitalist system was that it weakened the North. The Gramscian hegemony exercised by liberal ideology was severely undermined. By the mid-1970s Northern countries were generally reacting to, rather than initiating, proposals. The South would not have been able to accomplish this, regardless of its dissatisfaction with the existing system, without developing an alternative movement of thought.[49]

The South has been able to play upon divisions among Northern elites. Important groups within Northern society have come to endorse many of the policy proposals of the South. Their reasoning is based on a number of arguments of which the most pervasive is that the interdependent world of the last part of the twentieth century will be inherently unstable so long as the massive gap between the North and the South remains. There is widespread acceptance of Southern claims that the existing international order imposes impediments to Southern growth. A number of smaller European states, notably the Scandinavian countries and the Netherlands, have long taken a sympathetic attitude toward less developed areas. The Netherlands, for instance, supported proposals for a Special United Nations Fund for Economic Development (SUNFED) in the early 1950s, which represented one of the early demands for regime restructuring.[50] The leading Dutch spokesman on development issues during the mid-1970s was convinced not only that the existing system was unjust but also that it was subject to disruption by developing countries. Sweden and six other industrialized states voted for the Charter of Economic Rights and Duties of States, one of the resolutions that provided the foundation for the Third World's call for a New International Economic Order in the mid-1970s. Private groups in the North have attacked some multinational corporate practices.[51]

[49]Bernard Brodie has written, "In order to oppose an idea effectively, one needs more than superior authority—one needs in addition one or more alternative ideas" (*War and Politics*, p. 14).

[50]In a survey of members of the Dutch foreign policy elite, 31 percent said that external factors were the major causes; 14 percent that neither was of much importance, and 25 percent that internal causes were more important than external. (Baehr, "The Dutch Foreign Policy Elite," p. 252.) See also Hart, *The New International Economic Order*, pp. 118–120.

[51]Perhaps the most publicized instance of such an attack was the criticism evoked by the advertisement and promotion of baby formulas in the Third World by major multinational food companies, especially Nestlés. Formulas are usually not only nutritionally inferior to breast milk but also dangerous because of the poor hygienic practices followed in poorer countries. Church organizations in the North were very active. In 1976 a Swiss group secured a court order instructing Nestlés to "carry out a fundamental reconsideration" of

In general, the positions of Northern states regarding the NIEO varied across both countries and issue areas. In an analysis based on statements about access to markets, commodity trade, debt relief, and technology transfer made at the 1976 UNCTAD meeting, Jeffrey Hart concludes that Norway and the Netherlands were most favorably disposed, supporting the Third World's position on almost all issues, while Japan and Germany opposed almost all of the NIEO proposals.[52] Among the large industrialized states France, with its Gaullist tradition and less competitive industrial structure, was most supportive of Third World programs.[53] Although defending free markets, the United States was willing to make some concessions to the Third World. These concessions have been rationalized, however, as one step along the path that culminates in "graduation" to full and equal responsibility for maintaining open practices.

The ideological coherence of the Third World's position is but one of several variables accounting for the divergent positions of the North toward the NIEO program. Others include domestic political values, international economic interests, and party preferences.[54] The acceptance of Southern arguments did, however, contribute to the disunity of the industrialized countries.[55]

CONCLUSION

At the end of the Second World War the United States created a set of international regimes whose purpose was to promote general and long-term political objectives. American policymakers were able to employ a wide array of economic, ideological, and even military resources to sup-

its baby formula advertising program. *Wall Street Journal*, June 25, 1976, 24:2. The efforts of private groups culminated in a 1981 nonbinding World Health Organization resolution calling upon corporations to cease all advertisement and promotion of baby formula. This pressure did lead Nestlés to change its policies.

[52]Hart, *The New International Economic Order*, table 5.3.

[53]Ibid., p. 116.

[54]Ibid., chaps. 5–6.

[55]Hirsch and Doyle, *Alternatives to Monetary Disorder*, p. 60. See Tucker, *The Inequality of Nations*, passim, for an explanation of what he terms the "new political sensibility" in the North. For an exposition of a Northern position sympathetic to the South based on an interdependence perspective, see Hansen, *Beyond the North-South Stalemate*, and more especially the first Brandt Commission report.

port liberal principles, norms, rules, and decision-making procedures. LDCs had little control over these regimes. The objective of the South has been to move from market allocation toward authoritative allocation. The ability of the South to undermine and restructure regimes has varied across issue areas and over time as a function of three variables.

First, the power of the United States declined in some areas. Only rarely did this leave developing countries in any position to challenge IN preferences in most dyadic relationships, the disparity in resources between the larger countries of the North and virtually all countries of the South remained much too great for that. The decline of American capabilities, however, reduced both the inclination and ability of American central decision-makers to defend the regimes that they had themselves created. With increasing frequency regime stability was sacrificed to specific American economic interests. This made the liberal order more vulnerable to Third World attack.

The second attribute of the international system determining Southern influence was the degree of access provided by international organizations and the ability of the South to control their agendas and decisions. The international organizations created after World War II reflected both the style and interests of a hegemonic America. They were used to legitimate U.S. goals. To act effectively as a legitimating force, however, these organizations had to be accorded a substantial degree of independence. Membership was usually premised on the sovereign equality of all states. By the 1960s the Third World was able to take advantage of the loose connection between voting arrangements within organizations and the distribution of national power capabilities among states. The preferences of the more powerful states and the activities of international organizations diverged. There are dialectic elements in a hegemonic structure that make it likely that the behavior of international organizations will move from congruence to incongruence or even dynamic instability with the interests of the dominant state. The mid-1970s were an ideal time to take advantage of this situation. American leaders had lost control of international organizations but were still committed to them. During the course of the decade, however, American policymakers became more reluctant to accept unpalatable decisions supported by the Third World, which culminated in their rejection of the Law of the Sea Convention in 1982, and withdrawal from UNESCO and rejection of the World Court's jurisdiction in a case involving Nicaragua in 1985.

Finally, Third World states were able to increase their influence by articulating a coherent intellectual view. By effectively depicting the global economy as an engine of exploitation, developing countries were able to justify cognitively their demands for movement from liberal to authoritative norms and rules over a wide range of issues. Even more fundamentally, a coherent set of ideas created Third World unity by providing an intersubjective understanding of the common position shared by all developing countries because of their place in the world economic system. This subjective comprehension actualized the unity that was immanent in the objective domestic and international weaknesses of developing states. Finally, Third World ideas weakened the North by destroying the legitimating force of the liberal ideology espoused by the United States and by exacerbating fissures among Northern elites. Thus, despite the limited national material resources at the command of almost all Third World leaders, they were presented with opportunities to secure some of their meta-political objectives.

IV

Economic Performance and the Reaction to OPEC: Challenges to Economistic Interpretations

Many interpreters view Southern behavior as a response to inadequate economic performance. There is a widespread belief that the countries of the Third World are mired in poverty and stagnation. If the South is making radical demands, it is only because the existing international economic system has not provided satisfactory opportunities.

An examination of the actual experience of the Third World during the postwar period, however, belies such a simple picture. The South as a whole has grown faster than the North. Two groups of states, the oil producers and the newly industrializing countries (NICs) have done extraordinarily well, although impressive performances are not limited to these countries. Social indicators show an upward trend in virtually all developing countries. During the 1960s and early 1970s LDCs grew faster than most observers had anticipated, including policymakers from the Third World. Economic performance was especially good during the period immediately preceding the most strident Third World calls for the transformation of international regimes. None of this is meant to deny the extreme poverty of hundreds of millions of individuals in the Third World. But it does suggest that economistic interpretations of Third World behavior are too simple. If policymakers in developing countries were exclusively concerned with the well-being of their individual citizens, the frontal assault on an existing set of international regimes that has been associated with rapid aggregate growth in many countries would hardly seem appropriate.

However, rapid growth over time has not alleviated the gap between the North and the South, which continues to grow absolutely, but not relatively, because the initial disparity between the two areas is so great.

Diachronic performance is an indicator of economic progress within a country; the gap is an indicator of strength and vulnerability across countries. For most Third World countries, even very rapid economic growth cannot narrow their absolute gaps with the North or bring their relative positions to the point where their national capabilities would allow satisfactory control over the international environment. The meta-political strategy of the South cannot be explained in any straightforward manner by the failure of the extant international regime to provide economic benefits; it can be understood as a reaction to the insecurity and vulnerability experienced by the South within the existing rules of the game.

The Third World response to the quadrupling of oil prices that took place in 1973–1974 is also inconsistent with purely economistic explanations. While oil price increases benefited oil-exporting states, they hurt non-oil-producing LDCs. Energy import bills increased. Slower growth in industrialized countries, in part a result of higher oil prices, reduced the demand for primary and manufactured exports from the Third World. These losses were not offset by aid, or other capital flows from OPEC countries. Even so, the rise of OPEC was generally applauded by the Third World. While individual countries voiced reservations and tried to strike their own deals, OPEC's policies were not openly and collectively attacked despite their manifestly deleterious consequences for most poorer areas. It was not only that oil was the one major issue area in which developing states had succeeded in establishing a set of international practices, if not a full-fledged regime, but also that criticizing OPEC would have been inconsistent with the intellectual position on which Third World unity was based. In sum, the material presented in this chapter is not meant to demonstrate the empirical validity of the thesis that the NIEO is an effort to compensate for structural weakness at the international and domestic levels. The empirical data do suggest, however, that not all Third World behavior can be understood as a response to poor economic performance.

ECONOMIC PERFORMANCE

The Third World as a whole, and many individual countries, have experienced substantial material change in the postwar period. In this section I shall review data on national production and social well-being.

NATIONAL ACCOUNTS

The overall economic growth of the developing areas since 1950 has been impressive. They have grown at a faster rate than at any time in their own history. Their rate of growth has been more rapid than that of the industrialized market-economy countries.

Table 4.1 shows the ratio of GNP for 1975 to GNP for 1950, and average annual growth rates for the same period. The gross national product of the industrialized countries grew by a factor of 3.2 during the twenty-five-year period; that of the developing world by a factor of 3.91. Annual growth rates were at the historically unprecedented levels of 5.6 percent for LDCs and 4.7 percent for INs. With the exception of South Asia the increase in GNP for different areas of the Third World exceeded that of the developed countries.

Figures for per capita growth rates do not reveal such a positive relative experience for LDCs. The population growth rate of the Third World has been exceptionally high. The average annual rate for 1950–1975 was 2.4 percent. This compares with 1.0 percent for the industrialized countries. Population growth in the developing world has not only been much higher than in the past but also much higher than the past experiences of

TABLE 4.1
AGGREGATE GROWTH 1950–1975

	1975 GNP/ 1950 GNP	Average annual percent change
Africa	3.34	4.9
South Asia	2.67	4.0
East Asia (excluding Peoples Republic of China)	4.79	6.4
Middle East	8.60	8.9
Latin America	3.86	5.5
South Europe	4.30	6.0
OPEC	5.89	7.3
South Africa	3.35	4.9
All LDCs	3.91	5.6
Industrialized Countries	3.20	4.7

Source: Derived from figures in Morawetz, *Economic Development*, tables 1, A1, and A6.

now developed areas, with the exception of areas of overseas European settlement.[1] Table 4.2 shows per capita GNP growth rates for the period 1950–1975.

The growth rates of the developing world since 1950 are exceptionally high compared with the rates of the now industrialized countries during the nineteenth century. Table 4.3 shows annual percentage rates of growth for various areas of Europe for the years 1830 to 1910.

The growth rates of developing countries are also high compared with their own past experiences. For the period 1900 to 1913 the annual rate of per capita GDP growth for less developed countries was 1.2 percent; for 1913 to 1929, 0.9 percent, and for 1929–1952, 0.6 percent. Aggregate GDP growth rates for the same periods were 2.1 percent, 1.9 percent, and 2.2 percent.[2] For sixteen countries for which data are available for GNP growth rates for 1913–1950 and 1950–1968, only one, Malaya, experienced a lower rate in the later period.[3]

The aggregate economic performance of the Third World in the post-war era cannot be accounted a failure. Absolute growth rates were higher

TABLE 4.2
PER CAPITA GROWTH 1950–1975

	1975 per capita GNP/ 1950 per capita GNP	Average annual percent change
Africa	1.81	2.4
South Asia	1.52	1.7
East Asia (excluding Peoples Republic of China)	2.60	3.9
Middle East	3.55	5.2
Latin America	1.90	2.6
Southern Europe	3.01	4.5
OPEC	3.23	2.8
All LDCs (excluding Peoples Republic of China)	2.09	3.0
Industrialized Countries	2.20	3.2

Source: Morawetz, *Economic Development*, tables 1 and A1.

[1]Bairoch, *The Economic Development of the Third World*, chap. 1.
[2]Ibid., p. 184.
[3]Maddison, *Economic Progress and Policy*, p. 29.

TABLE 4.3
AVERAGE ANNUAL RATES OF EUROPEAN
ECONOMIC GROWTH, 1830–1910

	Total GNP		GNP per capita	
	1830–1910	1860–1910	1830–1910	1860–1910
Total Europe	1.74	1.88	0.92	0.96
Belgium, France, Switzerland, UK	1.80	1.72	1.25	1.16
Austria-Hung., Germany, Netherlands	1.98	2.24	1.10	1.24
Denmark, Finland, Norway, Sweden	2.26	2.51	1.33	1.60
Russia, Romania, Bulgaria	1.76	2.21	0.64	0.94
Greece, Italy, Portugal, Serbia, Spain	1.00	0.94	0.39	0.28

Source: Bairoch, "Europe's Gross National Product, 1800–1975," p. 280.

for developing areas than for industrialized ones for the period 1950–1975, and per capita growth rates were almost equal. Growth was faster than observers in either the developing or industrialized world had expected. The 5 percent target specified in the first U.N. Development Decade in 1960, a target understood to be more rhetorical than realistic, was actually exceeded. Projections of LDC growth rates made in the early 1960s were frequently too low.[4]

These aggregate statistics mask a wide range of country-level variation. Even when the experience of the Third World is examined at the national level, however, the growth rates for most countries are high both in comparison with the previous experience of poorer areas and with that of industrialized areas. Table 4.4 shows the distribution of average annual compound growth rates in GNP for developing countries for the period 1950–1975.

[4]Morawetz, *Twenty-five Years of Economic Development*, tables A4 and A5.

TABLE 4.4

DISTRIBUTION OF AVERAGE ANNUAL GNP GROWTH RATES
FOR LDCs, 1950–1975

Growth rate (%)	0–1.9	2.0–3.9	4.0–5.9	6.0–7.9	8.0<
Number of countries	4	20	31	16	6

Source: Derived from figures in Morawetz, *Economic Development*, tables A1 and A6.
Morawetz's study draws on World Bank data. Figures are not available for 22 countries.

Compared with Europe in the nineteenth century these are impressive increases. For the period 1830 to 1910 the average annual percentage rate of GNP growth for European countries ranged from 0.86 for Portugal to 2.62 for Denmark, with an average of 1.74; for the period 1860 to 1910, from 0.61 for Spain to 2.62 for Greece, with an average of 1.88.[5] The average growth rate for INs for the period 1950–1975 was 4.7 percent. Forty-three LDCs exceeded this figure, thirty-five failed to reach it. Because of recovery from the Second World War and other factors, this period was one of unusually rapid growth for industrialized areas.[6]

Country-level figures for per capita GNP growth rates do not present so favorable a comparison for LDCs because of their rapid population increase. Table 4.5 shows the distribution of per capita growth rates for developing countries for the period 1950–1975.

For the same period, the average per capita growth rate for industrialized countries was 3.2 percent. Only sixteen developing countries exceeded this rate. Current LDC per capita growth rates compare very favorably with European rates during the nineteenth century, which averaged 0.96 for the period 1830–1910, with a high of 1.86 for Denmark.[7]

If the growth experience of developing countries is broken down by time period it offers no explanation of why the New International Economic Order was so forcefully launched in the early 1970s. On the contrary, the late 1960s and early 1970s were the years during which the developing world enjoyed its most robust economic performance. The growth rates of gross domestic product and per capita gross domestic product for developing countries (excluding capital-surplus oil-exporting countries) are shown in table 4.6. In 1973, the year immediately before

[5]Bairoch, "Europe's GNP," p. 283.
[6]Organski and Kugler, *The War Ledger*, pp. 137–142.
[7]Bairoch, "Europe's GNP," p. 283.

TABLE 4.5

DISTRIBUTION OF AVERAGE ANNUAL PER CAPITA GROWTH RATES
FOR DEVELOPING COUNTRIES, 1950–1975

Growth rate (%)	Negative	0–2.0	2.0–4.0	4.0–6.0	6.0–8.0
Number of countries	8	35	26	9	2

Source: Morawetz, *Economic Development*, tables A2 and A3.

TABLE 4.6

AVERAGE ANNUAL REAL GROWTH RATES FOR DEVELOPING COUNTRIES
(EXCLUDING CAPITAL-SURPLUS OIL-EXPORTERS), BY PERIOD

	1950–1960	1960–1965	1965–1970	1970–1977
GDP	4.9	5.6	6.4	5.7
GDP per capita	2.7	3.1	3.8	3.2

Source: World Bank, *World Tables*, 2d ed., 1980, p. 372.

the major documents of the New International Economic Order were presented at the Sixth Special Session of the United Nations General Assembly, the non-oil developing countries as a group experienced their highest single increase in real gross national product, 6.1 percent, for the post-1950 period.[8] The most vigorous calls for a new international economic order came when the Third World was doing very well, not when it was doing badly.

In sum, the economic performance of the Third World through the mid-1970s was hardly a failure. On the contrary, absolute GNP increases were exceptionally high in comparison with the past experiences of developing and currently industrialized areas: the story for per capita growth rates is mixed. Compared with the past, these rates are quite high. But for the period 1950–1975 the average LDC per capita growth rate has been slightly less than that of the industrialized areas and, despite improvement in the 1970s, only 20 percent of LDCs exceeded the IN average for the 1950–1975 period. Furthermore, the developing world enjoyed its most vigorous rate of growth in the years immediately preceding the most strident attacks on existing regimes.

[8]IMF, *World Economic Outlook*, 1982, app. B, table 2.

SOCIAL INDICATORS

National income accounts are not the only measure of well-being. In recent years increased attention has been devoted to social indicators. Such indicators look at the extent to which fundamental human needs and aspirations, including health, education, and longevity, are being met. With regard to individual well-being, such figures may well be superior to national income accounts, which suffer from a number of deficiencies. Decisions about what to include in national accounts are determined by social structures and values. Only goods and services that enter the market are counted, creating a bias against developing countries where the proportion of nonmarket activity is higher than in industrialized areas.[9] Cross-national comparisons based on national accounts data also suffer from biases in exchange rate conversion figures, which understate the actual purchasing power of earnings in developing countries; purchasing power parity estimates of per capita LDC wealth are about three times as great as estimates based on official exchange rates.[10]

Social indicators are free of many of these difficulties. One of the more widely circulated indices is the Physical Quality of Life Index (PQLI) developed by the Overseas Development Council. This indicator is based on three variables: life expectancy at age one, infant mortality, and literacy. Data have been gathered beginning with 1950, and an index generated for each variable. The index ranges from 0–100. For literacy, the index is equal to the percentage of the population that is literate at age 15. For infant mortality, a scale is generated by assigning the value of 0 to the worst experience of an individual country (Gabon in 1950 with 229 deaths per 1,000 live births) and the value of 100 to 7 deaths per 1,000 live births, which is presumed to be the best that can be achieved. Similarly the value of 0 is assigned to the country with the lowest level of life expectancy at age one (38 for Vietnam in 1950) and the figure 100 is assigned to a life expectancy of 77, which is assumed to be the modal full life span for human beings.

The PQLI shows a substantial improvement over time for developing

---

[9]As Fred Hirsch pointed out in his brilliant essay, *Social Limits to Growth*, higher per capita GNP does not ensure greater satisfaction because the importance of positional goods increases; what counts is where individuals stand in relation to others, not their absolute levels of income. Development can provide adequate caloric intake for everyone, but there is only so much land on the ocean front. No matter how wealthy a society becomes, only those high up on the ladder will be able to rise to a white water view. Hirsch, *Social Limits to Growth*, passim. See also Kuznets, *The National Income and Its Composition*, chap. 1.

[10]Kravis et al., "Real GDP *Per Capita.*"

countries. For twenty-six Third World countries for which data are available for an extended period, the average PQLI increased from 54, circa 1950, to 63, circa 1960, to 71, circa 1970. For forty-seven countries for which data have been collected for 1960 and the early 1980s there is not one instance of a decline in the PQLI, even for countries that show declines in per capita income.[11]

There was a wide range in the PQLI in the early 1980s, however, from a low of 15 for Guinea-Bissau to a high of 98 for Sweden, Iceland, and the Netherlands. Table 4.7 shows the frequency distribution for PQLI for developing countries in the early 1980s, and percentage distributions for the early 1970s and early 1980s. The average PQLI for industrialized nations was 94 for both periods.

The pattern of improvement over time for developing countries in meeting basic needs is confirmed by other investigations. An International Labor Organization study of a large number of developing countries for the years 1960 and 1970 showed gains for virtually all countries in all categories. Literacy increases for all countries for which data are available; life expectancy falls in only one country, Ghana; caloric intake increases in 90 out of 103 countries; infant mortality declines in 52 out of 54 countries.[12]

James Wilkie has constructed one of the most complete international studies of various social indicators. His work is confined to Latin America

TABLE 4.7

DISTRIBUTION OF PQLI FOR DEVELOPING COUNTRIES

PQLI	0–19	20–39	40–59	60–79	80–100
Number of LDCs, early 1980s	6	33	27	27	27
% of LDCs, early 1980s	5	28	23	23	23
% of LDCs, early 1970s	9	35	20	14	22

Source: Derived from figures in Overseas Development Council, *The United States and World Development*, Agenda, 1977, pp. 160–171; and Agenda, 1982, table B-4.

[11]Morris, *Measuring the Condition of the World's Poor*, pp. 41–47, table 13; app. B, table 2; and app. C, table 1. Hansen et al., "U.S. Foreign Policy and the Third World," tables 5–8.
[12]Sheehan and Hopkins, *Basic Needs Performance*, pp. 16–17, 115–116.

and the United States. Wilkie has collected information on twelve variables related to health, education, and communication (HEC) for the years 1940, 1950, 1960, and 1970. Table 4.8 reproduces his data for Latin America. The HEC gap between the United States and Latin America increases in the 1940s but decreases in the 1950s and continues to decrease even more substantially in the 1960s.[13]

The experience of the Third World with respect to social indicators compares very favorably with earlier performances in industrialized countries. By the late 1960s life expectancy in LDCs was 49 years, a level reached by developed areas only in 1900.[14] In 1970 the average rate of infant mortality was 65 deaths per 1,000 live births for semideveloped countries and 123/1,000 for less developed countries, ranging from 19 for Hong Kong to 250 for Nepal. In 1900 the average rate of infant mortality for European countries was 166, ranging from 91 for Norway to 252 for Russia. Educational opportunity has increased more rapidly in the Third World in recent years than it did in industrialized areas during the nineteenth century.[15]

In sum, social indicators show positive performance for developing countries. In some cases improvements have been dramatic, in others modest. There is in general a curvilinear relationship between per capita income and social indicators of well-being, with fairly substantial increases up to per capita incomes of about $2,000 (1975 dollars) and modest changes thereafter.[16] Present Third World experience compares favorably with the past experiences of developed countries. With respect to social indicators the absolute gap between industrialized and some developing areas has declined during the postwar period.[17]

REACTIONS TO OPEC

The contention that Third World behavior cannot be understood simply as an effort to increase the transfer of resources is reinforced by the

[13]Wilkie, "Primary Social Change."

[14]Morawetz, *Twenty-five Years of Economic Development*, p. 48.

[15]Morawetz, *Twenty-five Years of Economic Development*, p. 48; Bairoch, *The Economic Development of the Third World*, p. 138; Sheehan and Hopkins, *Basic Needs Performance*, table 2.1 and app. 3; B. R. Mitchell, *European Historical Statistics*, table A4.

[16]Russett, "Marginal Utility of Income Transfers to the Third World"; Morris, *Measuring the Condition of the World's Poor*, p. 53.

[17]This is, however, not surprising, given the basic nature of these indices: social indicators have natural upper limits—100 percent literacy, a life expectancy of seventy-seven years—which are already closely approximated by industrialized areas.

reaction to oil price increases associated with the Organization of Petroleum Exporting Countries (OPEC). No other postwar economic event
had such an unambiguously negative impact on the economic well-being
of such a large number of developing countries. Higher oil prices con-

TABLE 4.8

LATIN AMERICA HEC ABSOLUTE DATA,
TOTAL AVERAGES BY COMPONENT, 1940–1970

Year	Life[1,a]	Infant[2,b]	Beds[3,b]	Doctors[4,b]	Dentists[5,b]
1940	38	146	578	2,779	10,382
1950	50	110	587	2,894	10,891
1960	57	88	511	2,491	8,874
1970	61	78	433	1,937	6,681

Year	Literate[6,a]	Primary[7,a]	Secondary[8,a]	College[9,a]
1940	50	45	5	1.0
1950	55	51	8	1.6
1960	66	64	15	2.1
1970	73	77	28	3.6

Year	News[10,a]	Telephone[11,a]	Motor[12,b]
1940	71	1.0	261
1950	63	1.5	140
1960	77	2.0	69
1970	78	3.0	45

Source: This table is reproduced from Wilkie, *The Narrowing Gap.*
[1]Life expectancy at birth.
[2]Infant mortality rate (deaths under 1 year per 1,000 live births).
[3]Persons per hospital bed.
[4]Population per physician.
[5]Persons per dentist.
[6]Literacy percentage for population at 15 and over.
[7]Percentage of school-age population (7–14) enrolled in primary school.
[8]Share of school-age population (13–18) enrolled in secondary school.
[9]College enrollment as a percentage of primary school enrollment.
[10]Newspaper circulation, copies per 1,000 persons.
[11]Number of telephones per 100 persons.
[12]Number of persons per motor vehicle (auto, buses, trucks) in use.
[a]High number is positive.
[b]Low number is positive.

tributed to balance of payment difficulties and slower growth rates. Financial assistance from OPEC states did not begin to compensate non–Arab Third World countries for higher oil bills. Yet the South did not castigate the oil exporters. Despite some criticism, OPEC was viewed more as a model to be emulated than as an exploiter to be condemned. This behavior is not consistent with interpretations that perceive economic development as the overriding objective of the developing world.

During the 1970s, oil prices increased in two major steps. During the winter of 1973–1974, prices quadrupled. There were several modest nominal increases in the period 1975–1978. Prices then rose by another 125 percent from the end of 1978 through the first quarter of 1980.

These changes had a substantial effect on non-oil developing countries. In the mid-1970s petroleum provided about two-thirds of the energy used by non-oil LDCs compared with 46 percent in the United States, 55 percent in West Europe, and 74 percent in Japan.[18] The pattern of trade between OPEC countries and non-oil LDCs is shown on table 4.9. The first increase in oil prices led to a jump of about $13 billion in the overall trade deficit between OPEC and the non-oil LDCs. However, the deficit then remained stable in nominal terms, and declined in real terms until the second round of sharp oil price increases in the late 1970s. For the years 1974–1978 the aggregate trade deficit of non-oil LDCs with industrialized countries was $81.5 billion, with oil-exporting countries, $90.8 billion.[19]

Financial assistance from OPEC countries did not offset the costs of higher oil prices for non-oil LDCs. For the period 1974–1978 OPEC countries provided $21.83 billion worth of overseas development assistance and another $6.90 billion on nonconcessional terms for a total of $28.73 billion. In terms of the GNP of OPEC countries this represents a substantial sum: the ratio of overseas development assistance to GNP for major OPEC donors, including Saudi Arabia, Iraq, and the U.A.E. (United Arab Emirates), was much larger than the comparable ratios for major industrialized-nation aid donors. The geographic distribution of OPEC aid was very skewed, however, with most assistance going to a small number of Islamic countries. For the period 1976–1978 Egypt received 25 percent of OPEC aid; Syria and Jordan accounted for an

---

[18]GATT, *International Trade*, 1978/1979, p. 58.
[19]Derived from figures in IMF, *Direction of Trade* annual, 1979, pp. 22–23, 28–29.

TABLE 4.9
NON-OIL LDC TRADE WITH OPEC COUNTRIES ($ MILLION)

	1963	1968	1973	1977	1982
Exports	405	725	2,345	8,840	19,070
Imports	1,950	2,060	7,455	26,700	51,885
Trade balance	−1,545	−1,335	−5,110	−17,860	−32,815

Source: GATT, *International Trade*, 1981/1982, table A25, and 1982/1983, table A23.

additional 25 percent. In 1978 the Yemen Arab Republic, Lebanon, and Mauritania received about 5 percent each. India (the only non-Muslim country to receive substantial amounts) and Pakistan accounted for another 11 percent. These eight countries received about 90 percent of OPEC's assistance.[20] For the period 1974–1978 these same eight countries had a cumulative trade deficit with OPEC countries of about $1.2 billion, an amount equal to only 1.3 percent of the cumulative trade deficit of all non-oil LDCs with OPEC for the same period. By 1980–1981 OPEC aid had become only slightly more widely distributed with thirteen countries (only one, India, being non-Islamic) receiving 81 percent of gross disbursements. In 1982 Syria and Jordan, the two largest recipients of OPEC aid, accounted for 32 percent of net disbursements.[21]

Non-oil-exporting LDCs financed their growing trade deficits, more than half of which was accounted for by transactions with OPEC countries, by increased borrowing. Their outstanding debt increased from $130 billion in 1973 to $664 billion in 1983. The debt service ratio (payments as a percent of exports) for all LDCs rose from 16 percent in 1973 to 24 percent in 1982 before falling back to 19 percent in 1983. Here, as in other areas, however, conditions varied across countries. A small number of high-income developing countries, notably Brazil and Mexico, accounted for most non-oil-LDC borrowing. At the other extreme, low-income LDCs experienced only moderate worsening of their balance of payment deficits and total debts. Debt service ratios for low-income countries fell from 15 percent in 1973 to 8 percent in 1979, before rising to 12 percent in 1982. Such countries were able to utilize official development assistance, with its low or negligible repayment obligations,

[20]OECD, DAC *Review*, 1979, p. 136 and table A.1.
[21]IMF, *Direction of Trade* annual, 1979, pp. 22–27; OECD, DAC *Review*, 1983, Tables III–6 and I.5.

while higher income LDCs were increasingly compelled to rely on private banks, which charged commercial interest rates.[22]

The increase in oil prices also had an indirect impact on the economic performance of less developed states. There has been a close relationship between economic growth in the North and the South. For the period 1973–1981, the correlation coefficient for the GNP growth rates of INs and non-oil LDCs, excluding China, was 0.71.[23] The OPEC decisions of 1973–1974 ushered in a period of severe economic strain for the more advanced countries. To sort out the contribution of various factors to the economic recessions of the mid-1970s and early 1980s is beyond the scope of this essay. Nevertheless, the sharp rise in oil prices was certainly an important variable. It contributed to higher rates of inflation. It led to a multibillion dollar transfer of real resources from the wealthier areas to the oil-exporting countries. It created intermediation problems for the international banking system. It increased the volatility of international exchange markets. By weakening the economic performance of the North, the sharp rise in oil prices also weakened that of the South.

Despite the negative, albeit varied, impact of higher oil prices, there was no concerted protest by the Third World against OPEC during the 1970s. African countries periodically criticized the oil-exporting states for not giving more aid. At UNCTAD-V a small number of developing countries, led by some Latin American states, sought to place the relationship between oil prices and development on the agenda, but they were not successful. Several countries complained about OPEC's refusal to offer concessional prices to the Third World. For those who adhere to fundamentally economic interpretations of Third World actions it "is astonishing to see how little the LDCs have done to press for lower prices given the central role of high oil prices in their financial difficulties."[24]

The failure to launch a public attack on OPEC, however, is consistent with a Third World strategy aimed at altering regimes and thereby enhancing both control and resource transfers. Third World behavior does conform with a meta-political strategy informed by substantive rationality even if it violates formal rationality based solely on maximizing economic growth. Aside from the movement for decolonization, the creation of OPEC was, during the mid- and late 1970s, the most effective exercise of power by the South against the North since the conclusion of the

[22]IMF, *World Economic Outlook*, 1983, tables 32 and 35.
[23]IMF, *World Economic Outlook*, 1981, tables 1 and 2.
[24]Beim, "Rescuing the LDCs," p. 728.

Second World War. The power of the major oil companies was severely curtailed. Exporting states assumed at least 50 percent ownership of all major concessions. National oil companies were formed. The percentage of oil sold by the majors precipitously declined. Prices and production levels were determined de facto by those oil-exporting states with surplus revenues, especially Saudi Arabia. In time, increased production from non-OPEC areas, weak macroeconomic performance, and more efficient use of energy in the North weakened the exporting states' hold on the market. But during the 1970s OPEC was the most dramatic example of the exercise of meta-power by Third World states.

The OPEC countries themselves strongly endorsed proposals for a New International Economic Order and identified themselves with the cause of the Third World. Oil-exporting states argued that the economic difficulties of developing areas were a product of transactions with the North. They persistently fought against isolating the oil issue in international forums, maintaining instead that any negotiations would have to address a full range of North-South issues. For instance, the Conference on International Economic Cooperation (CIEC) held at Paris in the late 1970s was initiated by the West in an effort to reach an agreement with oil-exporting states. OPEC insisted, however, on the participation of other LDCs. At CIEC and other international meetings, oil-exporting and non-oil-exporting Third World states worked closely together.

Aside from these reasons for supporting OPEC, there were two reasons for withholding criticism. The first, and most important, was that attacking OPEC would undermine one of the South's sources of strength, its ideology. By offering a coherent interpretation of international economic affairs, which depicted the existing system as a mechanism of exploitation, the Third World was able to delegitimate the liberal premises of the postwar order and forge Southern unity. Attacking OPEC for the consequences of higher oil prices on Third World development could destroy this ideological resource. Higher oil prices transferred resources from non-oil LDCs to the oil-exporting states at a ferocious pace. The pre-1973 regime, dominated by large international oil companies, was far more benign. Recognizing and accepting this situation would be incompatible with the belief system so effectively utilized by the South. OPEC was, therefore, generally ignored when it was not glorified; it was not publicly excoriated.

Criticism of OPEC would also have weakened the unity of the Third World in international organizations. The ability to use the U.N. system to formulate agendas, pass resolutions, and establish new institutional structures has been an important source of influence for developing countries. In organizations where votes are divided in proportion to contributions, particularly the IMF, OPEC countries have been accorded a larger role. If developing countries had systematically and persistently attacked OPEC, it would have been more difficult to maintain voting unity, and OPEC countries might have reassessed their support of Third World positions in international financial institutions.

CONCLUSION

Conventional interpreters of Southern behavior trace Third World demands to economic failure. This contention is not supported by the experiences of most developing countries. The Third World as a whole and most of its individual countries have grown faster during the postwar period than the industrialized areas. Despite extremely rapid population increases, the per capita growth rate of the North was only slightly higher than that of the South. Developing areas have grown at a much faster rate than the industrialized areas did during the nineteenth century. Social indicators of well-being reveal unprecedentedly large increases in infant survival, longevity, and literacy for the Third World during the postwar years. Furthermore, the Third World did not react negatively to OPEC, even though oil price increases led to higher trade deficits for almost all LDCs and greater debt service ratios for high- and middle-income developing countries.

These data are not presented to obscure the gap in physical well-being that still exists between the North and the South, or the human misery of those hundreds of millions of individuals living in abject poverty. I do not mean to imply that developing countries are uninterested in economic performance. The information presented in this chapter does suggest, however, that analysts who see material considerations as the fundamental motivation of Third World behavior do not have an adequate argument. Most Third World countries have experienced change, and the physical quality of life of their subjects has improved.

Although intertemporal and comparative examinations of rates of change are positive for developing countries, a focus on gaps between the North and South suggests a much more negative assessment. With the exception of the gap in social indicators between high- and middle-income

LDCs and industrialized areas, absolute differences in the performance of richer and poorer areas have grown dramatically during the postwar period. Some relative gaps have decreased, but still remain very large. If Third World leaders are concerned with gaps that are a measure of power differentials, of international weakness and vulnerability, and not just the intertemporal experiences of their own countries, which are a measure of changes in economic well-being, then their profound dissatisfaction with the postwar international order is more easily comprehended.

V

Reprise and Preview

REPRISE

Since the Second World War the structure of the international system has been profoundly changed by the creation of a large number of sovereign states with limited national power capabilities and weak domestic political systems. These states cannot control transnational flows or easily adjust to changes emanating from the international environment. This situation makes them vulnerable to external shocks.

For small, weak states, liberal international regimes based on market allocation are troubling even if they are associated with relatively high rates of economic growth. Such regimes leave Third World states exposed to a potentially volatile international environment whose fluctuations can destroy domestic political order. Authoritative regimes could not only provide the Third World with higher levels of material well-being but could also offer greater predictability and security. Under authoritative regimes, the allocation of resources would be more heavily influenced, directly or indirectly, by the decisions of states relying on their sovereign juridical powers. Direct allocation would involve the distribution of resources by state fiat. Indirect allocation would involve the truncation of private property rights.

The desire of the Third World to move away from liberal principles, norms, and rules toward regimes based on authoritative allocation can be seen across all the issue areas that have been salient in the North-South debate. In shipping, developing countries have sought a division of revenues based on the prescriptive rights of exporting and importing countries. In communications and space satellites they have called for an allocation of radio frequencies and geosynchronous orbits based on the sovereign equality of states rather than on existing needs. In trade they have pursued commodity agreements that would raise and stabilize prices by means of state-controlled quota systems or buffer stocks. They have endorsed the principle that the global commons is part of the common heritage of mankind, which cannot be simply appropriated by actors who possess the requisite capital and technology. The Third World has advocated principles that would make capital transfers automatic rather than subject to decisions taken by donor countries. Developing countries have argued that technology is part of the common heritage of mankind, not the private property of those who devised it.

Although the South has consistently fought for authoritative as opposed to market-oriented regimes, its success has varied across issue areas. This variation has depended on the degree of access afforded by existing institutions; more precisely, by the relevance of juridical sovereignty and the voting and membership arrangements of international organizations. Ideological unity and declining U.S. power, the other variables influencing Third World success, have not so much varied across issue areas as over time. The development and wide acceptance of a dependency-oriented approach to the world economy during the 1960s made it possible for the developing world to present a more intellectually coherent and consistent set of demands in the early 1970s. During this same period the United States remained committed to universal international organizations, but was unable to control them. Hence, in the early 1970s conditions were particularly propitious for calling for a New International Economic Order, not because developing countries were driven by economic desperation (during the late 1960s and early 1970s the Third World enjoyed the most rapid increase in the rate of its economic growth), but because the North had not yet begun to withdraw support from formal organizations and the South could forge a wide range of demands into a single coherent program.

In using this argument I do not mean to imply that developing states are uninterested in purely economic concerns, or that they are indifferent to their performance within existing liberal regimes. Most transactions between actors from the North and the South involve maximizing economic utility, given the present rules of the game. However, metapolitical behavior by Third World states, which is evident in international forums and is used to try and change international regimes—as opposed to relational power behavior, evident in other settings where LDCs accept existing principles, norms, and rules—cannot be adequately understood from an economistic perspective; that is, by those with a theoretical orientation who see economic performance as the fundamental, although not exclusive, motivation for Third World behavior. Aggregate growth rates for developing countries have been impressive in relation to their own pasts and to the contemporary and past experiences of industrialized countries. Even with very rapid increases in rates of population growth, the per capita growth of the Third World as a whole was almost equal to that of the North for the period 1950 to 1975. Indicators of social well-being have improved for virtually all Third World states. The NIEO program was launched during the years when the South was experiencing its very best economic performance. The Third World did not initiate a major public attack on OPEC even though the increase in oil prices had unambiguously damaging consequences.

Economistic interpreters are also challenged by the occasional willingness of LDCs to sacrifice wealth for control. For the most part the NIEO program has not been perceived as involving such a trade-off. The more authoritatively oriented regimes proposed by the South could increase both the level of transfers and the effective power of Third World states. However, there have been instances in which, when confronted with a trade-off, the Third World has opted for control. The South rejected Northern efforts to develop new international norms concerning population control even though these efforts were accompanied by promises of more aid. Such norms would infringe on the existing sovereign prerogatives of states. Moreover, the North's program was seen as an attempt to distract attention from the South's charge that the existing system was unfair. In the negotiations concerning a new international regime for the oceans, the South ultimately pressed for and won control over a broad swath of the ocean for littoral states. The extension of state sovereignty prevailed over other alternatives, one of which (initially supported by the United States) would have provided for a trusteeship zone in which exploitation would have been governed by the laws of the littoral state, but taxed for the benefit of the Third World as a whole. Such an arrangement would have provided more aggregate resources for the South, but at the cost of limiting the range of sovereign control.

Those using economistic approaches to North-South relations also confront anomalies in analyzing the specific provisions of the New International Economic Order. Some neoclassical economists have argued that many aspects of the NIEO would not be economically beneficial for developing states. For instance, debt cancellation would lower the total amount of capital available. International commodity agreements would encourage the development of substitutes. Truncating the property rights of multinational corporations would limit the transfer of technology. A link between aid and the distribution of IMF Special Drawing Rights would be inefficient and would have little impact on the least developed countries.[1] But if these arguments are correct, and developing countries are primarily concerned with economic growth, why then have they pursued such policies? The standard answers have been that they have made a mistake, or are ignorant, or have been misled by ideologues. Stupidity, however, is a descriptive, not an analytic, category. If developing states are understood to be interested in control as well as wealth, in political security as well as economic well-being, then the NIEO program is less puzzling. Authoritatively oriented regimes would lessen Third World vulnerability to external shocks by subjecting transnational flows to direct or indirect state control.

The coherence of the NIEO program across a wide range of issue areas can be comprehended by an interpretation based on the structural weakness of the Third World and the subjective unity derived from a shared interpretation of the exploitative nature of the existing global economic system. Economistic interpreters usually explain Third World unity as a product of logrolling the economic interests of individual states. However, only some logs have been rolled—those which emphasize authoritative, rather than market, allocation—and the objectives that have received the most attention in the NIEO, especially international commodity agreements, are not economically relevant for most Third World states.

The reaction of the Third World to economic gains under the prevailing liberal regime, the identification with OPEC, the occasional willingness to trade wealth for control, the deficiencies of the NIEO program from a neoclassical perspective, and the coherence of the NIEO program all suggest that an economistic interpretation of Third World behavior is inadequate. However, it must also be admitted that there is evidence that weighs in favor of economistic interpretations. For instance, LDC demands in the area of trade have included the very liberal objective of removing tariff barriers in the North. Furthermore, economistic interpreters do not have to make the arcane distinction between meta-power and relational power. All Third World behavior is seen as being guided by wealth-maximizing objectives. The difficulty of arriving at definitive analytic conclusions about the relative merits of realist and economistic interpretations is discussed at greater length in chapter 10.

In sum, I do not mean to imply with the argument presented here that

[1]Loehr and Powelson, *Threat to Development*.

developing states are uninterested in purely economic concerns. On the contrary, they have labored mightily to enhance their levels of well-being within the existing liberal order. At the same time, however, they have attempted to alter the basic rules of the game, to move from the liberal toward the authoritative end of the spectrum. More authoritatively oriented regimes could offer developing states both greater wealth and more control. Given their domestic and international weaknesses, such control is particularly attractive because it could mitigate vulnerability to shocks emanating from the international environment. The NIEO program is not rooted in misguided ideology or poor economic analysis; it is a manifestation of the basic structural condition of almost all Third World states—that of small size and political underdevelopment.

PREVIEW

The level of North-South meta-political conflict has been a function of the nature of the regimes confronting the Third World: the more liberal the existing principles, norms, and rules and the more accessible the decision-making organizations, the higher the level of conflict. Analytically, the most interesting issue areas are those that have not become part of the North-South debate, that have not been included in the call for a New International Economic Order. These issue areas all share one of two characteristics: either they are governed by regimes that are already based on authoritative rather than market-oriented principles and norms, or developing countries are not afforded access to the existing institutional structure. This does not preclude disputes over distribution within a given set of rules of the game, but it does imply that the basic nature of the regime itself will not or cannot be challenged. The debate within issue areas already governed by authoritative regimes is over relational rather than meta-political issues.

Table 5.1 shows a classification of issue areas according to whether there have been disputes between industrialized and developing countries over distributional issues or regime characteristics, or both.

The most populated category involves issue areas in which there have been North-South disputes over both the nature of the regime and the distribution of resources. These are issue areas governed by liberal market-oriented rules of the game that are generating patterns of resource distribution, which the South finds unsatisfactory. It is in this set that

TABLE 5.1

Typology of North-South Disputes

		Disputes over regime characteristics	
		Yes	No
	Yes	MNCs IFIs (partly) Trade Oceans Shipping Radio spectrum News reporting	Nonproliferation IFIs (partly)
Disputes over distribution of resources	No	Population control Human rights Basic human needs	Civil aviation Population movement Antarctica (until 1980s)

the New International Economic Order, the New International Information Order, and the New International Shipping Order are located.

Two issue areas, nonproliferation, and some aspects of international financial institutions (IFIs), illustrate a situation in which there has been conflict over the distribution of resources but not over basic principles and norms. The nonproliferation regime recognizes the primacy of authoritative allocation in the area of nuclear technology. International sales cannot be based solely on commercial judgments. Civilian power plants are subject to international inspection. These arrangements have been endorsed by developing countries despite the fact that the Non-Proliferation Treaty of 1968 makes a categorical distinction between the obligations of the five states possessing nuclear weapons (U.S., USSR, Britain, France, and China) and all the rest. However, developing countries have argued that the North has not honored its distributional obligations under the regime. In particular, industrialized countries have not provided adequate technical assistance for commercial nuclear activity in developing countries and have not reduced their own stock of nuclear weapons.

The international financial institutions—the World Bank, IMF, and the regional development banks—reflect Keynesian principles. Keynesians accept the need for state intervention to facilitate market functioning. This mix of authoritative and market allocation has met some of the concerns of developing states. However, officials of the two most important IFIs, the World Bank and the IMF, have been unsympathetic to most forms of direct domestic state intervention. There has been persistent conflict over both the level of resources provided by IFIs, and the content of specific projects or adjustment programs.

In the issue areas of population control, human rights, and basic human needs there has been conflict between the North and the South over the basic international rules of the game but not over the allocation of resources. In all of these issue areas the North has attempted to develop international principles and norms that would change the relationship between national states and their subjects. Some developed states have pressed for more population control, higher standards of human rights, and greater satisfaction of basic human needs. If these programs were endorsed by the international community—that is, if widespread international acceptance led to an expectation at the national level that such programs would be implemented—it would erode existing sovereign state autonomy and put additional demands on state resources. Prevailing international norms and practices place few inhibitions on a state's discretionary control over its own subjects. Even countries with ambitious population-control programs have opposed attempts to develop new international norms. Developing states have been willing to accept resources to meet specific population or basic human needs goals provided that these were not encumbered by efforts to legitimate these objectives in the international community. The South did not avail itself of all of the resources that were offered by the North for population control during the 1970s, an illustration of the independent standing of meta-political objectives.

Analytically, the most interesting issue areas are those in which there have been neither relational nor meta-power disputes between the North and the South. In civil aviation and population movement the South inherited existing regimes that were based on authoritative rather than market-oriented principles and norms. These regimes also provided satisfactory distribution of resources for the South. In the case of population movement and migration the existing international regime has recognized the right of states to control the movement of individuals across their borders. Although specific states have not always been able to exercise this right de facto (including the United States), the distribution of resources generated by this regime has not led the South to launch any major international initiatives. The "brain drain," for instance, remains largely an academic issue.

Civil aviation has not been an area of contention in North-South relations.[2] The absence of conflict reflects the fact that the regime for civil aviation, which the countries of the South have joined, limits the play of market forces. The regime legitimates direct state decisions about routes, frequencies, and fares. The principles and norms conditioning behavior in civil aviation have given precedence to security over efficiency. The right of the state to regulate movement within its own airspace has superseded any claims to territorial access based on purely commercial principles. When the United States has pushed for freer reign for the market, it has encountered opposition not only from the Third World but also from other industrialized countries.

The regime governing Antarctica offers an example of how existing institutional arrangements have severely impeded Third World access; the South has had difficulty putting the Antarctic regions on its agenda. Behavior in Antarctica is conditioned by the Antarctic Treaty, signed in 1959. Membership is restricted. The ostensible criterion for full participation in the regime is that countries must show sustained commitment, usually by establishing a wintering-over station, an expensive proposition. The original twelve consultative parties (two of which, Argentina and Chile, were from the Third World) had only expanded to sixteen by the early 1980s. Had the Antarctica issue emerged in the late 1960s, as opposed to the mid-1950s, the most salient operative principle would have been that the global commons was part of the common heritage of mankind. Antarctica might then have been treated in the same way as the oceans and space and become enmeshed in the larger arena of North-South disputes. The regime for Antarctica is a particularly graphic example of how important existing institutional structures are to an explanation of the variation in success enjoyed by developing countries in changing those international principles and norms with which they have been dissatisfied.

In the second part of this study, I shall investigate the issue areas of multinational corporations, the global commons (Antarctica and the oceans), transportation (civil aviation and shipping), and international

[2]A minor exception has been the passage of resolutions at ICAO conferences condemning Israel's annexation of the Jerusalem airport.

financial institutions in greater depth. In one of these issue areas, civil aviation, the Third World has no quarrel with existing regime structures. In a second, Antarctica, it has limited access. In the others, developing states confronted regimes informed to some degree by market-oriented principles and norms. Their ability to alter these principles and norms has been dependent on existing institutional arrangements—more specifically, on their ability to use their state sovereignty for direct intervention, and the access provided by existing international organizations.

Third World efforts to regulate multinational corporations have enjoyed considerable success. International regime change has been an adjunct of national regulation. The bargaining position of less developed host countries has improved over time as they have acquired knowledge of the market, technological skills, and capital. Juridical sovereignty gave a state the right to grant or withhold access to its territory. The Third World has also championed international rules of the game that would restrict the discretionary power of the multinational to transfer factors of production and limit the right of home countries to bring claims on behalf of their multinational corporations (MNCs). The formal outcome of this process is embodied primarily in national legislation, and secondarily in several international codes of conduct related to MNCs. LDCs have been able to place substantial constraints on multinationals, especially in primary-product industries.

The oceans are a second issue area in which developing countries have secured many of their regime objectives, although this may be a Pyrrhic victory. The most important determinant of this success was the creation of a formal organization structure, the United Nations Conference on the Law of the Sea (UNCLOS), which provided for universal membership and consensus decision-making. The Convention on the Law of the Sea, concluded in 1982, recognized those areas of the oceans beyond national jurisdiction as part of the common heritage of mankind, established exclusive economic zones of at least two hundred miles, and created an International Authority to regulate the exploitation of deep-seabed minerals together with an International Enterprise to participate in such development. All of these objectives had been strongly supported by the Third World. Had decision-making forums concerned with the oceans been as restricted as those associated with Antarctica (potentially another part of the global commons), the South would not have been able to incorporate as many of its regime preferences into the treaty. Third World accomplishments regarding the oceans were, however, marred by the refusal of the United States and several other industrialized states to sign the final agreement. By the early 1980s American policymakers had only limited commitments to those global universal organizations they could no longer control.

In shipping, existing institutional structures afforded LDCs some access. During the 1970s the Third World was able to secure wide but not universal acceptance of an UNCTAD code governing liner conferences. Liners, which ply regularly scheduled routes, carry about 20 percent of seaborne trade by weight and 80 percent by value. The rest is accounted for by tramps, dry bulk carriers, and tankers. Since the end of the nineteenth century, liner routes and fares have been governed by private cartels known as liner conferences. The objective of the UNCTAD Liner Code is to ensure free access to conferences for shipping lines from the Third World, to provide more bargaining power for shippers, and to divide revenues on a 40–40–20 basis between exporting country, importing country, and third parties. In other areas of world shipping, where no authoritative institutional structure was in place, developing countries have had less success in altering international principles, norms, and rules. Bulk carriers remain largely under the direct and indirect control of multinational corporations. Little headway has been made in eliminating flags of convenience. The Third World's share of shipping tonnage (excluding flags of convenience) is significantly less than its share of total cargo. In contrast, in civil aviation, where the existing regime legitimated authoritative allocation and offered easy access, almost all countries with established airlines, including LDCs, have been able to secure about 50 percent of the traffic originating within their territories.

Finally, in the area of official capital transfers, the Third World has accomplished some of its regime objectives. The principle that industrialized countries should contribute 0.7 percent of their GNP to foreign aid has been widely accepted, although not widely practiced. International financial institutions have become more important sources of aid for most developing countries. The formal power of LDCs within these institutions has increased over time, although it is still limited by weighted voting procedures. The institutions themselves have become more responsive to the preferences of their poorer members as the power of the United States has declined, and the organizations' future growth and vitality have become more dependent on Third World borrowers. However, these organizations ultimately remain dependent on the richer countries for funds. The regime for official international capital flows that existed in the years immediately after World War II, which legitimated the unilateral control of donor countries, has been whittled away; but the South has had only very limited success in establishing rules of the game that would obligate industrialized states to make substantial global resource transfers.

These arguments concerning the ability of developing states to secure their preferred regimes are summarized in table 5.2 for those issue areas examined in detail in the second part of this study.

In the case of civil aviation, developing countries enjoyed great success because they were afforded ready access to an existing regime that legitimated authoritative allocation. In the regulation of MNCs, Third World states could invoke juridical sovereignty but there were no functionally specific international organizations through which they could bring pressure, and they were forced to rely on UNCTAD. The level of Third World control of multinationals has increased, primarily in those areas where relational power conditions have changed in favor of host-country governments. With regard to the oceans, the UNCLOS, with its universal membership and consensus decision-making, allowed the Third World to secure a regime that legitimated extensive national control of offshore areas and resources (an augmentation of state jurisdiction and sovereign rights) and international control over seabed resources. In shipping, developing countries have had only limited success in altering existing market-oriented principles and norms; they had no functionally specific international organization through which to direct their program. In the case of Antarctica, the restrictive membership provisions of the 1959 treaty kept this item almost entirely off the South's agenda until the late 1970s. In the area of official capital transfers, developing countries have secured more control, and reinforced some preexisting authoritatively oriented norms largely through their ability to work within existing international financial institutions, where votes were weighted, and to establish new institutions, especially the United Nations Development Program (UNDP), which had egalitarian voting arrangements.

In sum, developing countries have pursued a coherent program for establishing or reinforcing international regimes based on authoritative rather than market allocation. Their success has varied across issue areas largely as a function of the access provided by existing international organizations or the relevance of their formal sovereignty. Third World states have been able to change, to some degree, all regimes to which they had some access, or in which their sovereignty could be used effec-

TABLE 5.2

INTERNATIONAL REGIMES

Issue area	Nature of regime after World War II	Relevance of juridical sovereignty	Access provided by existing international organizations	Conformity of present regime with Third World preferences
Civil aviation	Authoritative	High	High	High
MNCs	Market	High	Low	Moderate
Oceans	Market	Moderate for contiguous sea; low for deep seabed	High	High (for U.N. Convention)
Shipping	Market	High	Moderate	Moderate
Antarctica	Ambiguous	Low	Low	Low
Official capital transfers	Mixed	Low	Moderate	Moderate

Nature of the Regime: Authoritative refers to regimes that legitimate direct or indirect state allocation of resources. Market regimes legitimate allocation based on the endowments and preferences of private actors.

Relevance of Juridical Sovereignty: Juridical sovereignty is highly relevant if the state can alter behavior by blocking access to its territory; denying landing rights to planes is an example. It is low if blocking territorial access has no bearing on behavior, as in the case of the deep seabed or Antarctica.

Access Provided by International Organizations: Access is classified as high in one-nation, one-vote organizations with universal membership;

moderate in organizations with universal membership and weighted voting; low in organizations that severely restrict membership.

Conformity of Present Regime with Third World Preferences: Conformity is high if the present regime legitimates authoritative allocation and if LDCs are satisfied with existing resource distribution. Conformity is moderate if regime principles and norms are mixed and developing countries are not fully satisfied with behavioral outcomes. Conformity is low if market-oriented principles and norms continue to prevail and the actual distribution of resources is unsatisfactory.

tively. At the very least they have been able to undermine the liberal norms and principles that dominated the international system in the years immediately following the Second World War. The South has been able to take two legacies of the North—the organization of political units into sovereign states and the structure of existing international organizations—and use them to disrupt, if not replace, market-oriented regimes over a wide range of issues.

Part Two

Cases

VI

International Financial Institutions

Official large-scale, multilateral capital flows are a phenomenon of the post–World War II period. The International Bank for Reconstruction and Development (IBRD), or World Bank, and the International Monetary Fund (IMF) were created at the conclusion of the Second World War. The regional development banks—the Inter-American Development Bank (IADB), Asian Development Bank (ADB), and African Development Bank (AFDB) were established in the 1960s. Various other multilateral facilities, of which the United Nations Development Program is the most important, were also constituted after 1960.

There have been long and intense struggles between industrialized and developing countries over the policies of international financial institutions (IFIs), especially the IMF and the World Bank. However, these struggles should not be allowed to mask fundamental agreement on the basic norm that official agencies had to play an active role in the economy. The voting members of the IFIs are states. With few exceptions, loans must be guaranteed by the government of the borrowing country. The private market is not seen as the only mechanism for the international allocation of capital. For policymakers from the North, the World Bank and the Fund were the international projection of lessons drawn from the depression of the 1930s: state intervention was needed to rectify some market failures. While this Keynesian stance was not an endorsement of the South's preferences for authoritative determination of resource allocation, it was congruent with some Southern concerns about control.

There has been disagreement between the North and the South, however, over other meta-political as well as relational issues; that is, over the basic principles and norms of the regime as well as over distributional questions within the existing rules of the game. The enduring meta-political debate has been concerned with the extent to which international financial institutions can make their loans contingent on domestic economic policy as opposed to simply securing collateral that would guarantee repayment. Industrialized countries, especially the United States, have supported strong conditionality; the South has opposed it. Major distributional issues have included the level of resources provided by international financial institutions and the distribution of power and influence among industrialized countries, developing countries, and the international agency itself.

Over time, behavior has moved closer to the preferences of the South because there have been some changes in the older IFIs—the World Bank and the Fund—and because newer institutions, more closely approximating Southern predilections, have been created. The South's major source of leverage has been its ability to utilize existing institutional structures. The Keynesian underpinnings of the international regime for official capital flows accepted the legitimacy of state intervention in the allocation of capital. Juridical sovereignty gave developing countries access, albeit not equal votes, to the World Bank and the Fund, and through their membership in the United Nations they were able to establish the UNDP. The Inter-American and Asian Development banks were first discussed in regional U.N. agencies. The Third World's ideological unity contributed to a more coherent position in some of the older IFIs, and was embodied in the philosophy of the United Nations Development Program. The declining power of the United States led to some redistribution of votes, and created incentives for bureaucrats within IFIs to cultivate clients in borrowing countries.

The South, however, has not been able to alter institutional structures in ways that fundamentally change the underlying power capabilities of national actors. Although the target of 0.7 percent of GNP concessional resource transfers has achieved some salience and legitimacy, decisions about the allocation of resources to international financial institutions remain with the countries of the North. During the postwar period the regime for official capital transfers from the North to the South has moved from congruence (in which the characteristics of the regime mirrored the preferences of the most powerful state actors), toward incongruence (in which some regime characteristics are different from the preferences of the most powerful state actors), but there has been no trend toward dynamic instability in which the regime would become an instrument for upsetting the existing distribution of power among states.

THE IMPORTANCE OF INTERNATIONAL FINANCIAL INSTITUTIONS

International financial institutions have become a significant source of capital, especially aid (that is, capital provided on concessional terms), for developing areas. In the late 1940s the United States, through the Marshall Plan and Point IV assistance, dominated the official flow of resources. The only two international financial institutions, the World Bank and the Fund, were completely eclipsed. During the 1960s and especially the 1970s, however, multilateral agencies became more important for most LDCs. The percentage of net disbursement flows from multilateral sources increased from 7 percent in 1962 to 10 percent in 1965, to 12 percent in 1970, to 13 percent in 1976, and to 17 percent in 1982. These figures include bilateral and multilateral concessional and nonconcessional disbursements as well as changes in the private bilateral long-term assets of the nonmonetary and monetary sectors. The shift from bilateral to multilateral sources is stronger for official development assistance alone. Official development assistance is defined by the Organization for Economic Cooperation and Development (OECD) as flows to developing countries that are administered to promote their economic development and that are concessional in character and contain a grant element of at least 25 percent. The share of official development assistance from multilateral sources increased from 6 percent in 1962, to 14 percent in 1965, to 16 percent in 1970, and to 25 percent in 1977, and remained at about 25 percent through the early 1980s.[1]

Multilateral lending is particularly important for those poorer developing countries which do not have access to private capital markets. For instance, for the period 1975–1979, funds from the multilateral development banks (World Bank, IADB, ADB, and AFDB) accounted for 41 percent of total gross foreign flows to India, 42 percent to Tanzania, 29 percent to Bangladesh, and 25 percent to Kenya; but only 10 percent to Korea, 5 percent to Brazil, and 4 percent to Mexico.[2]

The bargaining position of LDCs is stronger in multilateral than in most bilateral situations. Although there is considerable variation across

---

[1]OECD, *The Flow of Financial Resources*, 1961–1965, tables A.1 and A.7; OECD, *Geographical Distribution of Financial Flows*, 1969–1975, pp. 266–267; and 1971–1977, pp. xii, xiii, and 266–267; 1979–1982, pp. 5, 13, 15, and 17.

[2]U.S. Treasury, *U.S. Participation in MDBs*, table 1.3.

international financial institutions (as set forth in the remainder of this chapter), they all share some characteristics that are attractive for Third World states. Recipient countries are members of the organization to which they are applying for assistance and have some influence on its policies. Since IFIs must maintain ongoing relations with their borrowers, decision-making styles are consensual, even in the conservative World Bank and IMF. The need to maintain the appearance of technical rationality and impartiality imposes constraints on the extent to which explicit political criteria can be introduced into IFI decisions. Over time, the staff and management within institutions have increasingly become the source of new policy initiatives. While these initiatives do not necessarily coincide with the predispositions of the South, they do provide a counterweight to preferences from the North. If nothing more, IFIs insulate Southern borrowers from Northern donors. The decision-making framework that exists in international organizations thus gives developing countries more leverage than they enjoy in bilateral aid negotiations where rules and norms are less clear and power asymmetries more apparent.[3]

The characters of international financial institutions vary substantially, however. With regard to the preferences of the North and the South, the organizations examined in this chapter can be ranked in the following order, beginning with institutions closest to the North: International Monetary Fund, World Bank, Asian Development Bank, Inter-American Development Bank, African Development Bank, United Nations Development Program, other United Nations funds.

THE IMF AND THE WORLD BANK

THE FUND (IMF)

The two enduring disputes between the North and the South in the International Monetary Fund have been about the level of resources available and the conditions imposed on the use of these resources. The South has made some marginal gains in both areas, but the IMF, more than any of the other IFIs, continues to reflect the basic orientation of the industrialized world, especially that of the United States.

[3]Gordenker, *International Aid*, pp. 57–58, 67.

The Articles of Agreement of the International Monetary Fund, negotiated at Bretton Woods in 1944, were designed for a world that never existed. The Fund was to preside over a pegged exchange rate system of freely convertible currencies. Its resources were to be used to finance temporary balance of payment difficulties. The policymakers at Bretton Woods did not appreciate the length of the postwar transition, or foresee the dominant role that came to be played by the United States dollar.

Through the 1950s the Fund's activities were limited. Reconstruction was handled by direct arrangements between the United States, and Europe and Japan. The gradual movement toward currency convertibility, achieved in 1958 for most industrialized areas, was facilitated by other institutions, such as the European Payments Union. Poorer countries accounted for a substantial proportion of Fund drawings, but only because they had no place else to go. No special provisions were made for the needs of LDCs.

IMF Resources

Table 6.1 shows the value of drawings from the Fund made by less developed and developed countries as well as the percentage of all drawings made by LDCs.

No long, clear trend emerges in the share of allocations to the two groups of countries until the sharp surge in LDC borrowing begins in 1979. The correlation between LDC drawings and IN drawings, which is 0.82 from 1947 through 1977, drops to 0.33 for 1947 through 1982. For the 1947–1977 period the coefficient of variability is 1.34 for less developed countries, and 1.53 for INs, meaning that the provision of Fund resources was somewhat more stable for poor countries than for rich ones.[4]

Initially there was only one way to get resources from the IMF—by borrowing from credit tranches. Each country's borrowing limits were determined by the size of its quota; that is, by the contributions that it had made to the Fund. In borrowing from the credit tranches, no formal distinction was made between more and less developed countries.

[4]If the trend increase in IMF activity over time is controlled for (assuming a linear relationship between time and LDC and IN drawings), then the wealthier countries show a slightly more stable borrowing pattern with a correlation coefficient of 0.55 for the industrialized countries and 0.48 for the developing countries for the 1947–1977 period.

TABLE 6.1

DRAWINGS FROM THE IMF

Year	Values of drawings made by LDCs (SDR millions)	Values of drawings made by INs (SDR millions)	LDC drawings as a percent of total
1947	31.3	438	7
1948	70.3	138	37
1949	72.5	30	71
1950	–0–	–0–	—
1951	35	–0–	100
1952	40.6	44	48
1953	80.5	151	35
1954	62.5	–0–	100
1955	17.5	–0–	100
1956	119	562	17
1957	388	582	40
1958	98	239	29
1959	130	51	72
1960	260	20	93
1961	688	1,769	28
1962	268	315	46
1963	282	50	85
1964	181	1,830	9
1965	487	1,948	20
1966	556	907	38
1967	410	426	49
1968	689	2,756	20
1969	395	2,073	16
1970	401	1,109	27
1971	362	1,478	20
1972	796	815	49
1973	315	417	43
1974	1,636	2,417	40
1975	2,048	2,550	44
1976	2,801	4,209	40
1977	724	2,700	21
1978	1,099	2,585	30
1979	1,460	382	79
1980	3,261	491	87
1981	6,156	925	87
1982	6,677	1,798	76

Sources: Derived from figures in IMF *International Financial Statistics*, May 1978, September 1983, and Supplementary Series no. 3 (1982).

Since the mid-1960s, a number of new facilities have been created. Some of these recognize the special situation of Third World countries and facilitate their access to the Fund's resources. By 1980 the Fund had established three permanent facilities that provided additional funds for less developed member states: the Compensatory Finance Facility, the Buffer Stock Financing Facility, and the Extended Facility. The Compensatory Finance Facility was established in 1963. It provides access to the Fund's resources without the usual restrictions, and beyond normal limits. Its objective is to meet short-term export fluctuations beyond the control of the member. The Buffer Stock Financing Facility, established in 1969, provides resources for members to contribute to international buffer stocks created by international commodity agreements when members of these agreements have balance of payment difficulties. The Extended Facility was created in 1974. It is designed to give LDCs long-term balance of payments assistance to correct structural imbalances by making loans for lengthier periods than would other Fund facilities.

In addition to these three permanent facilities, a number of temporary facilities, some of them exclusively related to developing countries, have also been organized within the IMF. The most important of these is the Trust Fund. At the IMF's meeting in Jamaica in 1976, agreement was reached to sell one-sixth of the IMF's gold holdings and to use the proceeds to create a special fund for less developed countries. In addition to loans from the Trust Fund, LDCs also received direct disbursements of $362.6 million, equal to 27.7 percent of profits from the sale of IMF gold. The Trust Fund was the first example of something resembling global taxation.

During the mid-1970s, the IMF ran a Special Oil Facility to provide funds to alleviate balance of payment adjustments precipitated by the quadrupling of oil prices. Almost seven billion SDRs (Special Drawing Rights) were borrowed at market rates. To facilitate the access of less developed countries, a subsidy account was established. Contributions of $195 million came from thirty-five industrialized and oil-exporting countries. This account made it possible to reduce the interest payments of LDCs from 7.7 percent to 2.7 percent. Funds from the Special Oil Facility were extended to more developed countries in 1974, 1975, and 1976, and to less developed countries in 1976, 1977, and 1978.

In 1979 the IMF introduced a Supplementary Financing Facility which was designed to increase the loans that could be granted to countries whose needs were large in relation to their quotas. New resources came from loans from more prosperous members. When the funds of the Supplementary Financing Facility were exhausted in 1981, the IMF adopted an enlarged access policy for the same purpose.[5]

As a result of the creation of these new facilities there was a sharp increase in the theoretical amount that a country could borrow in relation to its quota. Until the mid-1960s members were limited to 100 percent of their quota. With the creation of the extended and buffer facilities in the 1960s they could borrow up to 150 percent. Additional facilities and new policies with regard to the credit tranches made it theoretically possible for members to borrow up to 250 percent of their quotas by the mid-1970s, 455 percent by August of 1979, and 775 percent by May of 1981.[6]

The new facilities were, with the exception of the Oil Facility, specifically targeted to the developing world. Table 6.2 shows the total accumulated value of drawings from various Fund facilities as of July 1983 (December 1981 for administered funds).

Quotas have not increased at the same rate as global economic activity, however. In 1948 aggregate IMF quotas were equal to about 16 percent of total world imports. In 1980 they were equal to about 3 percent.[7] Thus, while the creation of new facilities specifically geared to developing areas represents a movement toward the preferences of the Third World, there has been little aggregate improvement in the level of resources that countries can secure from the Fund relative to their trading activity.

The second major enduring issue within the Fund has been the conditions associated with drawings. Third World countries have favored liberal conditionality. The United States has persistently advocated restrictive conditionality. Developing states have won only marginal battles. Loans have been extended for longer periods. Some conditionality terms have been relaxed. The Fund remains, however, firmly committed to the norm that it can negotiate policy conditions with borrowing countries.

The question of conditionality has persisted since the founding of the Fund. During the Bretton Woods negotiations, the British took the position that the Fund should respond passively to requests initiated by central banks, only making a judgment about whether a country would

[5]*Wall Street Journal*, June 15, 1978. See Williamson, *The Lending Policies of the IMF*, pp. 64–67, for an excellent summary of Fund facilities.

[6]Derived from figures in IMF, *International Financial Statistics, Supplementary Series No. 3*, 1982, and IMF, *Survey*, Supplement, November 1982, pp. 6–10.

[7]Dell, *On Being Grandmotherly*, p. 16.

TABLE 6.2
DRAWINGS FROM IMF (AND IMF-ADMINISTERED FACILITIES) AS OF JULY 1983

	Total (except trust fund)	Tranche	Extended, supplement, & enlarged access	Compensatory	Buffer	Oil	Administered accounts*
Percent drawn by LDCs (cumulative)	54	36	99	78	88	38	98
Value drawn by LDCs (cumulative SDR millions)	41,964	16,108	13,623	9,056	421	2,657	4,117
Total drawings (cumulative)	77,884	45,132	13,761	11,611	471	6,902	4,181
First date of use		1946	1975	1963	1981	1974	1976

Sources: *International Financial Statistics*, Sept. 1983, pp. 18–19. *International Financial Statistics, Supplementary Series No. 3*, 1982, pp. 10–11.

*These figures are as of December 1981.

actually be able to repay. Although the United States pressed for conditionality, no explicit provision was included in the Articles of Agreement. Over time, however, the United States, which was the major source of IMF resources, prevailed. The IMF's executive board accepted conditionality in 1952. Binding conditions were introduced in 1958. The Articles of Agreement were formally amended in 1969. The basic norm that emerged was that members would have free access to their first credit tranche (equal to 25 percent of their quota) but that borrowing from higher credit tranches would be subject to increasingly stringent conditions with regard to national economic policy and performance. Among the newer Fund facilities, borrowing from the Extended Facility and the Supplementary Finance Facility has been subject to high conditionality. By the late 1970s increased borrowing had pressed countries into the higher credit tranches, compelling them to negotiate standby agreements. One observer has acutely noted that, if the quotas of the Fund had been increased in proportion to world trade, a much higher percentage of current borrowing would have occurred in the lower credit tranches, which are not subject to high conditionality.[8]

The conditions imposed by the Fund are strongly influenced by conventional market principles. The Articles of Agreement state that the Fund should defend a liberal, open economic order. Trade restrictions are not an acceptable solution to balance of payment difficulties. With regard to domestic policy, the Fund is inclined to argue that the market should determine the allocation of resources. Standby agreements governing drawings from the Fund can thus specify aggregate and private sector credit, devaluation, and budget cuts; proscribe restraints on trade; and call for the reduction or elimination of domestic subsidies on staples and utilities.

Developing countries have made only limited headway in easing the conditions imposed by the IMF. The Compensatory Finance Facility and the Oil Facility were based on the norm that borrowing precipitated by external events beyond the control of the member states, such as higher oil prices, should be subject to low conditionality. In 1974 the Extended Facility introduced the possibility that the Fund would be able to make loans for longer than one year, giving borrowers more time to adjust. Multiyear lending was introduced for standbys in 1977.[9]

[8]Dell, *On Being Grandmotherly*, pp. 1–14, 31; Williamson, *The Lending Policies of the IMF*, p. 11.

[9]Williamson, *The Lending Policies of the IMF*, pp. 14, 28–33; Dell, *On Being Grandmotherly*, p. 20; Guitan, *Fund Conditionality*, pp. 17–18.

In 1979 the IMF's executive board announced what appeared to be an important change in policy. The board's decision stated that the Fund would "pay due regard to the domestic social and political objectives, the economic priorities, and the circumstances of members including the causes of balance of payments problems."[10] Performance criteria would normally be limited to macroeconomic policies. The Fund would pay more attention to supply side considerations and focus less exclusively on government budget deficits, subsidies, and public employment.[11]

Jacques de Larosiere, who became managing director of the Fund in 1978, stated in a number of speeches that the Fund would have to make loans for longer periods and that conditionality requirements would have to be reasonably liberal. He averred that "We have to cope with their [LDC] problems and consider them with a little more than just sympathy. We have to try and do something."[12]

These changes in policy were accompanied by alterations in IMF behavior. For the period 1979–1981 there was a significant increase in the percentage of multiyear loans. Also, a higher proportion of loans was approved without requiring prior devaluation, a distasteful condition for prospective borrowers, which is frequently provided for in standby agreements.

These changes in policy and behavior, however, did not herald a long-term trend toward greater liberality. After June 1981 the Fund tightened conditionality. Single-year standbys became more frequent; prior devaluations occurred more often. The IMF's managing director indicated that there had never been a change in fundamental policy.[13] There is an internal explanation for the sequence of developments: The period of liberal conditionality occurred when the Fund had ample resources. Like other financial institutions, it might simply have been trying to increase business. The changes in Fund policy, however, also correspond with changes in American policy. The Reagan administration strongly opposed liberalizing conditionality. Under Secretary of the Treasury Beryl Sprinkel stated that "We want to push the IMF's conditionality back to where it was."[14]

[10]Paragraph 4, Decision of March 2, 1979.

[11]*New York Times*, February 5, 1980, D1:3; *World Business Weekly*, April 2, 1980, and June 23, 1980, p. 50.

[12]Quoted in the *Wall Street Journal*, October 29, 1979, 6:1; see also IMF *Survey*, January 2, 1980, p. 26, and May 19, 1980, p. 157, for additional statements.

[13]Williamson, *The Lending Policies of the IMF*, pp. 44–51.

[14]Quoted in the *Wall Street Journal*, Sept. 21, 1981, 1:1.

In sum, Third World countries have not been hapless in their quest for more resources from the Fund under less stringent conditions. New facilities have been created. Resources have been increased. There has been some relaxation of the specificity of policies covered by standby agreements. But success has hardly been dramatic. This pattern of modest change toward the preferences of the Third World is reflected in some other issues related to the Fund.

During the late 1960s and early 1970s the proposal for a link between the creation of SDRs and financial assistance for less developed countries was a major issue. The Group of 77 wanted resources to be given directly to developing countries rather than having them allocated through some international financial organization such as the World Bank or the IDA (International Development Association). Developed countries, particularly the United States and Germany, rejected a link between development aid and the creation of new reserve assets on the grounds that it would be inflationary and would unduly complicate an already difficult procedure by confounding two separate policy areas, development and international liquidity. Initially the industrialized nations had not intended to include the LDCs in the allocation of SDRs at all. The final compromise provided for the distribution of SDRs according to IMF quotas. The LDCs had wanted some multiple of their quotas. Instead, this gave the LDCs about 28 percent of initial allocations, which was considerably higher than the amount they would have received based on their share of world trade (19 percent) or their share of world GNP (14 percent). Thus, while the LDCs did not get a clear link between development financing and the creation of new international liquidity, they have been able to share in the resources provided by the creation of SDRs.[15]

Alterations in voting arrangements within the Fund have also given LDCs more power. The share of LDC votes rose from 22 percent in 1947 to 35.8 percent in the early 1980s. Coincidentally, there has been an increase in the kinds of decisions that require special majorities of 70 or 85 percent. Article 9 of the IMF's Articles of Agreement initially specified nine kinds of decisions that required special majorities. This number was raised to eighteen in 1967 in the first revision of the Articles, and to thirty-nine by the second revision. These changes did not so much reflect a desire to mollify LDCs as an effort on the part of industrialized countries to maintain their vetoes. Provisions for special majorities added

[15]Cline, *International Monetary Reform*, pp. 48–49.

during the first amendment of the Articles were designed to give the European Economic Community (EEC) a veto over certain matters related to the creation of SDRs. Provisions for special majorities of 85 percent were added during the second revision of the Articles to protect the unilateral veto of the United States after the relative quota of OPEC countries was doubled. Nevertheless, the effect of these changes has been to give the Third World as well as Europe and the United States an effective unilateral veto over most, if not all, of the Fund's important decisions. This is reflected in the compromises that took place over the distribution of SDRs and the allocation of funds derived from the sale of gold. The effect of these changes has been to create a system approximating the rule of unanimity, at least so long as block voting prevails.[16] In addition to voting power, the number of executive directors from the Third World has increased from five out of thirteen in 1948 to eleven out of twenty-two in 1983.

The ability of the United States to block specific loans has also declined. In the 1950s the American executive director could exercise an effective veto over any large drawing. Proposals for large loans were cleared with American policymakers before being brought before the IMF's executive board. By the 1980s the United States could not block even the very largest Fund standbys. For instance, in 1981 the IMF approved a $5.8 billion standby for India, the largest given to that date. The U.S. executive director abstained on the final vote when it became apparent that there would not be enough votes to block the loan.[17]

An example of the increasing influence of the Third World within the International Monetary Fund was the creation of the Committee of Twenty in mid-1972. This group was charged with studying basic reforms in the international monetary system. It was composed of governors of the Fund. Nine of its members came from the Third World. Prior to the creation of the Committee of Twenty, discussions had been carried out by the Committee of Ten, whose members were drawn exclusively from industrialized countries. Protests from the Third World, supported by the collective veto power that the Third World already enjoyed in the Fund, forced the wealthier nations to accept a more broadly based committee.

These changes in practices and influence certainly do not mean that

[16]Gold, *Voting Majorities*, and Jekker, "Voting Rights of LDCs."

[17]Southard, "The Evolution of the IMF," pp. 19–20; *Wall Street Journal*, November 9, 1981, 6:1.

the IMF has been captured by the Third World. The voting arrangement that has developed in the Fund gives the Third World the ability to block some initiatives within the existing structure but not to change the structure. The norm of conditionality guided by market-oriented principles continues to determine the nature of standby agreements. The specific terms of these agreements can be discomforting for political leaders in the LDCs. Efforts by a number of institutions, including the IMF, to force Ghana to achieve external equilibrium contributed to severe domestic political unrest in the early 1970s. After staple subsidies were reduced in accordance with IMF standbys, there were food riots in Egypt, the Sudan, and Morocco, as well as in other countries. When Peru, which had fallen into a balance of payments crisis largely because of depressed world copper prices, was also compelled to impose a set of austerity measures to reach a standby agreement with the Fund, a period of prolonged political disorder ensued. There have been several cases in which discipline imposed on the domestic economy partly as a result of negotiations with the IMF have been associated with changes in political regimes.[18]

The leverage exercised by the IMF is considerable not so much because of the resources it can offer, which are often modest, but because over time other lenders have come to base their behavior on decisions taken by the Fund. This practice, initiated by the United States, began in the 1950s. American policymakers became concerned that aid funds were being used to bail out countries that had become overcommitted to private lenders. In several cases the United States made acceptance of IMF conditions a prerequisite for granting aid. The World Bank and other government institutions have often adopted the same practice. As private banks became active in less developed countries in the 1970s they also keyed their decisions to conditions set by the IMF. The Fund served an important political function in this regard. As an international institution it could set conditions that would have been unacceptable coming directly from another country or from a private bank.

In sum, within the IMF the influence of developing countries has increased. Their share of votes, however, is still well below 50 percent. Their most important acccomplishments have involved the creation of new facilities. The power to influence decisions and agendas has changed some of the rules and norms of the IMF, but only in modest ways. For

[18]Libby, "External Co-optation"; *World Business Weekly*, Sept. 3, 1979, p. 251; July 20, 1981, pp. 11–12.

LDCs, IMF conditionality is still excessively stringent.[19] The IMF remains far from the Third World's ideal of an institution liberally dispensing balance of payments assistance with a sympathetic understanding of the problems of LDCs and an automatic link between aid and new liquidity creation.

The genetic character of the Fund, set at its birth, continues to restrict its ability to respond to LDC preferences. The environmental forces exerted during its maturation, however, incline the IMF to a more sympathetic position. The future growth and scope of the Fund depend on its ability to work out satisfactory relations with Third World countries.

THE WORLD BANK (IBRD)

The World Bank, like the IMF, embodied Keynesian principles, which offered a rationale for state intervention in the market. The decision to establish the bank reflected policymakers' beliefs that private capital flows would not necessarily provide the resources needed to finance longer-term reconstruction and development. Loans must usually be guaranteed by the government of the borrowing country. States, not private actors, compose the membership of the bank. Final authority on specific loans rests with the executive board made up of representatives selected by one or more governments. These principles, norms, rules, and decision-making procedures are congruent with Third World preferences for a larger role for the state in resource allocation. Even with basic agreement on some aspects of the rules of the game, however, major areas of dispute involving questions of principle and distribution have persisted at the World Bank.

As in the IMF, one enduring area of concern has been the level of resources for LDCs. The World Bank's formal title, the International Bank for Reconstruction and Development, reflects its initial duality. The first article of the bank's Articles of Agreement explicitly mentions both rebuilding war-torn areas and promoting economic development in "less developed countries." The bank was charged with giving "equitable consideration to projects for development and projects for reconstruction alike." At Bretton Woods the Latin American countries had pressed for such a commitment. Harry Dexter White, the most influential American

---

[19]For one statement of the Group of 24, see IMF *Survey*, May 5, 1980, p. 137.

official concerned with planning for the bank during the Second World War, insisted that it should involve the rich as well as the poor. He saw the bank as an institution that would develop productive capacity, whether this was done through rebuilding or reconstructing was irrelevant. Indeed, he felt that it was difficult to distinguish between the two.

During its earliest years, however, economic development was clearly not the bank's major concern. The most important countries at Bretton Woods, with the exception of the United States, had been devastated by the war. They wanted resources for reconstruction. The first World Bank loans were made in 1947 to France, the Netherlands, Denmark, and Luxembourg. It quickly became apparent, however, that the bank did not have the resources to rebuild war-torn countries. After 1947 the major burden for reconstruction was carried by Marshall Plan funds. World Bank lending was piddling in comparison. Nevertheless, developed countries continued as the major clients of the bank into the 1960s. The division of resources between more and less developed countries is shown on table 6.3.[20]

With regard to total available resources the most significant institutional change at the bank was the creation of the International Development Association (IDA) in 1960. It makes loans for up to fifty years with no interest and a 0.76 percent service charge. This contrasts with the bank itself, whose loans run for shorter periods with rates tied to commercial interest charges. IDA resources have come directly from governments, with industrialized countries providing 90 percent of contributions and developing countries 10 percent. The bank has also transferred some of its earnings to the IDA.[21] The IDA's gross lending was equal to about 25 percent of the bank's total by 1980; its net lending to about 30 percent.[22]

In addition to the IDA, the Interest Subsidy Fund, or Third Window, was created in 1976. It offers loans at rates that are intermediate between those of the bank and the IDA. Funds equal to 4 percent interest came from voluntary contributions, thus reducing the obligation lenders must bear by an equivalent amount. A final facility within the Bank Group is the International Finance Corporation (IFC), founded in 1956. Its pur-

[20]Oliver, *Early Plans for a World Bank*, pp. 4, 27, 38, 43.

[21]IBRD, *The International Bank for Reconstruction and Development*, pp. 8–9; Mason and Asher, *The World Bank*, pp. 52–53 and chap. 12.

[22]Derived from information in OECD, *Development and Cooperation*, various years.

TABLE 6.3

TOTAL LOANS APPROVED BY IBRD-IDA

Fiscal years	Amounts ($ millions)			Percentages	
	Total	IDA	IBRD	IBRD to LDCs	Total to LDCs
1947	250		250	0	0
1948–1952	1,133		1,133	47	47
1953–1957	1,716		1,716	57	57
1958–1962	3,799	235	3,564	68	74
1963–1967	5,488	1,490	3,998	51	78
1968–1972	10,470	2,861	7,789	65	90
1973–1977	27,316	6,991	20,325	66	92
1978–1982	55,210	15,340	39,869	65	93

Source: Derived from figures in IBRD *Annual Reports,* 1947, 1948, 1954–1982. IDA Annual Reports, 1961, 1962, 1963.

pose is to make loans to private enterprises in developing countries. As opposed to the bank and the IDA, its loans do not have to be guaranteed by the government of the borrower. The funds from the Third Window and the IFC are modest compared with those of the bank itself and the IDA. The World Bank Group has, over time, come to provide greater resources for LDCs in a wider variety of ways, with easier terms.

The shift in the bank's lending pattern has been accompanied by changes in principles and norms, some of which were attractive to the South. The bank evolved from a conservative institution primarily concerned with preserving its credit rating and promoting the U.S. vision of a capitalist order to a broader-based development institution. The bank's second president, John J. McCloy (who replaced Eugene Meyer who held the office only six months) felt that his major task was to build confidence among American financiers, since the bank secured most of its resources by selling bonds on the American market. The bank was seen as merely a bridge between private capital markets and borrowing countries, not as an institution that would take initiatives or develop projects. McCloy did not regard the bank as a permanent organization;

he felt that over time its function would be taken over by private financial institutions.[23]

By the 1960s the bank's philosophy had begun to change. During earlier periods bank officials had generally argued that the main bottleneck to development was the lack of adequate projects presented by less developed member-states. By the mid-1960s officials were arguing that the lack of capital was the major bottleneck, implying that various kinds of aid activities had to be expanded. The bank began offering more technical advice and promoting local institutions so that more project proposals could be generated. However, the bank continued to emphasize infrastructure projects and to embrace conservative standards for judging performance and creditworthiness.

Under Robert McNamara, who became president of the bank in 1967, greater emphasis was placed on basic human needs. McNamara greatly expanded both the scope and the amount of the bank's lending. Projects that provided direct returns to the poor were emphasized. By 1978 poverty-oriented rural lending was the largest single lending sector—$1.7 billion, versus $1.1 billion for power and $1.1 billion for transportation. Agricultural projects in general accounted for 40 percent of the bank's loans by the mid-1970s.[24] In the late 1970s the IBRD also began making program loans, which supported general development programs as opposed to specific projects.

This change in the type of projects was not accompanied by any shift in the bank's neoliberal ethos. The aim of poverty-oriented projects was to increase investment, and therefore output, by the poor. Avoiding or eliminating price distortions introduced by the government remained a central tenet of bank advice.[25]

Within the bank the influence of the United States has declined. It has been supplanted not simply by greater influence for other states, including the Third World, but also by an increase in the power and autonomy of the bank itself.

The most manifest indicator of influence within the IBRD is voting power. Ten percent of votes in the World Bank are basic votes, which are distributed equally to all members; the rest are ostensibly distributed

[23]Oliver, *Early Plans for a World Bank*, chap. 10; Dell, *Inter-American Development Bank*, pp. 19–20; Ayres, *Banking on the Poor*, pp. 3–4.

[24]Ayres, *Banking on the Poor*, pp. 3, 46–50; and Hurni, *The Lending Policy of the World Bank*, pp. 45–47.

[25]Ayres, *Banking on the Poor*, pp. 74–75; *Economist*, Sept. 4, 1982; IMF *Survey*, p. 17.

according to financial contributions. This straightforward weighting formula, however, obscures what is in practice a much more attenuated relationship between voting power and financial contributions. All paid-in and callable contributions are counted in the allocation of votes. However, only hard currency, paid-in contributions, and callable capital from industrialized countries have provided fully usable resources for the bank, because callable capital from developing countries has not been used as collateral for IBRD bond issues. Initially the division of subscriptions was 2 percent paid-in in gold or convertible currency; 18 percent paid-in in local currency; and 80 percent callable (the percentage of callable has increased over time). As of 1981, paid-in capital was equal to 10 percent of total subscriptions. Developing states provided about 4 percent of the bank's usable resources in the form of paid-in subscriptions, but they held about 35 percent of total voting power.[26] A similar relationship between votes and contributions holds for the IDA. The IDA divided its members into two groups—Part I countries (more developed) and Part II countries (less developed). Part I countries were required to pay their entire subscription in gold or convertible currency. Part II countries had to pay only 10 percent of their subscription in gold or convertible currencies; the remainder could be paid in local currencies. Hard-currency replenishments of the IDA, which followed the pattern set by the initial subscription, have come almost entirely from industrialized countries. LDCs have been able to retain their overall share of votes, about 35 percent, even though they have contributed less than 5 percent of the IDA's total resources.

The declining influence of the United States is reflected in the outcomes of votes on several IDA and World Bank loans. During the 1940s and 1950s the voting power of the United States, coupled with its informal influence, almost always provided a blocking veto. By the 1970s this was no longer the case. In several instances the U.S. executive director abstained or opposed a World Bank or IDA loan, yet the loan was approved. American opposition has been motivated by a wide range of considerations including expropriation disputes, human rights violations, nuclear proliferation (in the case of India), and economic inefficiency. Table 6.4 shows the number of loans concluded by the IBRD and the IDA for fiscal years 1972 through 1982, on which the United States abstained or voted no. The numbers in parentheses indicate the number of countries involved.

[26]Derived from figures in World Bank, *Annual Report*, 1981.

TABLE 6.4
U.S. ABSTENTIONS AND NEGATIVE VOTES ON LOANS
APPROVED BY THE IBRD AND IDA

Year	IBRD	IDA
1972	3(3)	1
1973	1	1
1974	5(1)	0
1975	2(2)	9(1)
1976		10(4)
1977	2(2)	14(3)
1978	7(5)	7(5)
1979	2(2)	5(2)
1980	9(6)	3(2)
1981	7(6)	5(2)
1982	9(8)	4

Source: U.S. National Advisory Council on International Monetary and Financial Policies, *Annual Report*, various years. Dates refer to end of U.S. fiscal years. Number of countries in parentheses.

Although more voting power for LDCs, and even the outcomes of some votes, is too narrow an indicator of alterations of influence within the World Bank Group, it is consistent with other developments. The changes in institutional structure that have taken place in the IBRD, particularly the creation of the International Development Association, reflect pressure brought by less developed countries. During the 1950s LDCs constantly called for the creation of an international development fund under the control of the United Nations.[27] The industrialized states deflected this pressure by agreeing to create the IDA. They hoped that the IDA would meet Third World demands for greater resource transfers without involving any basic shift in control over those resources.

Even though the IDA ensnared developing countries within an institution that gave industrialized countries a majority of votes, was located in Washingon, D.C., and was presided over by an American, it still provided greater influence for some LDCs. In part this influence stemmed from the power of the weak. The industrialized countries were not

[27]This is elaborated on pages 165–167.

prepared to accept economic collapse in the poorest countries. India and Pakistan, in particular, were unable by the late 1950s to qualify for additional loans under the creditworthiness criteria used by the World Bank.[28] The alternatives were concessional loans or no loans. The industrialized countries accepted concessional transfers.

Once these procedures were in place, however, borrowing countries were able to bend them to their own needs. By the 1960s the financial position of the World Bank was more secure; its bonds were accepted in international capital markets. The level of activity within the bank came to depend as much on its ability to place loans as on its ability to secure funds from industrialized countries. Organizational growth dictated paying more attention to clients. Bank officials strongly supported the Third World initiative for the creation of a soft loan facility because without this option bank loans to the poorest countries would have been severely curtailed. The Bank's negotiating style emphasizes dialogue rather than confrontation. Bank representatives in individual countries have been particularly concerned about maintaining cordial relations with their counterparts in national finance and development ministries whose cooperation is critical for the formulation and implementation of projects. The bank has been very reluctant to terminate all activity in a particular country because renewing contacts then becomes highly salient politically.[29] Borrowers need lending institutions, but lending institutions also need borrowers.

Symbiosis made it easier for LDCs to influence the bank. For instance, India has been the largest recipient of IDA loans, accounting for 41 percent of disbursements through 1982.[30] Pressure from India has modified IDA policies. India was able to use IDA funds to subsidize loans to small farmers, even though such subsidies violated the Association's policies. The central government used IDA funds to enhance its control over agricultural policy, weakening the position of individual Indian states. Agricultural credit projects provided India with discretionary control of $400 million, of which only $54 million had to be repaid in hard currency. In the early 1970s India received loans for nationalized fertilizer plants and for oil tankers to transport oil from Iraq. The United States opposed the fertilizer loans (arguing that the industry should remain in

[28]White, *Regional Development Banks*, p. 38.
[29]U.S. Treasury, *U.S. Participation in MDBs*, p. 35; Ayres, *Banking on the Poor*, pp. 36–37; Ascher, "World Bank"; Gordenker, *International Aid*, chap. 2.
[30]World Bank, *IDA in Retrospect*, table 6.

private hands) and the tanker loans because Iraq had nationalized foreign oil companies without offering satisfactory compensation.[31] Thus, the Indian case does suggest an enhanced LDC capacity to manipulate the IBRD, a capacity that derives from the inherently symbiotic relationship of large lenders and borrowers.

The Bank can also bring pressure on borrowers, however. More than any other development bank (but not more than the IMF) it has been prepared to play an intrusive role. The bank's comprehensive economic surveys of countries, and its project reviews can influence decisions on loans. The bank has suggested actions such as tax reform, exchange rate changes, institutional innovations, and the use of foreign consultants as conditions for giving loans.

For program loans, the bank has required general development plans, giving it leverage on macroeconomic policies in borrowing countries. The bank's intrusiveness is even more pronounced in new-style basic-needs projects than it is in conventional loans for infrastructure and large-scale industrial and agricultural projects. The new-style projects must have considerable ongoing supervision. They require training new personnel, and frequent assessments by visiting teams. They involve the bank in the social and economic structures of the borrowing country at an intimate level.

The bank's own internal assessments indicate that it has been unable to influence major structural reforms without the support of national elites. Poverty-oriented programs have been particularly difficult to carry out because local officials have been indifferent or hostile. The bank's advice has been most readily accepted on questions of export promotion and trade liberalization.

The increase in the influence of borrowing countries has been accompanied by greater influence for the staff and management of the bank itself. The role of the executive directors, who must approve specific bank projects, has become less important. Under McNamara, the executive board did little more than ratify proposals presented to it by the bank's management. The management had great discretion over the general policy issues that would actually be presented to the board. As the bank's activities have grown and become more complex it has become increasingly difficult for executive directors to secure the information that would be needed to challenge the bank management's presentation.

[31] This paragraph draws from the excellent article by Moulton, "On Concealed Dimensions of Third World Involvement."

The institutional interests of the bank have been diverse, not simply responding to the preferences of the North or the South. The imperative of institutional growth and survival encourages the bank to develop programs that are acceptable to borrowing countries. The professionalism of the bank's staff has encouraged objective, quantifiable measures of project performance, sometimes in opposition to the preferences of the bank's management. Finally, the values of the bank's president, especially manifest in McNamara's poverty-oriented policies, have influenced bank activity.

Over time, the ability of the LDCs to influence specific World Bank decisions has thus increased. More than in the IMF, they share power over agenda setting with INs. The influence of the bank's management and staff has also grown. But the activities of the bank have not altered underlying national power capabilities. The United States, in particular, could still destroy the bank.

The most obvious indicator of the underlying power capability of the United States is the continued dependence of the World Bank Group on American funding. The bank cannot float bonds unless it has callable capital commitments. The IDA cannot make loans unless its resources are replenished by the industrialized countries. The United States donates the single largest amount; the American Congress has persistently failed to appropriate funds fully, even though commitments have been made by the administration. Under Reagan, the executive even failed to support pledges made by its predecessor. At the end of 1973 the United States was $1.5 billion in arrears to various international development institutions; by May 1980 it was $2 billion in arrears. Under Carter, the United States agreed to contribute $3.24 billion to the sixth replenishment of the IDA. But the Reagan administration did not make its first payment until 1982, and stretched the rest over a longer time period. Since other countries made proportionate reductions in their own contributions, the IDA was forced to scale down its new commitments in 1982 from $4.1 billion to $2.6 billion.[32]

The continued power of the United States to destroy the World Bank has placed clear constraints on the organization's activities. In particular, the bank has not been able to violate the basic foreign policy objectives of the United States. In the postwar period these objectives have been

[32]Gordenker, *International Aid*, pp. 79–80; Hurni, *The Lending Policy of the World Bank*, pp. 11–12, 94, 110–111; Ayres, *Banking on the Poor*, pp. 32–41, 57, 60, 66–67, 113–121; Ascher, "World Bank," pp. 417–421.

singularly oriented toward stifling Communist expansion. The only communist members of the World Bank are Yugoslavia, Rumania, Laos, Vietnam, and the Khmer Republic. Yugoslavia and Rumania have moved outside the immediate Soviet orbit, and loans to these countries can be seen as serving broader American foreign policy objectives. The World Bank did not make loans to Chile under the Allende regime, although it did extend credit to Pinochet, even though the economic performance of both was unimpressive. American consternation over a 1979 loan to Vietnam led McNamara to pledge that no further commitments would be made. U.S. officials up to and including the president have intervened on specific policy questions regarding the bank. A Treasury Department study initiated under the Reagan administration, and therefore unlikely to be biased in favor of the multilateral development banks (MDBs), concluded that in fourteen major conflicts during the 1970s the United States only failed outright on two.[33]

With regard to broader policy issues the stance taken by the Bank has at least been consistent with some major strands of opinion in the United States. The Bank has consistently endorsed liberal, as opposed to dependency, interpretations of development. McNamara's support of poverty-oriented programs corresponded to similar developments in the United States.[34] A major theme of A.W. Clausen's initial speeches (he became IBRD president in 1981) was that private enterprise had to play a major role in development, a position entirely consistent with that of the Reagan administration. These developments are not necessarily the result of U.S. pressure. But they do indicate that the bank is engaged in a dialogue whose intellectual agenda is consistent with conventional opinion in the United States.

In sum, the World Bank and the IMF embodied one principle of critical importance of the Third World—the legitimate right of the state to act in the economy. Despite weighted voting, both institutions gave Third World members a degree of formal power far in excess of their share of actual financial contributions. Over time, developing countries have secured more resources on better terms, especially as a result of the creation of the IDA, to a lesser extent because of new facilities in the IMF. As LDCs have become their major clients, both the IMF and the World Bank have become more solicitous of their opinions. The Bretton Woods institution remain wedded, however, to market-oriented policies.

[33]U.S. Treasury, *U.S. Participation in MDBs*, pp. 60–61.
[34]For instance, the Foreign Assistance Act of 1973 mandated concern for the poor.

While the United States has failed to block a number of loans that it opposed for primarily economic reasons, it has influenced IBRD and Fund policy related to central foreign policy objectives. The genetic characters of the IMF and the World Bank embodied in their ethos, voting arrangements, and funding sources have only slowly altered. The sources of leverage available to the Third World—equal voting, dependency ideology, and weakening Northern power—have been less relevant for the Fund and the bank than for any other major international organizations.

REGIONAL DEVELOPMENT BANKS

Third World countries were never satisfied with changes in the structure and behavior of the IBRD and the IMF. One counter has been the creation of new international economic institutions. For resource flows, the most important have been the Inter-American Development Bank (IADB) and the Asian Development Bank (ADB). The third regional bank, the African Development Bank (AFDB), has much more limited resources. Regional banks reflected the desire of developing countries to enhance their control. One study of regional development banks describes their creation as "essentially an act of political resistance against the developed countries' hegemony in the world economy."[35]

THE INTER-AMERICAN DEVELOPMENT BANK

The Inter-American Development Bank was founded in 1960. It was strongly supported by Latin American countries. They maintained that the World Bank was not paying enough attention to Latin America, was uninterested in regional integration projects, and was too concerned with past defaults. Latin American leaders wanted a regional bank not only because they felt it would increase capital flows but also because they believed they could play a leading role in such an institution. Although most contributions would have to come from the United States, Latin American influence would come from staffing and consultations. Their model was European participation in the Marshall Plan.[36]

---

[35]White, *Regional Development Banks*, p. 28.

[36]Mason and Asher, *The World Bank*, p. 579; Dell, *Inter-American Development Bank*, pp. 17–18.

From its inception the IADB pursued an independent course. The president of the bank has always been from Latin America. The bank management views itself as representing Latin American interests. The IADB has frequently taken positions at variance with the IMF, the World Bank, and the United States Agency for International Development. Unlike the IMF and the World Bank, it has not attempted to exercise leverage to change the general economic policies of its borrowers. During the 1960s, loans from the IADB were more heavily concentrated in agriculture, industry, and social projects; the World Bank continued, during this period, to emphasize infrastructure. In generating projects, the IADB relied heavily on negotiations with borrowing countries; the World Bank relied more on technical criteria. In a U.S. Treasury report it was concluded that the IADB is dominated by its Latin American members who "hold the majority voting power and who tend to present a united front on operational, administrative, and budgetary issues . . . [and that] management also tends to be more responsive to borrower concerns than in the World Bank.[37]

The IADB has been able to extend a substantial proportion of its loans on concessional terms. When the bank was founded, the United States contributed $394 million to a fund called the Social Progress Trust Fund (SPTF). The United States gave an additional $131 million in 1963. The purpose of the SPTF was to make loans for various social projects. The trust fund carried interest rates of 2.0–3.5 percent, and maturities of fifteen to thirty years. Moreover the loans were repayable in local currencies.[38] In 1965 the operations of the SPTF were absorbed into the other major soft loan operation of the IADB, the Fund for Special Operations (FSO). Prior to 1970, loans from the Fund for Special Operations carried interest rates of 3–4 percent. The borrowing country, however, was generally allowed to repay in local currencies. (Before 1970 only Mexico and Venezuela were asked to repay in U.S. dollars.) After 1970, repayments had to be made in hard currencies, but the terms of FSO loans were softened. Interest rates in 1979 were set at 1–4 percent and maturities ranged from twenty to forty years. Regular loans from the IADB carried interest rates of 8 percent and maturities of fifteen to thirty years.

[37]See U.S. Treasury, *U.S. Participation in MDBs*, p. 60 for quote; White, *Regional Development Banks*, pp. 173–186; Dell, *Inter-American Development Bank*, pp. 131–132; U.S. Congress, House Committee on Appropriations, *Foreign Assistance . . . for FY 1979*, Part 5, pp. 135–136, 206–207.
[38]White, *Regional Development Banks*, pp. 162–163.

The value of IADB lending provided by various windows through 1980 is shown in table 6.5.

TABLE 6.5
IADB AUTHORIZED LENDING BY FUND ($ MILLIONS)

Period	Ordinary capital	FSO & SPTF	Other, incl. interregional capital	Total authorized	Total disbursed
1961–1965	679	872	4	1,554	593
1966–1970	869	1,669	60	2,599	1,567
1971–1975	2,412	2,280	135	4,829	2,807
1976–1980	2,400	3,366	3,891	9,567	5,209

Source: Derived from figures in IADB, *Annual Report,* various years.

The United States has been the major provider of resources for the Inter-American Development Bank. Through fiscal year 1977 the United States had nominally contributed 33 percent of the paid-in ordinary capital of the IADB, 35 percent of the callable ordinary capital, and 54.2 percent of the funds for the Fund for Special Operations.[39] However, these figures substantially understate the share of real contributions made by the United States. A very large portion of paid-in as well as FSO contributions made by Latin American members of the IADB have been in the form of tied local currencies. They provide little increment in real resources available to the bank. Furthermore, until 1974 only the American share of callable capital gave the IADB any additional borrowing power; covenants in bonds issued by the IADB limited outstanding obligations to the value of callable capital authorized and appropriated by the United States. The IADB did not attempt to borrow on the callable capital authorized by members other than the United States because it wanted to maintain a high credit rating. Thus, before 1974, non-U.S. callable capital, which was about four times as large as paid-in capital, added nothing to the resources of the Inter-American Development Bank.

After 1974 the situation changed somewhat. A separate account, interregional paid-in and callable capital, was created. Contributions came from nonregional members who were first admitted in 1976 (Canada had

[39]U.S. Congress, Senate, Committee on Appropriations, *Foreign Assistance . . . for FY 1979,* p. 1272. Figures include regular and interregional capital.

joined in 1972) as well as from some regional members. Callable capital in the inter-regional account has also been used to support bond issues.

A close examination of the capital subscriptions to the IADB reveals the overwhelming importance of the United States. These subscriptions can be divided into three categories: subscriptions to regular capital, subscriptions to the FSO, and subscriptions to other special funds. Usable contributions to regular capital subscriptions consist of paid-in gold or convertible currency plus U.S. subscriptions to callable capital, plus callable subscriptions of other members to interregional capital. Usable contributions to the Fund for Special Operations and other special funds consist of U.S. dollars, gold, and convertible currencies. Table 6.6 shows the total usable contributions to the IADB as of 1977.[40]

TABLE 6.6

TOTAL UNRESTRICTED OR U.S. DOLLAR CONTRIBUTIONS TO THE
IADB AS OF 1977 ($ MILLIONS)

	Regular capital	FSO	Other funds	Total	Percent of total
United States	3,126	3,400	525	7,051	74
Other INs	700	496	154	1,350	14
Developing countries	549	141	400	1,090	11
Totals	4,375	4,037	1,079	9,491	100

Source: Derived from information in IADB, *Annual Report*, various years.

These figures, describing resources that could be used for something other than local currency expenses or very modest purchases, reveal a relationship between voting power and financial contributions that is much weaker than first appears from an examination of nominal contributions. Voting power in the Inter-American Development Bank is based on nominal contributions to the bank's regular capital. Only a very small percentage of votes are divided equally. The voting system in the bank appears to be one in which votes are closely related to financial contributions.

[40]Detailed discussion of the derivation of these figures can be found in Krasner, "Power Structures and Regional Development Banks."

This system is, to put the matter bluntly, a sham. Most of the contributions made to the IADB by its developing-country members have not provided any additional real resources. In 1980 the bank's Articles of Agreement guaranteed developing-country members at least 53.5 percent of voting power, the United States 34.5 percent, and Canada 4 percent. Nonregional members could have a maximum of 8 percent of the votes. This closely approximated nominal contributions to regular capital. It was wildly divergent from the share of usable resources (U.S. dollars or convertible currencies) offered by different groups of countries. Although the developing countries had 54 percent of the votes in the IADB, they had contributed only about 11 percent of the usable resources.

Precisely how formal voting power is translated into actual influence is not clear. Executive directors from developing countries, however, have always outnumbered those from industrialized countries and they do have a majority of the votes. By the late 1970s eight of the twelve directors were from Latin America or the Caribbean.

The inability of the United States to control the decisions of the executive board of the IADB is suggested in table 6.7, which shows cases in which the United States executive director either abstained or voted no on a loan that was subsequently approved.

In sum, there is a tremendous disparity between freely usable financial contributions to the Inter-American Development Bank and influence over the bank's ongoing operations. The IADB has not tried to compel borrowers to alter their macroeconomic policies as a condition for bank loans. Projects have been developed more through a process of negotiation between IADB staff and borrowing-country officials than through the application of ostensibly objective technical criteria. The IADB's staff is drawn largely from its developing-country members.[41] The United States has failed to block a number of regular loans it opposed. With regard to ongoing decisions, the developing-country members of the IADB have preponderant influence. With regard to agenda setting they share power with industrialized countries. This is a more agreeable situation for LDCs than exists in either the World Bank or the IMF.

The underlying national distribution of power, however, sets boundaries for IADB activities, which borrowing states cannot cross without jeopardizing the institution's financial base. The IADB, like other MDBs, has been subject to failures by the U.S. Congress to appropriate au-

---

[41]In 1979 only 27 percent of staff were U.S. nationals.

TABLE 6.7

U.S. ABSTENTIONS AND NEGATIVE VOTES ON LOANS
APPROVED BY THE IADB

Year	Number of projects	Number of countries
1972	1	1
1973	1	1
1974	0	0
1975	9	1
1976	10	4
1977	14	3
1978	9	4
1979	8	5
1980	10	5
1981	8	5
1982	5	3

Source: U.S. National Advisory Council on International Monetary and Financial Policies, *Annual Report*, various years. Years indicate end of U.S. fiscal years.

thorized contributions. Cuba is not a member of the IADB. When Allende came to power in Chile, loans were cut. In several instances the need to get additional resources from the United States led the Latin American and Caribbean states to accept policy changes that they could have blocked given their voting power. For instance, beginning in 1964 the United States tied FSO contributions to purchases from the United States, a policy that reflected the growing concern of American officials with the deterioration in the balance of payments. The decision to change the requirements for the amortization of FSO loans from payments in local currencies to payments in the currency borrowed (for loans made after 1972–1973) was accepted because of pressure from the United States.[42] There would not have been an IADB in the first place had the attitude of the United States not changed in the late 1950s. The Inter-American Development Bank was part of a larger policy, reflected also in the Alliance for Progress, in which the United States saw social and economic development as a prophylactic against communist takeovers.

[42]Dell, *Inter-American Development Bank*, p. 114.

THE ASIAN DEVELOPMENT BANK

Of the three regional development banks, the Asian Development Bank is the one most under the control of industrialized nations, in particular Japan. In both its formal arrangements and its actual practices the Asian Development Bank has not deviated far from the preferences of its donors. The constraints on developing-country members relate not just to the basic rules and norms of the organization but also to its everyday activities, to ongoing processes as well as general structures.

Industrialized nations were heavily involved in the formation of the Asian Development Bank. The impetus for the creation of a regional financial institution did not come from developing countries in the area, as was the case for the IADB, but rather from the Economic Commission for Asia and the Far East (ECAFE). The United States, in particular, was interested in creating a regional institution that would bolster support for the American effort in Vietnam. American leaders wanted to multilateralize aid to Southeast Asia, and to involve Japan more heavily in assistance efforts. It was also felt that the bank would build Asian support for U.S. policies. The membership of ECAFE included a number of nonregional industrialized countries. When the bank was founded in 1966, twenty-six of its members were developing countries, seventeen industrialized nations; again in sharp contrast to the Inter-American Development Bank in which the United States was the only founding developed-country member.[43]

The formal organizational structure of the ADB reflects the major role played by its donor members. Twenty percent of the votes in the bank are basic votes; that is, they are divided equally among all members. This compares with 10.1 percent for the IBRD, 3.2 percent for the IADB, and 50 percent for the African Development Bank. The bank's charter requires that nine out of the twelve executive directors be appointed by regional members and that 60 percent of the capital, and therefore at least 60 percent of the votes come from regional members. Although these procedures might appear, at first glance, to give developing countries substantial formal power, that is not the case. Japan, Australia, and New Zealand are counted as regional members. As of December 1982 industrialized-country members held 58 percent of the votes even though regional members held 64 percent. While this has not meant that develop-

---

[43]U.S. Congress, House, Committee on Foreign Affairs, *U.S. and MDBs*, pp. 26–27; White, *Regional Development Banks*, pp. 40–45.

ing countries have always lost, because the more advanced members are sometimes divided, it has meant that the LDC members of the Asian Development Bank have not had a blocking veto, in sharp contrast to the situation in the Inter-American Development Bank.

Despite the majority of votes held by industrialized countries, there is still a great disparity between actual financial allocations and votes. As in the case of the Inter-American Development Bank, votes are allocated on the basis of callable as well as paid-in capital. Contributions to soft loan windows, of which the Asian Development Fund's is by far the largest, are not included in allocating votes. These practices give LDC members far more votes than they would receive under a system based on their contributions to the bank's actual resources. As in the case of the IADB, the Asian Development Bank limits its borrowing to callable capital from industrialized countries. The callable capital contributions of less developed members raise their votes but do not increase the bank's resources. Table 6.8 shows the actual resources contributed to the Asian Development Bank by Japan, the United States, other industrialized countries, and less developed countries as of September 30, 1978.[44] The figures for the industrialized countries include all paid-in and callable capital, and contributions to the Asian Development Fund. The figures for less developed countries include the gold and convertible currency portion of their paid-in capital. As in the case of the Inter-American Development Bank, there is a tremendous disparity between voting power and actual contributions. Although LDCs have contributed only 4 percent of the ADB's actual resources, they hold about 45 percent of its votes. Executive directors, numbering twelve in 1980, have always been equally divided between industrialized and developing members.

The lending pattern and practices of the Asian Development Bank have been more conservative than those of the IABD. The Asian Development Bank has not been much concerned with regional integration or social reform. Its orientation has been highly technical. It has been market-oriented and has relied on economic incentives. The bank itself has never developed the dynamism and autonomy that characterize the World Bank. It has not been an initiator of new programs such as basic needs.[45]

The pattern of ADB lending suggests the central importance played by

[44]The following calculations do not include contributions to some smaller soft-loan windows whose funds do not exceed $50 million.

[45]U.S. Congress, House, Committee on Foreign Affairs, *U.S. and MDBs*, p. 26; White, *Regional Development Banks*, pp. 69 ff.

TABLE 6.8
FINANCIAL CONTRIBUTIONS AND VOTING POWER IN THE ASIAN
DEVELOPMENT BANK AS OF 30 SEPTEMBER 1978

	Total contributions ($ millions)	% of total contributions	% of total votes
United States	1,148.9	16.2	9.3
Japan	2,424.5	34.2	14.8
Other INs	3,244.6	45.7	32.1
Developing countries	279.1	3.9	44.8

Source: Derived from figures in Asian Development Bank, *Annual Report*, 1971; and U.S. House Committee on Appropriations, *Foreign Assistance and Related Program Appropriations for 1980*, 96th Congress, 1st Session (April, 1979), pp. 253 and 278.

Japan. The Japanese have contributed the largest amount to the bank. A Japanese citizen has always been president of the bank. The bank's pattern of loan allocations has been much closer to Japanese interests than to American ones, even though the United States and Japan initially contributed equal amounts to the bank's resources and the United States still contributes by far the second largest amount of funds to the bank. Table 6.9 shows product moment correlation coefficients between per capita Asian Development Bank lending and per capita net resource flows, overseas development assistance, total trade, exports, and imports from the United States and Japan by country.

The contrast between the Asian Development Bank and the Inter-American Development Bank suggests that it may be better for weak states to confront a truly hegemonic state than a normal power. A normal power is bound by the decisions of others and the structure of the international system. A hegemonic state does not confront the same constraints. It may be little concerned with those questions which are most vital to weaker states. It may provide international organizations with considerable independence (such as accepting the allocation of 53 percent of votes to recipients in the IADB) because it views these institutions as legitimators of a more general international order. Normal states are more concerned with their own immediate economic interests. Inter-

TABLE 6.9

CORRELATION COEFFICIENTS FOR PER CAPITA ASIAN DEVELOPMENT
BANK ALLOCATIONS BY COUNTRY (1971–1976) WITH PER CAPITA
INDICATORS OF JAPANESE AND AMERICAN ECONOMIC
INTERESTS BY COUNTRY

	Per capita net resource flows	Overseas development assistance	Per capita total trade	Per capita exports	Per capita imports
	1971–1976	1971–1976	1976	1976	1976
Japan	.54	.54	.76	.83	.88
United States	.16	−.20	.32	.38	.30

Source: Derived from figures in IMF, *Direction of Trade, Annual 1971–1977*; OECD, *Geographic Distribution of Financial Flows to Developing Countries, Dates on Disbursements 1971–1977* (Paris: OECD, 1978), World Bank, *World Bank Atlas*, 1977.

national organizations are seen more as instruments to be used to promote these interests than as legitimators of general norms. ADB activity has remained congruent with the preferences and interest of Japan. The IADB has drifted from narrow American preferences at least in some issue areas. Incongruence is more likely under conditions of hegemonic decline than under persistent multipolarity.[46]

THE AFRICAN DEVELOPMENT BANK

Of the three development banks, the African Development Bank (AFDB) has been the most independent, and the smallest. This conjuncture is no accident. The independence of the bank could only be purchased at the expense of limited financial resources. The African Development Bank illustrates the structural limits within which Third World countries must function: industrialized states, even hegemonic ones, have not been willing to transfer funds to institutions over which they have no control. Over time African states have dealt with the trade-off between resources and control by giving nonregional states more power, first by creating

[46]See Krasner, "Power Structures and Regional Development Banks," for an elaboration of these arguments.

an auxiliary institution, the African Development Fund (AFDF), and later by admitting nonregional members to the bank itself.

The creation of a regional development bank for Africa was initiated by African states. Unlike either the Inter-American Development Bank or the Asian Development Bank, industrialized countries were not involved. The initial proposals for a bank were made at the All-African People's Conference held in Tunis in January of 1960, and the bank was created in 1964. At an early stage a decision was made to exclude non-African states from membership. The plans for the bank did not receive much encouragement from developed countries. Voting power was allocated exclusively to African states according to a formula that tended to equalize influence. Basic votes, allocated equally to each member, accounted for 50 percent of the votes. The maximum ratio between the country with the largest number of votes and the one with the smallest was 5 to 1, while the maximum ratio for subscriptions was 30 to 1. For the IADB the ratio of the largest number of votes to the smallest is over 500 to 1, for the ADB, over 30 to 1. Decisions in the AFDB are made by a simple majority vote.[47]

The initial capitalization of the AFDB was $300 million. Fifty percent was paid-in convertible currency, the rest callable. These are not very impressive sums. The callable portion of the capital did not generate any additional funds for the bank since international financial markets were unwilling to accept it as collateral for bond issues. Members often failed to meet their paid-in obligations because they did not want to transfer scarce convertible currency. In the late 1960s only about 60 percent of the paid-in portion of subscriptions was received.[48]

Because of the limited resources that the African Development Bank itself was able to generate, efforts were made to bring wealthy countries into the institution, but only on the condition that this be done with a minimal loss of control for regional members. Discussions began in the mid-1960s for the establishment of a soft loan window, but they did not reach fruition until 1973 when the African Development Fund was created. Its membership consisted of the African Development Bank and a number of nonregional-state members, most of them industrialized countries. By 1981 Argentina, Brazil, Canada, Japan, South Korea, Kuwait, Saudi Arabia, the United Arab Emirates, the United States, Yugoslavia, and thirteen European countries had joined the AFDF.

[47]African Development Bank, *Annual Report*, 1969, Annex IV.
[48]Ibid., Schedule 2.

The African Development Fund, unlike the Asian Development Fund and the Fund for Special Operations of the IADB, is formally distinct from its parent institution, the African Development Bank. The two institutions have separate boards of directors. They are financially independent and neither organization is liable for the financial obligations of the other.

Voting power in the African Development Fund (AFDF) is equally divided between the African Development Bank and the nonregional-state members. Each group has the right to appoint six executive directors. The votes of the nonregional-state members are allocated exactly in proportion to their share of financial contributions to the AFDF. All operational decisions of the African Development Fund require 75 percent approval. Authorizations for general increases in subscriptions require 85 percent approval; a state has no obligation to contribute if it votes against the increase. The AFDF thus operates with a mutual veto-voting arrangement in which either less developed countries or nonregional-state members can block action.

In its day-to-day operations, however, the AFDF is controlled by the African Development Bank, and the bank is entirely controlled by African states. The African Development Fund has no staff of its own. It uses personnel from the AFDB to administer its projects. The bank is reimbursed for the use of these individuals. The president of the bank is also the president of the African Fund. He acts as the nonvoting chairman of the AFDF's board of directors and is empowered to propose operating and adminstrative budgets, develop overall programs, and set personnel policy.[49] The agenda for the African Fund is thus generated by the bank. The non-state members of the African Fund have the power to block programs, but not to take initiatives. The African Development Fund is a legal framework that has brought resources into the AFDB while still limiting the control of nonregional countries.

As in the case of other multilateral development banks there is a tremendous disparity between formal voting power and actual contributions. The African Development Fund began with an initial subscription of $142 million. By 1981 total subscriptions had risen to $1.09 billion with 2 percent coming from the AFDB, 4 percent from non-oil-exporting LDCs, 5 percent from oil-exporting LDCs, and 89 percent from INs. However, 50 percent of the votes are held by the African Development

---

[49]African Development Fund, *Annual Report*, various issues.

Bank, while nonregional developing countries hold 5 percent, and industrialized countries 45 percent. These relationships are summarized in
table 6.10.

TABLE 6.10

FINANCIAL CONTRIBUTIONS AND VOTING POWER IN AFRICAN
DEVELOPMENT FUND AS OF 31 DECEMBER 1981

	Percent of financial contributions	Percent of total votes
Developing countries, total	11	55
AFDB	2	50
nonregional states	9	5
Developed countries, total	89	45
Japan	15	7
United States	13	5
Canada	12	6

Source: Derived from figures in African Development Bank, *Annual Report*, 1981,
p. 109.

To a greater extent than any of the other regional development banks
the African Development Bank thus maintained its independence through
the 1970s. It set its own policies and hired its own staff. The bank's senior
officials were African, as opposed to the World Bank whose president
has always been American, the Asian Development Bank whose president
has always been Japanese, and the IADB, which has had a Latin American
president but a vice president from the United States. But the cost of
independence was a limited resource base. By the late 1970s the combined
funds generated by the AFDB itself and the AFDF were under one billion
dollars. This contrast with nearly $50 billion for the World Bank Group,
$7 billion for the Asian Development Bank and the Asian Development
Fund, and $8.5 billion for the IADB and the Fund for Special Operations.

The inability to generate substantial resources led to a change in policy.
In May 1979 the members of the African Development Bank decided to
admit nonregional members to the bank itself. In conjunction with the
admission of new members the AFDB's capital was increased from $1.5

billion to $6.3 billion. Twenty-five percent of initial new capital subscriptions were paid-in, the rest callable. The board of directors was expanded from nine to eighteen, with twelve chosen by African states and the remainder by nonregional members. African states hold two-thirds of the votes. Policy decisions require a 51 percent majority.[50]

In all international financial institutions, the countries of the Third World have achieved some of their meta-political objectives. The basic principle of all the IFIs is that the state plays a legitimate role in resource allocation. All the banks are conditioned by the norm that foreign assistance should not be merely an instrument of statecraft, unilaterally controlled by donor countries; the ability to influence ongoing activities is shared to some extent. In the Inter-American and African Development banks, routine decisions are effectively controlled by developing countries. The ability to set agendas is also shared to varying degrees, although the influence of the Third World is least in the International Monetary Fund and again greatest in the Inter-American and African banks.

The regime for official multilateral resource transfers has moved away from the Northern-dominated, even Northern-dictated, regime that existed at the conclusion of the Second World War. This movement has been facilitated primarily by the ability of developing countries to take advantage of existing regime structures. Because of their Keynesian principles, postwar international financial institutions were able to legitimate state intervention in the economy. Although weighted voting has been a target of Third World criticism, actual procedures in the IFIs gave developing states more power than they would have been entitled to on the basis of their contributions to usable financial resources. Over time, the declining power of the United States gave the bureaucracies of these institutions more leeway, as well as incentives to cultivate clients in borrowing countries. Ironically, the dominating position of the United States in the Western Hemisphere contributed to the creation of the IADB, an institution in which the relationship between specific American economic interests and bank behavior was more attenuated than in the case of the ADB where Japan, with its more specific economic needs, took the lead role. The development of a coherent ideology contributed to Third World unity in presenting a number of proposals, including the link and the relaxation of conditionality. Although none of the South's major initiatives has been accepted, the basic Keynesian principles and

<hr>

[50]AFDB, Press Release, IRP/B/8110, February 16, 1981.

norms of the regime for public capital flows, which legitimate state action, were coincident with the Third World's preference for authoritative over market allocation.

THE UNITED NATIONS

The objectives of the Third World with respect to the regime for official capital transfers are most clearly illuminated by actions taken within the United Nations. In the World Bank, the IMF, the Asian Development Bank, and the Inter-American Development Bank, the South had to contend with institutional structures, rules, and norms unilaterally created or heavily influenced by the North. The task of the South was to alter existing arrangements. In contrast, the United Nations offered developing countries the opportunity to play a major role from the outset. Their desire to create a regime for official capital transfers characterized by donor obligations to commit resources, rules determined by recipients, and institutional structures controlled by recipients is more apparent here than in the Bretton Woods institutions or in the Inter-American and Asian Development banks.

THE UNDP AND ITS PREDECESSORS

The first substantial United Nations aid program, the Expanded Program for Technical Assistance (EPTA), which was established in 1949, reflected American preferences. However, pressure by less developed countries for direct access to resources through the United Nations began as early as 1949. During the 1950s, the developing countries supported the creation of a Special United Nations Fund for Economic Development (SUNFED). SUNFED proposals described the agency as a supplement to private investment and World Bank loans. SUNFED would only provide resources for nonliquidating projects that could not meet World Bank loan criteria. The initial proposals were modest, calling for funding from member countries in their own currencies and providing for a veto over the use of these currencies. Later formulations were more ambitious, involving funding based on contributions equal to a specific proportion of the GNP of member states, and for voting allocations based on the principle of one nation, one vote. (The final LDC proposal in 1958, however, provided for an equal division of votes between donors and recipients and required majorities of two-thirds or three-quarters.) SUNFED was consistently rejected by most industrialized nations and never came into existence.[51]

The SUNFED proposals were the embodiment of the regime preferred by the Third World: the developing countries called not just for more resources but for effective control over these resources. Existing international institutions, such as the World Bank, where LDCs did not have effective control, were less than fully satisfactory vehicles. The conventional and conservative standards of the World Bank in the 1950s, which emphasized self-liquidating loans for infrastructure development (a position consistent with the liberal capitalist system supported by the United States), were questioned if not rejected by developing states, which wanted more flexible criteria and funding for state projects.

Although SUNFED was never endorsed, a compromise between the United States and developing countries did result in the creation of the United Nations Special Fund (UNSF) in 1959. The UNSF was not a direct loan-granting agency, which is what the LDCs wanted. Rather it engaged in preinvestment studies costing between $500,000 and $5,000,000. Special UNSF resources were also used for training, research, and the formulation of national development plans. During the 1960s all the resources allocated by the Special Fund were administered by one of the specialized agencies or a regional development bank. Thus, the UNSF did not have a strong independent operational presence. The specialized agencies did not have a direct hand in the formulation of UNSF policy. Rather, the activities of the Special Fund were overseen by a governing council of eighteen members elected by the Economic and Social Council (ECOSOC). Nine of the council representatives were from developing countries; nine from industrialized ones.[52]

The Third World achieved a major success with the creation of the United Nations Development Program (UNDP) in 1965. The UNDP was created by merging the UNSF and the Expanded Program for Technical Assistance. The institutional structure created for the UNDP gave the Third World power over both ongoing operations and agenda setting. The rules and norms that have evolved in the UNDP reflect the attitudes of the South. The UNDP has become a prime source of revenue for many

[51]Weaver, *The IDA*, pp. 23–25; Mason and Asher, *The World Bank*, pp. 328–383; Hadwen and Kaufmann, *How U.N. Decisions are Made*, pp. 85–99.

[52]Richards, *International Economic Institutions*, pp. 23–25; Auerback et al., "The U.N. Development Program," p. 512.

of the specialized agencies within the United Nations system and its influence has, therefore, spread over a wide network of organizations. The UNDP, however, relies on voluntary contributions and has not altered basic national power capabilities.

The UNDP is controlled by a governing council selected by the Economic and Social Council. The LDCs hold a majority of the seats in ECOSOC. The governing council of the UNDP initially consisted of thirty-seven members, with developing countries holding nineteen seats, industrialized market economic countries fourteen, and East European countries three, with the thirty-seventh seat rotating among these three groups on a nine-year cycle, each group holding the seat for three years. The size of the council was later expanded to forty-eight members with twenty-seven seats filled by developing countries, seventeen by industrialized market-economy countries, and four by East Europe. When the UNDP was created, the Third World was thus able to move beyond the even distribution of seats that had prevailed on the governing council of the UNSF.

Market-economy industrialized countries accounted for 87 percent of the contributions pledged to the UNDP, or its predecessor organizations, for the period 1959 through 1981. The United States contributed the largest single amount, providing 25 percent of all resources. The American share of contributions dropped, however, from 42 percent for the period 1959 through 1966 to 18 percent for the period 1977 through 1981. The largest contribution from the Socialist Bloc, which came from the Soviet Union, provided a little less than 1 percent of all pledges; India, contributing more than any other LDC, provided only a little more than 1 percent. Pledges grew from an annual average of $110 million for the period 1959–1966 to $268 million 1972, to $689 million in 1983. For the period 1973 through 1980, contributions to the UNDP were equal to about 9 percent of total overseas development assistance from industrialized countries.[53]

In its formal voting structure the UNDP provides the South with dominant influence. But the provision of resources comes from the North. The actual orientation of the program has been increasingly influenced by the views of the Third World. During its initial years the UNDP worked on a conventional project basis. But in 1970 the governing council

[53]Derived from figures in U.N. doc. no. DP/1983/6/Add 4, table 14.5; and DP/1980/6, p. 5.

voted to switch to a country-programming basis with funds being allocated to countries on a five-year funding cycle. This gave recipient countries considerably more leeway in their use of assistance from the UNDP. UNDP aid could be fitted into long-term development plans. Initiative for specific projects was left to recipients. The UNDP did not attempt to influence macroeconomic policies. The 1970 decision also mandated decentralization, with the UNDP resident representative assuming the major role for coordinating all United Nations aid activity. Recipient countries did not have to work primarily with a distant bureaucracy in New York, but could rely instead on a field representative whose success depended in part on his cordial relations with host-country officials and his ability to maintain a viable program.[54]

The administrator of the UNDP has always been an American. The first two adminstrators, Paul Hoffman and Rudolph Peterson, held to the conventional view of development problems, which attributed the condition of Third World countries primarily to their own national deficiencies. Technical assistance and capital transfers could break certain bottlenecks, but the fundamental problems of underdevelopment rested with the underdeveloped country.

The views of Bradford Morse, the third administrator of the UNDP who took office in January 1976, were much closer to the dependency positions favored by the Third World. He repeatedly argued that underdevelopment was a function of the world economic system, not just a characteristic of poorer areas. There was a clear shift in the tone of the *Annual Report of the Administrator,* from an emphasis on the program's growth and specific characteristics, with the world economy seen as offering benefits for everyone, to an emphasis on the need to restructure fundamentally the international economic system. In his first report Morse argued:

The entire international community is now straining to adjust to the demands of fairness and need—not merely the laws of supply and demand. Indeed, we are witness to a drive for a major restructuring of the global economy, with development as the primary aim and with greater equity and social justice as the driving force. [He went on to argue:] There is no doubt about it: the difficulties of the old "aid" relationship with its overtones of dependency, are giving way to the new difficulties involved in structural and institutional change on a global scale.

[54]See UNDP, *Report of the Administrator,* 1973, pp. 24–27, DP/48 for the 1970 decision; Gordenker, *International Aid,* p. 107 and chap. 5, for the position of field representatives.

Throughout the first generation of the development effort the lack of decisive strategies for external change considerably reduced the effectiveness of technical co-operation activities.[55]

In his 1978 report, Morse argued that "Development can no longer be viewed strictly as a matter of 'foreign aid' or capital assistance, or balance of payments adjustment support or technical co-operation. It has become a global process involving a restructuring of fundamental means of economic exchange and a more just and equitable division of labor among all nations."[56]

The UNDP has pointed out that it is prepared to deal with all types of economic systems. There is no formal commitment to the liberal ideals embodied in the Articles of Agreement of the IMF and the World Bank. UNDP assistance has gone to a wider variety of countries than have World Bank loans. The program has been responsive to the norms reflected in the call for a new international economic order. It has offered assistance to commodity producer associations, programs that enhance cooperation among developing countries, and made efforts to increase the bargaining power of LDCs vis-à-vis multinational corporations. The governing council has allocated special support for national liberation movements. The UNDP has avoided any efforts to use leverage to influence the macroeconomic policies of recipient countries. Resident representatives devote most of their time to the technical issues of specific projects, although individuals sometimes exercise influence on broader policy through personal ties with national leaders.[57]

THE UNITED NATIONS CAPITAL DEVELOPMENT FUND

In a little-noted episode in the mid-1960s the Third World countries attempted to create an institutional structure for official capital flows that would have approximated their ideal regime. In 1966, by a vote of 76–19–14, the General Assembly called for the establishment of a United Nations Capital Development Fund (UNCDF). No market-economy developed country supported the resolution. Contributions were to be based on a

[55]UNDP, *Report of the Administrator*, DP/255 1976, pp. 1–2.

[56]UNDP, *Report of the Administrator*, DP/380 1978, p. 7.

[57]UNDP, *Report of the Administrator*, DP/380 1978, p. 6; and DP/460 1979, p. 13; Ringen, "Fruits of the U.N.," p. 52; Gordenker, *International Aid*, chaps. 3–4.

fixed proportion of members' aggregate economic wealth. Votes in the Capital Development Fund's governing council were to have been equally divided among all members. The UNCDF was a revival of SUNFED, but in a more radical version, and by the mid-1960s the developing countries had enough votes in the General Assembly actually to pass such a resolution. The UNCDF resolution was adopted after the establishment of the IDA and the UNDP, actions which Northern policymakers thought would assuage Southern demands.

The UNCDF, however, never came into existence in the form envisioned by its initiators in their first resolution. The industrialized nations ignored the new organization. Greece was the only non–Third World country to participate in the first pledging conference at which pledges of $1,296,542 were made, mostly in local currencies. By May 1970 only $799,525 out of $3.4 million in pledges had actually been paid in, 90 percent in nonconvertible currency, with Greece continuing (with contributions of $3,000 per year) as the only non–Third World supporter of the organization.[58] Because of lack of financial support, plans to establish the UNCDF were modified. In 1967 the General Assembly voted to place the U.N. Capital Development Fund under the administration of the UNDP.

In 1973 the ECOSOC and the General Assembly adopted resolutions fundamentally reorienting the UNCDF toward small-scale projects in the least developed countries. This change prompted a number of wealthy countries led by the Netherlands to begin making contributions to the UNCDF. The Fund began full operations in 1974. By the end of 1982 cumulative commitments amounted to $277 million for 219 projects in forty-two countries. Total contributions were $178 million through 1982 with the Netherlands accounting for 33 percent, Sweden for 22, Norway for 15, Denmark for 7, and the United States for 6. Industrialized countries accounted for more than 80 percent of total contributions.[59] The UNCDF has worked through the UNDP, although its resources are kept separate. It explicitly does not attempt to negotiate with recipient governments' "internal policy reforms, whether dealing with the price structure, fiscal measures, land use or other national development elements."[60]

[58]Richards, *International Economic Institutions*, pp. 42–44; U.N., *Yearbook*, 1970, pp. 401–403; and 1967, p. 370.

[59]U.N. Doc. no. DP/361, pp. 7–10; DP/305, p. 5; DP/460, p. 22; DP/111, pp. 93–94; DP/1983/6/Add. 4, table 26; DP/1983/6/Add. 3, p. 2.

[60]U.N. doc. no. DP/251, pt. 1, p. 3.

In particularly clear form the U.N. Capital Development Fund illustrates the objectives and limits of Third World countries. Third World states wanted to create an institution for official resource transfers which they could effectively control, and through which they could make claims on the wealth of the North. They had to settle for a truncated institution, with voluntary contributions administered by the UNDP, rather than an organization functioning as an independent entity.

THE UNITED NATIONS REVOLVING FUND
FOR NATURAL RESOURCES

The United Nations Revolving Fund for Natural Resources (UNRFNR) is another example of the aspirations, possibilities, and limitations of Third World power. Like the U.N. Capital Development Fund, it represents an effort to change fundamentally the regime governing official capital transfers. However, in this case the South sought to gain independence and control through collective self-reliance rather than by locking the wealthy countries in a set of binding obligations.

The proposal for a Revolving Fund was initiated by the ECOSOC and passed by the General Assembly in 1973 by a vote of 106–0–18. Its funds are used to underwrite natural resource projects. The Revolving Fund is administered by the governing council of the UNDP, and the UNDP's resident representative channels all requests to it.[61]

The initial objective was to make the Revolving Fund self-sustaining by replenishing its resources from the earnings of successful endeavors. The Revolving Fund's procedures initially called for recipients to make payments equal to 2 percent of the value produced by the exploitation of minerals discovered with the aid of a Revolving Fund loan. Payments were to continue for fifteen years after the commencement of commercial production. A ceiling of fifteen times the original loan was established. The expectation was that these procedures would help to free developing countries from funding provided by the North.

As of 1982, voluntary contributions, needed to initiate the Revolving Fund's activities, totaled $31 million, with 71 percent provided by Japan, 11 percent by the United States, 6 percent by Belgium, and 5 percent by Canada.

[61]U.N. doc. no. DP/154, p. 2; DP/142, p. 9; UNDP, *Questions and Answers*, 1975, p. 32; U.N., *Yearbook*, 1973, pp. 399–400.

The Revolving Fund's operations did not go smoothly. There was considerable resistance from potential recipients during the 1970s. Four projects were approved in 1975–1976, none in 1977, six in 1978, and four in 1979. Negotiations between the Revolving Fund and governments have frequently broken down at the last moment with the government side withdrawing or preferring to work with private companies. Agreements were canceled because new regimes came to power or officials had a change of heart. The major problem, however, was the replenishment requirement. In 1981 an expert committee recommended that the rate of repayment be lowered to 1 percent per year for the least developed countries and that the ceiling on repayments be lowered to ten times the value of the original loan. These changes did lead to some increase in the Revolving Fund's activities. By the end of 1982, seventeen projects were under way or had been completed.[62]

The notion that assistance from the Revolving Fund would improve the bargaining power of host-country governments and therefore make them willing to accept replenishment payments has not worked out in practice. The exiguity of resources in Third World countries has made their policymakers reluctant to commit themselves to sharing resources even with other Third World states. Host-country governments worry that they might find it much more discomforting to alter repayment arrangements with a United Nations agency than they have in the past with multinational corporations. There is no expectation that the Revolving Fund will become self-sustaining in the foreseeable future. It has become one more operation dependent on voluntary contributions from the North.

It is hardly surprising that developing countries should have difficulties with collective goods and free riders. There is a persistent tendency to undersupply such goods in the international system.[63] Such problems are likely to be more acute for developing countries than for industrialized ones. The opportunity costs of carrying free riders are higher for developing countries because their resources are already heavily committed.

There are also a number of other special funds, administered by the UNDP, all funded by voluntary contributions. The Fund for Science and Technology, with targeted contributions of $250 million, was agreed to at the 1979 Vienna Conference on Science and Technology for Develop-

[62]U.N. doc no. DP/368, pp. 10–11, Annexes 2 and 4; DP/1983/34, Annex 2; and E/1981/23.
[63]Ruggie, "Collective Goods and Future International Collaboration."

ment. As of mid-1983, $35 million had been contributed. The Special Fund for Land-Locked Developing Countries, jointly administered with UNCTAD, was established by the General Assembly in 1976; by 1983 its resources amounted to only about $1.5 million. No industrialized country had participated. The United Nations Trust Fund for Assistance to Colonial Countries and Peoples provides resources to national liberation movements designated by the Organization of African Unity. Established by a General Assembly vote in 1975, it had resources of $17 million by the middle of 1978, $8 million of which was advanced by the UNDP's governing council, but by 1982 the Trust Fund's working balance was only $1.3 million.[64]

Within the United Nations system, developing countries dominate specific decisions and set agendas. The UNDP, the major U.N. capital transfer institution, was responsive to the new international economic order demands made by developing countries during the 1970s. Although an American, the program's administrator endorsed the dependency arguments used by the Group of 77 to justify fundamental restructuring of the international economic regime. Since its creation, developing countries have held a majority of seats on the UNDP's governing council. Industrialized countries have provided about 90 percent of the UNDP's resources. The UNDP has decentralized its operations and explicitly rejected efforts to pressure recipients to change their macroeconomic policies.

The Third World has not succeeded, however, in altering fundamental conditions governing the provision of resources to the program. Efforts to secure automatic contributions based on a fixed proportion of national income, a stipulation incorporated in the 1966 resolution establishing the United Nations Fund for Capital Development, were simply ignored by the North. The Revolving Fund for Natural Resources encountered difficulty because some Southern states have been unwilling to accept the replenishment requirement. In its economic activities, as well as in other ways, the United Nations has moved from congruence with the preferences of its most powerful member states to incongruence. However, the weak have not been able to use regime alteration to create conditions of dynamic instability; that is, to alter underlying national power capabilities.

[64]U.N. doc. no. DP/380, pp. 52–55; DP/1983/6/Add 4; tables 27 and 32; DP/1983/6/Add 3, p. 7.

CONCLUSION

From the outset the international regime for official capital transfers embodied some principles and norms that were coincident with the South's preferences for authoritative, rather than market, allocation. The Keynesian principles embodied in the World Bank and the IMF justified the need for state intervention. However, many other aspects of the regime were objectionable to the South. As a result of the declining influence of the United States, and the access provided by existing international organizations, the Third World was able to change some of these. In a less hegemonic world, IFIs had to cultivate support from a number of constituencies, including poorer borrowing countries. The American ability to dictate policies virtually unilaterally disappeared even in the IMF and the World Bank. The agenda-setting power of developing countries in the United Nations agencies facilitated the creation of new international financial institutions including the three regional development banks, the International Development Association of the World Bank, new facilities in the IMF, and the United Nations Development Program. These newer institutions were generally more responsive to the objectives of developing states. In the African Development Bank and the United Nations Development Program, developing countries have had the dominant influence. Even in the more traditional World Bank and IMF some concessions have been made to Third World preferences. The professional ethos and lending practices of these two institutions, however, continued to be dominated by a market-oriented approach.

The South's cognitive world view, emphasizing the inequities of the dominant market-driven rules of the game, contributed to altering some international norms. Aid is now generally viewed as an obligation rather than as a matter of discretion for wealthier countries. This norm has been recognized in several United Nations resolutions, which have been supported by the North as well as the South. It is implicitly embodied in the very existence of multilateral aid institutions, for these organizational structures inherently insulate aid recipients from donor pressures.

The norm that various common goods should generate resources for the whole international community, and not just be appropriated by the strongest, has been accepted. To date the only institutional manifestation is the IMF Trust Fund, which used the sale of gold to provide additional resources for developing countries. These allocations were subject to minimal supervision by the IMF. All countries have recognized that the deep seabed and outer space are part of the common heritage of mankind, and some of the profits from the exploitation of these areas will be devoted to economic development in the Third World.

The South has not just wanted to increase the level of aid. African states, for instance, resisted the direct membership of industrialized countries in the African Development Bank for twenty years because they wanted to maintain full control. The Third World rejected the International Resources Bank proposed by the United States at the 1976 UNCTAD meeting. For the Third World, the United Nations Revolving Fund for National Resources, firmly under the control of the UNDP, was a much more attractive repository for contributions from wealthier areas. Third World countries have persistently sought domination over both ongoing decision-making and agendas. They have promoted normative values that would deny the North discretion over the provision and allocation of aid resources. The Third World has pursued a meta-political strategy designed to alter principles, norms, rules, and decision-making procedures, as well as a relational power strategy solely related to distributional issues. The South has enjoyed success in both arenas because it has been able to utilize existing institutional structures, which legitimated direct state activity, take advantage of declining American power, and present a coherent intellectual alternative to liberal capitalism.

VII

Multinational Corporations

INTRODUCTION

In the period since the conclusion of the Second World War multinational corporations have become major actors in the world economy. During the 1960s, direct foreign investment from the thirteen OECD countries grew approximately one and a half times as quickly as the average growth rate. By the mid-1970s goods imported by American multinationals into the United States from their majority-owned affiliates accounted for about 30 percent of U.S. trade. On a global basis, intracorporate trade was estimated at 25 percent of all trade (excluding the centrally planned economies).[1] Multinationals command a dominant position in many of the leading technology industries. They have become a primary vehicle for the transfer of technology across national boundaries. They are an important source of transnational capital flows.

Despite their importance, however, the degree of general North-South conflict (as opposed to disputes of specific countries) over multinationals has not been as intense as it has been over other issues. Commodity agreements, trade, official capital flows including the behavior of the IMF and World Bank, and the Law of the Sea have all engendered more intense debate. Through the early 1980s the various international arrangements related to multinationals have taken the form of international codes or guidelines rather than definitive agreements or the creation of separate international institutions.

The somewhat moderated level of conflict concerning multinationals rests on the fact that the prevailing regime governing their behavior incorporates some of the major preferences of developing countries because of the significance of juridical sovereignty. All actors recognize that national states have the right to control economic behavior that takes

[1] OECD, *International Investment and Multinational Enterprises*, pp. 6–7.

place within their borders. A multinational cannot function without the sanction of the state. The notion of sovereignty at bay, so fashionable in the early 1970s, was never an accurate characterization. Despite their international and domestic weaknesses, Third World states have been able to use their juridical sovereignty, the constitutive principle of the present international system, to establish national principles and rules related to multinational corporations.

The specific character and effectiveness of national regulation have depended on the relative bargaining power of the host country on the one hand and the corporation on the other. The state's leverage has been derived, in the first instance, from its power to grant access to its territory. In addition, every state in the contemporary international system has at least formal control over a panoply of policy instruments that can be applied to economic actors. The extent to which a state can actually impose controls depends on its ability to provide itself with capital, technology, and market access. A state that must rely entirely on multinationals for these services cannot drive a very hard bargain. The extent to which developing countries control such resources has varied over time and across sectors. There has been a general intertemporal improvement in the bargaining power of host-country governments. Their power has been most extensive in the area of raw materials where they have been able to assert formal and effective control over most fuel and mineral exploitation. In the area of manufactures, LDC leverage is less impressive.[2]

In addition to national regulation, LDCs have supported new international rules of the game. The postwar liberal regime for multinational corporations (MNCs) emphasized national treatment, just and adequate compensation, and the right of companies to appeal to their home countries. The Third World has pressed for agreements that would legitimate the right to discriminate between national and multinational corporations, curtail the right of MNCs to alienate their property, and leave the determination of compensation and the resolution of any disputes to legal institutions in host countries. Industrialized states have advocated voluntary codes, whereas the Third World has preferred, but not insisted on, mandatory agreements.

New international principles and norms could enhance national bargaining power. New rules could coordinate the behavior of developing

[2]Huntington, "Transnational Organizations in World Politics"; Vernon, *Sovereignty at Bay*, chap. 3; Moran, *Multinational Corporations and the Politics of Dependence*.

states, making it more difficult for a multinational corporation to play one country off against another. They could change the expectations of corporate officials regarding treatment in Third World countries. Developing host-countries would be less susceptible to pressure from the home countries of multinationals if they could claim that their national regulations conformed to international arrangements, even voluntary codes. The various oversight and enforcement mechanisms associated with codes of conduct could provide additional information about the practices of both other states and multinational corporations.[3]

In sum, national juridical sovereignty provides all states with the ability to block the entrance of multinationals but not to compel multinationals to invest or to prevent their exit. Given that a corporation chooses to invest, the primary determinant of the division of gains is the extent to which the host country can command capital, technical skills, and knowledge of the market. New international rules of the game can enhance the bargaining power of Third World host countries by encouraging uniform treatment of multinationals, reducing the ability of corporations to play off one country against another, limiting the interventions that might be made by industrialized states on behalf of their companies, and providing additional information on MNCs.

THE PATTERN OF DIRECT FOREIGN INVESTMENT

Multinational corporations are not a new phenomenon. Many major industrial and raw-material enterprises were established on a global level by the end of the nineteenth century.[4] However, there has been a dramatic growth in transnational corporate activity since the 1950s. The net direct investment outflow from industrial market-economy countries rose from $3.3 billion in 1965, to $4.6 billion in 1970, to $13.0 billion in 1981. The stock of direct investment abroad for the developed market-economy countries increased from $105.3 billion at the end of 1967 to $287.2 billion at the end of 1976.[5]

Most of this investment has taken place among advanced industrialized countries, not between these countries and the Third World. The share

[3]For a discussion of the impact of codes, see U.N. Centre on Transnational Corporations, *Transnational Corporations: Third Survey*, pp. 393–403.

[4]Wilkens, *The Emergence of Multinational Enterprise*.

[5]World Bank, *World Tables*, 1983, p. 535; OECD, *International Investment and Multinational Enterprises*, pp. 39, 52.

of direct foreign investment (DFI) going to the Third World fell from 31 percent in 1967 to 26 percent in 1974, but rose again in the late 1970s. Despite the global economic slowdown during the latter period, the flow of investments to the developing world increased, rising from an average annual rate of $2.6 billion in 1967–1969, to $3.7 billion in 1970–1972, $6.0 billion in 1973–1975, $10.0 billion in 1976–1978, to $12.8 billion in 1979–1981.[6]

Foreign investment in the Third World is concentrated in more advanced or resource-rich LDCs. At the end of 1977 nearly 57 percent of direct foreign investment in the Third World was in thirty-four countries that had per capita gross national products in excess of $1,000, 18 percent in twenty-three countries with per capita GNPs between $750 and $1,000, and 7 percent in countries with per capita GNPs of less than $200.[7] In 1975, DFI was equal to about 9.5 percent of GNP for LDCs with incomes above $500 per capita (excluding tax havens and OPEC countries), 6.8 percent for those with incomes between $200 and $499, and 3.3 percent for those with incomes under $200.[8]

Table 7.1 shows the distribution across sectors for the stock of DFI in the developing countries from several major industrialized countries.

As the note to the table indicates, the categories are not consistent across countries, but the general pattern has been for the share of extractive industries to decrease over time, and manufacturing, and especially services, to increase.

NATIONAL REGULATIONS

Developing countries are involved in a mixed-motive game with multinationals. There is an inherent tension between the corporation's desire to integrate its activities on a global basis and the host country's desire to integrate an affiliate with its national economy. Maximizing corporate profit does not necessarily maximize national economic objectives. Conflict can develop over a wide range of issues. Host-country governments

[6]U.N. Economic and Social Council, *The Role of Transnational Corporations* (3), p. 12; U.N. Centre on Transnational Corporations, *Transnational Corporations: Third Survey*, p. 25.

[7]U.N. Economic and Social Council, *The Role of Transnational Corporations* (3), p. 13.

[8]U.N. Economic and Social Council, *Transnational Corporations: A Re-Examination*, p. 57; U.N. Centre on Transnational Corporations, *Transnational Corporations: Third Survey*, p. 3.

TABLE 7.1

PERCENTAGE DISTRIBUTION OF STOCK OF DFI
IN DEVELOPING COUNTRIES BY SECTOR

	Year	Extractive	Manufacturing	Services
United States	1976	17.9	39.1	43.0
United Kingdom	1974	19.6	47.6	32.8
Germany	1976	9.5	60.4	30.1
Japan	1974	24.0	50.8	25.2
Italy	1976	57.1	32.0	10.9

Source: U.N. Economic and Social Council, *Transnational Corporations: A Re-Examination*, Table III–38.
Note: For the United States and Canada, extractive refers to mining, smelting, and petroleum; for the United Kingdom, to agriculture and petroleum only, with mining and quarrying included in manufacturing; for Italy, to mining, agriculture, and fishing.

generally prefer that vertical links be established among operations within their national boundaries; MNCs may prefer to locate upstream and downstream facilities in other countries. The technology possessed by multinationals has usually been developed in industrialized countries. LDCs may prefer technology more suited to their local environment. Multinationals have been accused of introducing inappropriate products to developing countries, products that may be tolerable in wealthier countries but involve a misallocation of resources in poorer ones. Similarly, multinationals have been accused of generating tastes and preferences that reflect standards in rich countries but are inappropriate for poor ones. Fundamental decisions about corporate activity are taken by executives in advanced countries whose behavior cannot be directly controlled by host-country officials. Because they can affect economic performance, tastes, and the direction of development, MNCs pose a threat to the functional control a state can exercise within its own territorial boundaries.

These are not new problems. Conflicts with host countries are an inherent attribute of multinational corporate activity, especially in smaller and less developed countries. States have used a wide range of measures to control multinationals. For instance, since the nineteenth century, Finland has coped with multinationals by closely monitoring them, denying national treatment, excluding them from key economic sectors, promoting state-owned enterprises, and insisting on Finnish participation on boards of directors.[9] In the contemporary world virtually all countries prohibit foreign investment in some sectors, such as defense and communications. Governments have promulgated rules regarding the establishment of affiliates, repatriation of profits, debt financing, transfer payments, employment of nationals, disclosure of information, and tax rates.

One of the best-known Third World efforts to cope with MNCs has been formulated by the members of the Andean Common Market—Bolivia, Chile, Colombia, Ecuador, Peru, and Venezuela. (Chile withdrew in 1976.) The Foreign Investment Code of the Andean Pact provides for a coordinated investment strategy designed to rationalize production and prevent competitive bidding among its members. Technology transfer must meet legally stipulated criteria, which are enforced by an administrative body. Multinationals are compelled to share ownership with local actors. After three years, at least 15 percent of a firm must be locally owned. Depending on the member country, foreign corporations must phase out their holdings over a period ranging from fifteen to twenty-two years. Corporations that do not act in accordance with these provisions are denied the benefits of the community's customs-duty liberalization, and local capital markets.

Host countries have maintained that it is appropriate to renegotiate contracts and concessions despite the insistence of corporations that such agreements are binding. LDCs, in particular, have argued that multinationals often received excessively favorable treatment during the colonial era; that changes in general economic conditions are a legitimate reason for altering agreements; and that corporations often possess unfair advantages during initial contacts because of their superior knowledge and organization.[10] Host countries have argued that they have the unilateral right to establish grounds for nationalization, and the appropriate compensation should nationalization occur.

Formal rules and regulations, however, are one thing, effective control another. Juridical sovereignty provides a necessary but not sufficient condition for limiting the ability of multinationals to freely alienate property. The relative bargaining power of host countries and multinationals has varied across countries, time, and economic sectors as a function of

---

[9]Orton and Modelski, "Dependency Reversal," pp. 8–9.

[10]U.N. Economic and Social Council, *Transnational Corporations: A Re-Examination*, pp. 114–115.

the ability to command capital, technology, and market knowledge. The bargaining power of host countries has tended to increase over time. The number of multinational corporations has grown, giving host countries a wider range of choice. On a global basis there has been a decline in the concentration of firms in a number of major industries since the 1950s.[11] Multinationals have become more geographically diverse, with the U.S. share of DFI from the thirteen OECD countries declining from a peak of 60 percent for the period 1961–1967 to about 30 percent for the period 1974–1979.[12] Japanese and European corporations have been more responsive to some controls favored by Third World countries, especially those related to joint ownership. There has also been a long-term increase in the availability of information to Third World states. It has become commonplace, for instance, to publish mining contracts, giving policymakers in one country solid information on arrangements that have been made in others. If nationals with the appropriate training are not available, the services of foreign experts can be procured.

Holding particular industry characteristics constant, larger and more developed Third World countries have greater bargaining leverage. A consumer products manufacturing corporation will accept more controls to secure access to a country with a large market. Larger and wealthier developing countries, which have more capital of their own and greater access to international capital markets, can place greater controls on multinationals. Such controls can facilitate the transfer of technology and managerial skills. A number of developing countries have used international borrowing to establish state-owned corporations that have supplanted or challenged multinationals, a kind of jujitsu turning of the world capitalist system against itself.[13] Countries that are more advanced also have greater indigenous technological skill. Controls are most extensive in the more advanced Latin American countries, which have large markets and a well-trained managerial corps.[14]

Finally, the degree of host-country control has varied across industries. Manufacturing industries with advanced and dynamic technologies have

[11]Vernon, Storm Over the Multinationals, pp. 80–82.

[12]OECD, International Investment and Multinational Enterprises, p. 32; Miller, "An Economic Appraisal of the Proposed Code of Conduct for Technology," p. 129.

[13]See Frieden's fascinating discussion of this phenomenon in his "Third World Indebted Industrialization"; see also OECD, International Investment and Multinational Enterprises, p. 34.

[14]Miller, "The Proposed Code of Conduct for Technology," p. 129; Black, Blank and Hanson, Multinationals in Contention, pp. 48–54.

been more difficult to control. In such sectors multinationals offer a bundle of services that cannot be obtained elsewhere. Formal LDC participation may not make much difference because nationals lack the technical expertise to monitor corporate decisions effectively. Developing countries have had their greatest success in the raw-materials area where technical skill and market knowledge have been more accessible.

The increased capabilities of developing countries, especially in the larger states and in the raw materials sector, is reflected in major changes in practices related to multinationals. Ownership patterns have altered even in manufacturing. This is illustrated in table 7.2.

TABLE 7.2
PERCENTAGE OF WHOLLY OWNED MANUFACTURING AFFILIATES
IN LDCS BY PERIOD OF ESTABLISHMENT

	Before 1951	1951–1960	1961–1965	1966–1970	1971–1975
180 U.S.-based corporations	58.4	44.5	37.4	46.2	43.7
135 European-based corporations	39.1	31.6	20.9	18.9	n.a.
76 other transnational corporations	27.4	16.7	10.7	6.1	n.a.

Source: OECD, *International Investment and Multinational Enterprises*, table 13.

Nationalizations increased substantially during the period 1970–1976 as opposed to the 1960s.[15] Figures across sectors are shown in table 7.3. Aside from nationalization, there has also been an increased tendency to renegotiate contracts. This is illustrated for a sample of American corporations in table 7.4. None of these actions guarantees total and effective control, which is contingent on adequate managerial and technical capabilities. But the increase in the level of host-country intervention has been significant.

It is in the area of raw materials that changes have been most dramatic, reflecting the increased bargaining power of host countries. When multi-

[15]Jodice, "Sources of Change in Third World Regimes," pp. 180–181.

TABLE 7.3

NUMBER OF TAKEOVERS OF FOREIGN ENTERPRISES BY
MAJOR INDUSTRIAL SECTOR

	1960–1969	1970–1976	Totals
All	455	914	1,369
Mining	32	48	80
Petroleum	40	180	220
Agriculture	98	174	272
Manufacturing	76	145	221
Trade	28	20	48
Utilities	31	27	58
Bank and Insurance	133	216	349
Other	17	104	121

Source: U.N. Economic and Social Council, *Transnational Corporations: A Re-Examination*, Table III–29.

TABLE 7.4

DISTRIBUTION BY TYPE OF GOVERNMENT INTERVENTION
FOR A SAMPLE OF U.S. CORPORATIONS

	1946–1960	1961–1966	1967–1971	1972–1974
Expropriation	67	95	63	42
Intervention/renegotiation			14	25
Renegotiation of contract			8	25
Forced sale	33	5	15	8

Source: U.N. Economic and Social Council, *Transnational Corporations: A Re-Examination*, p. 66.

nationals first became involved in the international exploitation of minerals and petroleum they enjoyed enormous advantages. Host countries had little capital, virtually no technological skills, and limited knowledge of the market. They were not inclined to bargain vigorously because even initial payments could be a bonanza for hard-pressed treasuries. Direct or indirect colonial control limited possibilities for contract revisions.

Before World War II, concessions that gave one company, or a small consortium of companies, control over large tracts of territory (sometimes over a whole country) were the modal form of arrangement. There were no provisions for relinquishment if particular areas were not developed. Concessions were granted for time periods ranging from fifty to one hundred years. Host countries received modest royalties based on the amount, not the price or profit, of extracted materials. The corporations insisted that concessions had the same character as contracts between private parties and that they were inviolable except in selected circumstances. Thus, oil development in Saudi Arabia was at first controlled by Standard Oil of California and Texaco; in Kuwait by Gulf and British Petroleum; in Iran by British Petroleum (until 1951); in Iraq by a consortium composed of Exxon, Mobil, British Petroleum, Shell, and the Compagnie Francaise des Pétroles (CFP). Kennecott and Anaconda accounted for almost all of Chile's copper production, Anglo-American and Roan Selection Trust (controlled by American Metal Climax) for almost all of Zambia's.

The concession regime was swept away during the 1960s and 1970s as bargaining power shifted to host countries. Once discoveries were actually developed and large capital expenditures committed, it became more difficult for corporations to threaten to exit. Additional capital could be generated more easily by host countries whose nationals also acquired greater technical expertise and market knowledge. Almost all major foreign corporations working under old concession agreements were nationalized. New arrangements in the raw materials area have been much more favorable to host countries (perhaps too favorable). As table 7.3 indicates, takeovers of all kinds increased substantially for the period 1970–1976 as opposed to 1960–1969. The increase is especially marked in petroleum. Before 1960 there were only two major efforts to nationalize foreign oil companies, Mexico in 1938 and Iran in 1951. The first succeeded, at least in the sense that it was not reversed, but the Mexican oil industry languished until the 1970s. The second failed. Although the British Petroleum monopoly was broken, a newly created consortium of multinational oil companies assumed control of the Iranian industry. In contrast, the takeovers that have occurred in more recent years have transferred ownership to host countries.

There has been, moreover, a significant shift in actual control. In 1970, transnational corporations owned 94 percent of worldwide crude oil production, in 1979 they owned 45 percent. In 1973, the seven major oil corporations lifted 70 percent of OPEC oil; in 1978, 55 percent, in 1980 less than 33 percent. Oil-exporting states, not corporations, now have the major impact on production levels and prices. Throughout the 1970s they unilaterally changed contractual arrangements. It is not necessary to exaggerate the effectiveness of OPEC as a true cartel to assert that the regime for oil has fundamentally changed since 1970.[16]

A multiplicity of institutional forms has replaced the old concession regime. While investments in raw materials by American and British firms that previously dominated these sectors have fallen, firms from other countries, especially Japan, have increased their activity. Service contracts, production sharing, and technical assistance have become the dominant kinds of arrangements. Contracts have imposed time limits for multinationals to begin operations. They have set minimum levels of production. They have obligated firms to increase local processing. They have imposed criteria for purchases from local suppliers. In summarizing the situation related to raw materials, a comprehensive U.N. study states "So far, the greatest progress in achieving more balanced settlements has occurred in the field of natural resources. Many countries, large and small, have built up a knowledge and a capability that enables them to obtain a much more equitable share in the distribution of costs and benefits."[17]

In this discussion I do not mean to imply that developing countries can assert full and effective control even with regard to raw materials. Nor are multinationals anxious to place themselves in a vulnerable position. The largest new investors have been Japanese companies. They have abjured full ownership, but they have devised other ways to exercise control. Japan has itself pursued a conscious policy of diversifying sources of supply. Some exporting states are very dependent on Japanese markets. Japanese corporations have retained the most profitable stages of production for themselves while locating less profitable and highly polluting activities in producing countries. Control of transportation and logistics has also helped to enhance the power of Japanese multinationals.[18] The

[16]U.N. Centre on Transnational Corporations, *Transnational Corporations: Third Survey*, p. 197; *World Business Weekly*, June 30, 1980, pp. 33–36; Levy, "Oil and the Decline of the West," pp. 1003–1004; U.N. Economic and Social Council, *The Role of Transnational Corporations* (3), p. 18; and Keohane, "The Theory of Hegemonic Stability."

[17]U.N. Economic and Social Council, *Transnational Corporations: A Re-Examination*, p. 136. See pages 78–87 for a discussion of new contractual arrangements.

[18]Ozawa, *Multinationalism, Japanese Style*, chap. 5.

ability of host countries to influence multinationals is nevertheless much greater than it was in the 1960s.

The success developing countries have had in changing the rules of the game has had economic costs. Corporations have become increasingly reluctant to make substantial new raw-material investments in the Third World. Very few such commitments were made during the 1970s. The proportion of exploration expenditures in the mining industry devoted to developing areas fell from 35 percent for the period 1961–1965, to 30 percent for 1966–1970, to 14 percent for 1971–1975. During the 1970s, 68 percent of all seismic prospecting for petroleum and 91 percent of exploratory drilling took place in developed countries.[19] Confronted with the possible loss of large fixed-capital commitments, corporations have increasingly devoted their efforts to the United States, Canada, Australia, and South Africa, which offer less economic promise, because they have been heavily surveyed in the past, but more political stability. In a lengthy memorandum to the Common Market Commission, European mining companies explained their greatly decreased exploration activities in developing countries in the following terms: "What is new is the manner in which most governments can exploit a mining company's necessary vulnerability (in the early state of a project when very large funds are immobilized in the mine) to impose major changes in operating conditions with complete impunity and the general acquiescence of the international community."[20]

In sum, there have been substantial changes in the rules of the game for direct foreign investment. These changes have been most marked in the area of raw materials, and the proximate cause is the increased bargaining power of host-country governments. In specific terms, this bargaining power involves greater information about, and control over, capital, technology, and markets. The ability to impose these enhanced capabilities ultimately rests, however, on the principle of sovereignty, which accords the state the right to deny access to its territory and to regulate economic activity taking place within its boundaries. The increasingly effective assertion of control by national authorities has led to a change in international attitudes. International corporations and industrialized-country governments have come to accept, tacitly if not always

[19] Derived from figures in U.N. Centre on Transnational Corporations, *Transnational Corporations: Third Survey*, table V-2.
[20] Quoted in Ravenhill, "Asymmetrical Interdependence," p. 253b.

explicitly, the legitimacy of greater national control of multinational corporate activity. Sovereignty is not at bay. However, these new rules of the game have made corporations very wary of putting large amounts of capital at risk in the Third World.

MULTINATIONALS AND THE NIEO

For developing countries the major purpose of international regime change is to legitimate national efforts to control multinationals.[21] The prevailing liberal regime is based on neoclassical economic principles, which emphasize the mutually beneficial character of direct foreign investment, norms that call for the symmetrical treatment of national and multinational corporations, and rules and decision-making procedures that legitimate the multinationals' right to appeal to home-country governments. In contrast, the Third World has supported a set of principles that point to problems of unequal exchange, norms that justify differential treatment of national and multinational corporations, and rules and decision-making procedures that limit the right of foreign corporations to make appeals beyond the legal system of the host country. The Third World's program moves the international regime for direct foreign investment from the market toward the authoritative pole by legitimating national regulations that would limit the ability of multinationals to freely alienate goods and factors of production.

Several international organizations have been involved in efforts to generate principles and rules for multinational corporations. The OECD has adopted a number of resolutions, including a set of "Guidelines for Multinational Enterprises." In 1977 the International Labor Organization adopted the "Tripartite Declaration of Principles Concerning Multinational Enterprises and Social Policy." This declaration deals primarily with employment and labor relations. Multinationals were prominently mentioned in the major documents of the NIEO, the Charter of Economic Rights and Duties of States, and the Declaration on the Establishment of a New International Economic Order. UNCTAD has been involved in the negotiation of documents dealing with restrictive business practices and technology transfer, the first of which was accepted by a U.N. General Assembly resolution in 1980. The official title of this

---

[21]Keohane and Ooms, "The Multinational Firm and International Regulation," pp. 199–203.

document is "The Set of Multilaterally Agreed Equitable Principles and Rules for the Control of Restrictive Business Practices." Discussions about illicit payments have been conducted under the auspices of the U.N. Economic and Social Council. The ECOSOC also established an Ad Hoc Intergovernmental Working Group to deal with international accounting and reporting standards. Finally, the United Nations Commission on Transnational Corporations has attempted to negotiate a comprehensive code on multinational enterprises that would incorporate or take account of the provisions of other agreements.[22]

The multiplicity of activity reflects the diversity of actors and interests. Multinational corporations, industrialized countries, and developing countries all have some stake in successful international agreements. For the multinational, a stable international legal environment is attractive. Constantly changing rules of the game could, in the extreme case, make it difficult to play at all because assessing risks would become impossible. Some corporations have supported explicit international agreements, provided those agreements imposed obligations on states as well as on firms.[23]

In the industrialized countries there is general agreement on the benefits provided by multinational enterprise. There is commitment to giving national treatment. Principles and rules regarding nationalization and compensation are widely shared. International agreements, of which the OECD's 1976 Declaration on International Investment and Multinational Enterprises is the most prominent, are designed to coordinate policies, not to alter fundamentally bargaining power among countries or between governments and corporations. The OECD's 1976 declaration endorses the principle of national treatment, calls for international cooperation on incentives and disincentives for direct foreign investment, and addresses a set of guidelines directly to multinational enterprises. The guidelines state that "enterprises should" respect the policies of host countries and integrate themselves with the local economy and business community, provide information over and above that required by host-country laws to ensure adequate understanding of corporate functions, avoid anticompetitive practices such as restricting resales, refrain from using mechanisms such as transfer pricing to lower their tax obligations, re-

[22]U.N. Economic and Social Council, *The Role of Transnational Corporations* (3), pp. 27–29; U.N. Centre on Transnational Corporations, *Transnational Corporations: Third Survey*, pp. 105–123; Davidow and Chiles, "International Codes of Conduct," pp. 250 ff; and Black, Blank and Hansen, *Multinationals in Contention*, chaps. 8–10.

[23]Davidow and Chiles, "International Codes of Conduct," pp. 248–249; Miller, "An Economic Appraisal of the Proposed Code of Conduct for Technology, p. 124.

spect local labor-relations practices, and ensure that their scientific and technological activities are in conformity with local practices.[24]

For developing countries the purpose of international arrangements is to enhance their bargaining power and control. The major documents associated with the NIEO and endorsed by the General Assembly, and the codes on restrictive business practices and technology transfer discussed within the framework of UNCTAD, reject assumptions of natural symbioses between host countries and multinationals. One central norm especially strongly articulated in the Charter of Economic Rights and Duties of States and the Declaration on the Establishment of a New International Economic Order is that host countries have the right unilaterally to determine rules to be applied to multinationals operating within their boundaries. The coordinating mechanisms that have been endorsed by industrialized countries can be antithetical to the power-enhancing objectives of the Third World.

This issue of national control emerges clearly in the area of compensation for nationalized property. The industrialized countries have not denied that sovereign states have the right to nationalize property. They have insisted, however, that compensation should be prompt and adequate, and have supported the right of multinationals to appeal to their home countries in the case of dispute. The developing countries have sought a regime in which both compensation and nationalization would be unilaterally determined by the host country, and appeals by firms to their home country governments would be illegitimate. The 1962 General Assembly Resolution on Permanent Sovereignty Over Natural Resources endorsed the prevailing principles in stating that compensation for nationalized property should be based on "rules in force in the State taking such measures in exercise of its sovereignty and in accordance with international law."[25] The OECD guidelines also state that national law should be subject to international law and to international agreements to which the state has subscribed.[26] In contrast, the Declaration on the Establishment of a New International Economic Order does not mention compensation at all. The Charter of the Economic Rights and Duties of

[24]Keohane and Ooms in "The Multinational Firm and International Regulation" make the fundamental distinction between IN policies designed to facilitate coordination and LDC policies designed to alter bargaining power. The OECD Declaration is reproduced in Horn, "Codes of Conduct for Multinational Enterprises," pp. 452–461.

[25]Quoted in Weston, "The Charter," pp. 448–449.

[26]Baade, "The Legal Effects of Codes of Conduct," p. 19.

States allows that compensation should be paid, but that it should be determined by the nationalizing country. Disputes should be settled "under the domestic law of the nationalizing State and by its tribunals, unless it is freely and mutually agreed by all States concerned that other peaceful means be sought on the basis of the sovereign equality of States . . . (chap. 2, art. 2, para. 2 [c]). In the negotiations for a United Nations Code of Conduct on Transnational Corporations the position of developing states has been "that notions such as 'just' or 'adequate' compensation have a subjective element in them and should be replaced by the concept of appropriate compensation." Disputes should be settled by the courts of the host country. The right of the state to nationalize foreign property within its territory should be regarded as inalienable.[27] These norms are a break with past practice, which emphasized nondiscrimination, and international standards for compensation.[28]

The UNCTAD Set of Multilaterally Agreed Equitable Principles and Rules for the Control of Restrictive Business Practices, negotiated during the late 1970s, was formally approved without dissent by the General Assembly in December 1980. It focuses on the adverse effects of restrictive business practices on the trade and development of developing countries. Such practices include cartelization, monopolization, abuse of dominant market position, restrictions on the use of transferred technology such as requirements for tied purchases, restrictions placed on the export of affiliates in Third World countries dictated by the firm's global strategy, and artificial transfer pricing.[29]

The Group of 77 initially insisted that this set of principles be binding on both states and corporations. The industrialized countries adamantly rejected a binding code, supporting instead a set of voluntary guidelines. The Third World relented; the final agreement does not provide for enforcement. It does state, however, that implementation should be accomplished through national law and international agreements. The set of principles provides for the dissemination of information through UNCTAD, and the establishment of a permanent intergovernmental group of experts within UNCTAD.

[27]U.N. Centre on Transnational Corporations, *Transnational Corporations: Third Survey*, p. 119.

[28]Weston, "The Charter," pp. 438–443.

[29]Miller and Davidow, "Antitrust at the United Nations," p. 368; Czako, "The Set of Multilaterally Agreed Equitable Principles," p. 321; U.N. Economic and Social Council, *Transnational Corporations: A Re-examination*, p. 125.

Another major area that has received attention in the North-South dialogue is technology transfer. The Third World has insisted that it is at an inherent bargaining disadvantage because multinationals possess superior knowledge and managerial skills. An international agreement could create a more favorable (or equitable) environment. The Third World has pressed for a code that would encourage the autochthonous development of technology in developing areas and increase the overall flow of technology as well as enhance bargaining power. Group of 77 proposals have advocated international regulation, the unpackaging of technology at fair and reasonable prices, prohibition of restrictive practices, and effective performance of transfer arrangements. These proposals also give primacy to national laws in case of dispute, as opposed to the OECD guidelines, which emphasize arbitration. The Group of 77 proposals for the Technology Transfer Code are also much more specific with regard to the nature of contractual obligations than the OECD guidelines. Developing countries have insisted on a binding code.[30]

Running in parallel with discussion of codes on restrictive business practices and technology transfer have been discussions of an overall agreement on multinational enterprises. These discussions have been held under the auspices of the United Nations Commission on Transnational Corporations, which first met in 1975. Such a code would begin by endorsing a set of general principles for MNCs, such as respect for the sovereignty of host countries, obedience to local legal rules, and noninterference in indigenous political affairs. Drafts of the proposed code have admonished corporations to make positive contributions to host-country development efforts. Firms would also be encouraged to provide adequate information about their operations.

The Group of 77 initially insisted that the code should be binding and should apply only to corporations. Industrialized countries supported a nonbinding code that would apply to states as well as corporations. The Third World relented on the question of including states as well as firms but has continued to press for a binding agreement.[31]

How can this heterogeneous set of developments be explained? What

[30]Horn, "Codes of Conduct for Multinational Enterprises," pp. 76–79; Ghai, "Legal Aspects of Transfer of Technology," p. 20; Skelton, "UNCTAD's Draft Code of Conduct," p. 390; Miller and Davidow, "Antitrust at the United Nations."

[31]Asante, "Code of Conduct on Transnational Corporations," p. 11; Fatouros "The U.N. Code of Conduct," pp. 110–111; U.N. Economic and Social Council, *Transnational Corporations: A Re-examination*, pp. 31–42; and U.N. Centre on Transnational Corporations, *Transnational Corporations: Third Survey*, pp. 108, 121.

functions do various codes serve for developing countries? Why has some compromise occurred here, but not in other issues areas?

The restrictive-business-practices agreement was concluded because of a peculiar set of circumstances. Both INs and LDCs oppose restrictive business practices—the former because they are antithetical to the market, the latter because they weaken the bargaining power of host countries. In this area differing principles generated the same norm of opposing restrictive business practices. The industrialized nations had a well-developed legal framework and the code was consistent with these statutes. Developing countries did not have strong specific commitments. On the critical issue of the legal nature of the agreement a bargain was struck, with the industrialized nations agreeing that the code would not apply to state-sponsored cartels, and the Group of 77 accepting a non-binding arrangement. Several Third World states feared that a binding agreement would be used to challenge commodity cartels such as OPEC.

In contrast, in the area of technology transfer, differing principles generated different norms and rules. The Third World linked this issue to NIEO concerns about unfair bargaining advantage. Technology was identified as part of the common heritage of mankind. The South wants to legitimate national regulations that would lead to the rapid and cheap appropriation of technology by Third World actors. The North has maintained that technology is mutually beneficial for all and that its optimal generation requires a set of property rights that internalize the benefits derived from new inventions and techniques. The North supports the proprietary rights of developers.[32]

Even if formal agreement is not reached, however, negotiations can have benefits for developing countries. The basic purpose of the various codes of conduct related to multinationals is to enhance the effective power of host-country governments.[33] Third World countries want to use the codes to legitimate their own national policies and limit any negative reaction from corporations and industrialized countries.[34] The codes may become a source of national law. If an industrialized state endorses a code, even a voluntary one, there is an expectation that its

[32]Miller, "An Economic Appraisal of the Proposed Code of Conduct for Technology," pp. 135–138; Miller and Davidow, "Antitrust at the United Nations."

[33]Baade, "The Legal Effects of Codes of Conduct," p. 4; Horn, "Codes of Conduct for Multinational Enterprises," p. 54; Fatouros, "The U.N. Code of Conduct," p. 105.

[34]Miller ("An Economic Appraisal of the Proposed Code of Conduct for Technology," p. 130) notes that Mexico was forced to rescind a law on trademarks which violated prevailing principles and norms because of protests from industrialized countries.

policy will be appropriately altered. The existence of a code or a set of proposals lessens information problems for less sophisticated LDCs, and agreement encourages national action by signaling that there will not be a coordinated negative international response. UNCTAD is using the set of principles on restrictive business practices as a guide for developing a model national law.[35]

If a code were widely accepted over time, not just formally but in actual practice, it would enter the corpus of customary international law. It would then be regarded as binding even on those states which had not formally accepted it, provided that they had not persistently raised objections. If a developing country incorporated the provisions of a multinational enterprise code into its national law, and then acted against a corporation on the basis of those laws, the act of state doctrine as it is interpreted in the United States, Great Britain, and some other countries would prevent national courts from questioning the motives, fairness, and factual basis of a host country's claim that the code had been violated. If a transnational corporation failed to conform to a code, it could be subject to pressure from other actors; such a corporation might find it difficult to secure diplomatic protection or financing from international institutions. A code could encourage the renegotiation of old contracts that did not conform to its provisions. The very act of preparing a code focuses attention and educates the participants. Finally, a code could help to coordinate the behavior of developing countries, reducing the problem of competitive bidding for direct foreign investment.[36]

Few of these consequences are contingent on having codes that are binding on signatories; some effects derive from the process of negotiation itself. Even without any formal agreement, codes could result in new domestic legislation and greater coordination among developing countries. Some norms might be accepted even if no overall agreement were reached. The norm that LDCs have the right to regulate technology transfer to facilitate their development, even in ways that violate conventional liberal precepts, was accepted in UNCTAD negotiations by 1980, even though no overall agreement had been concluded.[37]

[35]Miller and Davidow, "Antitrust at the United Nations."

[36]Davidow and Chiles, "International Codes of Conduct Regarding Restrictive Business Practices," pp. 255–263; Horn, "Codes of Conduct for Multinational Enterprises," p. 61; Skelton, "UNCTAD's Draft Code of Conduct," p. 388; Fatouros, "The U.N. Code of Conduct," p. 108; U.N. Centre on Transnational Corporations, *Transnational Corporations: Third Survey*, pp. 121–123.

[37]Miller and Davidow, "Antitrust at the United Nations," p. 369.

CONCLUSION

Multinational corporations have become major actors in the international economic arena. Their success, however, is contingent on securing access to the territory of more than one state. The fundamental attributes of sovereignty provide even very weak governments with the ability to block such access. Thus, despite the asymmetry of economic power that can exist between corporations and states, host-country governments do have effective leverage. The major purpose of international negotiations and agreements has been to enhance the power of developing countries, not to alter the behavior of industrialized states or other international actors. This goal has made it easier to reach agreement in this arena than in others. LDCs have become more conciliatory on the question of binding versus voluntary codes since the difference is not likely to have much practical effect. Even a voluntary code can legitimate host-country controls and disarm MNC and home-country objections.

Developing countries have altered principles, norms, rules, and decision-making procedures related to direct foreign investment. National regulations are increasing. The sanctity of contracts can no longer be adequately defended. The proposition that under the old regime MNCs possessed unfair bargaining power has been widely accepted. Particularly in raw-material exploitation there has been a fundamental shift in effective control in favor of host countries. Multinationals have been compelled to alter their behavior. Simply by being sovereign states, by utilizing the constitutive principle of the international system, developing countries have been able to change the rules of the game for direct foreign investment. In other issue areas, where domestic action alone has more limited impact, the Third World has had a more difficult time.

VIII

Transportation

Civil aviation and shipping offer analytically revealing contrasts in the same functional area. In civil aviation many developing countries have their own national airlines, which carry a substantial share of the international passenger traffic generated within their own territories. Third World efforts in the area of shipping have been much less successful. Bulk carriers for petroleum and other bulk cargo, such as iron ore, coal, grain, phosphates, and bauxite/alumina, remain almost entirely under the control of owners from the industrialized world, especially multinational corporations. The South has not been able to translate its opposition to flags of convenience into new international rules. Only in the areas of liner conferences and cargo shipping procedures has the Third World made much headway in altering international practices.

The variance in outcome in these two major areas of international transportation was caused by differences in the preexisting regimes encountered by the Third World. The international regime for civil aviation is based on authoritative resource allocation, and has provided easy access for new entrants. The regime for shipping is based on market-oriented principles and norms, and does not provide easy access. In civil aviation, developing states and their airlines could become members of the International Civil Aviation Organization (ICAO) and the International Air Transport Association (IATA). In shipping, the South had to create a Shipping Committee within UNCTAD because the only functionally specific international organization, the International Maritime Consultative Organization (which became the International Maritime Organization in 1982), was an extremely weak agency whose activities were limited to noncommercial issues, such as safety and pollution. The principles underlying the regime for civil aviation generally give primacy to national security; those underlying shipping generally give primacy to economic efficiency. National security concerns are under the purview of the state; commercial objectives involve a wider variety of public and private actors.

Civil aviation has not been an area of dispute between the North and the South precisely because the existing regime already conformed to Third World preferences. Shipping has been an area of conflict in which developing states have created new forums, especially within UNCTAD, to place ocean transport issues on the international agenda.

CIVIL AVIATION

Civil aviation is distinguished from most other international regimes by the dominance of authoritative allocation over market allocation of resources. The fundamental principle of the regime governing civil aviation is that individual states have sovereign control of their own air space. From this principle, rules and procedures have evolved which allow states to regulate routes, fares, and schedules. This regime does not reflect the preferences or pressures of the Third World. Its basic configuration was established before the Second World War. But once this regime was in place, developing countries could regulate air traffic between their national territories and other states. They could secure a level of control and resources that would have been denied them by a regime governed by principles of market allocation.

The absence of conflict in the area of civil aviation indicates the importance of control as well as of resource transfers. Third World countries have secured a market share that is more or less proportional to their share of world airline passengers. Third World airlines have been able to compete with companies based in the industrialized world on an equal footing. It is difficult to think of another issue area where actors from developing and developed countries are perceived in such a symmetrical way. Air India, Avianca, and Korean Air Lines can challenge Pan American, Air France, and British Airways.

The central importance of the principle of authoritative allocation has been highlighted by the conflict arising from American efforts to make the regime for civil aviation more market-oriented. In the late 1970s American policymakers began to press for a more competitive international airline environment. This was an extension of the movement toward deregulation, which had been endorsed for domestic air travel.

American policymakers used bilateral pressure as well as international forums to promote a more market-oriented regime. This effort met with only modest success. It was resisted by other industrialized states as well as by the Third World. A regime governed by the principle of allocation based on existing endowments would put developing countries at a substantial disadvantage. It would be difficult for them to compete with the much larger airlines based in the West. Other industrialized countries as well felt threatened by American initiatives, and they were not ready to abandon a high level of state control over an infrastructural activity viewed as serving military and political as well as economic functions. In the end the United States limited its pressure to other industrialized states, especially those involved in the heavily traveled North Atlantic route. In August of 1982, eleven industrialized nations signed an agreement providing for some flexibility for North Atlantic fares around a reference price agreed to in the International Air Transport Association.[1]

More than any of the other issue areas investigated in this study, civil aviation illustrates the leverage that developing countries can secure from existing institutional structures. The ideology of dependency does not account for the Third World's success in this area. Declining American power tended to work against LDC preferences by increasing American desires for a more market-oriented regime. But the existence of a set of principles, norms, rules, and decision-making procedures that gave all states a presumptive right to participate in international civil air transport has allowed Third World countries to function with more equality in this area than in virtually any other.

THE EVOLUTION OF THE REGIME

The invention of flight presented policymakers with the challenge of constructing a new international regime. The most salient issue involved the treatment of airspace. The basic options were to give countries sovereign control over the airspace above their territories, or to regard the air as equivalent to the open oceans. Sovereign control was responsive to concerns about national security, open airspace to the goal of economic efficiency. At the first international conference on aviation held in Paris in 1910, France and Germany argued that airspace should be treated like

---

[1] *Economist*, May 8, 1982; *New York Times*, May 3, 1982, 1:3.

the sea beyond territorial limits. Great Britain argued for sovereign control. No agreement was reached. Britain then moved unilaterally, passing the Aerial Navigation Acts in 1911 and 1913, which gave the state the power to regulate flights. France and Germany promulgated similar laws. In 1913 an agreement was signed between Britain and France severely curtailing free flight; the agreement established narrow air corridors and required prior permission for landings.[2]

The overriding importance of security over economic optimization was reinforced by the First World War, in which fixed-wing aircraft were used for military purposes. The first major international agreement on rules and principles governing air flight was concluded at the Paris Peace Conference in 1919. The Aeronautical Commission of the conference, whose members were drawn almost entirely from the military services, formulated the Paris Convention of 1919. Its first article gave states unlimited sovereignty over the airspace above their territories. Although the second article noted the right of innocent passage, in practice, countries always negotiated prior approval for overflights or landings after 1919. The United States did not sign the convention, but did pass domestic legislation that closely approximated the principles and rules agreed to in Paris.

The Paris Convention set the basic parameters within which later disputes involving air travel were fought. The question of sovereign control had been settled. The issue was what kinds of customary rights would be granted. Would countries normally authorize use of their airspace for innocent overflights? Would they permit the embarcation and disembarcation of passengers traveling to and from third countries? How closely would international routes and fares be regulated by the state?

The positions taken by actors with regard to these issues have primarily reflected their economic interests. Countries with powerful commercial incentives to increase air travel have generally favored a generous interpretation of customary rights. Those with fewer competitive advantages have endorsed a narrower interpretation in which authoritative allocation by the state plays a more prominent role. For example, in 1919 the initial British proposal was extremely permissive. While recognizing sovereign control the British argued that commercial flights should be allowed to move freely, subject only to specific technical regulations. The United

[2]Cooper, *The Right to Fly*, pp. 20–24; Jonsson, "Sphere of Flying," pp. 276–277.

States also supported a more liberal regime. The technological position of the United States and Britain, and the long distances within the British Empire and the continental breadth of North America, made a relatively free regime attractive. The British position was not accepted, however, and practices during the interwar years were highly restricted. Landing rights were closely monitored and often linked to concessions in other issue areas. Overflights were blocked.[3]

At the conclusion of the Second World War, new efforts were made to codify an international regime for aviation. In 1944 an international meeting was held in Chicago. It resulted in the establishment of the International Civil Aviation Organization (ICAO). The ICAO dealt primarily with technical issues such as standardization and safety. Commercial and economic issues were codified in the Bermuda Agreement of 1946, a bilateral agreement negotiated between the United States and Great Britain, which set a model for other bilateral arrangements into the 1970s. It contained the following basic components: first, routes were established by government-to-government agreement; second, each state had the right to designate its own national carriers; third, carriers negotiated directly on questions of capacity and frequency; fourth, fares for the same route would be uniform; fifth, fares were negotiated within the context of the International Air Transport Association (IATA). IATA membership was made up of national airlines. Fares required unanimous agreement and were subject to the approval of national governments. The United States gave U.S. participants in IATA a waiver from antitrust regulations.

The Bermuda Agreement did provide for fairly liberal transit privileges. During the 1940s it became generally accepted that planes engaged in innocent commerce could overfly one country to reach a second and that planes could land for fuel and maintenance in transit from one country to another. These more liberal provisions reflected American desires for a more open regime while still recognizing the primacy of security concerns in the area of aviation. Both the Chicago Convention and the Bermuda Agreement reaffirmed the basic principle that states had sovereign control over the airspace above their territories.[4]

At the beginning of the postwar period, the Third World thus encountered an international regime for civil aviation based on the authoritative

[3]Jonsson, "Sphere of Flying," pp. 277–279; Cooper, *The Right to Fly*, pp. 27–31, 136–138.

[4]Jonsson, "Sphere of Flying," pp. 281–300; Cooper, *The Right to Fly*, pp. 164–184; Magdalent, "The CAB Show Cause Order," p. 84.

allocation of resources. States negotiated routes directly, and had the final right of approval for fares. States had the right to designate private actors in the system. Moreover, the accepted norm for the Chicago-Bermuda regime implied that national airlines had the right to 50 percent of the passenger load generated within their home territory.[5] Developing countries had the presumptive right to establish their own commercial international airlines. Capital and technical skills could be borrowed or bought from Northern firms. The postwar regime for civil aviation thus presented the developing world with an unusual opportunity to secure both resources and control, and to avoid the condition of dependence that characterized their interaction with the international system in so many other issue areas.

The opportunity was seized. Many developing countries formed their own airlines. Table 8.1 shows the number of developing countries with their own international airlines and the total number of countries with international airlines. The table includes only contracting parties of the International Civil Aviation Organization.

TABLE 8.1

	1947	1960	1971	1977
Number of LDCs with international airlines	4	49	75	82
Total number of ICAO members with international airlines	18	78	105	113

Source: Derived from information in ICAO, Statistical Summary, no. 1, *Air Transport* (April 1948), pp. i-ii; ICAO, Digest of Statistics, no. 85, *Traffic*, 1947–1960, pp. 37–45; ICAO, Digest of Statistics, no. 169, *Traffic*, 1961–1971, pp. 2–12; ICAO, Digest of Statistics, no. 228, *Traffic*, 1973–1979, pp. 8–22.

These data show that Third World countries have been able to enter the civil aviation market. It does not indicate what their market share is. This is brought out in table 8.2 which shows the ratio of the number of international passengers carried by the airline(s) of the indicated country to the number of passengers embarking and disembarking at major international airports within the same country. It offers an approximation of the share of traffic generated within a country which is carried by the airline(s) of that country.

Table 8.3 shows a summary of the frequency of these ratios.

[5]Jonsson, "Sphere of Flying," p. 300.

TABLE 8.2
CIVIL AVIATION PASSENGER MARKET SHARES, 1977

Ratio of the number of passengers carried by airlines of the indicated state to the number of international passengers embarking and debarking at major airports within that state in 1977.

Afghanistan	0.65	Ghana	0.59[1]
Algeria	0.50	Greece	0.29[1]
Argentina	0.36	Guatemala	0.27
Australia	0.54	Honduras	1.35[1]
Austria	0.60	Hungary	0.40[1]
Bahrain	0.27[1]	Iceland	1.66
Bangladesh	0.69[1]	India	0.52
Barbados	0.05	Indonesia	0.61
Belgium	0.43	Iran	0.54
Bolivia	n/a	Iraq	0.62
Brazil	0.47	Ireland	0.55
Canada	0.53	Israel	0.46
Chile	0.51	Italy	0.44
Colombia	0.61	Jamaica	0.58
Congo	0.64	Japan	0.53[1]
Costa Rica	0.51	Jordan	0.61
Cuba	0.37	Kuwait	0.47
Cyprus	0.52	Libya	0.43
Czechoslovakia	0.56	Madagascar	0.69
Denmark	0.59	Malawi	0.63
Dominican Republic	0.41	Malaysia	0.82
Egypt	0.30	Malta	0.42
El Salvador	0.71	Mauritius	0.09
Ethiopia	1.36[1]	Mexico	0.43[2]
Finland	0.78	Mozambique	0.53
France	0.46	Nepal	0.35
Gabon	n/a	Netherlands	0.60
Germany	0.50	Niger	0.67

TABLE 8.2

CIVIL AVIATION PASSENGER MARKET SHARES, 1977—*Continued*

Ratio of the number of passengers carried by airlines of the indicated state to the number of international passengers embarking and debarking at major airports within that state in 1977.

Norway	0.84[3]	Sweden	0.59[3]
Pakistan	0.81	Switzerland	0.60
Panama	0.34	Thailand	0.37
Peru	0.20	Tunisia	0.32
Poland	0.67	Turkey	0.27
Portugal	0.42	USSR	0.88
Republic of Cameroon	0.52	U.K.	0.68[4]
Singapore	0.59	U.S.	0.75
South Africa	0.43	Uruguay	0.45[1]
South Korea	0.74	Venezuela	0.44[1]
Spain	0.32	Yugoslavia	2.39
Sri Lanka	0.46[1]	Zaire	0.73

Source: Derived from figures in ICAO, *Civil Aviation Statistics of the World*, 1977.
[1]1976.
[2]Total 1977 figures for passengers, based partly on trend extrapolations.
[3]Includes arbitrary share of SAS.
[4]Includes Hong Kong and Belize.

TABLE 8.3

PERCENT OF INTERNATIONAL PASSENGERS
CARRIED ON NATIONAL AIRLINES (NUMBER OF COUNTRIES)

	0–20%	20–29%	30–39%	40–60%	61–70%	71–80%	80% <
LDCs	2	4	7	19	11	3	5
INs			2	18	2	2	3
Totals	2	4	9	37	13	5	8

Source: Derived from figures in table 8–2.

These statistics indicate that the tacit norm of ensuring a state 50 percent of the traffic from its own territory has been more or less implemented in practice. Forty-seven percent of the countries for which data are available from the ICAO have airlines that carry between 40 and 60 percent of the passenger fares generated within their country. While the 50–50 split is more apparent for industrialized countries, 37 percent of developing countries also have ratios of between 40 and 60 percent. The mean for fifty-one LDCs for which data are available is 53 percent, with a standard deviation of 27 percent; for twenty-one market economy countries the mean is 60 percent, with a standard deviation of 29 percent.

The regime for international civil aviation, with its fundamentally authoritative orientation, thus provided an environment within which developing countries were able to secure a larger share of their own international markets than they could have hoped for under a market-oriented regime. The airlines of industrialized countries were not able to realize fully the economic advantages generally associated with technology, skilled personnel, and large size. They could not simply land in a foreign country and offer a cheaper fare.

The central importance of the principle of authoritative as opposed to market allocation is illustrated by the reaction of developing as well as industrialized countries to American efforts to make the civil aviation market more competitive. Since the 1960s the United States has pushed for less state interference in the market for commercial flying. This initiative was a product both of an ideological commitment to the market and the strong position of American companies. The United States has generally favored regimes in which the state's role is limited. However, this commitment has been compromised in areas where American firms were at a competitive disadvantage, such as with dairy products or in shipping. In the area of civil aviation American companies were, by virtue of their size, in a good position to compete. At the end of 1977, 2,374 commercial turbojets were registered to U.S. airlines, about 43 percent of the world total. Great Britain, another country of registry for which figures are available, was next with 297 turbojets.[6]

Dissatisfaction with international regulation first surfaced in the 1960s, when the United States felt compelled to accept higher fares to Europe.

[6]Derived from figures in ICAO, *Civil Aviation Statistics of the World*, 1977, table 2–1. Breakdowns for Communist Bloc countries are not available.

This prompted the United States to initiate a policy of actively promoting charters and other nonscheduled flights. In the 1970s American efforts intensified, spearheaded by the Civil Aeronautics Board (CAB). The CAB had taken the lead in deregulating fares and routes within the United States. It moved to extend this policy to international flying. In August 1978 the Carter administration formally committed itself to a policy of promoting competition in international civil aviation. The CAB issued a show-cause order threatening to withdraw the antitrust waiver that had been given U.S. airlines to allow them to participate in IATA. Under U.S. pressure, IATA voted in November 1978 to allow members to withdraw from the traffic conferences which set rates while still remaining members of the organization. The CAB offered foreign carriers additional routes within the United States in exchange for more competitive practices designed to generate more air traffic. Previously, route rights had been exchanged for route rights. The large size of the American market led several countries, including Korea and Israel, to accept such agreements even though they would have preferred more restrictive arrangements. The United States also signed bilateral agreements with Belgium, the Netherlands, and Germany which provided that fares could be set by the country of origin or could be rejected only if both countries opposed a new rate. Under the existing regime, fares were subject to the veto of any one country. The CAB unilaterally gave eleven U.S. carriers the right to offer service to five Central American countries, even though formal agreements for liberalized service had only been concluded with two of these countries. U.S. airlines were told to negotiate their own landing rights, a break with the postwar Chicago-Bermuda regime, which called for such rights to be negotiated between states.[7]

These initiatives were vehemently opposed from several quarters. Within the United States, the State Department and the Transportation Department objected to the CAB's proposal to end the antitrust waiver for IATA negotiations. The State Department argued that it would damage U.S. relations with other countries and spill over into other areas.[8] Outside the United States, opposition to the CAB's proposal was almost universal. When the board held a number of meetings in foreign countries,

[7]Jonsson, "Sphere of Flying," pp. 285–287, CAB, *Annual Report*, FY 1978, pp. 59, 69–70, 87, 91; *Aviation Week*, October 29, 1979, p. 35; October 22, 1979, p. 29; May 21, 1979, p. 28; November 11, 1979, p. 24.

[8]*Aviation Week*, August 27, 1979, p. 23.

only Chile out of the forty-eight countries that appeared, expressed support for ending the IATA antitrust waiver. In December 1978 the ICAO council passed a resolution calling on contracting parties "to refrain from any unilateral action which would endanger multilateral fares and rate-setting systems." This was in response to the CAB's preliminary ruling in June 1978 that IATA agreements were no longer in the public interest. At the ICAO's second Air Transport Conference held in February 1980 resolutions were passed rejecting unilateral action that could have negative effects on multilateral agreements, and endorsing multilateral rate-setting through IATA.[9]

Developing countries were particularly unhappy with American moves to alter the basic principles, norms, and rules defining the regime for civil aviation. At the ICAO and other international forums they argued that a competitive system would destroy their equal participation in civil aviation. They maintained that their airlines, generally much smaller than those of industrialized countries, would be at a competitive disadvantage. They accused the United States of air imperialism. They endorsed multilateral IATA rate-setting because it gave them a stronger bargaining position than they would have in bilateral settings. For instance, the Ivory Coast delegate stated at a 1980 ICAO conference that his country "very much regrets any unilateral initiative which would tend to destroy IATA. We deplore the deregulation initiative and those measures designed to destroy IATA."[10] Air transport was included on the UNCTAD agenda for the first time in 1979. The Philippines sponsored a resolution at UNCTAD-V in Manila calling on developed countries to eliminate predatory tactics involving pitting their larger capacity against the infant airlines of many Third World countries. A resolution was passed stating that "in the transport sector particular attention should be given to the discriminatory practice of systems of duopoly in civil aviation, whereby special fares become an exclusive arrangement between two developed countries."[11]

As a consequence of domestic and international opposition the CAB was compelled to modify its stand. Foreign actors threatened refusal of

[9]*Aviation Week*, August 27, 1979, p. 23; ICAO, *Bulletin*, May 1980, pp. 18, 23, 30; Magdalent, "The CAB Show Cause Order," pp. 88–94.

[10]ICAO, *Bulletin*, May 1980, p. 24.

[11]Jonsson, "Sphere of Flying," p. 288; ICAO, *Bulletin*, May 1980, p. 25; UNCTAD, Resolution No. 119 (V), "Protection in the Service Sector"; Magdalent, "The CAB Show Cause Order," pp. 89–90.

landing rights, higher fees, withdrawal of fifth freedom rights (the right to pick up and discharge passengers in third countries), purchase of military equipment from other countries, retaliation in other issue areas, and cutthroat competition from subsidized government airlines. In December 1979 the CAB announced that it would limit its prohibition on IATA rate-setting to North Atlantic routes. At the second Air Transport Conference in February 1980 the United States was compelled to withdraw a proposal that would have legitimated country-of-origin and dual-disapproval rules for setting fares.[12] In 1982, after persistent pressure from the United States, nine European countries and the United States initialed an agreement providing for wider fare bands around IATA-agreed-on reference fares for North Atlantic routes. In exchange for this move toward greater market competition, U.S. policymakers agreed to extend the antitrust waiver for IATA participation even for the North Atlantic.[13] North–South routes were not affected. Civil aviation is basically an issue area in which international principles, norms, rules, and decision-making procedures coordinate and legitimate national state action. The United States has not been able to change the regime unilaterally, although the bargaining power derived from its size and economic importance has been reflected in a movement toward more market-oriented customary rights among INs.

Civil aviation illustrates in a particularly lucid fashion the importance of international regimes and the objectives of developing countries. The regime for civil aviation, which developed in the first part of the twentieth century and was codified in the Chicago Convention of 1944 and the Bermuda Agreement of 1946, was fundamentally based on authoritative rather than market allocation. It provided a framework that gave Third World countries easy access to civil aviation. Most developing countries have created their own national airlines, and most of these airlines have secured a substantial share of their own national markets. The existing regime for civil aviation thus satisfied the meta-political and relational objectives of developing countries; it provided both control and resources. For this reason, civil aviation is one of the few areas in which there has been little conflict between the North and the South. When the United States attacked the basic authoritative allocation principles of the postwar regime, it confronted opposition from other developed countries as well as from the Third World. Civil aviation was placed on the

[12]*Aviation Week*, October 29, 1979, p. 24; ICAO, *Bulletin*, May 1980, pp. 23–30.
[13]*Economist*, May 8, 1982.

UNCTAD agenda only after American action threatened the existing regime.

SHIPPING

INTRODUCTION

The other major form of international transportation, shipping, has presented developing countries with a situation very different from that surrounding civil aviation. Many aspects of the international regime for shipping have evolved over more than five hundred years, with roots in the practices developed by merchants during the late Middle Ages. Principles, rules, norms, and decision-making procedures associated with international shipping have generally been more concerned with facilitating commercial transactions than with national security. The international regime for shipping did not provide developing countries with easy access to resources and control.

Developing countries have tried to change the shipping regime. Their efforts have been most clearly manifest in a number of UNCTAD-sponsored conferences, some of which have led to new international agreements. The UNCTAD Code of Conduct for Liner Conferences, the most significant Third World initiative, gives developing countries a presumptive right to greater access and control over shipping by liners. The Convention on Multimodal Transport and rules governing the carriage of goods by sea, the Hamburg Rules, give shippers, including shippers from developing countries, somewhat more leverage over carriers.

Third World accomplishments have been limited, however. Proposals to eliminate flags of convenience, which are seen as an impediment to the development of national fleets, have not been accepted. Bulk carriers for crude oil, mineral ores, and grain are largely controlled by vertically integrated corporations from the North. The Liner Code has been rejected by the United States.

Existing international institutional structures have not given the Third World much leverage. The International Maritime Organization (IMO) has not been concerned with economic issues. The ideological cohesion of the Third World has been somewhat strained by Liberian and Panamanian support for flags of convenience. National cargo reservation has

been the most effective mode of attack on existing market-oriented practices, but only a limited number of developing countries have successfully
implemented such regulations. Through the 1970s the aggregate share of
Third World shipping tonnage remained far below its share of world
trade, and only a handful of LDCs were able to develop substantial
national fleets.

THE INTERNATIONAL REGIME FOR SHIPPING

The international regime for shipping has generally been shaped by
market-oriented principles and norms in the sense that the allocation of
resource has been determined by the preferences and capabilities of individual actors. This does not mean that the market for shipping is characterized by free competition among private actors. There has been a wide
range of constraints. Most bulk-cargo carriers are controlled by vertically
integrated multinational corporations. Rates and schedules for liners
(freighters plying regularly scheduled routes) are organized through cartels of ship owners known as liner conferences. State-owned shipping
fleets, especially from Eastern Europe, have been important competitors.
Hence, there have been very extensive departures from fully competitive
conditions, although most behavior has been consistent with market
allocation; that is, allocation based on the economic endowments of
public and private firms motivated by economic self-interest.

The extent of direct authoritative allocation by the state, as opposed
to private oligopolization, has been limited. The most important form of
authoritative allocation has been flag discrimination; that is, mandating
that certain shipments be carried on national bottoms. Subsidies and tax
programs have also been used to bolster national capabilities.[14] Among
the industrialized countries, the United States has violated competitive
practices more often than other major nations. American officials, however, have treated state intervention as an exception to, rather than an
attack on, a competitive market-oriented regime; for instance, by justify-
ing requirements that goods purchased with foreign aid be carried on

---

[14]This analysis does not deal with the construction of ships, which has frequently been
heavily subsidized. This is also true for civil aviation, where major American airframe,
engine, and avionics companies have benefited from spillovers from defense spending, and
European firms have been directly supported by the state.

American bottoms, with the argument that such shipments would not exist at all were it not for state intervention.[15]

In the postwar period liberal principles and norms have been codified in several international agreements. In 1961 a Code on Invisibles, including shipping, was negotiated within the context of the OECD. The GATT also states that shipping is part of the more general liberal regime for trade. The IMO endorses a competitive market. Liberal principles were largely adhered to in actual practice. Through the 1960s less than 10 percent of cargo was reserved through state intervention.[16]

Some of the liberal aspects of the international shipping regime have deep historical roots, especially those related to practices covering the carriage of goods, such as forms for bills of lading, insurance, liability, and packaging. A set of rules, principles, norms, and decision-making procedures known as the Law Merchant dates back to the twelfth century. The Law Merchant was transnational law that covered a certain class of people (merchants), in certain places (fairs, seaports, and other points of trade), and was administered by merchants, not judges. Equity was the overriding principle. Speed and informality were central characteristics. The Law Merchant reinforced practices that were essential for the growth and development of trade, such as the legally binding character of informal contracts and the survival of the rights and obligations of one partner in a partnership should the other partner die. Early merchants sought to limit the encroachment of political power into their routine practices, an encroachment that would almost certainly discourage maximizing market efficiency.[17]

As national states became stronger and cultural influences more diverse, however, the universal Law Merchant of the late Middle Ages was weakened but not eliminated. Rules for the transport of goods were increasingly set by national legislation, which was strongly influenced by older commercial practices. The Law Merchant was incorporated into national law. Moreover, because of the economic advantages of uniform contractual arrangements, national legislation has been coordinated by international agreements, many of which remain private. For instance, transnational trade associations have promulgated rules in various issue

---

[15]Cafruny, "Ruling the Waves," pp. 72–74.
[16]Ibid., pp. 113–114.
[17]Trakman, "The Law Merchant," pp. 4–5, 11–12; Berman and Kaufman, "The Law of International Commercial Transactions," pp. 225 ff.

areas, and have provided for compulsory arbitration rather than recourse to national courts to settle disputes.[18]

The Third World thus confronted an international regime for shipping which emphasized market rather than authoritative allocation, even though distortions introduced by private restraints on trade were tolerated. The IMO, the only public international organization exclusively concerned with shipping, was very weak. Its operational activities were limited to safety and pollution, and it did not provide developing countries with leverage over economic practices.[19] National reservation of cargo by industrialized countries did offer LDCs a useful precedent for making demands for more direct or indirect state allocation. The situation is similar to that surrounding developments in the oceans, where American claims over fishing and the continental shelves immediately after World War II offered LDCs an opening for attacks on more general liberal principles and norms. While the United States regarded its oceans claims and cargo reservation as exceptions to a liberal order, developing countries could justify the same practices with principles and norms legitimating authoritative state allocation. In the case of the oceans, however, developing countries had a very effective forum, the United Nations Conference on the Law of the Sea. In shipping, the Third World had to create a forum in a more peripheral venue, UNCTAD's Committee on Shipping, which had less legitimacy in the North. Thus, in international shipping, developing countries confronted a market-oriented regime in an institutional environment, which provided them with only limited leverage.

SHIPPING MARKETS AND DEVELOPING COUNTRIES

The regime for shipping with its fundamental adherence to market principles has not left developing countries in a strong position with regard to establishing and nurturing their own merchant fleets. In a world of markets, few LDCs are in a strong position. With the exception of those countries which are used for flags of convenience (more on this shortly) very few developing countries have been able to generate merchant fleets whose size is proportional to the goods generated by their ports.

[18]Berman and Kaufman, "The Law of International Commercial Transactions," p. 228.
[19]Cafruny, "Ruling the Waves," p. 304.

There are two main classes of ships—freighters and bulk carriers. Freighters, in turn, can be divided into several categories. Liners are ships that ply regularly scheduled routes. Tramps are freighters that solicit cargo where it is available. Freighters may be containerized or semicontainerized. These distinctions, especially containerization, which is a new technology, have had an impact on Third World efforts at regime change. Few developing countries have secured a share of shipping tonnage proportional to their share of cargo in any of these categories, although their success has been greatest for liners. In December 1970, nationals from LDCs controlled only about 7 percent of all commercial shipping. In 1978, Third World countries generated 30 percent of all bulk cargoes and 90 percent of all tanker cargoes, but accounted for only 8.6 percent of deadweight shipping tonnage. Seventy-eight percent of the companies offering liner service to developing areas are based in industrialized countries. About two-thirds of iron ore, and bauxite and alumina, are carried on ships controlled by multinational corporations. The Third World's share of liner tonnage did, however, increase from 8.7 percent in 1965 to 18.4 percent in 1978.[20]

Table 8.4 shows a summary of the relationship between merchant-fleet size and shipments for all countries for which figures were available for the late 1970s. The table shows the ratio of each country's share of world merchant deadweight tonnage in 1979 to the country's share of goods loaded and unloaded in 1976. The share of world shipping is based on beneficial ownership, not nominal flag; that is, ships flying flags of convenience have been classed with their country of beneficial ownership rather than with their country of registration. If a country's fleet were proportional to its share of goods loaded and unloaded, the figure would be "1." Figures larger than "1" indicate that a country's merchant fleet is proportionally larger than its share of world cargoes; figures less than "1" that its fleet is smaller.

The distribution of these ratios is summarized in table 8.5.

The commercial tonnage of nearly half of the LDCs is less than 10 percent of their share of world cargo, whereas the commercial tonnage of 50 percent of the industrialized nations is greater than their share of world cargo. The contrast with civil aviation is striking: 68 percent of the LDCs for which figures are available from the ICAO have national

---

[20]U.N. doc. no. TD/B/C.4/203, pp. 10, 21; Lawrence, *International Sea Transport*, pp. 12, 16; Neff, "The U.N. Code of Conduct," p. 398; Cafruny, "Ruling the Waves," p. 249.

TABLE 8.4
Proportional Shares of World Shipping

Ratio of share of world merchant deadweight tonnage in 1979 to share of total world goods loaded and unloaded in 1976

Developing countries		Developing countries	
(Africa)		*(Caribbean & C. America)*	
Angola	0.14	Bahamas	0.03
Benin	0.06	Barbados	0.01
Congo	0.02	Cuba	0.53
Egypt	0.43	Dominican Republic	0.08
Ethiopia	0.20	El Salvador	0.01
Gabon	0.07	Guatemala	0.05
Gambia	0.20	Haiti	–0–
Ghana	0.41	Jamaica	0.01
Ivory Coast	0.25	Mexico	0.56
Kenya	0.06	Nicaragua	0.08
Liberia	0.79	Panama	2.57
Madagascar	0.52	Trinidad and Tobago	–0–
Mauritania	–0–		
Mauritius	0.47	*(South America)*	
Morocco	0.21	Argentina	1.32
Nigeria	0.05	Brazil	0.42
Republic of Cameroon	0.18	Chile	0.38
Senegal	0.08	Colombia	0.83
Sierra Leone	–0–	Ecuador	0.21
Sudan	0.27	Guyana	0.04
Tanzania	0.15	Peru	0.48
Togo	0.06	Uruguay	1.07
Tunisia	0.06	Venezuela	0.08
Zaire	0.63		

TABLE 8.4

PROPORTIONAL SHARES OF WORLD SHIPPING—*Continued*

Ratio of share of world merchant deadweight tonnage in 1979 to share of total world goods loaded and unloaded in 1976

Developing countries		Developing countries	
(Asia)		*(Asia)*	
Bahrain	0.06	Yemen Arab Republic	0.03
Burma	0.05	Yemen, Democratic	
Cyprus	−0.08[1]	Republic of	0.03
Hong Kong	17.85		
Indonesia	0.17	*(Other Areas)*	
Iran	0.06	Papua New Guinea	0.13
Iraq	0.21	Malta	0.15
Jordan	−0−	Yugoslavia	1.78
Kuwait	0.37		
Lebanon	0.80		
Malaysia	0.03	Industrialized countries	
Oman	−0−	Canada	0.37
Pakistan	0.59	United States	1.66
Philippines	0.83	Japan	1.32
Qatar	0.06	Belgium	0.29
Saudi Arabia	0.09	Denmark	2.59
Singapore	0.59	Finland	1.07
South Korea	1.08	France	0.83
Sri Lanka	0.30	West Germany	1.34
Syria	0.02	Greece	23.37
Thailand	0.20	Iceland	1.09
Turkey	0.85	Ireland	0.09
UAE	0.03	Italy	0.87

TABLE 8.4
PROPORTIONAL SHARES OF WORLD SHIPPING—*Continued*

Ratio of share of world merchant deadweight tonnage in 1979 to share of total world goods loaded and unloaded in 1976

Industrialized countries		Communist bloc countries	
Netherlands	0.31	Bulgaria	0.60
Norway	7.45	East Germany	1.32
Portugal	0.94	Poland	0.83
Spain	1.11	Rumania	1.14
Sweden	0.82	USSR	1.40
United Kingdom	1.96		
Australia	0.13		
New Zealand	0.14		

Source: Derived from figures in the following: United Nations, *Statistical Yearbook,* 1978, table 160 for goods loaded and unloaded; Lloyd's *Register of Shipping,* 1979, table 1 for deadweight tons by flag of registration; and UNCTAD Trade and Development Board, Committee on Shipping, *Review of Maritime Transport, 1979,* TD/B/C.4/198, 22 May 1980, table 6 for beneficial ownership of flags of convenience.

¹Because flag registration and beneficial ownership were derived from two separate sources, discrepancies can arise. This is reflected in the negative figure for Cyprus where UNCTAD's *Review of Maritime Transport* lists a larger non-Cypriot beneficial ownership for Cypriot flag ships than Lloyd's *Register of Shipping* lists under nominal Cypriot registration

airlines that carry approximately 50 percent or more of the international passengers departing from their airports.

LDCS AND REGIME CHANGE IN SHIPPING

The market-governed and predominantly commercial nature of the international regime for shipping, the weak market position of virtually all developing countries, and their consequent failure to secure a share of the world's commercial fleet proportionate to their share of the world's cargo, encouraged developing countries to try to alter the principles, norms, rules, and decision-making procedures governing world shipping.

TABLE 8.5

RATIO OF SHARE OF WORLD SHIPPING TO
SHARE OF WORLD CARGO

	(Number of countries, and percent, in each category)					
	.00–.09	.10–.24	.25–.49	.50–.74	.75–.99	1.00 <
LDCs	34 (46%)	12 (16%)	10 (13%)	6 (8%)	5 (7%)	6 (8%)
INs	1 (4%)	3 (11%)	3 (11%)	1 (4%)	5 (19%)	13 (50%)

Source: Derived from figures in table 8.4.

Here, as in other issue areas, their efforts have been directed toward establishing a regime that would more readily legitimate direct state allocation or the truncation of private property rights. Such a regime would enhance LDC control and provide a presumptive right to a greater share of the revenues generated by the ocean transport of goods.

Third World dissatisfaction with prevailing principles and practices in shipping is long-standing. Latin American countries objected to the rate structure imposed by liner conferences as early as 1940. In 1957 the economic conference of the Organization of American States passed a resolution complaining that maritime rates were higher for Latin America than for other areas, and that this discouraged international trade. Shipping was discussed at the first UNCTAD meeting in 1964, and a permanent Committee on Shipping was established in 1965. In 1969 a group of twenty-three LDCs led by Brazil placed a proposal before UNCTAD calling for the formation of an organization that would allocate shipping routes and sailing schedules to ensure nondiscriminatory treatment for LDCs. The model for this effort, which was withdrawn as a result of opposition from industrialized nations, was the regime for civil aviation.[21]

During the 1970s there was a more comprehensive and coherent effort to change the nature of the regime. Here, as in other issue areas, the ideology of dependency and unequal exchange provided a unifying force

[21]Lawrence, *International Sea Transport*, p. 225; Brown, *Transport and Economic Integration*, p. 145; Holderness, "The U.N. Code of Conduct," p. 858.

and sense of direction. Developing countries maintained that the existing regime for shipping was exploitative. The market was inherently unfair because the bargaining power of the parties was so asymmetrical. Lack of knowledge made it difficult for LDCs to enforce the provisions of bills of lading. The Third World argued that liner conferences used discriminatory rate structures, did not provide adequate service for developing areas, perpetuated center–periphery trade routes, blocked access to decision making, and drained foreign reserves. In the area of bulk shipping, an UNCTAD report noted that Third World countries generating cargoes such as bauxite/alumina and iron ore could not penetrate the bulk-shipping market because it was dominated by vertically integrated corporations. The small proportion of bulk cargo controlled by developing countries is, UNCTAD argued, "attributable largely to the attitudes of the TNCs [transnational corporations] concerned and to their failure to appreciate the need for developing countries to develop and diversify their economies and not to remain merely passive suppliers of raw materials."[22]

Third World efforts to restructure the international regime for shipping were codified in three agreements proposed in the 1970s. The first dealt with liner conferences, the second with the ocean transport of goods, and the third with multimodal transport. Developing countries also pressed for a revision of the rules and norms affecting flags of convenience and the distribution of resources in the area of bulk transport. In some countries these international efforts were accompanied by national shipping programs.

The United Nations Code of Conduct for Liner Conferences

Third World efforts to create allocative regimes based on the sovereign equality of states is, in the area of shipping, most clearly reflected in the United Nations Code of Conduct for Liner Conferences, which was concluded in 1974 but not ratified by the requisite number of states for a decade. Liners account for about 20 percent of world cargo by weight and about 80 percent by value. Since the 1870s, shipping companies

---

[22]Quote is from U.N. doc. no. TD/B/C.4/203, pp. 21–22. See also, Selvig, "The Hamburg Rules, the Hague Rules," pp. 303–304; Cafruny, "Ruling the Waves," p. 151.

operating liners have been organized into liner conferences. In the 1970s there were about 360 liner conferences with from two to forty members each. Conferences usually cover only one direction of trade. Their primary function is to specify rates for highly differentiated classes of products. They are, in effect, cartels that maintain their position by using customer rebates, stipulating contractual liabilities for shipping with non-conference members, and giving low priority to goods from "disloyal" shippers.[23]

Liner conferences were first organized in response to the overcapacity resulting from the development of steamships. They have remained as durable features of the industry because of the endemic tendency to cutthroat competition resulting from low barriers to entry, inelastic supply, and very high ratios of fixed to variable costs. The basic economic characteristics of the industry encouraged departure from a competitive market, but left control with well-endowed private corporations.[24]

UNCTAD's Committee on Shipping began a detailed study of liner conferences in 1969, which led to the United Nations Code of Conduct for Liner Conferences, adopted in April 1974 by a vote of 72–7–5. The function of this code is to provide Third World countries with greater access and control. Potentially, its most important provision states that in trade between any two countries cargo should be equally shared between the lines of the exporting and the importing nation, and that third parties have the right to a "significant part, such as 20 percent, in the freight volume." Thus, the code sets a target of a 40–40–20 division between exporting, importing, and third-party carriers. The code guarantees the shipping companies of all countries equal access to liner conferences serving their national ports. The traditional practice had been to admit new members to a conference only if they posed a commercial threat. The code gives shippers the right to invoke its dispute-settlement mechanism if they have a conflict with carriers; under the traditional regime, shippers had no standing, a particularly troubling situation for actors from developing countries who usually lacked expertise and resources. The dispute-settlement mechanism covers such issues as refusal to admit a shipping line to a conference, expulsion of a line from a conference, practices inconsistent with the code, changes in freight rates and surcharges, and loyalty arrangements with shippers. While participa-

[23]Neff, "The U.N. Code of Conduct," p. 399, Deakin, *Shipping Conferences*, pp. 1–3.
[24]Neff, "The U.N. Code of Conduct," p. 401; Deakin, *Shipping Conferences*, pp. 21–22, 43.

tion in the dispute-settlement mechanism is mandatory, the recommendations of independent conciliators are nonbinding. Developing countries had originally called for binding arbitration; industrialized countries had supported a purely voluntary mechanism.[25] In sum, the U.N. Code of Conduct moves power and control away from the members of established liner conferences, provides developing-country carriers with a presumptive right to a share of the market, and gives shippers from developing countries more leverage against liner companies.

The Code of Conduct was endorsed by a number of industrialized countries. With the partial exception of the United States, more-advanced countries were motivated by narrow calculation of economic interest. States with relatively large fleets tended to oppose the code, those with small ones to support it. Within Europe, France supported the code from the outset and West Germany eventually accepted it as a second-best solution. Britain, Denmark, and Greece opposed efforts at regulation. After extensive bargaining during the 1970s the European Community finally ratified the code while preserving competitive market-oriented rules for activities among its own members. Japan, solicitous of Third World concerns, also endorsed the code. The United States opposed, even though its own liner fleet was limited, arguing on ideological grounds for competitive open markets. American policy was, however, inconsistent: the Federal Maritime Commission had approved a number of cargo-shipping arrangements for shipping between the United States and several Latin American countries; the United States heavily subsidized its own merchant fleet. The conflicting interests of the industrialized states, the ideological coherence of the Third World's position, and the forum provided by UNCTAD made it possible to secure approval for an international agreement that embodies principles, norms, rules, and decision-making procedures preferred by the Third World.[26]

The United Nations Convention on Liner Conferences alone does not enable LDCs to develop substantial merchant marines, if only because liners make up only one part of international shipping. But if a developing country can secure the resources to buy or charter vessels, the code legitimates national efforts to penetrate international markets. The code, with its targeted market shares and emphasis on access to conferences,

---

[25]Herman, "The Code of Conduct," pp. 265–267; Holderness, "The U.N. Code of Conduct," p. 859; Neff, "The U.N. Code of Conduct," p. 412.

[26]For an excellent discussion of debates within the North and policy more generally, see Cafruny, 'Ruling the Waves," pp. 197–202 and chap. 6.

offers the clearest example in the area of shipping of the norms underlying the Third World's New International Economic Order.

It is not certain that the code or any consequent alteration in the share of liner shipping will enhance economic efficiency for developing countries. If shipping lines from LDCs were as competitive as those based in industrialized countries, they would have an easier time penetrating international markets. Given the competition from tramps, non-conference liners, and Eastern European freighters, it is not likely that existing shipping conferences would have been able to raise rates much above what they would have been under competitive conditions. The balance-of-payment effects of buying or chartering liners may not be positive. By bringing less efficient fleets into service and assuring them a share of the market, the code may even result in higher freight rates for developing countries.[27] However, if the narrow economic impact of the code is uncertain, its effect on power is much less ambiguous. The implementation of the code makes developing countries less dependent on the vagaries of systemic forces over which they previously had limited influence.

The Hamburg Rules and the U.N. Convention on Multimodal Transport

In 1978 an UNCTAD-sponsored conference, meeting in Hamburg, West Germany, adopted a new set of rules governing the oceanborne transport of goods. In 1980 another UNCTAD conference adopted a set of rules governing the multimodal transport of goods; that is, carriage by more than one means of transport. Developing countries played a large role in both of these exercises. The venue of the decisions was itself significant since earlier agreements had been negotiated by private transnational organizations. Both of the agreements enhance the bargaining power of shippers as opposed to carriers by increasing the responsibility and liability of carriers and by establishing dispute-settlement mechanisms open to shippers as well as carriers.

The ability of developing countries to secure access to negotiations dealing with the rules governing the oceanborne transport of goods was in part a reflection of overarching regime characteristics, including the

[27]Holderness, "The U.N. Code of Conduct," pp. 862 ff; Neff, "The U.N. Code of Conduct," p. 412.

principle of the sovereign equality of all states and the existence of universal international organizations. The leverage of developing countries was also enhanced by the need for some standardized form of contract. Given the number and diversity of transactions, it would be very costly if the terms of each shipment had to be negotiated ad hoc. However, the actor who sets the general rules can secure economic and political benefits.

Discussions concerned with setting the rules for the oceanborne carriage of goods have been going on for more than a hundred years. The primary topic has been the rules for shipping contracts (bills of lading). Such contracts cover issues such as liability, description of goods, and format. Initially, the rules were set by shippers. Dissatisfaction with this regime led to the negotiation of the Hague Rules in 1921 under the auspices of the Comité Maritime International, a private law organization composed of national shipping organizations. The Hague Rules set limits on liability for each package, an unattractive situation for shippers because inflation and currency devaluations reduced the real liability of carriers. In response to pressures from shippers, the Visby Rules, which increased liability, were adopted in 1968. All of these negotiations were conducted in private international forums with LDCs playing only minor roles.[28]

The developing countries began actively to attack existing ocean-carriage practices in the 1970s. They saw the extant regime as a device for guaranteeing the privileges of carriers, almost all of which were from industrialized countries. They felt excluded from decision-making procedures. Revisions of the Hague-Visby rules and the multimodal convention were identified with the liner code as part of a new international economic order for maritime transport. One industrialized-country observer felt that, at the 1978 negotiations leading to the Hamburg rules, the Hague-Visby rules were "a dragon to be slain with whatever means could be brought to bear."[29]

The basic impact of the Hamburg Rules was to increase the liability of carriers. The Hamburg Rules, as opposed to the Hague-Visby Rules, presume the fault of the carrier, and place the burden on the carrier to show innocence in matters of navigational and vessel management. The

[28]Moore, "The Hamburg Rules," pp. 1–3; Selvig, "The Hamburg Rules, the Hague Rules," p. 301.

[29]Moore, "The Hamburg Rules," p. 5. UNCTAD's Secretary General argued at a 1979 meeting on multimodal transport that the new agreements were "Part of the continuing efforts to create a new maritime order, as one of the main elements in the restructuring of international economic relations" (U.N. doc. no. TD/MT/CONF/12/Add. 1, p. 4).

nominal liability of carriers for each package is increased, although an upper limit is still set. The time to sue carriers is extended. Clauses limiting the venue of disputes to the domicile of the carrier are invalidated; carriers can no longer prevent shippers from taking disputes to the latter's national courts. Under pressure from LDCs the Hamburg Rules came into force after having been ratified by only twenty states.[30]

The United Nations Convention on Multimodal Transport was adopted by consensus in May 1980. The Final Act of the Conference on Multimodal Transport was signed by all major industrialized countries as well as LDCs. A number of INs, however, including Great Britain, Japan, the United States, Spain, and France expressed reservations about various aspects of the convention. The preamble to the convention states as its first basic principle that "a fair balance of interests between developed and developing countries should be established and an equitable distribution of activities between these groups of countries should be attained in international multimodal transport." The second basic principle is "that consultation should take place on terms and conditions of service, both before and after the introduction of any new technology in the multimodal transport of goods, between the multimodal transport operator, shippers, shippers' organizations and appropriate national authorities." The substantive provisions of the convention specify the form and content of documentation for multimodal transport, liability for loss or delay, jurisdiction for dispute settlement (in which the plaintiff can choose the country where the goods were taken in charge or delivered, or where the defendant has a place of business), and customs regulations affecting multimodal shipments.[31]

Like the Hamburg Rules, the Convention on Multimodal Transport thus increases the responsibility of carriers, most of whom are from industrialized nations; makes it easier for shippers to bring suit in their own national courts; and gives shippers a presumptive right to invoke dispute-settlement procedures. The convention gives LDCs the right to participate in discussions related to capital-intensive new technologies, such as containerization, which could make it more difficult for them to develop national fleets. Both the Hamburg Rules and the Convention on Multimodal Transport provide developing countries with leverage they did not have under the previous regime.

[30]Moore, "The Hamburg Rules, pp. 7–10; Selvig, "The Hamburg Rules, the Hague Rules," pp. 305–307.
[31]U.N. doc. no. TD/MT/CONF/16/Add. 1, pp. 2, 6–10, and the text of the Convention.

Flags of Convenience

A final area in which the Third World has been pressing for a restructuring of the existing shipping regime is flags of convenience. Flag of convenience refers to a situation in which there is little or no real economic link between the country of registration and the ship that flies its flag. For shipowners, flags of convenience offer a number of advantages, including low taxation, unrestricted capital movements, and lower operating costs. UNCTAD treats the Bahamas, Bermuda, Cyprus, Liberia, Panama, Singapore, and Somalia as open-registry, or flags-of-convenience, countries. Liberia and Panama are the most important. Their share of gross merchant-fleet tonnage increased from 10 percent in 1955 to 28 percent in 1976. Flags of convenience are used mainly by oil tankers and bulk-ore carriers.[32]

Third World complaints against flags of convenience are of relatively recent vintage. The issue was first raised at UNCTAD-II in 1968. It was then taken up in UNCTAD's Committee on Shipping. An Ad Hoc Intergovernmental Working Group was convened in 1978. This group and the Committee on Shipping have passed several resolutions condemning flags of convenience.

The gravamen of the Third World position has been that flags of convenience hamper the development of national fleets. Although the Liner Code and the Code on Multimodal Transport have given developing countries some control over freighters, they do not affect bulk carriers. UNCTAD and the Group of 77 have argued that developing countries have not been able to penetrate this market, in part because flags of convenience provide shipowners from industrialized countries with unfair economic advantages. Shippers have difficulty bringing suit against carriers flying flags of convenience because their owners cannot be identified. Shipping investments in developing countries are less attractive because of the financial advantages offered by open-registry countries. These economic effects reinforce the barriers to entry confronting LDCs, which are already imposed by vertically integrated multinational corporations that control much of the world's bulk-carrier fleet. Without these barriers, the cheap labor offered by many developing countries would provide a natural economic incentive to shift registration.[33]

[32]U.N. doc. no. TD/B/C.4/168, pp. 6, 23, 54, 65, and 73.
[33]U.N. doc. no. TD/B/C.4/168, pp. 65–66, 74; TD/B/C.4/177, pp. 15–17; Cafruny, "Ruling the Waves," pp. 20–22.

At the conclusion of the first session of the Ad Hoc Intergovernmental Working Group, the Group of 77 forced through a resolution stating in part that: "The expansion of open-registry fleets has adversely affected the development and competitiveness of fleets of countries which do not offer open-registry facilities, including those of developing countries."[34] At a meeting of the Committee on Shipping held in the summer of 1981, the Group of 77 used its voting power to pass a resolution calling for the phasing out of flags of convenience. All the industrialized countries voted against the resolution with the exception of France and Belgium, which abstained. Liberia voted with the North. Panama abstained.[35]

Developing countries have not, as yet, made much headway against flags of convenience. It is one of the few areas in which there is a split within the South. Liberia, the largest beneficiary of fees from vessels flying a flag of convenience, has defected from the Group of 77. Both public and private actors in the North have been more unified on this issue than on liner conferences. Powerful economic interests in the North, especially multinational mineral corporations, have supported flags of convenience. The practice has been legitimated by court decisions in major industrialized countries, especially the United States. During the 1960s labor union efforts to end open-registry practices, which did not use union seamen, were completely unsuccessful.[36]

In all areas of shipping, the Third World has challenged prevailing market-oriented principles and norms. Lacking national capabilities, LDCs have tried to change the rules of the game so that they could more easily develop their own merchant fleets. They were able to utilize the general principle of the sovereign equality of all states, and the existing structure of international organizations, especially UNCTAD, to force shipping issues onto the international agenda. In the cases of the Liner Code and open registry, the UNCTAD secretariat played a major role. Sovereignty gave the LDCs the right to demand that they be included in decision-making forums. Once they were participants, their views had to be taken into consideration in negotiating the Hamburg Rules and the Code on Multimodal Transport because general consensus was necessary for a smoothly functioning system. There were significant splits among

[34]Quote from U.N. doc. no. TD/B/C.4/177, Annex, p. 1; U.N. doc. no. TD/B/C.4/168, pp. 65–66, 74; TD/B/C.4/177, pp. 15–17.

[35]*World Business Weekly*, June 29, 1981, p. 8.

[36]Cafruny, "Ruling the Waves," p. 214.

industrialized countries. While common ideology and interest bound the Third World (with the exception of Liberia and Panama), the North divided according to economic interest, particularly with regard to the UNCTAD Code of Conduct for Liner Conferences. Countries with small fleets and maritime ambitions supported the code, those with large fleets opposed it.

For LDCs the ultimate benefit of new international regimes is to enhance their own national efforts to develop merchant fleets. Many Third World states have already acted unilaterally in the area of shipping. Argentina, Bolivia, Brazil, Burma, Chile, India, Indonesia, and Egypt among others have passed legislation favoring national vessels (a practice, it should be noted, also followed by the United States). Brazil, Argentina, and India have outlawed deferred-rebate systems and insisted on open conferences. During the 1970s a number of LDCs concluded bilateral treaties providing for 50–50 or 40–40–20 splits for freighter cargo. Latin American states, all of which reserve cargo for their national lines, were particularly active. Virtually all Latin American liner shipping is now governed by bilateral agreements providing for a 50–50 division between exporting and importing countries, and many Latin American fleets do, in fact, carry 50 percent of national liner cargo. These developments were made possible by growing national capacity. But, as in the case of multinational corporations, LDC efforts were facilitated by changes in international regimes, which legitimated national policies and coordinated Third World behavior making it more difficult for Northern actors to retaliate.[37]

In sum, in shipping as in other issue areas, the Third World has sought to undermine existing market-oriented regimes and supported rules of the game legitimating authoritative state allocation. These efforts have not been entirely ineffective. But Third World accomplishments in shipping have been limited to liners and rules for carriage. Most of the world's shipping continues to be governed by market-oriented behavior.

CONCLUSION

In civil aviation and shipping, the Third World has pursued similar objectives but enjoyed very different levels of success. In both areas,

[37]U.K., Board of Trade, Comm. on Inquiry Into Shipping, *Report*, May 1970, Cmnd 4337, pp. 437–439; Strange, "Who Runs World Shipping?" p. 358; Hearn, "Cargo Preference and Control," pp. 483–490; Oribe-Stemmer, "Flag Preferences in Latin America," pp. 124–125; Cafruny, "Ruling the Waves," pp. 220–232.

developing countries have defended an allocative regime, which would provide them with more power and resources even at the cost of economic efficiency. In civil aviation, developing countries got what they wanted because it was there already. The existing regime was authoritatively allocative rather than market-oriented. American efforts to move toward more market-governed behavior have been limited to North Atlantic routes. Third World countries do have a substantial share, usually close to 50 percent, of the traffic they generate. In the area of shipping, they have secured some changes in the regime but most of the world's fleet remains firmly in the hands of actors from industrialized countries.

The difference in outcomes is largely a result of the nature of the existing regimes encountered by developing countries. In the area of civil aviation, the North had created a regime that reflected a concern with security. States have been heavily involved in establishing routes, fares, and service frequencies. Existing norms gave Third World countries a presumptive right to develop their own national airlines and to a substantial share of the international passenger travel generated within their borders. In contrast, world shipping has been governed by market-oriented principles. Allocation has been determined primarily by the endowments of individual firms, although highly competitive conditions are rare because of the oligopolistic practices of liner conferences and multinational corporations; shipping has been characterized by market, but not perfect market, conditions. Developing countries were not given any presumptive right to specific cargo shares. Existing structures such as liner conferences, the control of vessels by vertically integrated companies, and flags of convenience have made it difficult for LDCs to develop national merchant fleets. Developing countries have begun to change the rules of the game in shipping primarily through national legislation mandating cargo reservation. But the Third World has had little success at the international level except with regard to liner conferences and rules of carriage. Northern unity has been greater, and the relevance of juridical sovereignty less, in the area of flags of convenience. In shipping, the existing regime inhibited the development of national carriers in the Third World; in civil aviation, it encouraged it.

IX

The Global Commons

Several areas of international concern have been placed under the rubric of the global commons. These include the oceans, Antarctica, space, and the electromagnetic (radio) frequency spectrum. It is not obvious that all these issues share the same characteristics. Analytically, a commons refers to an area that is difficult to enclose or privatize. This may be the result of externalities, uncertainties about the value of different parts of the commons, the high costs of enforcing private property rights, or indivisibilities associated with the product of the commons. Without a joint regime, under these conditions each individual has an incentive to over-exploit the commons area, leading to a Pareto-suboptimal outcome. Some issues associated with the concept of the global commons, such as the electromagnetic spectrum, do have one or more of these characteristics. Others, such as deep seabed nodules, do not.[1]

The link among global commons issues has not been a set of shared analytic characteristics, but rather a shared legal history. Areas associated with the global commons have been viewed as beyond national jurisdiction but open to free use. The classic example is the high seas. The debate over the global commons has dealt primarily with the legitimacy of this construction in the face of changing technological and political circumstances.

The basic objective of the Third World has been to bring areas that have been open to free use under the control of either some universal international organization or individual sovereign states. Under the old market regime, actors with the ability to exploit an area were free to do so. In the absence of externalities this is a very attractive situation for those whose resources permit unilateral action. Under a common heritage

[1] Wijkman, "Managing the Global Commons," p. 515. For a skeptical view of the need for joint regimes, see Conybeare, "International Organizations and the Theory of Property Rights."

regime, the use of common spaces would be regulated by an international organization for the benefit of the whole world community. For developing countries with limited national capabilities, a common-heritage regime is far more attractive than a market-oriented one.

An alternative strategy for Third World states is national appropriation of areas that have previously been regarded as beyond sovereign jurisdiction. National control allows the state to set the rules of the game under which exploitation takes place. Actors from the North, such as multinational corporations, can be regulated, taxed, or even excluded altogether. LDCs successfully implemented this strategy with regard to contiguous seas, but failed with regard to broadcasting-satellite orbits.

In all the issue areas associated with the global commons, the Third World has supported regimes in which allocation would be based more on direct or indirect authoritative allocation than on the endowments of individual public or private actors. The Third World has argued that space is part of the common heritage of mankind. This claim is reflected in the 1967 Outer Space Treaty, which states that space "shall be the province of all mankind," and is firmly embodied in a 1979 General Assembly Resolution for a Draft Agreement Governing the Activities of States on the Moon and Other Celestial Bodies, which declares that the moon and all of its resources are part of the common heritage of mankind. The Outer Space Treaty has been ratified by a large number of states, but has been subject to alternative interpretations by the North and the South. By the fall of 1983 the Moon Treaty had been signed by only eleven countries (including one IN, the Netherlands) and ratified by only four. The industrialized states were not, by the early 1980s, prepared to accept constraints on their relational power capabilities emanating from nothing more than Third World United Nations' majorities.

Commons issues have also arisen in areas of communications related to the allocation of the radio spectrum, direct satellite broadcasts, and geosynchronous orbits. These issues, along with the question of news reporting from the Third World by Northern press agencies, have been conjoined as the program for a New International Information Order. The conventional regime for allocating radio frequencies was based on the principle of maximum use, given existing capabilities. The radio spectrum was allocated on a first come, first served basis according to guidelines drawn up at World Administrative Radio Conferences (WARCs). Frequencies were registered with the International Frequency Registration Board, a technical organization that is part of the International Telecommunication Union (ITU). The board, traditionally composed of private-sector engineers (who were not appointed by their governments), approved registrations provided that they did not interfere with existing broadcasts. By 1980 this regime had resulted in a situation in which the United States and the Soviet Union used about 50 percent of the radio spectrum, and 90 percent of the spectrum was utilized by 10 percent of the world's population. Similarly, the limited number of geosynchronous, or stationary, orbits, which are the optimal configuration for communications satellites, were rapidly being appropriated by Northern actors because of their superior technical skill, larger capital resources, and greater market opportunities.[2]

Developing states have challenged the existing regime and called for an allocation of resources that would not be based on market principles. In WARC meetings and in the United Nations Committee on the Peaceful Uses of Outer Space they have defended principles, norms, rules, and decision-making procedures that would legitimate a greater role for direct state allocation. Despite the lack of technical expertise, a common ideological perspective facilitated the formulation of a coherent set of proposals. Third World states argued that each nation should be allocated a share of the radio spectrum regardless of its present demand. They maintained that some orbital slots should be reserved for interested states even if they did not have the existing capacity to launch a satellite. In 1976 eight equatorial states signed the Bogotá Declaration, which asserted national sovereignty over geosynchronous orbits above their territories. Developing states also demanded that prior consent be obtained before direct satellite broadcasts were beamed at their territories or Landsat satellites were used to collect or disseminate information about geological and agricultural conditions.[3]

In part, because of the cohesion provided by their common ideology, and the access to decision-making arenas provided by WARCs, the ITU, and the United Nations, developing countries have had success in some areas. In addition, LDCs do have at least potential relational power with regard to the radio spectrum. If they developed capacity that would actually require the use of more frequencies, they could interfere with

[2]Soroos, "The Commons in the Sky," pp. 671–672; Wijkman, "Managing the Global Commons," p. 534; Alexandrowicz, *The Law of Global Communication*, pp. 66–69.

[3]Willard, *Political Determinants*, pp. 43–44; Soroos, "The Commons in the Sky," p. 674; Wijkman, "Managing the Global Commons, p. 535; Kroloff, "The View from Congress," p. 166.

existing broadcasts, a prisoners' dilemma situation that provides a high incentive for arriving at some mutually acceptable allocative mechanism. Recent WARC conference members have recognized that some part of the radio spectrum should be distributed on the basis of future need. With regard to Landsat activities, LDCs failed to secure any agreement on their demand for prior consent, but a number of developing states have worked out bilateral agreements with the United States for the dissemination of information. Sovereign prerogatives give developing states leverage in this area because the actual exploitation of any mineral located with the aid of space-sensing requires state approval. LDCs have had less success in enforcing their claims to geosynchronous orbits where, unlike the contiguous sea (which is examined in more detail later in this chapter), sovereign assertions were not bolstered by even minimal relational power. It is much easier to force a tuna boat to port than to alter the orbit of a satellite.

In this chapter I examine in greater detail the two other major issue areas treated as part of the global commons—the oceans and the Antarctic regions. Analytically, they are particularly revealing because the institutional arrangements and negotiating procedures associated with them differed dramatically. In the case of the oceans, the United Nations Conference on the Law of the Sea (UNCLOS), a universal-membership negotiating forum dealing with a wide range of issues, gave developing countries ready access to decision-making forums and invested them with more influence and power than they could ever have claimed on the basis of their national power capabilities. The oceans were a prominent issue in the North-South debate during the 1970s. In the case of the Antarctic, a treaty signed in 1959 specified restrictive criteria for participation in decision-making procedures. The Antarctic has not been a focus of dispute between the North and the South. While this may be explained partly by the fact that two Third World countries (Chile and Argentina) have been consultative members of the treaty from the start, an exclusionary negotiating forum made it difficult for the Third World to place the Antarctic on its agenda. Only in 1983 was the Antarctic issue brought before the United Nations. The UNCLOS was a highly contentious negotiating forum that ultimately failed to produce a universally acceptable treaty; procedures followed to produce the Antarctic Treaty created a generally cooperative environment that subsequently led to the conclusion of several modest additional agreements. Negotiations concerning the oceans offer an example of an effort to come to terms on principles, norms, rules, and decision-making procedures in a situation in which there were fundamental differences in interests, power capabilities and, therefore, preferences among the actors involved. Negotiations regarding the Antarctic offer an example of a situation in which disagreements over basic issues of principle were placed in abeyance in favor of specifying rules that were acceptable to a small number of states. The United Nations Conference on the Law of the Sea set a precedent that should be avoided; the Antarctic Treaty system followed a strategy that ought to be emulated.

OCEANS

The development of an international regime for the oceans illuminates, in a particularly clear fashion, the objectives pursued by developing countries and the extent to which the realization of these objectives is facilitated by universal international organizations. After a decade of negotiation at the Third United Nations Conference on the Law of the Sea (UNCLOS-III) more than one hundred countries signed the United Nations Convention on the Law of the Sea in December 1982. (All these countries will not necessarily ratify the convention.) The treaty was endorsed by major developing countries, with the exception of some important Latin American states, including Venezuela and Argentina. It was also signed by the Eastern Bloc countries. Although France, Japan, and several small industrialized countries including Canada, Australia, and the Netherlands supported the agreement, it was rejected by several richer market-economy states. The opposition of the United States, which was particularly vehement, was engendered by the provisions of the convention dealing with deep-seabed mining.

The treaty gave the coup de grâce to an older, weakening regime whose central principle was that the oceans belong to no one, and whose basic norm was freedom of the seas beyond narrow territorial limits. The U.N. convention legitimates the extension of control by littoral states and treats the oceans' deep-seabed resources as the common heritage of mankind. Freedom of the seas was the ideal norm for a market-oriented allocation of resources; it gave individual actors carte blanche to take what they could get. Resource allocation reflected the endowments and preferences of these actors. The provisions of the Convention on the Law of the Sea are infused with the principle of authoritative state allocation, which has been the central norm of the program for a New International Economic

Order. The treaty recognizes the right of state actors to dictate the rules of the game. Coastal states can select the criteria they will use in determining resource allocation in the territorial sea and in their exclusive economic zone. Seabed mining is governed by the International Sea-Bed Authority composed of parties that have signed and ratified the convention.

Analytically, the program pursued by the Third World concerning the oceans is particularly significant because it is a case in which there was a trade-off between maximizing economic returns and pursuing regime objectives associated with state control. The primary economic beneficiaries of the agreement concluded in December 1982 are countries with long coastlines, and those which are land-based mineral producers. These states will benefit from restrictions on the production of minerals from the seabed, and from the extension of littoral states' control over the resources in as much as 350 offshore miles of ocean. Many of the countries in this set are developed; most developing countries are not in this group. The economic resources available to the Third World as a whole would have been much greater if the control of coastal states had been circumscribed. However, the developing world as a bloc opted for the extension of state control.

The ability of developing countries to secure an international treaty that embodied their preferred principles and norms was facilitated by a decision-making structure that provided equal, formal access for all states, and which gave many Third World states entrée to the private, specialized negotiating groups where the text was actually formulated. Such an arrangement would have been unthinkable in the nineteenth century, when the major maritime nations set and enforced rules for the ocean. However, as a result of precedents established in the 1930s, the availability of the United Nations as a forum, and the leverage Third World states secured from their ability to assert unilaterally, even if they could not always enforce, claims to extensive territorial oceans, the law of the seas convention was negotiated in a universal forum concerned with a wide range of issues—the optimal milieu for the exercise of power by the Third World.

THE CONVENTION

The 1982 United Nations Convention on the Law of the Sea was the product of more than a decade of negotiation. Its 320 articles and 9 annexes addressed almost all the major questions that had been subjects of international debate. These included the breadth of the territorial sea; navigational rights in territorial waters, straits, and archipelagic states; the creation of exclusive economic zones for coastal states; control of the continental shelf; rights of access for landlocked states; the exploitation of deep-seabed resources; environmental protection; and scientific research. In addition the convention established several new institutions, the most important of which was the International Sea-Bed Authority.

The convention was imbued with the principles and norms supported by the Third World, which have been reflected in other programs associated with the New International Economic Order. The most significant economic provisions of the treaty involved the extension of coastal state control. The convention provided for a twelve-mile territorial sea with right of innocent passage. It established an exclusive economic zone, which extends for 200 miles for living resources, excluding whales, and up to 350 miles for mineral exploitation beneath the continental shelf. While there were some modest concessions to international commitments in the exclusive economic zone, which gave coastal states something less than full sovereignty, the basic impact of the convention was to affirm state control over a much wider area than was previously accepted.

The regime established for the exploitation of deep-seabed nodules incorporated authoritative principles and norms supported by the Third World. The convention endorsed the proposition that the deep seabed is part of the common heritage of mankind, which should be regulated by the international community. The treaty established a complicated set of institutional structures to carry out this task. All states endorsing the convention become members of the International Sea-Bed Authority. The Authority has three organs—an assembly, a council, and a secretariat. In the assembly, which is described as "the supreme organ of the Authority," each nation has one vote. Questions of procedure can be settled by simple majority, those of substance must have at least a two-thirds' majority. The assembly elects the council, which has thirty-six members chosen from five different classes: four large consumers of metals (including one from Eastern Europe); four major investors in nodule exploitation (including one from Eastern Europe); four land-based producers (including two LDCs); six LDCs with special interests (including landlocked and large population); and eighteen states from designated geographic regions. The United States would probably be assured of a seat on the council in the last category if it were a member of the assembly; the total number of market-economy industrialized states on the council would then fall between eight and thirteen. The council makes decisions about seabed exploitation subject to the approval of the assembly. Substantive decisions require majorities ranging from two-thirds to consensus (that is, no stated opposition), depending on the issue. A major industrialized country would thus have a veto only on those issues decided by consensus, and might not be able to block decisions requiring a three-quarters' majority.[4]

The convention also created the Enterprise, which is the operating organ of the International Sea-Bed Authority. The Enterprise engages in the exploitation of resources from the deep seabed. Private corporations are obligated to make technology available to the Enterprise "on fair and reasonable terms" (Annex III, Art. 5). When a group of developing countries applies for a contract, private corporations are obligated to make technology available on the same terms as it is provided to the Enterprise. Private corporations can take the initiative in designating mining sites, but these sites must be divided into two parts. The Enterprise then selects one of the two parts, leaving the other for the private corporation. Terms agreed to at the final negotiating session of the U.N. Conference on the Law of the Sea initially provided eight sites for what are termed "pioneer" investors, and two for the Enterprise. The Enterprise has some financial advantages over private investors because it does not have to pay prospecting costs, and can secure technology and capital on concessional terms.[5]

The convention limits the production of deep-seabed nodules for twenty-five years after the initial start of production to levels that will not have any substantial negative effect on the earnings of land-based producers. If Third World countries are adversely affected, the Assembly can provide for a system of compensation. The Authority can become a member of international commodity agreements (Art. 151).

Finally, the treaty provides for a Review Conference fifteen years after commercial exploitation begins. Article 155 urges that decisions at this conference be taken on a consensus basis. If consensus cannot be reached, the convention can be amended by a three-quarters' majority vote.

The international regime for the deep seabed is the closest the Third

---

[4]Wijkman, "UNCLOS and the Redistribution of Ocean Wealth," p. 46, argues that the total number of states representing consumer interests, including two LDCs, would be nine. Voting arrangements are described in Articles 151–161 of the Convention.

[5]Annex III Article 5; Wijkman, "Redistribution of Ocean Wealth," p. 43; Wasserman, "Sea Convention Adopted," pp. 441–442.

World has come to constructing its ideal regime. The initial position of the developing world was that activities should be centrally planned and controlled by an Authority in which each nation had one vote. Actual exploitation would have been carried out exclusively by the Enterprise. The initial position of the market-economy countries was that the Authority should merely register claims for mining corporations. The final agreement is closer to the basic principles and many of the rules endorsed by the Third World. It is the Authority that is designated to organize, carry out, and control activities "on behalf of mankind as a whole."[6] Power is distributed on a one-nation, one-vote basis in the assembly. Even if all the major industrialized countries ratified the convention they would not have a veto over some substantive decisions taken by the council and, in fifteen years, the treaty could be changed without their acquiescence.[7]

Other aspects of the convention do not necessarily violate the preferences of industrialized states. The guarantees of freedom of navigation were important for the leading maritime powers. The United States in particular was concerned about restrictions on the movements of its naval vessels, a concern that the convention assuaged by endorsing free passage through straits, and by extending coastal state jurisdiction through the new device of exclusive economic zones rather than enlarging the territorial sea, which would have implied full sovereign control. The extension of coastal state jurisdiction had economic benefits for rich nations as well as for poor ones. In the area of the deep seabed, the Third World did, nevertheless, conclude an agreement that violated the expressed preferences of wealthier, more powerful, more technologically capable states.

THIRD WORLD OBJECTIVES

The Convention on the Law of the Sea illuminates the two central analytic questions of this study: First, what are the objectives of the Third World? Second, what determines the extent to which these objectives are realized?

The law of the sea is one of the few areas where it is possible to make a distinction between behavior designed to secure wealth, and behavior designed to increase control through the creation of authoritative regimes.

---

[6]Article 153.
[7]Wijkman, "UNCLOS and the Redistribution of Ocean Wealth," pp. 38–39; Friedheim and Durch, "Seabed Resources Agency," p. 379; Barkenbus, "Ocean Exploitation," p. 687.

In most cases, regime transformation corresponds to a redistribution of wealth, which can plausibly be seen as positive for the Third World. Most aspects of the NIEO program are consistent with both economistic and realist interpretations. The oceans, however, are one issue area where an analytic distinction can be made. Neither the basic North-South cleavage that came to dominate the conference nor the substantive program pursued by the Group of 77 can be easily understood from a wealth-maximizing perspective.

In the three Law of the Sea Conferences—the first in 1958, the second in 1960, and the third, which ran from 1972 to 1982—there were three cleavages: East versus West; landlocked and shelf-locked states versus those with extensive coastlines; and North versus South. The East-West split dominated the first two conferences, but not the third. The littoral-versus the landlocked-states cleavage was central only in the early and mid-1970s. There was a clear division of interest between these two groups of states. Landlocked and shelf-locked states would have benefited most from a regime that limited coastal state control and treated ocean resources as the common heritage of mankind. During the 1972–1973 session a group of landlocked states, led by Austria, was organized in the U.N. Sea-Bed Committee. Its ability to block the extension of national control, most strongly favored by a number of Latin American states, depended on breaking the unity of the Group of 77. Of the 103 LDCs that attended the second UNCLOS-III session, 22 were either landlocked or shelf-locked. These states, in combination with wealthier landlocked countries, would have had the votes necessary (one-third) to block action by the conference. However, this coalition ultimately collapsed. The negotiating text that emerged during the mid-1970s did little for the landlocked and shelf-locked countries. The behavior of coastally deprived Third World countries was, in the end, determined by the North-South cleavage.[8]

A further examination of some alternative proposals also reveals the primacy of political objectives associated with control through authoritative regimes. The final decision for extensive coastal state economic control, a decision that did not maximize economic benefits for the Third World as a whole, was not foreordained. At the beginning of UNCLOS-III most industrialized states were not committed to such a regime. In

[8]Barkenbus, "Ocean Exploitation," p. 691; Miles, "Introduction," pp. 163–164, 177, 233–234; Swing, "Who Will Own the Oceans?" pp. 532–533.

particular, until the early 1970s, military concerns led the United States to favor a policy of relatively limited littoral state jurisdiction. Because of the American Navy, policymakers, particularly in the Defense Department, were anxious to avoid any international agreements that could limit freedom of navigation. During the early 1970s, however, U.S. policy shifted decisively toward favoring more extensive coastal state control.[9]

This change was a result of both domestic and international pressures. American oil companies wanted national control, and guarantees against expropriation. They found support in the Interior and Commerce departments and in the Senate Interior Committee. Coastal-fishing interests also preferred more extensive state control, but they were opposed by distant-water interests. The oil companies were able to forge alliances with states that supported broad coastal jurisdiction, including some LDCs. The Group of 77 as a whole was, by 1973, strongly pressing for the expansion of national control. In the face of these developments the United States adopted a coastal position by 1974, including support for a 200-mile economic resource zone.[10]

Had the major developing countries favored a maritime rather than a coastal position, it is conceivable that the outcome of the UNCLOS would have been different. The Defense Department would have found allies rather than opponents in the U.N. Sea-Bed Committee. The oil companies would have confronted a situation in which extensive coastal state regulation would not appear to be a feasible option. Under these conditions an international regime based on the free right of transit, narrow territorial seas, limited economic zones, and the regulation of resource extraction from the ocean by some international arrangement reflecting the common heritage of mankind principle could have emerged. Such a regime would have had more economic benefits for the Third World as a whole than the agreement that was ultimately concluded in Geneva.

Most economically viable ocean resources are located in the exclusive economic zone now controlled by coastal states. Out of the ten largest beneficiaries of the zone, six are industrialized nations. Industrialized nations with 25 percent of the world's population get 50 percent of the exclusive economic zone area. The area under the jurisdiction of the

[9]Hollick, *U.S. Foreign Policy and the Law of the Sea*, p. 137; Wenk, *Politics of the Ocean*, p. 259.

[10]Hollick, *Law of the Sea*, pp. 256–280; Keohane and Nye, "Transgovernmental Relations."

United States was increased more than that of any other country—an ironic outcome for a program vigorously supported by the Third World and only hesitantly endorsed by the United States.[11]

Table 9.1 shows estimates of the percentage distribution of ultimately recoverable petroleum within various ocean boundaries. A seabed regime providing for narrow sovereignty (12 nautical miles) would have left 80 to 95 percent of the petroleum beneath the ocean floor as part of the common heritage of mankind. Petroleum is by far the most economically important resource that the oceans will yield. Its potential value is far higher than that of the other two primary sources of marine wealth—fisheries and seabed nodules. Such a regime was never seriously considered by the Third World.

Instead, the Convention on the Law of the Sea gives coastal states exclusive control over oil and other mineral resources for 200 nautical miles. Between 200 nautical miles and the end of the continental shelf, to a maximum claim of either 350 nautical miles or 100 nautical miles beyond the 2,500-meter isobath, the coastal state has resource jurisdiction but must share revenues with the International Sea-Bed Authority. In this mixed zone, the Authority gets 1 percent of the value of production beginning in the sixth year of production at any site, rising 1 percent a year to a maximum of 7 percent. These resources are to be distributed to the members of the convention "on the basis of equitable sharing criteria" (Art. 82). One scholar estimates that even though only 5 to 20 percent of petroleum lies *beyond* 200 nautical miles, the revenues involved in the full development of this resource could amount to $3 billion to $6 billion per year. This is no trivial amount, but it is at most only one-quarter of the resources that may be produced *within* 200 nautical miles. Moreover, the taxes imposed by the convention may make it uneconomical to exploit oil beyond 200 nautical miles.[12]

With regard to fisheries, 99 percent of the catch is made within the exclusive 200-mile economic zone. The annual value is about $20 billion. Although the treaty specifies that landlocked and geographically disadvantaged states "shall have the right to participate, on an equitable basis, in the exploitation of an appropriate part of the surplus of the living resources of the exclusive economic zone," the coastal state can unilaterally set the allowable catch and its own harvest, and thus the surplus. It

[11]Wijkman, "Managing the Global Commons, p. 530; Nye, *Should We Cut Our Losses?* p. 90.

[12]Wijkman, "UNCLOS and the Redistribution of Ocean Wealth," pp. 34–36.

TABLE 9.1

CUMULATIVE PERCENTAGE DISTRIBUTION
OF RECOVERABLE PETROLEUM

	U.S.	World
Within 12 nautical miles	10–25%	5–20%
Within the 200-meter isobath	55–70%	55–70%
Within 200 nautical miles	75–94%	80–95%
Within the base of the continental slope	86–99%	90–98%
Within the edge of the continental rise	98–100%	98–100%

Source: International Economic Studies Institute, *Raw Materials . . .* , p. 233.

can also charge a fee for fishing rights (Arts. 69 and 70). The most lucrative fishing grounds are in temperate waters. Table 9.2 shows the distribution of the catch between developed and developing areas for the year 1972, the last year before unilateral extension of fishing limits began.

The fishing provisions of the convention thus favor coastal over non-coastal, and rich coastal over poor coastal states. Since noncoastal states had a blocking veto at the UNCLOS this is hardly the outcome that would be predicated based on a calculation of economic interests.

There were alternative regimes suggested for minerals and living resources. In 1970 the United States offered a plan that would have subjected a much greater share of economic resources to international distribution. President Nixon proposed to the U.N. Sea-Bed Committee that a special trusteeship zone be established between the 200-meter isobath and the edge of the continental slope. Within this trusteeship zone the coastal state would have the authority to license exploration and development. However, one-third to one-half of the net revenue from oil exploration would be set aside for international uses. Beyond the edge of the continental slope, resources would be fully subject to an internationally established regime. This proposal was endorsed by the United Kingdom and Canada.[13] The taxing of fishing, oil, and mineral revenues from beyond the 200-meter isobath could have yielded $4.5 billion by the mid-1980s. This proposal was not supported by Third World states. Richard Cooper, an economist and under secretary of state in the Carter administration, mused that "Coming from a country with a long

[13]Quigg, *A Pole Apart*, p. 171.

TABLE 9.2

WORLD FISH CATCH DISTRIBUTED BY REGION AND VESSEL OF CAPTURE IN 1972

	Total catch		Catch by nonlocal fishermen		Catch by nonlocal fishermen from developed countries		Catch by nonlocal fishermen from developing countries	
	Million metric tons	% of total catch	Million metric tons	% of col. 1	Million metric tons	% of col. 1	Million metric tons	% of col. 1
Catch in developed-country areas	41.1	73.3	11.1	27.0	11.1	27.0	0.0	0.0
Catch in developing-country areas	15.0	26.7	5.2	34.7	4.7	27.3	1.1	7.3
Totals	56.1	100.0	15.3	29.1	15.2	27.1	1.1	2.0

Source: Reproduced from Wijkman, "Redistribution of Ocean Wealth," table 1, p. 31.

coastline, this was an extraordinarily generous proposal, and it is one of the many baffling aspects of the politics of relations between developed and less developed nations that this proposal was received very coolly by the less developed countries and that it was never seriously considered."[14]

The rejection of this proposal is only baffling from an economistic perspective. The trusteeship zone would have enhanced revenue for the Third World as a whole but would not have provided clear control. The littoral state, acting as a trustee for the international community, would have retained the right to license economic activity. There would have been no direct responsibility to any international organization. The American trusteeship proposal is one of the few cases where some less developed countries were clearly confronted with a trade-off between resource transfers and political power. These countries, which had limited coastlines or were landlocked or shelf-locked, had the option of siding with more coastally well-endowed developing states or breaking Third World unity and allying with the North. They rejected an alliance.

THIRD WORLD POLITICAL LEVERAGE

The provisions of the United Nations Convention on the Law of the Sea reflect the expressed preferences of the Third World. Although some developing countries were unhappy with the outcome, in the end they went along. The South prevailed even in the area of seabed mining despite the intense opposition of the Reagan administration, a level of opposition that ultimately led the United States to reject the treaty. How was this possible?

An analysis based on national power capabilities may explain the preferences of the Third World, but not how they were achieved in the oceans issue area. Weak states prefer allocation by authoritative political decisions rather than by the market. Developing countries do not have the technological or economic resources to exploit seabed nodules. Their naval capacities are limited. Yet the terms of the convention related to seabed exploitation embody principles, norms, rules, and decision-making procedures that are far closer to those initially proposed by the South than to the preferences of the North.

[14]Richard C. Cooper, "The Oceans as a Source of Revenue," p. 112. See also Swing, "Who Will Own the Oceans?" p. 535; Hollick, "Bureaucrats at Sea," pp. 28–40; Stevenson, "Legal Regulation," pp. 53-54.

Developing countries utilized two major sources of leverage. First, as sovereign states they could claim, even if they could not defend, more extensive control over contiguous seas. Second, the universal multi-issue negotiating forum presented by the United Nations Law of the Sea Conference offered the opportunity to transform unilateral claims into universally legitimated sovereign rights. Existing regime structures—the plausible rights of sovereignty and the United Nations—were the critical determinants of Third World success. In addition, the ability of the Group of 77 to formulate a coherent program around the principle of a common heritage of mankind, and the inability of the United States to provide effective leadership for the North enhanced Third World negotiating effectiveness at the UNCLOS.

Until the middle of the twentieth century the primary issue associated with the oceans was the breadth of the territorial sea. During the nineteenth century the major maritime nations, especially Great Britain, wanted to maintain freedom of navigation. At the beginning of the twentieth century only six or seven states claimed more than the customary three-mile limit. Their claims were rejected by the great naval powers, which acted unilaterally to enforce the three-mile limit. In the nineteenth century landlocked states did not participate in ocean rule making.[15]

During the twentieth century, however, the decision-making structure based on unilateral action by the major naval powers broke down. In 1930 an international conference was held at the Hague to codify ocean law. The agenda was drawn up by the International Law Committee of the League of Nations. The meeting was attended by forty states. The legitimacy of the right of the great naval powers to set and enforce rules for the ocean was undermined.[16] The Hague Conference established an important precedent for future negotiations.

After the Second World War more states made claims to extensive national jurisdiction. Ironically, the United States itself provided an important impetus for this movement. In 1945 President Truman issued two proclamations. One asserted American control over established fisheries, especially those that had been developed by American nationals; the other over natural resources of the continental shelf contiguous to the United States. These claims were not a product of America's ambitious postwar hegemonic future but of the 1930s and the Second World War when

[15]Keohane and Nye, *Power and Interdependence*, p. 124; Nye, "*Should We Cut Our Losses?*" p. 3.
[16]Keohane and Nye, *Power and Interdependence*, p. 93.

narrower and more specific concerns arose. The assertion of rights over traditional fisheries was inspired by a dispute with Japan over salmon-fishing off Alaska, which had festered during the 1930s. The United States saw long-range Japanese fishing encroaching on an industry that had been developed by U.S. interests. During the 1930s technological improvements in drilling made it possible to exploit offshore oil to a greater depth, opening the possibility for new resource development beyond the traditional three-mile limit, especially in the Gulf of Mexico. Anxious to ensure adequate supplies of petroleum during the war, the Roosevelt administration initiated policies designed to exclude European powers from the Gulf by establishing coastal state control of shelf resources. Both the fishing and mineral initiatives came to fruition in policies announced by Truman shortly after Roosevelt's death. The United States spent the next thirty years trying to undo actions by other states that were partly inspired and justified by the Truman proclamations.[17]

In the 1950s and 1960s a large number of countries, especially in Latin America, made ambitious claims. In 1950 Mexico, Argentina, and Costa Rica unilaterally proclaimed sovereignty over their continental shelves. In 1946 Chile, Ecuador, and Peru proclaimed 200 nautical miles of territorial sea, at the same time providing for continued recognition of the right of innocent passage. Argentina, Brazil, Nicaragua, and Panama made similar claims. Indonesia, Singapore, and Malaysia asserted control over the Strait of Malacca. By the 1960s Canada and Australia, which had traditionally allied with the great naval powers, were taking a more coastal view of their interests. For instance, in 1970 Canada extended its jurisdiction over commercial vessels to 100 miles in an effort to control pollution.[18]

This pattern of creeping jurisdiction coupled with the precedent of the 1930 Hague Conference for negotiating ocean issues through convention diplomacy provided the two major sources of leverage for developing countries. The first two United Nations Conferences on the Law of the Sea were held in Geneva in 1958 and 1960. The 1958 meeting, attended by eighty-seven countries, concluded four conventions which dealt with the territorial sea and contiguous zones, high seas, fishing and the conservation of living resources, and the continental shelf. These agreements,

---

[17]Hollick, *U.S. Foreign Policy and the Law of the Sea*, chap. 2.
[18]Joyner, "The Exclusive Economic Zone," p. 694; Keohane and Nye, *Power and Interdependence*, p. 95; Wenk, *Politics of the Ocean*, p. 254; Brown et al., *Regimes*, p. 41.

however, did not clearly delineate the breadth of the territorial sea. The right of coastal states to exploit the continental shelf was defined by technological capability, an inherently ambiguous criterion, given technological change. The 1960 UNCLOS was called to resolve the territorial sea and contiguous zone questions, but failed to do so.

Both the 1958 and 1960 conferences were dominated by the East-West cleavage. As a continental land power with a limited navy the Soviet Union supported a 12-mile territorial sea. This was opposed by the United States and Great Britain. The United States was also reluctant to jeopardize relations with Latin American states by challenging their ocean claims on a bilateral basis. American policymakers saw convention diplomacy as the format to follow to promote American interests; creeping jurisdiction could be checked by negotiating agreements at universal international forums. [19]

The strategy of conference diplomacy did not work, however. Claims to more extensive national control continued during the 1960s. New issues were placed on the agenda, of which the most important was the regime for the mining of deep-seabed nodules. These potato-sized rocks scattered along parts of the deep ocean floor contain nickel, copper, cobalt, and manganese. By the mid-1960s it was technologically possible to exploit this new resource. But there were no accepted rules of the game covering such activity.

For the major powers, the optimal strategy would have been to separate the deep-seabed issue from questions of coastal state control. In the former issue area, the industrialized countries had sufficient national power capabilities to act on their own. In the latter, the exercise of sovereign power to make unilateral claims could not be ignored. By severing the seabed from international control, the North (including the Soviet Bloc) could have established its own rules of the game for exploiting the deep seabed.

[19]In *Power and Interdependence* Keohane and Nye argue that recent developments regarding the oceans reflect changes in the international system toward a pattern of complex interdependence (p. 150). Whether there has been a systemic change or simply an alteration in military strength (in which states claiming broad jurisdiction now have relatively stronger navies), need not be resolved here. Regardless of the general theoretical interpretation, for the purposes of this analysis the critical point is that the United States was prepared, even anxious, to have ocean issues dealt with in a universal, multi-issue forum in the 1950s. The North-South cleavage had not yet congealed and American policymakers felt that they would be able to cope with Communist Bloc ambitions. Hollick, *U.S. Foreign Policy and the Law of the Sea*, pp. 127–135.

By the 1960s, however, a series of international precedents had been set for settling ocean-related questions through conference diplomacy. More importantly, the South was intent on linking seabed exploitation to other issues in the context of a major United Nations conference. This tactical linkage was the only source of leverage that the Third World had over the resource exploitation issue. During the mid-1960s a number of initiatives were taken in the Economic and Social Council and in the General Assembly. The South pressed for a comprehensive oceans regime including the seabed. In August 1967 Arvid Pardo of Malta proposed that seabed resources be controlled by the United Nations for the benefit of developing areas. He argued that the wealth of the oceans should be viewed as part of the common heritage of mankind, and he placed this principle in the context of the North-South debate. Pardo's speech led to the creation of the United Nations Sea-Bed Committee in 1967 and eventually to the UNCLOS-III, the Third United Nations Conference on the Law of the Sea. As early as June 1968 the North-South cleavage was clearly manifest in the Sea-Bed Committee. By the early 1970s the Latin American and African groups within the G-77 had resolved their differences over coastal state control, and landlocked LDCs were aligned with their more coastally well endowed brethren.[20]

Both the Soviet Union and the United States initially resisted linking the seabed with other issues. However, several General Assembly resolutions supporting this strategy were passed over American objections. By 1970 American officials had resigned themselves to a universal multi-issue forum. Policymakers hoped that they would be able to trade off concessions in the area of the seabed for a comprehensive treaty that would guarantee security interests related to rights of free navigation. The United States supported the 1970 United Nations resolution calling for a new conference. The initial meeting of UNCLOS-III in Caracas, Venezuela, in 1973 was attended by 137 nations, each with one vote.[21]

The existence of the United Nations as a venue for debating oceans issues, and the leverage that the developing countries secured from their ability to assert control unilaterally over contiguous ocean areas thus produced a negotiating forum in which there was limited congruence between underlying national power capabilities and the distribution of

[20]Wenig, *Structure and Process*, pp. 19–33; Nye, "*Should We Cut Our Losses?*" p. 5; Wenk, *Politics of the Ocean*, pp. 260–263.

[21]Wenk, *Politics of the Ocean*, p. 284; Laursen, "Security versus Access," pp. 202–203; Nye, "*Should We Cut Our Losses?*" p. 5.

voting power. To provide both Upper Volta and the United States with one vote in deciding what should be done about coastal state control, navigation, and deep-seabed mineral development was bizarre. Although the United States and the other maritime powers did secure many of their navigational objectives and enjoyed economic benefits from the exclusive economic zone, differences over the deep-seabed regime led the United States and several other major industrialized countries to reject the agreement that was ultimately concluded in 1982.

AMERICAN REJECTION OF THE LAW OF THE SEA CONVENTION

It is possible to argue that the Reagan administration's rejection of the Law of the Sea Convention was grounded in domestic American politics, not in international structures. Rather than flowing from the incongruence between underlying national power capabilities and international institutional arrangements, the outcome of the UNCLOS might be attributed to electoral outcomes, pressure group politics, or ideological commitments.

First, it can be argued that if Carter had been reelected the executive would have backed the convention. Elliot Richardson, the chief American negotiator during the Carter administration supported the final terms of the treaty and argued that ultimately the United States would have to sign because there were no alternatives.[22] In 1980 it appeared that the United States was committed to concluding a treaty.

Second, powerful private actors opposed the Law of the Sea Convention. The American rejection of the treaty can be seen as a response to interest group pressure. A representative of the American Petroleum Institute argued that the agreement would enhance the right of LDCs to expropriate foreign corporations, provide special advantages for the Enterprise, result in mandatory technology transfer, arbitrarily limit production, and set an adverse precedent for future international arrangements.[23]

In expressing its opposition, the American Mining Congress emphasized that the convention would jeopardize access for American corporations, fail to provide security of tenure over the long term even for

---

[22]U.S. Congress, House, Committee on Foreign Affairs, *U.S. Foreign Policy and the Law of the Sea*, pp. 89–92.
[23]Ibid., pp. 256.

successful ventures, distort the market through the imposition of production controls, and give undue advantage to pioneer enterprises from countries that had not made extensive research and development expenditures. A variety of other private groups also testified against the convention.[24]

Third, ideological concerns about the new international economic order were manifest in a number of statements against the Law of the Sea Convention. Congressman Don Young of Alaska, testifying before his fellow members in the House, argued that the "treaty does not protect the U.S. interest in mining, oil and gas development, defense or fisheries. If the intent of the United States is to share our wealth with less developed countries let us do so directly and not through the sort of robbery which is envisioned in the new international economic order." Trent Lott of Mississippi stated that "'Common heritage' became the rallying cry for radical leftist Third World ideologues hellbent to establish the new international economic order."[26] The 1980 Republican party platform included a statement that "too much concern has been lavished on nations unable to carry out seabed mining, with insufficient attention paid to gaining early American access."[26] Hence, it is possible to argue that the U.S. rejection of the convention was determined by domestic electoral, pressure group, or ideological considerations.

To some extent this domestically oriented interpretation can be challenged on its own terms. There was considerable opposition within the Carter administration to the final shape of the U.N. Law of the Sea Convention. The United States might have acted in the same way had Carter been reelected. Moreover, the reaction of the private sector was mixed. Some of the large oil companies were in favor of the convention because they felt it would give them a more stable operating environment. State behavior was not simply hamstrung by private pressures.

It is also possible, however, to interpret much of the evidence about the motivation of American central decision-makers from a broader systemic perspective. The statements made by the Reagan administration focused on questions of economic interest and power. Testifying before the House Foreign Affairs Committee in June 1982 James Malone, the assistant secretary of state for Oceans, Environment, and International Scientific Affairs, stated that the nonseabed provisions of the convention

[24]Ibid., pp. 216–227.
[25]Ibid., pp. 30, 49.
[26]Quoted in Wasserman, "Law of the Sea," p. 82.

were "consistent with U.S. interests," but that the deep-seabed mining provisions did "not minimally meet U.S. objectives."[27] He maintained that the treaty would discourage mining, force the transfer of technology, fail to establish a predictable environment, and allow enterprises from the Soviet Union, Japan, and other countries to secure pioneer status even though they had made only limited investments compared with American companies. Malone went on to note that although the United States would probably be assured of a seat on the Authority its influence would still be limited. The convention could be changed after fifteen years even if the United States and other industrialized countries disapproved. The Authority could restrict output over the objections of the United States. Finally, revenues collected by the Authority could be allocated to national liberation movements. No academic devotee of *realpolitik* could have written a more sober rationale for U.S. rejection of the convention.[28] Furthermore, other industrialized states objected to the seabed mining provisions, suggesting that an analysis of domestic American policies is a less than fully adequate explanation for the failure of the UNCLOS to reach a consensus.[29]

It is difficult to see how serious problems could be avoided even in a seabed regime in which all of the major industrialized states participated. LDCs would be able to set the policy of the International Sea-Bed Authority in several important areas. Conflicts between the Authority and major private mining interests would be inevitable. Yet the ability of the Authority to enforce its writ would depend critically on the participation of INs. Empirically, it has been extremely unusual for a stable regime to be created when there is incongruence between national power capabilities and the new rules of the game. Incongruence is less likely to lead to instability in long-established regimes, which can be sustained by custom, habit, social knowledge, uncertainty about the consequences of change, and vested interests.[30]

It is too simple to blame the outcome of the UNCLOS on the vagaries of American politics. The United States made a fundamental, but under-

[27]U.S. Congress, House, Committee on Foreign Affairs, *U.S. Foreign Policy and the Law of the Sea*, p. 86.

[28]Ibid., pp. 84–89.

[29]See statements of Belgium and Britain in A/CONF.62/PV.188, p. 56; A/CONF.62/PV.189, pp. 80–83.

[30]On the distinction between regime maintenance and regime creation, see Krasner, "Regimes and the Limits of Realism."

standable, strategic error in agreeing to a multi-issue universal international forum to deal with oceans issues. Ample precedents, including the 1930 Hague Conference, and UNCLOS-I and UNCLOS-II made the United Nations the natural venue for a meeting to discuss the oceans. In the late 1960s U.N. diplomacy was not dominated by the North-South cleavage. Had purely economic calculations determined state policies the final outcome might well have coincided with American preferences regarding relatively narrow coastal state control and free access to the deep seabed. The American decision to participate in UNCLOS-III was a sensible option in the late 1960s.

If the United States was not simply naive, the Third World was not simply blustering. Developing countries were not intent on pushing through a treaty that would be rejected by the North. The Third World wanted an agreement that would legitimate direct authoritative state allocation of resources; the extent of this legitimation depended on Northern participation. The final outcome was hardly optimal for the South. By 1980 or 1981, however, the developing countries were locked into a negotiating text that had been largely agreed to by the North. Last-ditch compromises regarding the status of pioneer ventures and a seat for the United States on the International Sea-Bed Authority were made in an effort to end the misgivings of the Reagan administration. But when these were rejected the Third World, ultimately with the support of the Soviet Bloc and a few advanced industrialized market-economy countries, decided to proceed even without the support of the United States. The final result, after more than a decade of negotiations, was an international agreement that did not offer a stable environment. The future of seabed mineral exploitation is clouded. The rights of nonsignatories with regard to some of the provisions of the convention, such as passage through straits, is uncertain.

The use of convention diplomacy to negotiate a new international regime for the oceans was blighted from the outset. International regimes have developed in two ways. First, they may emerge over a period of time from routinized practices. Habit and custom becomes institutionalized, imbued with normative significance, and rationalized through general principles. Second, regimes have been created by powerful states to promote their own interests. The first option was not feasible in the oceans issue area. Indeed, long-established practices were under attack. The second option required a venue other than the United Nations.

From the perspective of the United States, the optimal strategy would have been to delink various ocean issues and to make agreements only with those states that had the capabilities to undo arrangements that might be concluded without them. Issues related to the territorial sea, navigation, and the exclusive economic zone should have been negotiated with coastal states. Issues related to the exploitation of the deep seabed should have been negotiated with those states that have the technological capability or naval power to influence the pattern of exploitation unilaterally. In the late 1960s it was difficult, perhaps impossible, to consider such a strategy seriously because of American assumptions about the efficacy of conference diplomacy and the ability of the Third World to link seabed and navigation issues at the United Nations. Given the problematic outcome of the Conference on the Law of the Sea, more particularistic interest-oriented strategies now look more attractive.

ANTARCTICA

While the oceans became the subject of a major North-South confrontation during the height of the NIEO debate during the 1970's, the regime for another issue area, with many similar characteristics, evolved in a radically different way. Like the deep seabed, the Antarctic region may contain significant wealth. Krill, a small crustacean that swarms in Antarctic waters, is already being commercially harvested. There is evidence of mineral and hydrocarbon deposits. National claims to these resources are tenuous. Yet through the 1970s Antarctica was not an area of conflict between the North and the South.

Since 1959, behavior has been governed by a set of agreements that are modest in scope and limited in membership, and which sidestep fundamental disagreements related to territorial claims to various parts of the Antarctic. The Antarctic Treaty system began in 1959 with twelve full members, known as consultative parties, including two Third World states, Chile and Argentina. By 1984 only four additional consultative parties had been added, including two more LDCs, Brazil and India, which joined in 1983. The criterion for admitting new, full-voting members is that they demonstrate a functional capacity in the region by launching significant Antarctic research activity. To date, all the consultative parties have sought to maintain exclusive control in the region, although the policies of Brazil, and especially India, have not yet been fully revealed. The issue was successfully kept out of the United Nations until the First Committee of the General Assembly discussed the Antarctic in the fall of 1983 and called for a study by the secretary general.

The Antarctic Treaty system is extremely weak. There is virtually no enforcement mechanism. Formal discussions of one major problem, mineral exploration, were regarded as potentially so conflictual because of competing territorial claims that they were put off until the early 1980s. Given that the fundamental issue of national claims has not been resolved, it may be inappropriate even to label the Antarctic system a regime. Rather, it is a set of rules and decision-making procedures, reflecting weak norms associated with scientific exploration, disarmament, and environmental protection, which is designed to coordinate the behavior of states so that they can avoid mutually undesirable outcomes. The calculations of the actors are short term. Agreements have been violated. The treaty system is not strong enough to deter one of its members from a behavioral change if power or interests alter.[31]

The Antarctic system is incomplete. It is not logically coherent. But it has worked. Major conflicts have been avoided. The environment has not been degraded. The commercial harvesting of krill has begun. The system has worked because the relationship between underlying power and interests and regime characteristics has not become attentuated. States that cannot undermine agreements in the region have been excluded from the treaty system. In a world in which there are fundamental differences over principles and norms, which flow from outlandish disparities in national power capabilities, the Antarctic system offers one example of a feasible strategy for coping with common problems. Rather than striving for fundamental accords that are unattainable, it concentrates on modest goals that are segregated and disaggregated. Rather than creating open, universal decision-making forums that encourage frustration and bitterness, it works through closed meetings restricted to a small number of countries. In a world characterized by basic differences over principle, unresolvable conflicts are most likely to be avoided by arrangements designed to reconcile specific, clear-cut, short-run interests.

[31]The Antarctic system is a manifestation of what Arthur Stein has called the "dilemma of common aversions." The system is designed to prevent mutually undesirable outcomes. (See Stein, "Coordination and Collaboration.") On the need to define regimes as including principles and norms, not just rules and decision-making procedures, see Krasner, "Structural Causes and Regime Consequences."

THE CREATION OF THE ANTARCTIC
TREATY SYSTEM

The negotiations that led to the conclusion of the Antarctic Treaty of 1959 were initiated by the United States. In 1958 President Eisenhower invited the eleven other states that had participated in the Antarctic phase of the International Geophysical Year to a conference.[32] The twelve participants disagreed about the most basic issue associated with Antarctica: whether or not states could claim territory and exercise sovereignty. Seven states had made territorial claims—Argentina, Australia, Chile, France, New Zealand, Norway, and the United Kingdom. Belgium, Japan, South Africa, the USSR, and the United States had not made claims of their own and rejected the claims of others. The American position has been that there are no legitimate sovereign claims in the Antarctic; the area should be open to any country capable of exploiting it; and the Arctic oceans should be treated as high seas since there is no land-based sovereign.

Despite this basic difference, an agreement was reached. The Antarctic Treaty of 1959 prohibits military activity, nuclear explosions, and the disposal of radioactive waste in the area. It promotes scientific progress by providing for the exchange of information and personnel. The issue of sovereignty is left open: Article IV states that nothing in the treaty affects existing claims. Unanimous consent of full members known as the consultative parties, is required for any action. The treaty does not have any real sanctions. Although inspections have been provided for, they have rarely taken place. No international secretariat has been created. Regular meetings have taken place only once every two years. After thirty years, that is, in 1991, any consultative party can call for a review conference.[33]

The scientific norms of the International Geophysical Year served as a convenient pretext for the United States. The basic American objective was to stabilize strategically the Antarctic area. U.S. policymakers confronted two problems. First, there was anxiety about conflict with the Soviet Union. If the Suez Canal were destroyed, shipping would be

[32]The International Geophysical Year was a major international undertaking designed to collect and disseminate basic geophysical information.

[33]Auburn, *Antarctic Law*, pp. 104, 139–143, 154–155, 175; Joyner, "The Exclusive Economic Zone," pp. 704–705, 719–720; Mitchell and Kimball, "Conflict Over the Cold Continent," p. 125.

forced around the Cape of Good Hope and the Antarctic could, American officials feared, be used as a submarine base. In the late 1940s the United States had proposed that the region be governed by a condominium of states that would exclude the Soviet Union. But Russian protests and resistance from allies with territorial claims undercut this endeavor. The International Geophysical Year brought the Soviets actively into Antarctica for the first time. In December 1958, the Russians announced that they would make their scientific stations permanent, year-round facilities. This led other states, which had intended to leave, to follow suit, and catalyzed negotiation of the treaty. The Antarctic Treaty was the first accord signed by the two superpowers after the initiation of the Cold War.[34]

The second strategic problem for the United States was the danger of conflict among Western powers with conflicting territorial claims. The polar segments claimed by Great Britain, Argentina, and Chile overlap. This has led to numerous confrontations. Argentina and Chile sent naval forces into areas claimed by Great Britain in the early 1950s. Before 1958, diplomatic protests concerning infringements of sovereign territories by scientific expeditions were routine. In 1952 a British meteorological expedition was forced to withdraw because of gunfire from an Argentine ship. In 1953 British officials, accompanied by marines, dismantled huts built by Argentine and Chilean nationals and arrested two individuals. Argentina and Chile attempted to use the Rio treaties to secure U.S. support for their territorial claims against Great Britain. By imposing a moratorium on the issue of sovereignty, the treaty resolved, or at least delayed, intra-allied conflicts into which the United States would inevitably be drawn, as it was into the Falkland Islands (Maldives) war.[35]

EVOLUTION OF THE ANTARCTIC SYSTEM

The Antarctic system has displayed an impressive ability to perpetuate itself in the face of changing circumstances. The signatories to the treaty have tacitly adopted policies designed to maintain their monopoly position. While the East-West strategic issue that precipitated action in the

[34]Taubenfeld, "A Treaty for Antarctica," pp. 261, 281; Auburn, Antarctic Law, p. 89; Quigg, A Pole Apart, pp. 142–147; Hanessian, "The Antarctic Treaty," pp. 436–447.
[35]Burton, "New Stresses," pp. 472–473; Quigg, A Pole Apart, pp. 120–122; Auburn, Antarctic Law, pp. 56–57; Luard, "Who Owns the Antarctic?" p. 1178.

first place has faded, the maintenance of functional control over economic as well as scientific activity has become the main concern of the consultative parties.

Membership has been limited. Article IX of the Antarctic Treaty says that a state can become a consultative party by demonstrating "its interest in Antarctica by conducting substantial scientific research activity there, such as the establishment of a scientific station or the dispatch of a scientific expedition." Over time, the consultative parties have come to interpret this provision to mean that a state must establish a permanent wintering-over station or carry out major scientific research projects. This is generally a fairly substantial proposition both in direct expenses and in the provision of polar scientists. Icebreakers cost more than $50 million. In one season the United States had seven air crashes. Belgium stopped research in 1961 because of the financial burden. Through 1983 only four new countries had become consultative members—West Germany, Poland, India, and Brazil. Whereas Poland's station cost only about $3 million, West Germany's ran to over $100 million. India's and Brazil's efforts were not as ambitious as those of most of the other consultative parties but were elaborate, sophisticated, and expensive enough to be beyond the reach of all but a very few LDCs. For instance, in December 1983 India sent eighty-three individuals to establish a permanent scientific station.[36] As of 1983, thirteen other countries had acceded to the treaty, but they did not enjoy consultative status and therefore did not vote in meetings where decisions were actually taken. Membership in the system's scientific arm, the Scientific Committee for Antarctic Research (SCAR), is limited to nationals from consultative-party states even though it is officially a nongovernmental scientific body. The treaty also makes a distinction between the original signatories, who can remain members even if they cease active Antarctic activity, and new consultative members, whose continued standing is contingent on their sustaining scientific research, making any substantial expansion of membership even more unlikely.[37]

The treaty does not provide for any direct role for the United Nations system, which would have diluted the power of the signatories. Scientific cooperation with specialized agencies has been limited and carried out

[36]*Economist*, Jan. 30, 1982, p. 48, and Jan. 7, 1984, p. 46; *New York Times*, Aug. 29, 1983, A9:5, and Sept. 13, 1983, B17:2.

[37]Auburn, *Antarctic Law*, pp. 3–4, 181–182; Joyner, "The Exclusive Economic Zone," p. 705; Shapley, "Antarctic Problems," p. 505.

primarily through the Scientific Committee for Antarctic Research. Exchange of information has frequently omitted international organizations; for instance, recommendations about information on nuclear issues have not mentioned the International Atomic Energy Commission; on transportation questions there has been no mention of the International Civil Aviation Commission; on pollution matters, the International Maritime Organization has been ignored.[38]

For a long period, discussions among the consultative parties were carried out in secret; more recently, adherents have attended as observers. Originally this may have reflected the delicate domestic political position that sovereignty claims involved for some of the signatories, especially Chile and Argentina. But over time this exclusionary practice was perpetuated by apprehension about outside pressures from other states, U.N. agencies, or private corporations. According to one American official, the consultative parties were "anxious not to raise a red flag for the Third World."[39]

Since its founding, the central problem for the Antarctic Treaty system members has been to increase the treaty system's scope to include the development of the region's economic potential without destroying the framework of the system itself. The 1959 accord does not deal with economic issues. In part, this reflects the fact that commercial activity was not seen as imminent at the time. But the more important reason for avoiding the question of economic exploitation was that it could not have been resolved in the face of conflicting territorial claims. Scientific expeditions posed a less direct challenge to sovereignty. By giving each consultative party the right to license its own expeditions, and providing for the mutual recognition of such licenses, it was possible to find a formula that satisfied both claimant and nonclaimant states. The exploitation of marine living resources and, more especially, minerals is more intimately linked to sovereignty claims, especially given the acceptance of 200-mile exclusive economic zones for the oceans. The challenge for the consultative parties was to extend the scope of the system, despite their fundamental disagreements over sovereign territorial control, without losing their effective decision-making monopoly. This extension has been carried out through a series of incremental steps involving the negotiation of new conventions rather than by amendments to the original treaty. The 1959 treaty has been preserved at the core of the system while, at the same

[38]Auburn, *Antarctic Law*, pp. 121–128.
[39]*Yale Law Journal* 87. "Thaw in International Law?" p. 836, n. 150.

time, membership in satellite agreements has been offered to other states with competencies in particular functional areas.

The first new arrangement was concerned solely with conservation. The Agreed Measures for the Conservation of Antarctic Fauna and Flora was concluded by the consultative parties in 1964. Its objective was to protect native vegetation and wildlife. It stated that disturbances to natural habitats were to be minimized. Hunting and capturing wild animals required special permits issued by signatories to the agreement. Although this arrangement has generally been regarded as a success, it has still not been actually ratified some eighteen years after its conclusion. There are no enforcement mechanisms. Implementation has been dependent on voluntary compliance through national legislation.[40] The Agreed Measures, like much of the Antarctic Treaty itself, provided a set of rules that allow signatories to accomplish some shared objectives (in this case related to environmental protection) despite serious disagreements over basic principles.

The Convention for the Conservation of Antarctic Seals, which was concluded in 1972, does address economic questions. There are six species of seals in the region and some had been caught commercially, primarily for their fur. The convention sets catch limits on three of the species and prohibits outright the killing or capturing of the other three. No secretariat, however, was established. There is no mechanism for enforcement. The veto rule of the Antarctic Treaty system was extended to the issue of sealing. The convention to protect seals has not had any real test because exploratory ventures suggested that commercialization would not be profitable.

By maintaining a monopoly on decision-making power for the consultative parties, negotiating outside of the formal Antarctic Treaty arrangements, and providing for minimal joint enforcement, the convention on seals set a precedent for the 1980 Convention on Marine Living Resources.[41] Krill are the most economically important living marine resource in the Antarctic region. They occupy a critical place in the food chain of the region, serving as a basic source of nutrition for many larger marine animals, including seals and whales.

A number of pressures led the consultative parties to the Antarctic Treaty to take some action with regard to marine living resources. Several countries, including Japan, the Soviet Union, Poland, East Germany,

---

[40]Auburn, *Antarctic Law*, pp. 236 and 270.
[41]Auburn, *Antarctic Law*, p. 210; Scully, "Marine Living Resources," pp. 347–348.

West Germany, Taiwan, Chile, Norway, and South Africa, had actually begun to harvest krill. Since some fishing took place within two hundred miles of claimed land areas there were fears that disputes could arise that would make it impossible to obfuscate sovereignty issues. The members of the Antarctic Treaty system were also anxious to preempt efforts by other organizations to assert jurisdiction.[42]

Fifteen states signed The Convention on Marine Living Resources on August 1, 1980. The contracting parties are Argentina, Australia, Belgium, Chile, France, East Germany, West Germany, Japan, New Zealand, Norway, Poland, South Africa, the Soviet Union, the United Kingdom, and the United States. The explicit purpose of this convention is to forestall the wasteful development of resources by establishing targets for sustainable harvests. Unlike the Antarctic Treaty itself, the Marine Living Resources Convention established an international organization in the form of a concomitant commission. Each signatory of the convention has one vote on the commission. The commission must act on the basis of consensus. The convention also established a secretariat, which is charged with conducting required scientific investigations.[43]

The Convention on Marine Living Resources, like the other agreements in the Antarctic Treaty system, is weak and permissive, imposing few restrictions on signatories. The treatment of sovereignty is as opaque as in the Antarctic Treaty itself. The convention reaffirms the 1959 treaty's statement that nothing in the agreement should be taken to affect claims of sovereignty one way or the other. Publicity is the only enforcement mechanism. The commission is empowered to inform the contracting parties of action by a member which affects the goals of the convention. Conflicts can be settled by arbitration, but only if both parties agree. A state need only give ninety days notice to opt out of a decision it disagrees with even though decisions are taken by consensus.[44]

As in the Antarctic system, a critical objective of active states has been to create a decision-making arena that restricts membership. While the Marine Living Resources Convention was formally concluded outside the framework of the Antarctic Treaty, it was actually negotiated by the consultative parties to the treaty and presented as a *fait accompli*. Mem-

[42]Peterson, "Antarctica," p. 383; Shapley, "Antarctic Problems," p. 504–505; Auburn, *Antarctic Law*, p. 207.

[43]Stone, "International Agreements," p. 195; Auburn, *Antarctic Law*, pp. 211–213; Quigg, *A Pole Apart*, pp. 183–193.

[44]Auburn, *Antarctic Law*, pp. 220, 232; Quigg, *A Pole Apart*, p. 187; Luard, "Who Owns the Antarctic?" p. 1181.

bership in the commission is limited to the original consultative parties plus East Germany, and states that are actively engaged in the harvesting of, or research on, relevant marine living resources. As in the case of the treaty, states in the latter category which cease their activity are dropped from the commission. Both Poland and West Germany engaged in the level of scientific activity necessary to qualify as consultative parties to the Antarctic Treaty, in part because of their interest in krill. They wanted a guarantee that they would be involved in any relevant decisions. Because the convention is based upon a consensus voting arrangement, some states have been excluded that have met functional criteria. The Soviet Union has blocked the admission of South Korea and Taiwan even though both are engaged in krill harvesting.[45]

The consultative parties have also discussed rules for mineral development. This issue was consciously avoided when the Antarctic Treaty was being formulated because it bore so directly on the unresolved issue of territorial claims. It is highly unlikely that any exploitation will take place on the thick and shifting ice pack that covers the Antarctic continent itself. The most promising possibilities involve oil development on the continental shelf. The consultative parties began considering the question of mineral development in the early 1970s. No serious conversations took place until the late 1970s, however, and formal negotiations began only in 1982. It was recognized that agreement on a minerals regime was contingent on the successful conclusion of the negotiations dealing with marine living resources since minerals were bound to present more difficult problems. The consultative parties were also prompted by the possibility that more intensive surveying and new technologies might lead to a commercially exploitable discovery, and by apprehension that if they did not act the venue for decision making might move to the United Nations.[46]

Although the shape of any final agreement on Antarctic minerals is not yet clear, not least because claimants and nonclaimants continue to disagree about sovereignty, the consultative parties have reached consensus on several points. They have asserted that they will continue to play an active role, and that the integrity of the Antarctic Treaty will be maintained. They have agreed that claimant states will get a larger share of the wealth generated by mineral exploitation on territories they have claimed

[45]Auburn, *Antarctic Law*, pp. 153–154; 216–224; Quigg, *A Pole Apart*, pp. 189–190.

[46]Quigg, *A Pole Apart*, pp. 197–198; Reuters North European Service, Feb. 27, 1984; *The Financial Times*, Feb. 16, 1984, p. 6; *Metals Week*, Feb. 6, 1984, p. 7.

(although this hardly resolves questions of conflicting claims), and they have recognized that some revenue sharing with the world community or the Third World is inevitable.[47] In dealing with mineral resources, the consultative parties intend to act as they have acted in the past, maintaining a regime whose membership is severely restricted by the requirement that states demonstrate functional capacity before they are given an equal voice in determining the rules of the game for Antarctica.

THE THIRD WORLD AND ANTARCTICA

Given the point in time when it was created, it is not surprising that the Antarctic system did not reflect North-South issues. In the late 1950s a coherent, ideological orientation, based on dependency theory and emphasizing unequal exchange, was not widely disseminated. Although the developing countries had made protests against many specific aspects of international regimes, they had not formulated a coherent overall position that would have allowed them to make claims readily in new areas. Had the Antarctic issue developed a decade later, other principles, most notably the concept of the common heritage of mankind, would have been widely promoted. The analogy between the oceans and Antarctica would have been readily at hand. It is not likely that a small number of states could have monopolized decision-making power regardless of the principles they invoked.

Once the regime was in place, however, it became more difficult for the Third World to act. Unlike space, where regime creation was initially embedded in the United Nations, or oceans, where the old order was disintegrating, the regime for Antarctica has functioned effectively. Developing states were unable to place the issue before the United Nations until the fall of 1983. India attempted but failed to have it discussed by the General Assembly in the mid-1950s. In 1975 efforts were made to include Antarctica on the agenda of the United Nations Environmental Program. In the same year, Sri Lanka raised the issue in both the General Assembly and ECOSOC. In 1976 the Group of 77 proposed that a joint FAO/UNDP project concerned with fisheries in the Southern Hemisphere be administered by both developing and industrialized nations, and called for a new Antarctic Treaty to carry out this program. Libya and

[47]Quigg, *A Pole Apart*, pp. 194–198.

Algeria suggested in 1977 that Antarctica could be placed under the International Authority that would be created by the Law of the Sea Treaty.[48]

The consultative parties worked to prevent any of these initiatives from coming to fruition. The region was not discussed openly at the UNCLOS meetings because of the efforts of treaty-nation diplomats. One American official stated in 1977 that: "Off the record, Antarctica could blow the conference right out of the water. Antarctic claimant nations would rather not have a sea law treaty than one that impaired their sovereignty in Antarctica."[49] The consultative parties succeeded in removing Antarctic issues from the United Nations Environmental Program agenda, arguing that they constituted a special case. Efforts by the Food and Agriculture Organization to develop a food program involving krill were successfully resisted.[50]

This situation changed in the early 1980s. The Seventh Summit Meeting of the Non-Aligned Countries, held in New Delhi in March of 1983, called for a comprehensive United Nations study of Antarctica. Antigua and Barbuda, and Malaysia, introduced a resolution to this effect at the 1983 General Assembly. One of the arguments made by the representative from Antigua and Barbuda was that there "are now 157 nations which sit in the United Nations, and 14 [sic] of these nations can no longer expect, without accountability, to manage as they see fit an area of land that is one-tenth of the earth's surface."[51] The representative from Malaysia referred to the Antarctic regime as the "last vestigial reminder of the colonialist order" and suggested that the "Treaty and its system have become mired in the obsession to maintain a status quo regime advantageous to the privileged few."[52] Third World spokesmen also persistently argued that Antarctica should be treated as part of the common heritage of mankind. After negotiation between the consultative parties to the Antarctic Treaty and a number of Third World states, a compromise resolution was agreed on and adopted by consensus. This resolution called upon the secretary general to undertake a comprehensive study

[48]Taubenfeld, "A Treaty for Antarctica," p. 278; Quigg, *A Pole Apart*, pp. 167–168; Hanessian, "The Antarctic Treaty," pp. 449–452.

[49]Quoted in Shapley, "Antarctic Problems," pp. 504–505.

[50]Mitchell, "Antarctica," p. 65; Auburn, *Antarctic Law*, p. 126; Burton, "New Stresses," pp. 503–504.

[51]U.N. doc. no. A/C.1/38/PV.42, p. 6.

[52]Ibid., pp. 12, 16.

of Antarctica "taking fully into account the Antarctic Treaty system and other relevant factors" and seeking "the views of all Member States."[53]

There are two factors that can explain the timing of the Third World's attention to the Antarctic. First, there was growing interest in potential mineral and hydrocarbon development. At least ten of the consultative parties, including the United States, the Soviet Union, France, Britain, and Japan, had engaged in some geological surveying by 1983. No proven reserves had been discovered, however, and it was known that development costs for any offshore oil would be at least twice those incurred in Alaskan fields. Still, the activities of Northern states could only raise apprehension among developing countries, which lack both membership in the regime and the technical and economic resources to undertake any activities on their own.[54] Second, the conclusion of the United Nations Law of the Sea Conference cleared away a major impediment to discussion of Antarctica. Had this issue been raised earlier it might have been folded into the negotiations on the law of the sea. This would have complicated an already difficult set of problems. It would have threatened further tension within the Third World delegation because Chile and Argentina, which had sovereign claims in Antarctica, were adamantly opposed to having the region placed under the common heritage rubric.

If the analysis of this study is correct it is unlikely that the launching of a discussion of the Antarctic in the United Nations will lead to any substantial change in the regime. The Law of the Sea Convention has already demonstrated that the industrialized states are prepared to walk away from international agreements that do not conform with relational power capabilities; commitment to conference diplomacy has waned. There is as yet no break within the community of consultative parties. The only real element of uncertainty in this regard is India, which had pressed for a more open regime before it became a consultative party. India kept a low profile at the 1983 General Assembly debate, but its behavior could change. However, Chile and Argentina have remained steadfastly committed to the Antarctic Treaty. They have fought to keep Antarctic issues out of general membership forums. Their success in this endeavor during the 1970s, and the compromise resolution adopted by

[53]U.N. doc. no. A/C.1/38/PV.43, p. 18. The U.N. debate can be found in U.N. doc. no. A/C.1/38/PV.42 and 43. The statement of the Non-Aligned summit is reproduced in U.N. doc. no. A/48/495/S/16035. See also Peterson, "Antarctica."

[54]*Oil and Gas Journal*, Nov. 14, 1983, p. 24; *Washington Post*, Dec. 1, 1983, p. A33; Luard, "Who Owns the Antarctic?" p. 1182.

consensus at the 1983 General Assembly have thus far prevented an explicit split among developing countries. If the Third World aggressively pushed for a common heritage regime, Chile and Argentina would almost certainly break ranks. Because these two countries, and India and Brazil as well, have relational power capabilities in this issue area, they do not need a universal membership organization. In sum, the institutional commitments that have grown up since 1959, the participation of Argentina and Chile, the co-optation of Brazil and probably India, the weakening Northern acceptance of conference diplomacy, and the negative lessons of the Law of the Sea Conference make it unlikely that any initiative taken in the United Nations will substantially alter the regime for Antarctica.

CONCLUSION

The Antarctic system offers a striking contrast to the Law of the Sea negotiations. In the former, a limited number of states have been able to monopolize decision-making; in the latter, negotiations were conducted in a universal international forum. The members of the Antarctic Treaty system have explicitly recognized that they cannot reconcile their differences over the most basic issue of principle—whether or not national sovereignty can be exercised in the region. The countries engaged in the UNCLOS did agree to the principle that the deep seabed was part of the common heritage of mankind, even though they disagreed on the norms and rules that flowed from this principle. The consultative parties to the Antarctic Treaty have dealt with issues on a piecemeal basis. Agreements regarding flora and fauna, seals, and marine living resources have been negotiated since 1959. The last two were concluded outside of the formal framework of the treaty itself, thus making it easier to preserve the core membership. The UNCLOS incorporated an extremely wide range of issues, which were not necessarily organically linked. The rules for the deep seabed did not have to be tied to the question of exclusive economic zones for littoral states.

In the final stages of negotiation, North-South conflict emerged as the basic cleavage in the UNCLOS. In contrast, the Third World has not to date been able to insinuate itself into decision-making for Antarctica. The treaty members have been able to maintain their monopoly through the good fortune of having begun their regime in 1959, and by the political acumen associated with effectively opposing or weakening Third World demarches and expanding the scope of the treaty system to deal with new issue areas. Chile and Argentina have consistently fought against any substantial role for the United Nations; pressure for a common heritage regime would split the Third World.

Which regime or set of agreements—the Antarctic Treaty and related conventions or the Law of the Sea—offers a better guide for policy? The former is a logical shambles. There is no agreement on the basic question of sovereignty although scientific progress, environmental conservation, and demilitarization have provided some permissive norms that have guided the formulation of specific rules. Enforcement mechanisms are basically nonexistent. But the Antarctic Treaty system has worked. Major conflict among members has been avoided. The area has been demilitarized. Scientific investigations have continued. Commercial development of krill has begun.

The treaty system could easily fall apart. It is very weak. Nonsignatories can simply ignore any of its provisions. But if it did collapse it would not bring in its train any major shocks. The Antarctic Treaty conventions have never moved very far from the underlying power capabilities that sustain them.

The Law of the Sea offers fundamental contrasts. There was little relationship between underlying power capabilities and formal participation in the UNCLOS, although in informal working groups that was less true. The most important consequence of the negotiations was the legitimation of the extension of sovereignty of littoral states over vast areas of the seabed, a conclusion that is congruent with the fundamental NIEO objective of moving from market-oriented to authoritative allocation.

In the final analysis, the UNCLOS accord failed to secure the support of a number of major states. The United States, Britain, and West Germany opposed the treaty outright. Some that signed the convention may not ratify. This is likely to create serious problems for the commercial exploitation of deep-seabed nodules. The area is in legal limbo. The Law of the Sea treaty may evolve over time into an effective international regime. Corporations may engage in activity sanctioned by the Authority, even if they are based in the United States. But stability is not likely. There is too much incongruence between underlying power capabilities and decision-making within the regime. If vital interests were at stake, major countries would simply ignore the dictates of the Authority. Alternatively, the Reciprocating States Agreement, negotiated among several industrialized countries, could become the basis of a future regime for seabed mining. But its prospects would be clouded by the rival norms and rules embodied in the U.N. Law of the Sea Convention.

From the perspective of he United States, it is the Antarctic system, not the Law of the Sea, which should offer a model for the future. Efforts to create and maintain rules of the game should be restricted to states that have the power to disrupt agreements that might be concluded. There are fundamental disagreements about general principles and norms between the industrialized and the developing countries. These disagreements reflect international power disparities that cannot be overcome. Such deep-seated antagonisms preclude the formulation of coherent and durable regimes except in specific areas where there are tangible shared interests. Efforts to create universal-membership regimes are likely to lead to recriminations and distrust. Even if such agreements are, fortuitously, concluded, they are likely to disintegrate under the pressure of changing circumstances, given the absence of agreement on principles and norms, and the substantial disparities of interest among various states. Mutually desired patterns of behavior are more likely to emerge from arrangements focused on specific problems and rules rather than on general principles. Such arrangements may even generate shared principles and norms over time. When principles and norms are accepted in the first instance, it is possible to work from the top down. When they are not, it is better to work from the bottom up. This is not a comforting strategy for those pursuing major breakthroughs in North-South relations, but it is an approach that recognizes that most international behavior is driven by short-term calculations of interest and by the power that can be brought to bear to accomplish such objectives.

Part Three

Conclusions

X

Proscriptions, Prescriptions, Predictions, and Analytic Conclusions

INTRODUCTION

The conflict between the North and the South, the powerful and the weak, has become one of the defining characteristics of the present international system. The establishment of more than seventy-five states with limited material resources since the conclusion of the Second World War has led to tensions between the material power capabilities of individual actors and major international regimes. The most important regimes governing international economic transactions are infused with liberal, market-oriented principles whose consequences can exacerbate the political vulnerabilities of many countries of the South. The basic objective of the New International Economic Order program has been to establish new rules of the game that would legitimate authoritative allocation by states acting directly to distribute goods, or indirectly to limit the right to alienate private property. This can be accomplished either by legitimating national regulation or by creating or transforming international institutions. This agenda is not rooted in transitory ideological preferences, irrational hatred of former colonial masters, economic ignorance, or miscalculation of the material consequences of existing or proposed regimes. Rather, it reflects enduring political realities grounded in the international and domestic weaknesses of almost all Third World countries. Any Northern effort to develop a coherent policy response to the South as a group, or to specific developing countries, must take cognizance of this basic structural characteristic of the contemporary international system.

This analysis *proscribes* two types of policy: conference diplomacy, and attempts to change a state's treatment of its own subjects. Conference diplomacy, involving a multiplicity of issues and universal state participation, is bound to end in frustration. The basic principles advocated by the North and the South are fundamentally in conflict, and support for these principles reflects the extremely skewed distribution of national material power capabilities in the international system, which will not change in the foreseeable future, if ever.

The arguments presented here also imply that efforts to promote policies that infringe on the accepted sovereign powers of developing states with regard to income distribution or the rights of individuals (and in other areas as well) will be politically barren. The recognition of sovereignty, of the right of the state to exercise the sole legitimate authority within a defined geographical area, is of critical importance for the Third World. The scope of sovereignty can be challenged, however. Because of their lack of national power capabilities, Third World states are bound to resist such challenges. They are dependent on the transnational recognition of juridical sovereignty to provide a defense against foreign encroachments and internal dismemberment.[1] The South will be unenthusiastic about Northern efforts to change international norms in areas like population control, human rights, and basic human needs, which are associated with the way in which states deal with their own subjects, even if acceptance of Northern initiatives would bring additional material resources.

The arguments made in this book *prescribe* three kinds of policies for the North. First, there are many specific deals that can be struck on a bilateral or limited multilateral basis within the existing rules of the game. This is especially true for the NICs and some raw-material exporters. Second, there are specific functional international regimes, which can be supported, because authoritative allocation is already the governing principle. Civil aviation and, more ambivalently, official resource transfers, have already been examined in some detail. But there are several others, including migration, nuclear nonproliferation, and security in general, where authoritative state allocation is the accepted norm. Third, there may be some issue areas in which the North could benefit from movement away from a market-oriented regime. The defining analytic characteristic of such issue areas is that a group of less developed countries can inflict costs on the industrialized world. New international regimes based on authoritative allocation could benefit the North and the South. Trade and investment in some raw materials offers one example.

In most issue areas, however, the prospects for regime maintenance

---

[1]Jackson and Rosberg, "Why Africa's Weak States Persist."

and cooperation are not bright. Difficulties between the North and South will not disappear even if they become more muted. Developing and industrialized countries are more likely to be able to agree on specific rules than on general principles. The best existing model for future cooperation is the international regime for Antarctica, a regime whose members have explicitly chosen to suspend disagreement on fundamental principle (sovereignty over Antarctic territory); that is limited to countries with a direct ability to disrupt arrangements; that includes developing, industrialized, and Communist states; and that has grown incrementally in response to changing technological capabilities and knowledge.

The basic *prediction* of this study is that, given the skewed distribution of power that characterizes the present international system, tension and conflict will dominate North-South relations, even though many mutually advantageous deals may be struck. There are, however, three developments that could mitigate this tension. First, some developing countries may generate the national power capabilities needed to cope effectively with the existing international system. That is more likely to occur as a result of increasing domestic competence than as a result of growing international strength. More LDCs may generate domestic institutional structures that will allow them to adjust to pressures emanating from the international system. It is this capacity to adjust, not just rapid economic growth, that distinguishes the Southeast Asian NICs and explains their relative indifference to NIEO demands. There are also a small number of developing countries which, just because of their size, have the capacity to cope with the international environment. China, although not usually seen as part of the Third World, is the most obvious example.

Second, tension between the North and the South may decline because convention diplomacy will atrophy. The United Nations system has been critical for the South because it has provided developing countries with a forum that has guaranteed some attention from the North. This level of attention is, however, likely to wane. And as it wanes, the United Nations and those ancillary institutions which have been established in response to Southern demands, such as UNCTAD and UNIDO, will decline in importance. If major industrialized states do not pay attention to what happens at the United Nations, or do not fund its activities, the South will have a program without an audience. Given the extreme incongruity between national power capabilities and organizations in which each state has an equal vote, the North will increasingly treat such institutions with indifference. Without a forum for presenting NIEO demands, tensions between the North and the South may abate. This is not because the basis for the demands will disappear, but because they cannot be effectively voiced.

Finally, there is a more utopian prospect, which is unambiguously the most attractive from a realist perspective—the disengagement of the North and the South. Given fundamental disagreements over principles and norms, many interactions between the North and the South will be laden with tension and uncertainty, even if they provide mutual economic benefit. Commitments to principles and norms will not change, because they are grounded in unalterable (at least for the foreseeable future) disparities in national power capabilities. Tensions could be lessened, however, if the degree of interaction between the North and the South declined. Although there are some modest contemporary trends in this direction, they are not large enough to lead to any widespread delinking between the First and Third worlds.

This study concludes with a review of the evidence in support of realist or structural, as opposed to economistic, interpretations. Most of the empirical data are consistent with either interpretation. The behavior of developing states can be seen as a function of economic concerns, which include demands for more participation in existing liberal international regimes, or as a response to structural weakness, which leads to demands for more authoritative regimes that would enhance both wealth and control. There are few cases in which LDCs have sacrificed power for wealth, or wealth for power. The problem of arriving at a firm "scientific" decision about the merits of economistic and realist approaches is compounded by theory laden observation: underlying each approach is a different conception of the world. Many economistic arguments focus on the behavior of individuals and groups. From this orientation, the investigation of the beliefs and attitudes of discrete policymakers is a fruitful research endeavor. Realist interpretations focus on the behavior of states as collectivities. From this orientation, the beliefs and attitudes of individual decision-makers are less revealing than final policy output. Although the phenomena examined under economistic and realist approaches are not composed of mutually exclusive sets, the overlap is limited. Different basic theoretical orientations imply not only different independent variables but also different dependent ones. Although the failure to oppose OPEC, the intellectual coherence of the Third World's program, some specific instances in which wealth has been sacrificed for control, and the reluctance to recognize the benefits of the existing liberal regime all weigh in favor of a realist interpretation, it would be disingenuous to suggest that conclusive evidence has been presented, or even that a definitive test of economistic and realist interpretations is possible.

PROSCRIPTIONS

CONFERENCE DIPLOMACY AND THE NORTH-SOUTH DIALOGUE

In July of 1983, UNCTAD-VI ended a month-long session which disappointed all the major participants. The industrialized nations refused new aid commitments of almost $90 billion, which had been proposed by the developing countries. The United States disassociated itself from the final statement of the conference. The spokesman for the Group of 77 said that the meeting had achieved "meager results."[2] UNCTAD-VI, which took place nearly a decade after the South's call for a New International Economic Order, was one of a long series of frustrating multifunctional exchanges. Various United Nations sessions have produced "meager results." The 1981 North-South Summit at Cancun accomplished nothing. Even when some agreement has been reached, as was the case with the Common Fund for Commodities or the UNCTAD Liner Code, implementation has been slow and the final outcome problematic. The Law of the Sea Conference failed to produce a document that could be endorsed by all major actors. One observer concluded that the "North-South dialogue is virtually moribund."[3]

The analysis presented here suggests that these failures are not the result of transitory factors. It is not the narrow-mindedness of the North or the rhetorical flights of fancy of the South that have led to a breakdown of the dialogue. There are fundamental differences between the international regime preferences of the North and the South which are a product of underlying disparities in national power capabilities. These preferences will not change, even if the economic performance of the South improves.

The basic theme of arguments that have been presented to support the continuation of the North-South dialogue is that interests vital to the

[2] Quoted in the *Wall Street Journal*, July 5, 1983, p. 25.
[3] Rothstein, *The Third World and U.S. Foreign Policy*, p. 19.

North are linked with the resolution of issues raised in the NIEO. A wide range of specific points has been made. Because of increasing economic links, prosperity in the North depends on prosperity in the South. Developing countries provide vital raw materials. Population growth in poorer areas and the consequent demand for food have global inflationary effects. Starvation and poverty spawn political unrest that will inevitably spill over into richer areas. Failure to reach international agreement will turn developing countries toward the Soviet Union. Progress in specific functional areas, where both sides acknowledge possibilities for mutual benefit, will be difficult without some progress in the North-South dialogue.[4]

Leaving aside the merits of these specific points, Northern policymakers are unlikely to be convinced, because the alleged benefits of accepting Southern demands are long term and uncertain, while the costs are immediate and tangible. Theoretically and empirically it has been difficult to establish any systematic link between economic development, political unrest, and foreign-policy behavior. Rapid growth may be politically destabilizing.[5] Economic stagnation may lead to political passivity rather than to activism. Progress in specific functional issue areas is more likely to be driven by immediate interests and bargaining power than by the level of cooperation achieved in the North-South dialogue. The 1970s provided some examples of the creation of new functional arrangements, the maintenance of existing regimes based on authoritative allocation, and the growth of North-South trade in relative and absolute terms, despite the high level of conflict and minimal specific accomplishments of convention diplomacy. It is thus difficult to establish clear links between the tangible political and economic interests of the North and progress on NIEO demands. Without such links Northern policymakers are unlikely to be persuaded by arguments emphasizing the overall interdependence of the North and the South.

Furthermore, convention diplomacy has costs. The South was able to present its case so forcefully because of the access provided by existing international organizations. These multifunctional, universal-membership, equal-voting institutions, of which the United Nations General Assembly is the exemplar, generate conflict rather than cooperation. The South can formulate alternatives to liberal principles and norms, set

[4]The first Brandt Commission report offers the most salient exposition of many of these arguments.

[5]Olson, "Growth as Destabilizing."

agendas, develop political coalitions, and establish linkages across issue areas; but these institutions cannot give the Third World the material resources that are needed to implement the NIEO program. The existence of the United Nations system thus invites the South to make demands that cannot be fulfilled without the acquiescence of the North. That acquiescence is not likely to be forthcoming. This is a situation that contributes to instability rather than to stability. Rather than helping to resolve specific functional or bilateral problems, it can exacerbate them.

ENCROACHMENTS ON EXISTING
SOVEREIGN-SUBJECT RELATIONS

A second policy conclusion that emerges from this analysis is that Northern efforts to influence domestic policies in developing countries by generating new international principles and norms will be resisted and will not lead to an international consensus. This remains the case even when LDCs could secure more resources by acceding to the preferences of the North. For developing countries, international norms related to meeting basic human needs or controlling population may not only threaten traditional values and disrupt existing political patterns, they also infringe on accepted juridical sovereign prerogatives. If these prerogatives were eroded, many developing states would find themselves even more exposed to external and internal pressures.

Foreign policies have domestic consequences. Defense pacts, trade agreements, IMF standbys, exchange rates, monetary aggregates, weapons procurement, or armament exports can all affect the level and distribution of domestic resources. When one state pressures another to change such policies, it is tampering with domestic, not just international, transactions. Such classic foreign policy instruments, however, should be distinguished from Northern attempts to promote the political and economic well-being of individuals in the South, especially when they attempt to do so by creating new international regimes. Efforts such as meeting basic human needs or controlling population and promoting political rights do not have proximate direct or tangible foreign policy consequences. Prevailing international norms and rules treat these issues as being within the purview of each state's sovereign prerogatives.

Enhancing the political and economic well-being of individual human beings in the South is an attractive policy for humanitarian reasons. From theoretical perspectives that identify political development and democracy with economic prosperity, such a policy also appears to promote America's long-term milieu goals. But, for political leaders in developing countries, Northern policies aimed directly, not incidentally, at their domestic affairs are a threat to the integrity of the state and the stability of the political order, not only because they are intrusive but also because they challenge existing sovereign prerogatives.

Experience in the area of population control offers an example of Southern resistance to Northern initiatives aimed directly at individual citizens. Despite diplomatic and financial initiatives from the North, especially the United States, no international consensus, no agreement on principles or norms, has emerged for population problems narrowly defined. The Third World has insisted that population issues must be placed within a context that is concerned with social and economic development broadly conceived. Even Third World countries with active population control programs have rejected efforts to promulgate new transnational values. Developing countries have, at times, turned down offers of financial assistance and have resisted attempts to place specific population-control issues on the agendas of international organizations.

Northern countries have led the effort to make population growth an international issue. Early initiatives came from Sweden and Denmark. In the United States the Rockefeller and Ford Foundations became active in the 1950s. The Johnson administration firmly embraced population control. The United Nations Fund for Population Activities was created in the mid-1960s largely because of American support; the United States has been the major source of funds for international population-control activities.[6]

American policymakers and private elites had a variety of rationales for supporting population control in the Third World. Endemic malnutrition and episodic famines were dramatic reminders of the humanitarian consequences of existing conditions. Rapid population increases were seen as a fundamental impediment to economic development and thus were associated with the general American rationale for economic assistance to the Third World, which linked economic development to political development, political development to democracy, and democratic regimes to an international system compatible with American interests and values.[7] In 1980 the State Department coordinator of population

---

[6]Marden et al., *Population in the Global Arena*, pp. 39–48; Crane and Finkle, "Organizational Impediments to Development Assistance," p. 542.

[7]Packenham, *Liberal America and the Third World*.

affairs argued that rapid population increases led to a demographic distribution skewed toward younger cohorts and that "Recent experiences, in Iran and other countries, show that this younger age group, frequently unemployed and crowded into urban slums, is particularly susceptible to extremism, terrorism, and violence as outlets for frustration. On balance these factors add up to an increasing potential for social unrest, economic and political instability, mass migration, and possible international conflicts over control of land and resources." He went on to state that the basic objective of the United States "is a strong and sustained international consensus which can support, and influence, national leaders in their approach to population issues." The United States was supported by most other industrialized countries. As president of the World Bank, Robert McNamara made the issue an important component of his agenda.[8]

The Third World's reaction to these initiatives at the international level, which first surfaced at the 1974 World Population Conference in Bucharest, has been negative. This Conference was seen by the North as the culmination of nearly a decade of effort to make population a major international issue. Resolutions had been passed in a number of United Nations agencies. Extensive consultation had taken place at the national level. Several major Asian countries, including India, had supported population-control objectives. But Bucharest, attended by representatives from 137 countries, was a disappointment for its supporters. The Third World turned the meeting into a discussion of the New International Economic Order. Population issues were subordinated to more general goals. The Draft Plan which had been prepared by members of the United Nations Secretariat was thrown out. The final resolution contained explicit endorsements of national sovereignty and did not prescribe any specific population policy.[9] The executive director of the U.N. Fund for Population Activities stated that "At Bucharest it became clear that opposition to what was regarded as Western thinking on population was much deeper-rooted than had been thought."[10]

After 1974, developing countries continued to resist attempts to develop an international consensus on population control that was not incorporated into a broader conception of development. Population was not on the agenda of the Seventh Special Session of the U.N. General

[8]U.S. State Department, *Current Policy*, no. 171 for quote. For a statement from McNamara after he left the bank see his article, "The Population Problem."

[9]Finkle and Crane, "The Politics of Bucharest."

[10]Salas, *International Population Assistance*, p. 317.

Assembly held in 1975. A 1976 resolution, which endorsed a set of principles for the allocation of resources by the United Nations Fund for Population Activities favoring national decision-making, was one of the few actions on population taken by the General Assembly.[11] Aside from the one at Bucharest, the only other global international meeting on population during the 1970s involving political actors was a gathering of parliamentarians held at Colombo in Sri Lanka in 1979. It was attended by representatives from only fifty-eight countries and the declaration adopted at the conclusion of the meeting strongly endorsed linking population and development programs. The United Nations International Conference on Population held in Mexico City in 1984 reaffirmed the Plan of Action adopted at Bucharest. The final declaration of the conference stated that "Growing international disparities have further exacerbated already serious problems in social and economic terms" before going on to note that "population growth, high mortality and morbidity, and migration problems continue to be causes of great concern requiring immediate action."[12] World Bank field representatives did not press population programs, despite McNamara's concern, because the finance and planning ministries, on whom bank officials depended for formulating and implementing projects, were not interested.[13] Although the United Nations Fund for Population Activities grew in size, and ECOSOC continued to have a Population Committee, no major institutional initiatives, like the formation of UNCTAD or UNIDO, were carried out.

Third World reaction to Northern attempts to develop an international consensus on population control cannot be explained by some narrow economic considerations. During the 1970s the money available for population planning from international agencies exceeded the demand from developing countries. In the late 1970s Mexico turned down a World Bank loan that stipulated that some of the funds were to be used for birth control. More significantly, even countries with ambitious population planning programs, such as India, have rejected the North's position at international conferences. The South has maintained its unity despite major differences among individual countries, even in an issue area where the North has offered additional resources.[14]

---

[11]U.N. General Assembly Res. 31/170.

[12]The Colombo Declaration is reprinted in *Population and Development Review* 5, 4, December 1979, pp. 730–735. The Mexico City declaration can be found in the *New York Times*, Aug. 16, 1984, p. 8.

[13]Crane and Finkle, "Organizational Impediments to Development Assistance," p. 527.

[14]Crane and Finkle, "Organizational Impediments to Development Assistance," p. 540;

Spokesmen for developing countries have argued against narrowly defined international population policies for a variety of reasons. Some Third World countries, Argentina being the most notable example, see themselves as underpopulated. The general reaction from Third World officials has been that development questions must not be subordinated to population issues. Population cannot be treated in isolation. Demographic trends are determined by more general considerations. Northern efforts to link aid and population planning have been particularly resented. Intellectuals influenced by Marxist traditions also reject antinatalist arguments, which are seen as part of a Malthusian heritage that ignores the importance of capitalist institutions in the generation of poverty and exploitation. The ambiguous empirical relationship between population growth and per capita income growth, and between population growth and explicit policies, has provided support for LDC rejection of the North's agenda.[15]

An explicit theme of many Third World arguments, and one that explains why even developing countries with ambitious domestic programs have rejected efforts to generate international principles and norms in the population area, is that such norms would encroach on state sovereignty. Population control involves changing the behavior of individuals. Some governments support such programs; others reject them; many are indifferent. But LDCs, which rely heavily on de jure sovereign powers, do not want these prerogatives to be constrained by new international antinatalist norms and principles.

There is another characteristic of Northern population efforts that is inherently threatening to weak and vulnerable states. In the case of population control, the North is not making the standard offer associated with most foreign aid—economic resources for political compliance. Population control is rationalized in the North as a long-term contribution to domestic and international political stability. The state in the South is only a conduit for funds. It does not have to alter its foreign policy. This logic is in tension with existing norms associated with the principle of sovereignty, which proscribe interference in the domestic affairs of other states. Southern resistance to Northern efforts to develop

---

New York Times, June 10, 1980, D1:3; Marden et al., *Population in the Global Arena*, p. 98; Finkle and Crane, "The Politics of Bucharest," p. 105.

[15]Marden, et al., *Population in the Global Arena*, pp. 94, 96; McCoy, "Linkage Politics and Latin American Population Policies," pp. 85–86; Stycos, "Politics and Population Control in Latin America," passim.

international population norms is not simply a product of specific national values, or evidence of a concern that antinatalism may be a ploy for subordinating development aid, but is also a reflection of the deep adherence of Third World states to the prerogatives of sovereignty.

This conclusion is not meant to imply that individual Third World countries will necessarily reject family planning or population control programs. Some developing countries were pioneers in this area. By 1980 some thirty-five LDCs had programs aimed at reducing population growth, and another thirty-one had expressed official support for family planning.[16] After the Bucharest Conference, two American observers concluded that the "developing nations will not turn away from their demographic dilemmas merely to spite the West. They are more likely to follow the example of China, India, Mexico and Egypt in pursuing the cause of a new economic order in the international system—while simultaneously carrying out population policies as part of their development plans at home."[17]

Population control is one of several areas in which Northern policies threaten the recognized powers of national states. Basic human needs offers a second example. During the 1970s, the basic human needs approach was supported by a number of political leaders in the North, who saw such programs making an important contribution to milieu goals by eliminating the abject poverty that they associated with political instability. Their initiatives have not been welcomed by the South, however, even though the Bariloche Foundation of Argentina made an important contribution to the early formulation of this approach.[18] Manuel Perez Guerrero, secretary general of UNCTAD in the late 1970s, wrote in 1983 that "it was obvious that the new approach [basic needs] was conducive—perhaps intentionally—to distracting attention from the objective of restructuring international economic relations through changing the rules of the game. It was also obvious that the resources that would be required for making an impact on the problem of basic needs would not be forthcoming from the financial assistance of the industrialized countries. Help could only result in time from the basic changes inherent in the task of restructuring."[19]

Human rights are a third area in which Northern efforts to create new

[16]Marden et al., *Population in the Global Arena*, p. 79.
[17]Finkle and Crane, "The Politics of Bucharest," p. 109.
[18]Hart, *The New International Economic Order*, p. 13.
[19]From Guerrero's "Foreword" in Hart, *The New International Economic Order*, p. xi.

international norms that would alter the state's sovereign prerogatives with regard to its own subjects have been resisted by the South. Third World policymakers have not frontally challenged the notion of human rights. Rather, they have sought to alter Northern conceptions by focusing on economic and social rather than political and civil rights, and by emphasizing the collective rights of peoples rather than the inalienable rights of individuals.

The human rights issue has been addressed in a number of major United Nations actions. The U.N. Charter endorses human rights, an action reaffirmed by the Universal Declaration of Human Rights of 1948. In 1968, after extensive debate and conference diplomacy, the General Assembly approved two documents—the International Covenant on Economic, Social, and Cultural Rights, and the International Covenant on Civil and Political Rights. As of July 1982, seventy-three states had ratified the former, and seventy states had ratified the latter.[20] In 1977 the General Assembly passed a resolution, sponsored by the Third World, which held that it was impossible to have civil and political rights without first providing for economic, social, and cultural rights. One commentator has argued that during the first twenty years of United Nations activities, social and economic rights were virtually ignored, whereas during the subsequent period civil and political rights have been ignored.[21]

The sovereign prerogatives of states, not financial resources, have been directly at stake in this debate. Historically, sovereignty has not been synonymous with absolute power.[22] The claims of the state have been to some extent legitimated or delegitimated by the international community. De jure sovereign prerogatives are particularly important to most states in the Third World because of their relative lack of other kinds of capabilities. The conception of human rights, pressed especially by the United States since World War II, would limit the juridical prerogatives of the state. The United States has tried to universalize American practices, which are grounded in Lockean conceptions of society based on atomistic individuals possessing inalienable political and civil liberties.[23] It can be inferred from such a conception that an individual could make

[20]U.N. doc. no. ST/HR/4/Rev. 4, p. 18.
[21]Donnelly, "Recent Trends in U.N. Human Rights Activity."
[22]Delbrueck, "International Protection of Human Rights," pp. 569–573.
[23]Zvobgo, "A Third World View," p. 93; Delbrueck, "International Protection of Human Rights," p. 573.

claims against the state that could not be easily accommodated to either the practice or theory of most political regimes in the Third World.

Policymakers and intellectuals from the Third World have maintained that Western conceptions of human rights are culture-bound. They have suggested that Third World cultural traditions emphasize the group rather than the individual. Human rights are only conferred through membership in a larger social community. Furthermore, political and civil rights cannot be severed from economic and social rights, as the Lockean conception suggests. Without economic progress, Third World leaders have argued, political and civil rights are meaningless.[24] While one Western commentator has stated that economic rights are "'incoherent' assertions of human rights . . . [because] . . . they may involve redistribution of privately held resources,"[25] Third World spokesmen have argued that the implementation of the New International Economic Order is central to the attainment of human rights.[26]

Because of the Third World's voting majority in the United Nations, there has been a general movement away from Western approaches. The Lockean values embodied in early global declarations have not been rejected by the South for any specific economic reasons. On the contrary, endorsement of Western values might have created an atmosphere in which advanced market-economy countries took a more forthcoming attitude toward economic transfers. As in the case of population control and basic human needs, developing states have resisted Northern efforts related to political and civil rights because new international norms would undermine the accepted juridical prerogatives of the state.

In sum, an analysis of North-South relations that begins with the weakness and vulnerability of developing states implies that conference diplomacy will be ineffective. Efforts to create new international norms and principles concerning the relationship of states to their own subjects will be rejected by the Third World when they encroach upon the recognized prerogatives of sovereignty. Both should be avoided by the North.

PRESCRIPTIONS

An argument that understands the distribution of national power capabilities to be the basic determinant of the foreign policy behavior of

[24]See discussion in Donnelly, "Recent Trends in U.N. Human Rights Activity," p. 649; and Zvobgo, "A Third World View," passim.

[25]D'Amato, "The Concept of Human Rights Activity," p. 1129.

[26]Donnelly, "Recent Trends in U.N. Human Rights Activity," p. 650, n. 35.

individual states does not preclude a wide range of cooperative exchanges between the North and the South. Three types of activity can be specified. First, there are many specific deals that can be struck between the North and the South. Second, there are already issue areas in which authoritative allocation of resources is legitimated by international regimes. Such regimes are not necessarily free of conflict since distributional questions may be unresolved, but developing and industrialized countries do share the same principles and norms. Third, new regimes may be created, but only if they mitigate the vulnerability of the South by legitimating authoritative rather than market-oriented principles.

SPECIFIC TRANSACTIONS

Nothing in this analysis suggests that the many specific transactions, especially economic exchanges, that go on between the North and the South will necessarily decline. The period of the Third World's most vigorous protests against the existing international economic order coincided with a substantial increase in international trade between rich and poor countries. The value of exports from developing to industrialized areas (excluding the Eastern Bloc) increased from $31.4 billion in 1968, to $79.5 billion in 1973, to $251.1 billion in 1978, to $363.3 billion in 1981. These totals include amounts contributed by Third World states that were not traditional oil exporters: $20.5 billion in 1968, $47.1 billion in 1973, $104.0 billion in 1978, and $160.2 billion in 1981.[27] Table 10.1 shows the relative importance of trade with developing areas for the industrialized North.

There was also a dramatic increase in the flow of capital from industrialized to developing areas during the 1970s, particularly from private banks. Through the 1960s, private-bank dealings with Third World states were modest. In 1971 bank loans accounted for 12 percent of all disbursed debt held by LDCs. By 1981 this figure had increased to 33.5 percent. In absolute terms, disbursed bank loans to developing countries amounted to $11 billion in 1971 and $180 billion in 1981. This increase occurred in an environment of considerable uncertainty and high levels of Southern criticism of existing international regimes.[28]

Direct foreign investment from developed to developing areas also increased during the 1970s in absolute terms. The value of direct invest-

[27]Derived from figures in GATT, *International Trade*, 1981/1982, table A25.
[28]Derived from figures in OECD, *External Debt of Developing Countries, 1982 Survey*.

TABLE 10.1

TRADE (EXPORTS PLUS IMPORTS) WITH DEVELOPING AREAS
AS A PERCENTAGE OF TOTAL TRADE
FOR SELECTED INDUSTRIALIZED AREAS

	1968	1973	1978	1981
North America*	23.3	24.7	33.8	36.2
Japan	38.7	40.0	49.1	51.1
Western Europe**	15.6	13.9	17.7	20.0
All industrialized areas	19.5	18.8	24.5	27.6

Source: Derived from figures in GATT, *International Trade,* 1981/1982 (Geneva, 1982),
table A25.

*Includes intra-North American trade.

**Includes intra-Western European trade.

ment in developing countries from the United States rose from $21.0
billion in 1971 to $29.1 billion in 1976, from the United Kingdom from
£1.9 billion to £2.7 billion, from Germany from DM 6.7 billion to DM
14.2 billion, and from Japan from $1.8 billion to $8.1 billion. Investment
in LDCs as a percentage of total foreign direct investment fell, however,
from 25 to 21 percent for the United States and from 28 to 24 percent
for the United Kingdom. It rose from 28 to 32 percent for Germany and
from 49 to 51 percent for Japan. The areas of most active growth
were manufacturers and services; investments in mining and petroleum
declined or stagnated.[29]

This review is not meant to imply that North-South transactions will
continue to grow across all issue areas. Auction markets for standardized
products, which require no long-term commitments and where each
transaction is independent of any other, can function effectively without
international regimes. But customer markets—which involve long-term
commitments—can only work effectively when there are institutional
arrangements that provide confidence, predictability, and continuity.[30]
Without a stable institutional environment it is difficult to conclude
specific agreements in customer markets.[31] The more time that must be

[29]Derived from figures in OECD, *International Investment: Recent Trends*, table 10.

[30]Diaz-Alejandro, "Delinking North and South," p. 114.

[31]See Keohane, "The Demand for International Regimes," for a discussion of the distinction between specific agreements and regimes.

bridged before an exchange is concluded, the higher the level of uncertainty. Actors will be reluctant to enter into long-term engagements when the rules of the game are not well established. Without stable international regimes, specific agreements will be altered unilaterally as the interests and bargaining power of the actors change. *Ceteris paribus*, the longer a contract is in effect in an international environment where behavior is not conditioned by accepted principles, norms, rules, and decision-making procedures, the more likely it is that the contract will be arbitrarily rewritten. Confronted with such prospects, actors, particularly private corporations, will be reluctant to involve themselves in long-term transactions, especially with states.

As agreement on international regimes governing North-South transactions decayed, a differential impact across issue areas began to emerge by the early 1980s.[32] International trade, where the time needed to conclude an exchange is relatively short and where auction markets are important, was not much affected by the erosion of the rules of the game. Although the global recession of the early 1980s had a negative impact on the absolute value of world trade, exports from developing areas as a percentage of total world exports rose from 18.4 percent in 1968, to 19.1 percent in 1973, to 23.4 percent in 1978, to 27.4 percent in 1981.[33] Much of this increase was, however, accounted for by traditional oil-exporting states.

In the area of bank lending, developments in the early 1980s were not so sanguine. Financial intermediaries bridge time and space. During the 1970s private banks recycled petrodollars by accepting short-term deposits from oil-exporting states and extending medium- and long-term loans to developing countries. Banks became increasingly exposed not only to unforeseen economic changes but also to unilateral action by borrowing countries. Some borrowing countries discussed the possibility of a debtors' cartel.[34] Some loans were rescheduled by debtors without consulting lenders. Smaller debtors could set off a chain reaction by declaring de jure default. As economic difficulties beyond the control of the immediate actors increased in the early 1980s, the private banks moved to decrease their exposure by shortening and altering credit terms. The ratio of short-term bank credits to medium- and long-term credits (excluding guaranteed export credits) to non-OPEC developing countries

[32]For a discussion of decay, see Haas, "Words Can Hurt You," p. 193.
[33]Derived from figures in GATT, *International Trade*, 1981/1982, table A25.
[34]*Wall Street Journal*, March 22, 1983, 33:1.

increased from 0.53 in 1977 to 0.74 in 1982. Floating, as opposed to fixed-interest, debt as a percentage of total net non-OPEC LDC debt increased from 23 percent in 1978 to 41 percent in 1982.[35] Banks also reduced the absolute level of their lending. Between 1981 and the middle of 1983 bank lending as a proportion of total lending to LDCs fell from 60 to 30 percent. Smaller countries, in particular, were having difficulty securing new funding.[36] The absence of agreed-upon principles, norms, rules, and decision-making procedures exacerbated the already high risks created by changing economic conditions. Even with improved conditions, private banks will move with much more caution.

The consequences of unstable regime structures for economic behavior are most clearly illustrated in the area of direct foreign investment for raw materials. The exploitation of natural resources involves large, non-fungible capital commitments. New projects often take several years to develop. Physical assets are subject to the jurisdiction of host countries. Private corporations are unlikely to undertake such enterprises without some guarantee that the rules of the game will remain stable. During the 1960s and 1970s, however, developing countries dramatically altered principles, norms, rules, and decision-making procedures for major mineral developments. The regime of concessions, in which private corporations were given long-term control over vast areas, was unilaterally changed. Corporations could continue to bear the risk of exploitation and development but they could no longer be sure that they would reap any ensuing benefits.

Multinationals engaged in exploitation of raw materials responded by trying to decrease their exposure. They moved toward management contracts and away from equity holdings. They raised capital for new projects by borrowing rather than committing corporate funds. They sought to involve financial institutions and customers in third countries to enhance their transnational alliances.[37] Manufacturing companies with more rapidly changing product lines, more dynamic technology, and less financial exposure were not as attractive as targets for nationalization. Between 1973 and 1976 the proportion of the stock of American direct investment in extractive industries in developing countries fell from 36.4 percent to 17.9 percent, and in absolute terms dropped from $8.3 billion to $5.2

[35]OECD, *External Debt of Developing Countries, 1982 Survey*, tables 18 and 8.

[36]*Wall Street Journal*, July 13, 1983, 1:6.

[37]Moran, "Transnational Strategies of Protection"; Leff, "Multinationals in a Hostile World," pp. 26–29.

billion. During the same time period the stock of investment in the manufacturing sector rose from $7.8 billion to $11.3 billion, and in services from $6.7 billion to $12.5 billion.[38]

It is not simply that the form of corporate activity in Third World extractive industries has changed, however. The amount of exploration and development activity in developing areas is lower than it would have been in a more secure environment. By the late 1970s industrialized countries—primarily the United States, Canada, Australia, and South Africa—were the targets of most new activities even though they had already been more intensely investigated than developing areas. In 1981, industrialized areas accounted for 67 percent of worldwide expenditures (excluding the Eastern Bloc) for geophysical surveys for petroleum, and 70 percent of expenditures for mineral surveys.[39] A 1980 United Nations report stated that it "appears that changes in the pattern of ownership and the reactions of transnational corporations to their perception of unstable investment conditions (particularly in the mineral sector), as well as cyclical factors, have led to a considerable decline in transnational corporation investments in certain minerals."[40]

In sum, in some environments in which international regimes are unstable it is possible to maintain a high level of economic interchange. The longer the time needed to conclude a transaction, however, the more difficult this becomes. *Ceteris paribus*, it is easier to sustain commodity trade than bank lending, and easier to sustain bank lending than investment in extractive industries.

EXISTING AUTHORITATIVE REGIMES

Cooperation between the North and the South is not necessarily limited to specific transactions. There are existing international regimes that provide the context for mutually satisfactory agreements. The defining characteristic of these regimes is that they embody principles that legitimate allocation based on the authoritative decisions of the state. Civil aviation, international travel, and nuclear nonproliferation offer examples.

[38]U.N. Economic and Social Council, *Transnational Corporations in World Development*, Table III–38.

[39]Derived from figures in *Geophysics: The Leading Edge* 1, 4, p. 31. Figures for South Africa are not included in these totals.

[40]U.N. Economic and Social Council, *The Role of Transnational Corporations* (3), p. 18.

Civil Aviation

Civil aviation has already been discussed. The principles, norms, rules, and decision-making procedures related to civil aviation heavily favor authoritative state allocation. Airspace above a state's land area is treated as national territory. Landing rights must be granted by political authorities. Fares are subject to political review. Under this regime, a large number of Third World countries have been able to develop viable national airlines, which transport about 50 percent of the passengers traveling to or from their home territories. American efforts to move the civil aviation regime more toward market-oriented principles and norms have been resisted by states from the North as well as from the South. In the International Civil Aviation Organization and the International Air Transport Association, the North-South cleavage has not been salient.

International Travel

The movement of individuals offers a second example of a regime in which authoritative state action is widely accepted. Individuals do not have the right to cross state borders freely; they are subject to the regulations imposed by political authorities.[41] Prior to the late eighteenth century, movement was relatively unencumbered. In 1793, however, the British government passed legislation to stem the influx of refugees from France, some of whom were thought to harbor revolutionary sympathies. The French followed with their own regulations. By the end of the nineteenth century the general norm was that the state had full control over emigration and immigration. The passport, one clear institutional manifestation of the regime governing the movement of individuals, came into widespread use after the First World War. States are recognized as having the right to deny entry to an individual without a proper passport. The conditions for issuing a passport are left to national authorities.[42] Although there have been assertions that the right to travel is a basic human right not subject to the arbitrary dictates of national states, this position has not won many adherents. Virtually all states hold that they have the right to control the movement of individuals across their borders.

[41]Diaz-Alejandro, "Delinking North and South," p. 125.
[42]Plender, *International Migration Law*, pp. 43 ff; Goodwin-Gill, *International Law and the Movement of Persons*, pp. 25–50.

There has been no dispute between the North and the South over the basic principles governing international travel. There has not been international agitation to create an organization to challenge the existing regime. The "brain drain" from developing to industrialized countries has received relatively little attention.[43] Third World countries have not demanded that their impoverished populations be given the right to migrate to more affluent areas, yet such demands would be no more inherently quixotic than is the call for an international tax on armaments or the now widely accepted proposition that some revenues from deep-seabed mining be allocated to poorer countries.

Nonproliferation

A third example of a regime governed by authoritative allocation is nuclear proliferation. This issue area is particularly instructive because it is one where there has been considerable North-South conflict over distribution but not over the basic rules of the game. Most developing states have ratified the Non-Proliferation Treaty (NPT) even though it is the only major agreement since World War II that makes a juridical distinction between classes of states—those with and those without nuclear weapons. Although some observers have been skeptical about the durability of the nonproliferation regime, the analysis presented here suggests that the prospects for success are enhanced because there is agreement on basic principles and norms.

Nuclear power is not a piece of cake. States have recognized that nuclear technology and materials cannot be treated as normal commodities. The market-oriented principles and norms of the trading regime have never been applied. In 1943 the United States, Great Britain, and Canada agreed not to communicate information to third parties without mutual consent. The United States attempted to deny plutonium technology to Britain and Canada. After the war the basic thrust of American policy was to maintain as much control as possible.[44] By the early 1950s, however, Soviet atomic explosions had demonstrated that a monopoly was impossible.

The international regime for nonproliferation began with the American Atoms for Peace Program in 1953. This program explicitly confronted

---

[43]See UNCTAD, *Monthly Bulletin*, no. 195, pp. 6–8, for a discussion of U.N. activity.
[44]Goldschmidt, "Nonproliferation Policies," pp. 70–72.

the basic problem of the nonproliferation regime: distinguishing between the dissemination of nuclear technology for civil and for military purposes. The United States offered to share civilian technology if recipients would accept inspections and controls. These international safeguard procedures, which were first developed in bilateral agreements, were embodied in the Statute of the International Atomic Energy Agency (IAEA) opened for signature in 1956 and the Non-Proliferation Treaty (NPT) opened for signature in 1968, the two central institutional manifestations of the nonproliferation regime.[45] The IAEA Statute provides for safeguards (that is, inspections) to prevent the diversion of nuclear material from civilian to military purposes, for all projects that receive technical assistance from the IAEA. Bilateral agreements, too, sometimes call for IAEA safeguards. The NPT provides for IAEA inspections of all nuclear facilities in signatory states that do not have nuclear weapons.[46]

Participation in the nonproliferation regime is extensive. By the mid-1970s, 109 states, including all countries with nuclear programs, had become members of the IAEA. The NPT has been more controversial. Two nuclear-weapon states, France and China, did not sign; a number of other states with major nuclear programs, including India, South Africa, Israel, and Spain, also had not signed the NPT by 1980. Three nuclear weapons states, however—the United States, USSR, and Great Britain—and 111 other states had ratified the treaty. Several Latin American states that had refused to sign the NPT endorsed the Treaty for the Prohibition of Nuclear Weapons in Latin America (Treaty of Tlaltelolco) which came into force in 1969. Moreover, almost all nuclear facilities were covered by IAEA safeguards. As of 1977 there were 506 nuclear facilities covered by safeguards and only 11 (one in Egypt, six in India, two in Israel, one in South Africa, and one in Spain) that were not.[47] Virtually all countries have endorsed some aspect of the nonproliferation regime.

The widespread participation of Third World countries in the regime cannot be treated as a foregone conclusion. First, the system of safeguards infringes on the prerogatives of the home state. Second, the

[45]Nye, "Maintaining a Nonproliferation Regime," p. 17; Yager, *International Cooperation in Nuclear Energy*, p. 28.

[46]Yager (*International Cooperation in Nuclear Energy*, pp. 27 ff) offers a convenient summary of the provisions of the regime.

[47]U.S. Congress, Committee on Governmental Affairs, *Nuclear Proliferation Factbook*, pp. 419, 421. See also Mabry, "The Present International Nuclear Regime," p. 164.

Non-Proliferation Treaty makes an explicit distinction between the five nuclear-weapon states (U.S., USSR, Great Britain, France, and China) and nonnuclear-weapon states. The provisions of the treaty obligate only nonnuclear-weapon states to subject all of their nuclear activity to IAEA inspection. The NPT has been described as the first unequal treaty since the end of the colonial era.

Third, developing countries have bitterly contested the behavior of industrialized states, especially the nuclear-weapon states, arguing that they have not lived up to the norms and rules of the regime. At the first NPT Review Conference held in 1975, the North-South cleavage was highly salient. Third World countries objected to proposals for tighter safeguards on nonnuclear-weapon states, while nuclear-weapon states continued to reject inspections of all their nonmilitary nuclear facilities. Developing countries argued against national underground tests and in favor of an international organization to conduct peaceful nuclear tests. They called for the implementation of Articles IV and VI of the NPT, which provide for disarmament and technical assistance for peaceful nuclear endeavors. North-South disputes were so intense at the second NPT Review Conference held in 1980 that it was impossible to agree on a final document. Developing countries were particularly upset by the efforts of industrialized states, led by the United States, to place tighter controls on the export of nuclear technology and materials through the London Suppliers' Group; by the provisions of the 1978 Nuclear Non-Proliferation Act, which required that existing U.S. bilateral agreements be renegotiated to provide full-scope safeguards (safeguards for all nuclear facilities within a country); and by American, Canadian, and Australian pressures for the acceptance of full-scope safeguards even by countries that had not signed the NPT. Even in the ostensibly more technically oriented environment of the International Nuclear Fuel Cycle Evaluation (INFCE), which was held during the late 1970s, North-South issues were prominent. The communiqué initiating the INFCE exercise in 1977 stated that the participants "recognized that special consideration should be given to the specific needs of and conditions in developing countries."[48]

These North-South conflicts led some observers to predict the demise

---

[48]U.N. doc. no. INFCE/PC/2/9, p. 1; McGraw, "The NPT Review Conference"; Epstein, *Retrospective on the NPT Review Conference*; Yager, *International Cooperation in Nuclear Energy*, pp. 32–38; Atlantic Institute for International Affairs, *Nuclear Non-proliferation and Safeguards* (statements by Argentine and Brazilian representatives).

of the nonproliferation regime.[49] The analysis presented here, however, suggests a more hopeful prognosis. Aside from the fact that there are interest-oriented calculations weighing against proliferation (if country A secures a bomb, country A knows that country B is very likely to get a bomb too), agreement on basic principles and norms make the nonproliferation regime more stable than many other international arrangements.[50] The North and the South (and the Communist Bloc as well) agree that the international movement of nuclear technology and material must be subject to state decisions rather than to the market. The debate within the IAEA and the NPT is a relational, not a meta-power, debate. While there is no guarantee that disagreements will be satisfactorily resolved, at least the players agree on the basic rules of the game.

In sum, civil aviation, international travel, and nonproliferation offer examples of existing regimes governed by authoritative, rather than market-oriented, principles. In these areas the North and the South have at least agreed on the basic principles and norms. In the case of civil aviation, they have generally agreed on distributional issues as well. Shared principles and norms do not preclude disputes, as the nonproliferation regime demonstrates, but they do make it more likely that a durable, mutually acceptable pattern of behavior will be established.

CREATING NEW REGIMES

Regime creation is more difficult than regime maintenance. There are, however, some possibilities for specific issue-area regime creation involving the North and the South. The necessary condition for such an exercise is the acceptance of authoritative, rather than market-oriented, principles and norms by the First World as well as the Third World. Developing states will not support the establishment of new regimes unless they reduce vulnerability as well as enhance resource transfer. The North would have to be convinced that market-oriented principles and norms would not (and could not) provide adequate security, or they could accept authoritative allocation as a second-best solution because they were convinced that markets would not work.

International commodity agreements offer a possible area for future

[49]See, e.g., Yager, *International Cooperation in Nuclear Energy*, p. 38.
[50]For a discussion of the incentives against proliferation, see Quester, "Preventing Proliferation."

cooperation between the North and the South. The endemic problem confronting commodity producers is that inelasticities of supply and demand can lead to severe price fluctuations. For mineral products, supply is likely to be stable, but demand fluctuates with the business cycle in consuming countries. For food producers, demand is likely to be stable, but supply can fluctuate because of environmental conditions. While price fluctuations are inconvenient for the North, they can be devastating for particular Third World states; monocultural economies, in which government revenues are highly dependent on trade taxes, are particularly vulnerable.

For the Third World, the Integrated Program for Commodities, the most important item on its agenda during the mid- and late 1970s, was not disposed of satisfactorily. The centerpiece of the South's proposal was a Common Fund that would provide resources for specific commodity control as well as support for the development of forward linkages in developing countries, such as marketing and processing. Coupled with the fund was an initial list of some fifteen commodities that would be subject to specific agreements. Not much progress was made. The Common Fund was finally accepted by the North, but funded at a meager level. Some existing commodity agreements, such as the International Coffee Agreement and the International Tin Agreement, continued. A few new arrangements were concluded, the most important of which dealt with natural rubber.

But the resistance of the North, especially the United States, to international commodity control remained intense. American private and public actors viewed commodity agreements as unfortunate departures from the liberal, market-oriented principles governing the movement of most traded goods. American leaders have actively taken the lead only in formulating international commodity agreements that were seen as part of a broader political strategy. For instance, the United States helped to create the Inter-American Coffee Agreement at the outset of World War II to cement relations with Latin American states, and the International Coffee Agreement in 1960 to promote economic and political development in conjunction with the Alliance for Progress.[51] But in the absence of general political goals, American leaders have usually taken a negative view of authoritative intervention in international raw-material markets.

[51]Krasner, "Business-Government Relations," and "Manipulating International Commodity Markets."

There are a number of economic benefits that could accrue to the United States, however, if it accepted an authoritative, rather than a market-oriented, allocation for raw materials. The real challenge for industrialized consumers is to make sure that they have adequate supplies. Stockpiling and supplier diversification are two prudent measures that can be taken. Commodity agreements offer a third possibility. Production is likely to be more stable if producers are confident of their export earnings. Greater predictability would facilitate capital investments. Political instability and consequent economic disruption associated with fluctuations in export earnings would be mitigated.

Raw-materials investment offers another area where the rules of the game might be changed to the mutual advantage of the North and the South. The breakdown in concession agreements has led to a decline in natural-resource investments in developing countries. When investments have been made, corporations have acted to limit their own financial exposure. Given repeated renegotiation of contracts, nationalization, and even expropriation, corporate executives have not been anxious to make large, nonfungible, long-term investments in the Third World. However, this situation decreases security of supply for consuming nations as a whole by leaving the level of production and the number of producers lower than they would otherwise be. An international regime that encouraged investment could be beneficial to both the North and the South. Such a regime would have to satisfy Southern concerns with sovereignty and control as well as Northern concerns for security of supply.

This might be accomplished by increasing the role of international financial institutions (IFIs) in Third World raw-materials investment. Both industrialized and developing countries have accepted the basic rules of the game associated with IFIs. They are an important postwar institutional innovation in which the authoritative role of the state is clearly recognized. Developing countries do have significant voting power, even in the IMF and the World Bank. IFIs could provide direct loans for natural-resource projects or they could cofinance with multinational corporations. In either case they could act as a buffer between MNCs and host countries. International-organization involvement in a project might also leave LDC political leaders less exposed to accusations that they had sold out to international capitalism.

The proposal for a special World Bank energy affiliate, made during the early 1980s, offers one example of an attempt to establish a more active role for international financial institutions. This proposal was supported by most industrialized countries. It was opposed by the United States, however. The deputy secretary of the Treasury explained the U.S. position in the following terms: "Bluntly put, this was [sic] an area that the private sector can and will adequately serve. The energy affiliate would have simply substituted less expensive public development capital for available private capital."[52] Would that it were so. The kindest interpretation of American behavior is that policymakers have misunderstood the impediments to smoothly functioning markets for large, nonfungible, long-term investments in Third World countries. The influence of the private oil companies and doctrinaire commitments to the market in the Reagan administration are (perhaps) less generous explanations. Where developing countries want significant control and multinational corporations require contractual stability, the market will not produce an optimal outcome over the life cycle of a raw-materials investment. Greater authoritative allocation, in the form of a more active role for international financial institutions, could increase the aggregate level of welfare.

Even in an area like raw materials, where a strong case can be made for the mutual benefits that could be derived from new rules of the game, it is difficult to be sanguine about agreement between the North and the South. In the present international environment the prospects for establishing new regimes are not bright. It is easier to sustain an existing set of principles, norms, rules, and decision-making procedures than to create a new one.[53] Regime creation has generally been associated with the emergence of a new hegemonic power, such as the United States at the conclusion of the Second World War. The hegemon has resources to induce other states to accept its vision of international order, to tolerate free riders, and to provide collective goods. In the absence of a hegemonic power, problems related to public goods and questions about distribution are more difficult to resolve. Existing regimes generate information, which reduces uncertainty, and beneficiaries that provide political support. Negotiating new regimes may also be more difficult in the post-NIEO era because there are institutional structures for the South, such as bloc voting in UNCTAD, which automatically link issues and aggregate demands.[54]

---

[52]U.S. Treasury Department, *Treasury News*, R-560, January 7, 1982.

[53]Keohane, "The Demand for International Regimes."

[54]Roger Hansen has argued that the level of overall conflict between the North and the South is so high that agreement on specific functional issues will be very difficult. This

In sum, the analysis presented here suggests that the United States, and the North in general, should abandon efforts to conclude global agreements with the South. Policies such as meeting basic human needs, population control, and human rights, which infringe on the recognized sovereign prerogatives of the state, will be resisted by the South and will not generate stable international regimes. Many mutually acceptable transactions are possible, however, especially when they can be completed in a short period of time in auction markets. Existing international regimes guided by authoritative principles, such as civil aviation and nonproliferation, have and will continue to provide opportunities for cooperation between the North and the South. New regimes, based on a greater role for the state in the allocation of resources, may be created. Raw-material investments and international commodity agreements offer examples. But given the difficulties associated with regime creation in the absence of a hegemonic state, the prospects for establishing new regimes, as opposed to sustaining old ones, are poor.

PREDICTIONS

The most important proposition of this study is that conflict between the North and the South is endemic. It is a product of deep asymmetries of power that leave almost all developing countries exposed to shocks from the international environment. This structural situation compels the Third World to attempt to alter the rules of the game in ways that would lessen their vulnerability. Relational power behavior, designed to maximize economic returns within existing market-oriented regimes, is not a substitute for meta-power behavior, designed to create new regimes that would legitimate behavior based on authoritative state resource allocation. The demands for a New International Economic Order, which were especially salient during the 1970s, are the clearest manifestation of the South's challenge to the market-oriented regimes that govern most kinds of international transactions, especially in the critical areas of trade, private capital flows, and direct foreign investment.

---

conclusion appears too pessimistic given successful North-South cooperation in some regimes. Robert Rothstein, in an analysis much closer to the one presented here, endorses differentiation and selectivity for the United States with a focus on specific short-term issues. (See Hansen, "North-South Policy," p. 1123; and Rothstein, *The Third World and U.S. Foreign Policy*, pp. 209–210.) For problems associated with UNCTAD commodity regimes see Rothstein, *Global Bargaining*.

The NIEO was not an exercise in empty rhetoric, an agglomeration of half-baked ideas, or the product of logrolling among developing countries. The kinds of demands embodied in the call for a New International Economic Order will not disappear, because the structural conditions that prompted them are enduring characteristics of the international system. However, there are three developments that would lessen the intensity of the North-South conflict: greater capabilities in some developing countries, less Northern concern with existing international organizations, and (less likely) more collective self-reliance for the South and consequent delinking from the North.

THIRD WORLD CAPABILITIES

Meta-political efforts aimed at altering the basic nature of international regimes are prompted by the vulnerability experienced by weak states in a market-governed environment. At the national level this vulnerability can be mitigated in three ways. First, a large state may be able to disengage from the world economy. Second, a state may have the resources to intervene effectively in an international market. Third, a country may be able to adjust effectively to changes in the world market if its factors of production are sufficiently mobile.

Disengagement

At the aggregate level there are few developing countries whose overall size offers the prospect of escape from the vicissitudes of the world economy. The economies of most developing countries are small and nondiversified. The economic costs of an autarkic policy, even assuming that one could be enforced, would be very high. There are few examples of such efforts. Burma attempted to pursue a policy of self-reliance. Official World Bank figures show that trade (imports plus exports) fell from 40 percent of GDP for the period 1950–1960 to 26 percent for the period 1960–1970, to 13 percent (one of the lowest figures for any LDC) for the period 1970–1977.[55] Much higher unofficial estimates have been suggested, however, which take account of smuggling. Only the very

[55]World Bank, *World Tables*, 1980, p. 51.

largest nonindustrialized states are likely to be able to limit their involvement with the world economy. Table 10.2 shows the distribution of the
ratios of trade to GDP for ninety-one developing countries. Nepal,
Ethiopia, and Burma are among the eight countries with trade below 25
percent of GDP; the first being small and remote, the second experiencing civil war, and the figure for the third failing to take account of
a large black market. There are five developing countries—Argentina,
Bangladesh, Brazil, India, and Mexico—that are large and, at least during
the early and mid-1970s, not very heavily involved in the world economy
as indicated by figures for trade. However, Brazil, Mexico, and Argentina
became the Third World's three largest debtors. By the early 1980s they
were compelled to impose severe restrictions on their domestic economies
to meet their international obligations. Among the non-Communist developing countries, only India emerges as highly disengaged from the
world economy.

China offers the clearest example of a poor country that is separated
from the world economy. In the late 1970s China's gross national product
was about three times as large as Brazil's and four times as large as India's,
the two other continental size developing countries. During the 1970s
the ratio of Brazil's trade to its GDP was 18 percent, India's was 11
percent, and China's was 5 percent. Neither India nor China has borrowed heavily on private international capital markets. Both severely
control direct foreign investment and technology transfers. Thus India
and China are the two developing countries that are substantially disengaged from the world economy, and are likely to remain so. They need
not be as concerned with the nature of international regimes as smaller
countries.

TABLE 10.2

TRADE (EXPORTS PLUS IMPORTS) AS A PERCENTAGE
OF GDP 1970–1977 (NUMBER OF LDCs)

	<25%	25–49%	50–74%	75–99%	99%<
Number of developing countries	8	27	24	14	18

Source: Derived from figures in World Bank, *World Tables*, 2d. ed. (Baltimore: Johns
Hopkins University Press, 1980) pages by country, Economic Data Sheet I. For some
countries, only part of the time period is covered.

State Intervention in International Markets

In a market-oriented regime, allocation is a function of the resources and preferences of individual actors. States as well as private corporations can be players in the market. If an actor from a developing country, especially the state, can intervene effectively in a market, there is less reason to embrace authoritative international regimes. Under these circumstances there will be relational power conflict between the North and the South over the distribution of returns, but there may not be meta-power conflict over the principles and norms of the regime.

During the 1970s, states in industrialized countries increasingly acted to create comparative advantage in high-growth industries as well as to promote direct sales in foreign markets.[56] Few developing countries, however, have the administrative capacities or technical skills needed for such programs. Only the NICs have been able to move in these directions.[57] Interventions by other Third World countries have been limited to situations in which they have enjoyed a monopolistic or oligopolistic position in a particular market. But even here the successes have been limited in number. Oil in the 1970s is the sole example of sustained market control by Third World countries. Other groups of raw-material producers have tried to intervene in global markets, but with limited success. The conditions for effective market control are stringent. Supply and demand must be price-inelastic. If more than one producer is involved, then stability is an endemic problem because financially strapped states are likely to cheat or lead others to think that they will. With the exception of the surplus-oil-exporting states (Saudi Arabia, Kuwait, UAE, and Libya) no Third World producer of minerals has had the economic reserves needed to provide assurances against cheating. Oil will remain the exception with regard to Third World cartels.[58]

Internal Factor Mobility

Third World states that have mobile factors of production can adjust to, even if they cannot control, changing international market conditions.

---

[56]Zysman and Cohen, "Open Trade."

[57]Yoffie, *Power and Protectionism* and "Newly Industrialized Countries and the Political Economy of Protectionism."

[58]Krasner, "Oil Is the Exception"; Varon and Takeuchi, "Developing Countries and Non-Fuel Minerals."

Such mobility may come from a combination of efficient domestic factor markets and state direction. The Southeast Asian NICs offer the most arresting examples of such capabilities, with Hong Kong strongly relying on the market, and Korea, Taiwan, and Singapore employing both state and market mechanisms.[59] Brazil and Mexico also have highly developed institutional structures. Factor mobility is closely related to general economic and political development. The example of the NICs, especially Taiwan and South Korea, shows that effective development is at least possible within the context of the existing world political economy.[60]

Very few developing countries can hope to decrease the absolute gap between their national power capabilities and those of the larger industrialized states. Many LDCs, however, may be able to develop vibrant internal markets or effective political economic institutions. Such states could live with open international markets because they could adjust to them even if they could not control them. They would come to resemble the small industrialized states in their relationship to the global economy. A world of more agile Third World countries would mitigate North-South conflict.

In sum, greater Third World capabilities with regard to overall size, market power, or domestic factor mobility would make markets more acceptable to the South and would decrease North-South dissension over basic principles and norms. Fewer than five developing countries, however, are of continental proportions, and only oil producers have been able to intervene effectively in world markets. Other developing states may follow the path pioneered by the NICs and rely more heavily on a relational power as opposed to a meta-power strategy, but there is as yet no evidence of widespread changes in the ability of LDCs to adjust to global markets. Still, domestic development in the South offers the best hope for reconciling LDCs to market-oriented regimes.

THE DECLINE OF INTERNATIONAL INSTITUTIONS

Tension between the North and the South may also decrease because developing countries lack effective forums at which to present their de-

---

[59]Cumings, "The Origins of the Northeast Asian Political Economy."

[60]Singapore and Hong Kong are so small that they might better be viewed as entrepôts. The ratio of trade to GDP was 200% for Hong Kong and 270% for Singapore during the 1970s.

mands. The NIEO program could not have developed without the United Nations system, even with the same structural conditions and ideological commitments. The principle of the sovereign equality of all states and the correlative rule of one nation, one vote made it possible for developing states to set international agendas and create new institutional structures such as UNCTAD. However, the effectiveness of universal forums has depended, in the final analysis, on the continued attention of the North. This attention has begun to falter.

Symbolically, the United Nations compound on the East River in New York is coming to resemble the Guantánamo Naval Base in Cuba. Both are an affront to the principles and norms of the territories that surround them and both are vestiges of past power configurations. Without the commitment of American resources, the United Nations would not exist. American leaders expected United Nations decisions to legitimate their foreign policy preferences. They no longer do. The rise of the Third World and the loss of Gramscian hegemony has left the United States on the defensive. By the mid-1960s the United States was voting with the General Assembly majority less than 50 percent of the time, and had begun casting vetoes in the Security Council.[61]

American willingness to support the United Nations and other international organizations has not collapsed, but it has declined. In the immediate postwar years, the United States provided 39 percent of the assessed budget of the United Nations; this figure fell to 33 percent between the mid-1950s and the mid-1970s; and then to 25 percent in 1974. The political standing of U.S. ambassadors to the United Nations has declined from major political figures like Adlai Stevenson to career foreign service officers like Donald McHenry, or minor political figures like Jeane Kirkpatrick. In 1977 the United States temporarily withdrew from the International Labor Organization after the International Labor Conference refused to accept a report from one of its major committees which monitored compliance with ILO human rights resolutions. The report cited the USSR, Czechoslovakia, Ethiopia, Liberia, Uganda, Argentina, Bolivia, and Chile for deficiencies. The United States refused to sign the Law of the Sea Convention arguing that the provisions related to the mining of deep-seabed nodules were unfair to multinational corporations and incompatible with national security interests involving strategic materials. The United States negotiated an agreement with

[61]Haas. "Words Can Hurt You," p. 230.

a small number of industrialized countries and empowered the U.S. National Oceanic and Atmospheric Administration to issue regulations for the exploitation of seabed minerals by American companies. In 1982 the Reagan administration refused to pay a $1 million U.N. assessment for a commission created by the Law of the Sea Convention. It was the first time the United States had claimed the right not to pay such an assessment. In 1984 the United States announced that it intended to withdraw from UNESCO unless there was a fundamental change in the organization's administration and philosophy. UNESCO had become the major venue for the Third World's presentation of the New International Information Order (NIIO) which, among other measures, called for greater national regulation of the international flow of news. The NIIO program was based on the principles that existing arrangements presented a biased view of developments in the Third World, imposed Northern, or Western, cultural values on the South, reinforced the unequal exchange of information, and impeded greater interchange among developing countries. The United States quit UNESCO in 1985, and also, for the first time, refused to participate in a World Court case.[62]

Increasingly, the United States has carried out policy in forums with limited membership or functionally specific tasks. Major budgetary support has been provided only for selected U.N. programs. For instance, in 1975 American contributions accounted for 40 percent of the budget for the United Nations Force in Cyprus, 69 percent for the Cyprus Relief Fund, 52 percent for the U.N. Disaster Office, and 86 percent for the U.N. Fund for Drug Abuse Control.[63] New institutional structures have been created and old ones used more actively. Negotiations about export financing have been discussed within the context of the OECD. Regular summit conferences among the leaders of the most powerful advanced market-economy countries began in the mid-1970s. These are not institutional settings which the South can use to present the NIEO program. In some, they have no access at all. As Northern commitment to universal multifunctional organizations declines, the demand for a New Interna-

<hr>

[62]For figures on American contributions, see U.S. State Department, *United States Contributions to International Organizations*, various years, Appendix tables. The United States temporarily withdrew from the ILO in the late 1970s. For a short presentation of the reasons for this action, see U.S. State Department, *U.S. Participation in the United Nations*, 1975, pp. 196–197. For the seabed decisions, see *San Francisco Chronicle*, December 31, 1982, p. 7. For the World Court, see *New York Times*, January 19, 1985, p. 1.

[63]U.S. State Department, *United States Contributions to International Organizations*, 1976, table facing p. 102.

tional Economic Order may wane, not because the objectives of the South have changed but because they cannot be expressed. The North has the option of exit as its loyalty to U.N. agencies erodes; the South has only the option of voice.[64]

DELINKING THE NORTH AND SOUTH

Northern indifference and Southern development are two ways in which conflict over basic principles and norms could be mitigated. A third would be to delink the North and the South. Collective self-reliance would not eliminate the difficulties experienced by Third World countries in the international environment, but would turn dissatisfaction away from the North. The vulnerabilities of individual Southern states (at least with regard to intentional pressures from other states as opposed to systemic disturbances) might be eased because power asymmetries among LDCs are less than those between industrialized and developing states. Policymakers from developing countries would find it easier to agree on international regimes based on authoritative allocation.

Analysts with very different theoretical orientations have arrived at similar conclusions. Breaking with the North is the most important policy prescription of dependency theory. If the world capitalist system is milking the periphery through unequal exchange, perverting its political development through the triple alliance, and undermining its cultural autonomy with bourgeois Northern products and advertisements, then the most desirable course of action is to sever or restrict relations with the center. Third World leaders have not embraced all aspects of dependency theory (since it frequently depicts them as dupes or allies of the North, such an embrace would be awkward), but they have supported the concept of collective self-reliance for the South.

Selective delinking, if not a wholesale break in relations, has also been supported by nonradical analysts in the North. Carlos Diaz-Alejandro defended such a policy in a volume prepared for the Council on Foreign Relations 1980s Project. He noted that self-reliance must be contingent on the fact that the "basic needs of the country are not at the mercy of the caprice of external markets or vulnerable to external blockades."[65] While the economic arguments for delinking lack both theoretical rigor

[64]Hirschman, *Exit, Voice, and Loyalty.*
[65]Diaz-Alejandro, "Delinking North and South," p. 112.

and powerful empirical support, political incentives arising from the constraints imposed by an unregulated market system make delinking attractive.[66] Robert Rothstein has argued that "(A)nything that the developing countries can do for and among themselves is likely to contribute to the construction of an international system that is relatively less dominated by conflict."[67] In another volume for the 1980s Project, Fred Hirsch and Michael Doyle concluded an article on the international monetary system with the contention that a "degree of controlled disintegration in the world economy is a legitimate objective for the 1980s and may be the more realistic one for a moderate international economic order."[68]

Given the fundamental asymmetries of power that exist in the present international environment, the domestic political weakness of Third World regimes, the unwillingness or inability of a declining hegemonic power (the United States) to provide decisive leadership, domestic economic problems in the North at the macro and sectoral levels, and the public-choice problems associated with coordinating policies among advanced industrialized states, the world would be safer with less involvement rather than more. From a structural realist perspective a reduction in the level of involvement between the North and the South is the most attractive evolutionary path.

There are some modest indications that the level of economic interaction among developing countries is becoming more important. Table 10.3 shows the relative level of intra–Third World trade. Overall, there was a modest increase (from 21 percent to 26 percent) in the importance of intra–Third World trade between 1963 and 1981. The most dynamic trading partners, the East Asian NICs and the traditional oil exporters experienced virtually no change over that entire period, although both did increase their share of intra-LDC trade during the 1970s. In 1981 these two groups of countries (Indonesia is included in both) accounted for 79 percent of intra-LDC trade. Third World trade as a percentage of total world trade increased from 4 percent in 1973 to 7 percent in 1981.[69]

The level of capital flows within the Third World is modest. The

[66]Ibid., p. 91.

[67]Rothstein, *The Third World and U.S. Foreign Policy*, p. 116.

[68]Hirsch and Doyle, *Alternatives to Monetary Disorder*, p. 55. For similar arguments, see O'Leary, "Controlled Dis-Integration"; and Calleo, "The Decline and Rebuilding of an International Economic System."

[69]Derived from figures in GATT, *International Trade*, 1981/1982, table A25.

TABLE 10.3
EXPORTS TO DEVELOPING AREAS AS A PERCENT OF
TOTAL EXPORTS FROM DEVELOPING AREAS

	1963	1968	1973	1977	1981
Central and South America	17	20	21	25	28
South and East Asia	35	31	28	30	33
West Asia	21	20	22	23	26
Africa	11	10	12	13	13
Traditional Oil Exporters*	22	15	18	19	22
All Developing Countries	21	20	20	22	26

Source: Derived from figures in GATT, *International Trade, 1981/1982* (Geneva, 1982), table A.5.

*Traditional oil-exporters also included in geographic areas.

percentage of total LDC debt owed to other developing countries increased from 5.2 percent in 1975 to 5.6 percent in 1980. The 0.4 percent gain was entirely accounted for by OPEC lending, which grew from 3.2 percent to 3.8 percent of all Third World obligations.[70]

There has been an increase in the level of direct foreign investment (DFI) among developing countries. By 1980 the stock of DFI held by firms from LDCs was $5–$10 billion. Asia was by far the largest source of direct investment, followed by Latin America, the Middle East, and Black Africa. As of 1980, Hong Kong and Brazilian firms were estimated to have $2 billion each in equity abroad, Indian firms more than $100 million, and firms from South Korea, Taiwan, Argentina, Mexico, and Venezuela $50–100 million. For India the outward flow of direct investment was greater than the inward. Most investments have gone to neighboring LDCs.[71] As compared with multinationals from industrialized countries, those from the Third World advertise less, have local partners more often, and repatriate capital at a lower rate.[72] They also generally utilize less capital-intensive technology, an attraction for developing areas

[70]Derived from figures in OECD, *External Debt of Developing Countries, 1982 Survey*, Annex 1

[71]Figures are from Lall, "The Rise of Multinationals," and Wells, *Third World Multinationals*, chap. 1.

[72]Wells, *Third World Multinationals*, pp. 138–140.

with surplus labor. A number of international organizations, especially UNCTAD and UNIDO, as well as individual LDC policymakers, have pointed to the growth of Third World multinationals as an example of collective self-reliance.[73]

As in the case of trade and capital flows, absolute levels of activity are very modest, however, even if the trend line indicates more interaction within the South. In 1976 the total stock of direct investment abroad from the major industrialized countries amounted to $287 billion.[74] Even under the most generous estimates, Third World DFI amounted to only a little more than 3 percent of this total. There have been no major initiatives to promote direct foreign investment within the South. Some Third World countries have encouraged such activity, others have discouraged it.[75] There are very few examples of successful joint ventures involving several developing countries despite the explicit commitments of organizations like the Andean Pact.[76]

There are genuine political advantages for the South in pursuing a policy of collective self-reliance, even if the economic consequences cannot be confidently estimated. Starting from a very low base, Southern interaction in trade, capital flows, and direct foreign investment has increased. But the absolute level of activity is still paltry—7 percent of world trade, 6 percent of capital flows, perhaps 4 percent of direct investment. Moreover, explicit Southern efforts at regional integration have had only limited success. Even when there is agreement in principle, it has been impossible to resolve distributional conflicts. Such conflicts are particularly trying for policymakers with limited economic slack. Andean Pact efforts to create joint enterprises came to naught. The East African Federation disintegrated. Other regional efforts have fared poorly. There is no decisive movement toward collective self-reliance in the South, although the North would do well to encourage and support developments that would promote such a trend. Both the North and the South would find themselves in a more stable environment if the South were more self-sufficient, less dependent on the global economy.

In sum, trends do not indicate any transformation of the basic structural

[73]Ibid., pp. 146–149.

[74]OECD, *Direct Investment Trends*, 1981, p. 39.

[75]For instance, Indonesia has tried to limit investment from Hong Kong and Singapore because of concern about the influence of ethnic Chinese. Wells, *Third World Multinationals*, p. 137.

[76]Ibid., p. 148.

conditions generating tension between the North and the South over regime principles and norms. A few extremely large developing countries, notably China and India, are very self-sufficient. Several LDCs—Taiwan, Singapore, South Korea, possibly Mexico and Brazil—have domestic political and economic institutions that make it possible for them to adjust to external changes. There has been an increase in economic interaction among Southern states, but the absolute levels of trade, capital, and investment flows are modest and the more ambitious efforts at institution building, such as the Andean Pact, have had limited results.

ANALYTIC CONCLUSIONS

Major intellectual perspectives have three components: analytic, hermeneutic, and prescriptive.[77] Most analysts of North-South relations have emphasized the central importance of economic phenomena. This holds true for non-Marxists as well as for Marxists. Analytically, those with non-Marxist economic approaches have maintained that Third World political leaders are motivated by the desire to improve the economic well-being of their societies as a whole or the individual citizens within them. This contention does not preclude consideration of political power, but it does view this goal as instrumental and subordinate to more fundamental wealth-maximizing motivations. Hermeneutically, those following economistic approaches describe global interaction as a mixed-motive game played by individual utility-maximizers. Official action may reflect pressures from a wide range of sources, including societal groups, private firms, classes, and individuals within the government who, for personal or other reasons, have a variety of different objectives. The term *state* is a meaningless and misleading reification. Prescriptively, economistic analysts suggest that enhancing the economic well-being of the South should be a central policy goal of the North. Southern prosperity would be beneficial for the rich as well as the poor. The tensions that exist between industrialized and developing states would be ameliorated by improved material conditions in the Third World.

The modified realist (or modified structural) argument presented in this study offers a radically different perspective. Analytically, the basic contention of this book is that in international forums concerned with global

[77]Ashley, "Political Realism and Human Interests."

regimes the most important motivation of the Third World is to reduce vulnerability by supporting principles, norms, and rules that legitimate authoritative allocation rather than market-oriented allocation. Hermeneutically, I speak in this study of a world of states struggling to maximize stability and control. Insecurity is an ever-present condition. Prescriptively, my analysis suggests that North-South conflict is endemic because the power gap is already so great that vulnerability will persist. Only very large Third World states, or those which develop political institutions that can adjust to the perturbations of the global system, will reconcile themselves to liberal international regimes. The most prudent policy for the North is to limit the membership of regimes, recognize that auction, not consumer markets, are the most appropriate for transactions with the Third World, and encourage collective self-reliance.

The comparison and assessment of two such radically different perspectives is problematic at best. They are drawn from different intellectual traditions. They not only emphasize different explanatory variables but, more importantly, they investigate different dependent variables. For those with economistic perspectives, the main problem is to analyze the behavior of utility-maximizing individuals. For those with realist approaches, the problem is to explain the behavior of the state. The state defined as a set of central decision-making roles and institutions is a meaningful concept because the foreign policy behavior manifested by these institutions is primarily determined by the distribution of power in the global system and the place of the particular state in that system. The motivation of specific individuals can only be significant within the structural constraints imposed by the balance of power. Those working from an economistic perspective suggest that an appropriate methodology for understanding Southern behavior is to probe the beliefs and attitudes of policymakers.[78] Those with a modified realist perspective suggest examining the final policy decisions of states. Data generated from individual interviews are more likely to reveal disparate goals and objectives than empirical findings based on U.N. votes or national policy. Given these differences between economistic and realist perspectives, conventional scientific tests of alternative explanations must be approached with some skepticism. If two theories do not agree on the nature of the dependent variable, do not see the same "real world," then it is chimerical to expect a definitive empirical result. Conventional exercises in falsification are

[78]See, e.g., Jacobsen et al., "Revolutionaries or Bargainers?" and Hart, The New International Economic Order.

much more easily conducted between those who argue within the same basic paradigm or intellectual tradition than between those who argue from different paradigms.

The situation confronted here, however, is not one of complete theory incommensurability. It is appropriate to conclude with a review of the evidence that bears on the merits of economistic and modified realist interpretations of Southern behavior. The dependent variables suggested in the two approaches are different, but not mutually exclusive, sets. In most cases the collective behavior of the South is consistent with either interpretation. Only a few cases offer the possibility for discriminating between the two arguments. While most of the evidence presented in this book does weigh in favor of a modified realist perspective, there are exceptions.

This study sets forth my claim that, in meta-political situations, the Third World has consistently attempted to move regimes from market-oriented toward authoritative modes of allocation. This claim does not deny the importance of economic objectives. The more authoritative regimes proposed by developing states would provide them with both greater control and more material wealth. Moreover, there are many relational power situations in which developing countries have been solely concerned with getting the best possible economic deal given existing liberal institutions. Economistic interpreters have maintained that the desire to improve economic well-being is the most important motivation of Third World behavior. However, most of those holding economistic arguments have also been sensitive to the political demands of the Third World. They have interpreted these demands as an effort to play a larger role in setting the rules for prevailing liberal regimes. Thus, both the modified realist approach elaborated in this study, and sophisticated economistic interpretations, see both power and wealth as motivations of Third World behavior.

The best evidence for discriminating between modified realist and economistic interpretations is located in the off diagonal cells of table 10.4. The column entries assume that power is increased through regimes that legitimate more authoritative modes of allocation. If, in issues associated with the rules of the game, developing countries endorse liberal norms because they want more wealth, this supports economistic interpretations. If they sacrifice wealth for control, this supports a modified realist perspective. Behavior that falls in the upper left-hand cell is consistent with either orientation. If LDCs get more wealth and more power

TABLE 10.4
POLICY CONSEQUENCES

		Increase power	
		Yes	No
Increase wealth	Yes	Modified realist Economistic	Economistic
	No	Modified realist	X

their behavior can be satisfactorily interpreted by advocates of economism or realism. These possibilities are outlined in table 10.4.

A further distinction is that in the analysis presented in this study, I maintain that Third World unity is the result of a structural similarity among developing states, not a logrolling strategy designed to incorporate a wide range of economic demands. The unity of developing countries is a product of their objective situation and subjective self-understanding. The objective conditions confronting almost all developing states are their international and domestic weaknesses. The exceptions are China and India, because of their large size, and the East Asian NICs because of their ability to make domestic adjustments. The subjective communality of all Third World states has been provided by a movement of thought that sees the poverty of the South as a function of the workings of the world capitalist system; in particular, a series of mechanisms that inevitably produce unequal—that is, inequitable—exchange. Thus, a modified realist interpretation suggests that the unity of the Third World will be robust, and support for authoritative principles, norms, and rules will be consistent across a wide range of issue areas.

In contrast, economistic interpreters imply that individual developing states would not be reluctant to break ranks in meta-political struggles if the economic stakes were significant. Logrolling coalitions would be more unstable. There would be less consistency with regard to general principles and norms across issue areas.

The empirical evidence is not conclusive despite the fact that the data presented here are more likely to support modified realist than economistic interpretations, given the theoretical assumptions that guided their collection. This is not, I hope, because the selection of the evidence has been biased but because the nature of the evidence—collective state decisions as opposed to individual attitudes and beliefs—naturally weighs in favor of a realist position. Although in this study I have attempted to survey a wide range of issue areas, it would be disingenuous to argue that all of the material that would weigh against a modified realist interpretation has been garnered. Even with these biases some cases presented here are more easily interpreted from an economistic orientation. For instance, in the area of trade, the Third World has demanded that industrialized states eliminate their trade barriers on manufactures from developing countries. This is a straightforward liberal objective. It stands in contrast to other demands in the trade area which have called for special and differential treatment. In the area of flags of convenience there has been a break in the unity of the Third World. Panama and Liberia have refused to support the Third World's call for an end to flags of convenience. They benefit economically because they are the largest open-registry countries.

There is, in addition, an epistemological consideration, which weighs in favor of an economistic, rather than a modified realist, perspective—elegance or parsimony. The realist argument I presented in this study required that I make a fundamental distinction between relational and meta-power behavior; economistic interpretations do not require such a distinction. Relational power behavior refers to efforts to maximize returns within a given set of rules. In the context of North-South relations it generally implies maximizing economic well-being, given liberal international regimes. Meta-power behavior refers to efforts to change the rules of the game. If the arguments of this study are persuasive, the reader will conclude that Third World meta-power behavior has been designed to move regimes from market-oriented toward authoritative principles, norms, and rules. This position does not challenge the assertion that the ongoing relational power pattern of North-South transactions is driven by wealth maximization. It is only in arenas particularly concerned with regime definition, maintenance, and change that meta-political behavior has been manifest.

Economistic interpreters do not find it necessary to distinguish between relational and meta-power behavior. The Third World is assumed to be interested in wealth maximization in both arenas. Political control is a secondary consideration. The motivations that inform bargaining over the sale of a bale of cotton, boxload of televisions, or a ton of copper are the same ones that guide discussions about the principles, norms, rules, and decision-making procedures that influence policy concerning trade, multinational corporations, radio frequencies, or deep-seabed nodules. For economistic interpreters, it may be useful to make a nominal distinction between relational and meta-power behavior, but the analytic apparatus used to explain action is the same for both arenas. Although a modified realist approach may provide an explanation for patterns of behavior that are anomalous from an economistic perspective, this can only be done by bifurcating Third World behavior and applying different causal arguments for different situations.

In addressing the relative merits of modified structural as opposed to economistic interpretations of North-South relations there are two kinds of claims that can be made. The first is that there is very little evidence that is inconsistent with a modified structural, or realist, interpretation. There are very few cases in which developing states have sacrificed control for wealth in meta-political arenas. The evidence is at least as consistent with a modified realist argument as it is with an economistic one. The stronger claim is that there are patterns of behavior that are inconsistent with economistic interpretation but consistent with realist ones: behavior in which the South has been willing to trade off wealth for control, or at least behavior that is peculiar from an economistic perspective but readily comprehended from a modified realist one. Several specific cases and general patterns of such behavior have been presented in this study.

For instance, in the early 1970s the Nixon administration suggested creating a trusteeship zone for the oceans. This zone would have been administered by littoral states, but part of the revenues generated from resource exploitation would have been committed to international development. The Third World rejected this proposal even though it would have provided more transfers for developing areas as a whole than the regime of expansive exclusive economic zones, which was finally incorporated into the Law of the Sea Convention.

Third World resistance to Northern efforts to establish new norms exclusively related to population control is more consistent with modified realist than economistic interpretations. Even states with ambitious population control programs of their own have opposed new international norms that could infringe on existing sovereign prerogatives and therefore weaken state control. Some developing states have rejected foreign aid packages because they include stipulations regarding population policy. Had the South supported Northern initiatives in this area, additional resources might have been forthcoming.

Developing states have taken a number of positions that were bound to antagonize the North even when no material benefits were at stake. Through UNESCO the South has attempted to legitimate a New International Information Order. Some parts of this effort, such as the call for allocating radio frequencies on the basis of future rather than current needs, are related to material interests. The most publicized aspect of the Third World's program, however, calls for greater national control over the international press corps. Such controls are antithetical to liberal Northern values. They would not provide developing states with additional material resources, but they would give political leaders in the South greater control over the transnational flow of information, a flow that can affect domestic as well as foreign developments. Third World efforts to prevent the international legitimation of political and civil rights have also led to confrontations with industrialized market-economy countries. Given the commitment of the United States to political rights, a commitment enshrined in some provisions of foreign aid legislation, these confrontations can only damage prospects for greater material flows from the North to the South. Resisting Lockean conceptions of individual rights does, however, preserve the sovereign prerogatives of Third World states.

A defense of modified realist interpretations must also rely on arguments other than those that show a trade-off between wealth and power, because examples could be multiplied for both of the off-diagonal cells of table 10.4. The most important of these arguments can be summarized here. First, Third World unity is difficult to explain from an economistic perspective, especially the maintenance of unity with the OPEC countries. The quadrupling of oil prices imposed substantial economic costs on virtually all non-Islamic Third World countries. But this did not lead to an open break with oil-exporting states. The natural cleavage would have been between oil-exporting and oil-importing countries. An attack on OPEC pricing in alliance with the North would have been less whimsical than many other Third World demands. However, no alliance ever developed between industrialized and developing oil consumers. Likewise, the natural economic cleavage in the UNCLOS would have been between littoral and landlocked states, a cleavage that would have allied Austria and Upper Volta. However, early efforts to create a united bloc of land- and shelf-locked states gave way to an overriding North-South cleavage by the end of the conference.

Second, there is intellectual coherence in the policies presented by the Third World across a wide range of issue areas. With the exception of demands for eliminating trade barriers in the North, developing states have consistently put forth programs that are based on authoritative rather than liberal principles. These programs are designed to enhance the direct or indirect control of the state. Allocation based on existing endowments and preferences, the defining principle of a market, has been rejected. This is reflected in endorsement of special and differential treatment in trade, international commodity agreements, global taxation to enhance capital flows to the Third World, international control of the exploitation of deep-seabed nodules, presumptive market shares in civil aviation and shipping, allocation of radio frequencies on the basis of anticipated rather than current needs, national sovereignty over geosynchronous orbits, regulation of the news media, rejection of Western conceptions of human rights, resistance to the creation of international norms related exclusively to population control, nonproprietary treatment of technology, limiting the property rights of multinational corporations, and loosening the conditionality imposed by the IMF.

This set of demands, neatly packaged in several United Nations resolutions during the mid-1970s, can be treated as merely empty rhetoric, the daydream of foreign office officials who are far removed from critical economic decisions. Such an approach contains the implication that Third World political leaders should not be taken seriously. While Northern officials are regarded as prudent representatives of their states' interests, Southern officials are viewed as their states' mouthpieces, full of empty rhetoric, pompous or ill-educated windbags, rather than as serious statesmen.

Finally, a modified realist perspective provides an explanation for the exceptional level of Southern alienation from the prevailing postwar liberal regime. Under this regime the Third World as a whole, and most individual countries, have grown at rapid rates compared with their own past experiences or with the contemporaneous or historical experience of the North. Social progress in the form of longer life spans and higher levels of education has occurred in almost every developing country. Some LDCs have done spectacularly well adopting a strategy of export-led growth. None of this denies that there are still hundreds of millions of individuals who live at the bare subsistence level at best, or that a substantial number of countries, especially in Africa, have faltered in their drive for economic development. However, Third World experience since World War II, even with its unattractive blemishes, can hardly be interpreted as a failure. If it is true that developing states were driven primarily by economic considerations, it is difficult to understand why the North-South cleavage has become so salient. At the very least one would have expected greater division in the Third World, with more successful countries endorsing the existing system and less successful ones rejecting it. No such embrace has been encountered, however, at least not at global negotiating forums concerned with international regimes.

From a realist perspective, the defining characteristic of Third World polities is vulnerability. This vulnerability has not been reduced by economic growth. Meta-political efforts to mitigate this condition by supporting international regimes that legitimate authoritative allocation have been facilitated by a subjective unity cemented by the widespread acceptance of theories of unequal exchange. To admit the benefits of the postwar liberal order would imply rejecting these theories and undermining the very notion of the Third World. The most strident period of Third World demands, which occurred in the early 1970s, followed the most rapid period of Third World economic growth. No theory based on relative economic deprivation could explain this pattern of behavior.

None of this evidence is decisive, however. Most aspects of North-South relations are consistent with both modified realist and economistic interpretations. The cases that fall in the off-diagonal cells of table 10.4, in which power is sacrificed for wealth, or wealth sacrificed for power, are limited. A more convincing test of these competing perspectives must await future developments. Economistic interpretations contain the suggestion of at least the possibility of long-term North-South cooperation and stability, if economic progress continues. Those with modified realist orientations are much more pessimistic.

In 1648 the Peace of Westphalia codified the triumph of sovereignty as the constitutive principle of the international system. The regime of sovereignty has displaced all other forms of political organization at the international level. Tributary states, empires, trusteeship zones, commonwealths, all are historic relics. In the present international environment, however, the triumph of sovereignty has caused major incongruities between underlying power capabilities and transnational principles and norms. Decolonization imbued Third World states with a level of de jure and de facto control which they could not have attained or defended through their national power capabilities. The principle of the sovereign equality of all states has legitimated Third World challenges to the dominant market-oriented regimes favored by the North; international organizations created and funded by the North have become forums where such challenges can be voiced; the weakness and vulnerability of developing countries compels such challenges to be made. Yet, the exiguity of their national power resources precludes any decisive victory. They can attack and undermine existing international regimes but they cannot destroy or replace them. This paradox has been a basic source of tension between the North and the South. It cannot be mitigated by economic development alone. A few Third World states may resign themselves to, or accept, market-oriented regimes because they are very large or domestically agile. But most will not. The North-South conflict will be an enduring characteristic of the international system. There are some problems for which there are no solutions.

Glossary

ADB	Asian Development Bank
ADF	Asian Development Fund
AFDB	African Development Bank
AFDF	African Development Fund
ASEAN	Association of Southeast Asian Nations
CAB	Civil Aeronautics Board
CIEC	Conference on International Economic Cooperation
CIPEC	*Conseil Intergouvernmental des Pays Exportateurs Cuivre* (Intergovernmental Council of Copper-Exporting Countries)
DFI	Direct foreign investment
ECAFE	Economic Commission for Asia and the Far East
ECLA	Economic Commission for Latin America
ECOSOC	Economic and Social Council
EEC	European Economic Community
EPTA	Expanded Program for Technical Assistance
FAO	Food and Agriculture Organization (of the United Nations)

FSO	Fund for Special Operations
GATT	General Agreement on Tariffs and Trade
GDP	Gross domestic product
HEC	Health, education, communication
IADB	Inter-American Development Bank
IAEA	International Atomic Energy Agency
IATA	International Air Transport Association
IBRD	International Bank for Reconstruction and Development (World Bank)
ICAO	International Civil Aviation Organization
IDA	International Development Association
IFC	International Finance Corporation
IFI	International Financial Institution
ILO	International Labor Organization
IMF	International Monetary Fund
IMO	International Maritime Organization
IN	Industrialized nation
INFCE	International Nuclear Fuel Cycle Evaluation
IPC	Integrated Program for Commodities
ITO	International Trade Organization
ITU	International Telecommunication Union
LDC	Less developed country

| MDB | Multilateral development bank |
| MNC | Multinational corporation |

NAM	Non-Aligned Movement
NI	National Income
NIC	Newly industrializing country
NIEO	New International Economic Order
NIIO	New International Information Order
NISO	New International Shipping Order
NPT	Non-Proliferation Treaty

OAU	Organization of African Unity
ODC	Overseas Development Council
OECD	Organization for Economic Cooperation and Development
OPEC	Organization of Petroleum Exporting Countries

| PQLI | Physical Quality of Life Index |

SCAR	Scientific Committee for Antarctic Research
SDR	Special Drawing Rights
SELA	Latin American Economic System
SPTF	Social Progress Trust Fund
SUNFED	Special United Nations Fund for Economic Development

| TNC | Transnational corporation |

UNCDF   United Nations Capital Development Fund

UNCLOS   United Nations Conference on the Law of the Sea

UNCTAD   United Nations Conference on Trade and Development

UNDP   United Nations Development Program

UNIDO   United Nations Industrial Development Organization

UNRFNR   United Nations Revolving Fund for Natural Resources

UNSF   United Nations Special Fund

WARC   World Administrative Radio Conference

References

All references are included below with the exception of some public documents cited by their document number.

African Development Bank. *Annual Report* (various years).

African Development Fund. *Annual Report* (various years).

Alexandrowicz, Charles Henry *The Law of Global Communication.* New York: Columbia University Press, 1971.

Amacher, Ryan C., and Richard J. Sweeney. "International Commodity Cartels and the Threat of New Entry: Implications of Ocean Mineral Resources," *Kyklos* 29 (1976).

Amin, Samir. *Unequal Development.* New York: Monthly Review Press, 1976.

———. *The Maghreb in the Modern World.* London: Penguin, 1970.

Ardant, Gabriel. "Financial Policy and Economic Infrastructure of Modern States and Nations." *In* Charles Tilly, ed., *The Formation of National States in Western Europe.* Princeton: Princeton University Press, 1975.

Asante, Samuel K. B. "Code of Conduct on Transnational Corporations," *In* Kamal Hossain, ed., *Legal Aspects of the New International Economic Order.* London: Frances Pinter, 1980.

Ascher, William. "The World Bank and Development," *International Organization* 37 (Summer 1982).

Ashley, Richard. "Political Realism and Human Interests," *International Studies Quarterly* 25 (June 1981).

Asian Development Bank. *Annual Report* (various years).

Atlantic Institute for International Affairs. *Nuclear Non-Proliferation and Safeguards: A Conference Report.* Paris: Atlantic Institute, 1981.

Auburn, F. M. *Antarctic Law and Politics.* London: C. Hurst and Company, 1982.

Auerback, Kenneth D., and Yoshinobu Yonekawa. "The United Nations Development Program: Follow-Up Investment and Procurement Benefits," *International Organization* 33 (Autumn 1979).

Aviation Week (various issues).

Axelrod, Robert. "The Emergence of Cooperation Among Egoists," *American Political Science Review* 75 (June 1981).

Ayres, Robert. *Banking on the Poor*. Cambridge: MIT Press, 1983.

———. "The 'Social Pact' as Anti-Inflationary Policy: The Argentine Experience Since 1973," *World Politics* 28 (July 1976).

Baade, Hans W. "The Legal Effects of Codes of Conduct for MNEs." *In* Norbert Horn, ed., *Legal Problems of Codes of Conduct for Multinational Enterprises*. Antwerp: Kluwer, 1980.

Bachrach, Peter, and Morton Baratz. "The Two Faces of Power," *American Political Science Review* 56 (December 1962).

Baehr, Peter R. "The Dutch Foreign Policy Elite: A Descriptive Study of Perceptions and Attitudes," *International Studies Quarterly* 24 (June 1980).

Bairoch, Paul. *The Economic Development of the Third World Since 1900*. Berkeley, Los Angeles, London: University of California Press, 1975.

———. "Europe's Gross National Product, 1800–1975," *Journal of Economic History* 52 (Fall 1976).

Baldwin, David. "Power Analysis and World Politics: New Trends vs. Old Tendencies," *World Politics* 31 (January 1979).

Baran, Paul. *The Political Economy of Growth*. New York: Monthly Review, 1957.

Baran, Paul, and Paul Sweezy. *Monopoly Capitalism*. London: Penguin, 1966.

Barkenbus, Jack N. "The Politics of Ocean Resource Exploitation," *International Studies Quarterly* 21 (December 1977).

Bates, Robert H. *Markets and States in Tropical Africa: The Political Basis of Agricultural Policies*. Berkeley, Los Angeles, London: University of California Press, 1981.

Bauer, P. T., and B. S. Yamey. "Against the New Economic Order," *Commentary* (April 1977).

Baumgartner, Tom, et al. "Unequal Exchange and Uneven Development: The Structuring of Exchange and Development Patterns." *Working Paper* Nr. 45, Institute of Sociology, University of Oslo, 1976.

———. "Meta-Power and Relations Control in Social Life," *Social Science Information* 14.

Baumgarnter, T., and T. R. Burns. "The Structuring of International Economic Relations," *International Studies Quarterly* 19 (June 1975).

Beim, David O. "Rescuing the LDCs," *Foreign Affairs* 55 (July 1977).

Bell, Wendell, and J. William Gibson, Jr. "Independent Jamaica Faces the Outside World," *International Studies Quarterly* 22 (March 1978).

Benjamin, Roger. "The Political Economy of Korea," *Asian Survey* (1982).

Berman, Harold J., and Colin Kaufman. "The Law of International Commercial Transactions *(Lex Mercatoria)*," *Harvard International Law Journal* 19 (Winter 1978).

Black, Robert, Stephen Blank, and Elizabeth C. Hanson. *Multinationals in Contention: Responses at Governmental and International Levels.* New York: The Conference Board, 1978.

Brandt Commission. *North South: A Programme for Survival: Report of the Independent Commission on International Development Issues.* Cambridge: MIT Press, 1980.

Brodie, Bernard. *War and Politics.* New York: Macmillan, 1973.

Brown, Robert T. *Transportation and the Economic Integration of South America.* Washington, D.C.: Brookings Institution, 1966.

Brown, Seyom, et al. *Regimes for the Ocean, Outer Space, and Weather.* Washington, D.C.: Brookings Institution, 1977.

Bull, Hedley. *The Anarchical Society.* New York: Columbia University Press, 1977.

Burton, Steven J. "New Stresses on the Antarctic Treaty: Toward International Legal Institutions Governing Antarctic Resources," *Virginia Law Review* 65 (April 1979).

CAB. *Annual Report* (various years).

Cafruny, Alan W. "Ruling the Waves: The Structure of Conflict in the International Shipping Regime." Unpublished Ph.D. diss. Cornell University, 1983.

Calleo, David P. "The Decline and Rebuilding of an International Economic System: Some General Considerations," *In* David P. Calleo, et al. *Money and the Coming World Order.* New York: New York University Press, 1976.

Cameron, David R. "The Expansion of the Public Economy: A Comparative Analysis," *American Political Science Review* 72 (December 1978).

Caporaso, James. "Dependence, Dependency, and Power in the Global System: A Structural and Behavioral Analysis," *International Organization* 32 (Winter 1978).

Cardoso, Fernando Henrique. "Associated-Dependent Development:

Theoretical and Practical Implications." *In* Alfred Stepan, ed., *Authoritarian Brazil: Origins, Politics and Future*. New Haven: Yale University Press, 1973.

———. "Dependency and Development in Latin America," *New Left Review* 74 (July–August 1972).

Cardoso, Fernando Henrique, and Enzo Faletto. *Dependency and Development in Latin America*. Berkeley, Los Angeles, London: University of California Press, 1979.

Chalmers, Douglas A. "Developing on the Periphery: External Factors in Latin American Politics." *In* James N. Rosenau, ed., *Linkage Politics*. New York: Free Press, 1969.

Chase-Dunn, Christopher, and Richard Rubinson. "Toward a Structural Perspective on the World-System," *Politics and Society* 7 (1977).

Christian Science Monitor

Claude, Inis I., Jr. "Collective Legitimization as a Political Function of the United Nations," *International Organization* 20 (1966).

Cline, William R. *International Monetary Reform and the Developing Countries*. Washington, D.C.: Brookings Institution, 1976.

Colson, David A. "The Antarctic Treaty System: The Mineral Issue," *Law and Policy in International Business* 12 (1980).

Conybeare, John A. C. "International Organization and the Theory of Property Rights," *International Organization* 34 (Summer 1980).

Cooper, John C. *The Right to Fly*. New York: Henry Holt and Company, 1947.

Cooper, Richard C. "Economic Interdependence and Foreign Policy in the Seventies," *World Politics* 24 (January 1972).

———. *The Economics of Interdependence*. New York: McGraw-Hill, 1968.

———. "The Oceans as a Source of Revenue." *In* Jagdish N. Bhagwati, ed., *The New International Economic Order: The North-South Debate*. Cambridge: MIT Press, 1977.

Coppock, Joseph D. *International Trade Instability*. Westmead, Farnborough, Hants., England: Saxonhouse, 1977.

Cox, Robert, and Harold Jacobsen. *Anatomy of Influence: Decision Making in International Organization*. New Haven: Yale University Press, 1973.

Craig, Gordon, and Alexander George. *Force and Statecraft*. New York: Oxford University Press, 1983.

Crane, Barbara B., and Jason L. Finkle. "Organizational Impediments to Development Assistance: The World Bank's Population Program," *World Politics* 33 (July 1981).

Cumings, Bruce. "The Origins of the Northeast Asian Political Economy: Industrial Sectors and Political Consequences, 1900–1980," *International Organization* 38 (Winter 1984).

Czako, Judith M. "The Set of Multilaterally Agreed Equitable Principles and Rules for the Control of Restrictive Business Practices," *Law and Policy in International Business* 13 (1981).

Dallek, Robert. *Franklin D. Roosevelt and American Foreign Policy, 1932-1945.* New York: Oxford University Press, 1979.

D'Amato, Anthony. "The Concept of Human Rights in International Law," *Columbia Law Review* 82 (October 1982).

Davidow, Joel, and Lisa Chiles. "The United States and the Issue of the Binding or Voluntary Nature of International Codes of Conduct Regarding Restrictive Business Practices," *The American Journal of International Law* 72 (April 1978).

Deakin, B. M., in collaboration with T. Seward. *Shipping Conferences: A Study of Their Origins, Development, and Economic Practices.* Cambridge: Cambridge University Press, 1973.

Delbrueck, Jost. "International Protection of Human Rights and State Sovereignty," *Indiana Law Journal* 57 (Fall 1982).

Dell, Sidney. *The Inter-American Development Bank: A Study in Development Financing.* New York: Praeger, 1977.

———. *On Being Grandmotherly: The Evolution of IMF Conditionality,* Essays in International Finance 144. Princeton: International Finance Section, Princeton University, 1981.

———. "Stabilization: The Political Economy of Overkill," *In* John Williamson, ed., *IMF Conditionality.* Washington, D.C.: Institute for International Economics, 1983.

Diaz-Alejandro, Carlos F. "Delinking North and South: Unscheduled or Unhinged?" *In* Albert Fishlow, et al., *Rich and Poor Nations in the World Economy.* New York: McGraw-Hill, 1978.

Dolan, Michael B., et al. "Foreign Policies of African States in Asymmetrical Dyads," *International Studies Quarterly* 24 (September 1980).

Dominguez, Jorge I. "Consensus and Divergence: The State of the Literature on Inter-America Relations in the 1970s," *Latin American Research Review* 13 (1978).

———. "Mice That Do Not Roar: Some Aspects of International Politics in the World's Peripheries," *International Organization* 25 (1971).

Donnelly, Jack. "Recent Trends in U.N. Human Rights Activity: Description and Polemic," *International Organization* 35 (Autumn 1981).

Duvall, Raymond D., and John Freeman. "The Techno-Bureaucratic Elite and the Entrepreneurial State in Dependent Industrialization," *American Political Science Review* 77 (September 1983).

Eckes, Alfred. *A Search for Solvency*. Austin: University of Texas Press, 1975.

Economist

Ehrlich, Thomas. "Statement Before the House Committee on Foreign Affairs, February 5, 1980." *Department of State Bulletin*, vol. 80, no. 2036.

Ehrlich, Thomas, and Catherine Gwin. "A Third World Strategy," *Foreign Policy* 44 (Fall 1981).

Emmanuel, Arghiri. *Unequal Exchange*. New York: Monthly Review Press, 1972.

Epstein, William. *Retrospective on the NPT Review Conference: Proposals for the Future*. Occasional Paper 9, Stanley Foundation, Muscatine, Iowa, 1975.

Evans, Peter. *Dependent Development*. Princeton: Princeton University Press, 1979.

Fagan, Richard R. "The Realities of U.S.-Mexican Relations," *Foreign Affairs* 55 (July 1977).

Fatouros, Arghyrios. "The U.N. Code of Conduct on Transnational Corporations: A Critical Discussion of the First Drafting Phase." *In* Norbert Horn, ed., *Legal Problems of Codes of Conduct for Multinational Enterprises*. Antwerp: Kluwer, 1980.

Feis, Herbert. *Europe: The World's Banker, 1870–1914*. Clifton, N.J.: A. M. Kelley, 1964.

Finkle, Jason L., and Barbara B. Crane. "The Politics of Bucharest: Population, Development, and the New International Economic Order," *Population and Development Review* 1 (September 1975).

Fishlow, Albert. "A New International Economic Order: What Kind? *In* Albert Fishlow, et al., *Rich and Poor Nations in the World Economy*. McGraw-Hill, 1978.

Frieden, Jeff. "Third World Indebted Industrialization: International Finance and State Capitalism in Mexico, Brazil, Algeria, and South Korea," *International Organization* 35 (Summer 1981).

Friedheim, Robert L., and William J. Durch. "The International Seabed Resources Agency Negotiations and the New International Economic

Order," *International Organization* 31 (Spring 1977).

Gardner, Richard. *Sterling-Dollar Diplomacy*. New York: McGraw-Hill, 1969.

GATT. *International Trade* (various issues).

Geophysics: The Leading Edge of Exploration 1 (September 1982).

Ghai, Yash. "Legal Aspects of Transfer of Technology." *In* Kamal Hossain, ed., *Legal Aspects of the New International Economic Order*. London: Frances Pinter, 1980.

Gilmore, William C. "Requiem for Associated Statehood?" *Review of International Studies* 8 (January 1984).

Gilpin, Robert. *War and Change in World Politics*. New York: Cambridge University Press, 1981.

———. *U.S. Power and the Multinational Corporation*. New York: Basic Books, 1975.

Gold, Joseph. *Conditionality*. Washington, D.C.: International Monetary Fund, 1979.

———. *Voting Majorities in the Fund: Effects of the Second Amendment of the Articles*. Washington, D.C.: International Monetary Fund, 1977.

Goldschmidt, Bertrand. "A Historical Survey of Nonproliferation Policies," *International Security* 2 (Summer 1977).

Goldstein, Judith. "A Re-Examination of American Trade Policy: An Inquiry into the Causes of Protectionism." Unpublished Ph.D. diss. University of California, Los Angeles, 1983.

Good, Robert C. "State Building as a Determinant of Foreign Policy in the New States." *In* Laurence W. Martin, ed., *Neutralism and Nonalignment*. New York: Praeger, 1962.

Goodwin-Gill, Guy S. *International Law and the Movement of Persons Between States*. Oxford: Oxford University Press, 1978.

Gordenker, Leon. *International Aid and National Decisions*. Princeton: Princeton University Press, 1976.

Gosovic, Branislov, and John G. Ruggie. "On the Creation of a New International Economic Order: Issue Linkage and the Seventh Special Session of the U.N. General Assembly," *International Organization* 30 (Spring 1976).

Grant, M. A. "Domestic Determinants of Mexican Foreign Policy: The Case of Echeverria's 'New Foreign Policy.'" Paper presented at the 1977 annual meeting of the American Political Science Association, Washington, D.C., September 1977.

Grindle, Merilee S. "Policy Content and Context in Implementation."

In Merilee S. Grindle, ed., *Politics and Policy Implementation in the Third World*. Princeton: Princeton University Press, 1980.

Guitan, Manual. *Fund Conditionality: Evolution of Principles and Practices*. Washington, D.C.: International Monetary Fund, 1981.

Gunder Frank, Andre. "Latin America: Underdevelopment or Revolution." New York: Monthly Review Press, 1969.

Gwin, Catherine B. "Poverty and Inequities: Strategies for Change." *In* W. Howard Wriggins and Gunnar Adler-Karlsson, *Reducing Global Inequities*. New York: McGraw-Hill, 1978.

———. "The Seventh Special Session: Toward a New Phase of Relations Between the Developed and Developing States?" *In* Karl P. Sauvant and Hajo Hasenpflug, eds., *The New International Economic Order: Confrontation or Cooperation Between North and South?* Boulder, Colo.: Westview Press, 1977.

Haas, Ernst B. "Why Collaborate? Issue-Linkage and International Regimes," *World Politics* 32 (April 1980).

———. "Words Can Hurt You: Or, Who Said What to Whom About Regimes," *International Organization* 36 (Spring 1982).

Hadwen, John G., and Johan Kaufmann. *How United Nations Decisions are Made*. Leyden: A. W. Sythoff, 1961.

Haggard, Stephan, and Chung-in Moon. "The South Korean State in the International Economy." *In* John G. Ruggie, ed., *The Antinomies of Interdependence*. New York: Columbia University Press, 1983.

Halle, Louis J. *The Cold War as History*. New York: Harper & Row, 1967.

Handel, Michael. *Weak States in the International System*. London: Frank Cass, 1981.

Hanessian, John. "The Antarctic Treaty 1959," *International and Comparative Law Quarterly* 9 (July 1960).

Hansen, Roger D. *Beyond the North-South Stalemate*. New York: McGraw-Hill, 1979.

———. "North-South Policy—What Is the Problem?" *Foreign Affairs* 58 (Summer 1980).

———. "The Political Economy of North-South Relations: How Much Change?" *International Organization* 29 (Autumn 1975).

———. *U.S. Foreign Policy and the Third World, Agenda 1982*. New York: Praeger, 1982.

Haq, Mahbub ul. *The Poverty Curtain: Choices for the Third World*. New York: Columbia University Press, 1976.

Hart, Jeffrey. *The New International Economic Order*. New York: Macmillan, 1983.

Hartz, Louis. *The Liberal Tradition in America*. New York: Harcourt Brace and World, 1955.

Hearn, George H. "Cargo Preference and Control," *Journal of Maritime Law and Commerce* 2 (April 1971).

Hechter, Michael, and William Brustein. "Regional Modes of Production." *American Journal of Sociology* 85 (March 1980).

Helleiner, G. K. "International Technology Issues: Southern Needs and Northern Responses." *In* Jagdish N. Bhagwati, ed., *The New International Economic Order: The North-South Debate*. Cambridge: MIT Press, 1977.

Herman, L. L. "The Code of Conduct for Liner Conferences: Frustrations on the Road to Utopia," *The Canadian Yearbook of International Law* (1976).

Hinrichs, Harley H. *A General Theory of Tax Structure Change During Economic Development*. Cambridge: Harvard Law School, 1966.

Hinsley, F. H. *Power and the Pursuit of Peace*. Cambridge: Cambridge University Press, 1963.

Hirsch, Fred. *Social Limits to Growth*. Cambridge: Harvard University Press, 1976.

Hirsch, Fred, and Michael Doyle. *Alternatives to Monetary Disorder*. New York: McGraw-Hill, 1977.

Hirshman, Albert. *Exit, Voice, and Loyalty: Responses to Decline in Firms, Organizations, and States*. Cambridge: Harvard University Press, 1970.

——. *National Power and the Structure of Foreign Trade*. Berkeley: University of California Press, 1946.

Hoadley, J. Stephen. "Small States as Aid Donors," *International Organization* 34 (Winter 1980).

Holderness, Clifford G. "Economic Analysis of the United Nations Code of Conduct for Liner Conferences," *Stanford Law Review* 29 (April 1977).

Hollick, Ann L. "Bureaucrats at Sea." *In* Ann L. Hollick and Robert E. Osgood, *New Era of Ocean Politics*. Baltimore: Johns Hopkins University Press, 1974.

——. *U.S. Foreign Policy and the Law of the Sea*. Princeton: Princeton University Press, 1981.

Holsti, Ole. "The Three-Headed Eagle: The United States and System

Change," *International Studies Quarterly* 32 (September 1979).

Holsti, Ole, and James N. Rosenau. "Vietnam, Consensus, and the Belief Systems of World Leaders," *World Politics* 32 (October 1979).

Horn, Norbert. "Codes of Conduct for MNEs and Transnational *Lex Mercatoria*: An International Process of Learning and Law Making." In Norbert Horn, ed., *Legal Problems of Codes of Conduct for Multinational Enterprises*. Antwerp: Kluwer, 1980.

Huntington, Samuel P. *Political Order in Changing Societies*. New Haven: Yale University Press, 1968.

―――. "Transnational Organizations in World Politics," *World Politics* 25 (April 1973).

Hurni, Bettina S. *The Lending Policy of the World Bank in the 1970s: Analysis and Evaluation*. Boulder, Colo.: Westview Press, 1980.

IBRD. See under International Bank for Reconstruction and Development, and World Bank.

ICAO. *Bulletin* (various issues).

―――. *Civil Aviation Statistics of the World* (various issues).

―――. *Digest of Statistics, Traffic* (various years).

―――. *Statistical Summary, Air Transport* (various years).

IDA. *Annual Report* (various years).

Independent Commission on International Development Issues (Brandt Commission). *North-South: A Program for Survival*. Cambridge: MIT Press, 1980.

Inter-American Development Bank (IADB). *Annual Report* (various years).

International Bank for Reconstruction and Development. *The International Bank for Reconstruction and Development, 1946–1953*. Baltimore: The Johns Hopkins Press, 1954.

IMF (International Monetary Fund). *Direction of Trade* (various issues).

―――. *International Financial Statistics* (various issues).

―――. *Survey* (various issues).

―――. *World Economic Outlook* (various issues).

International Nuclear Fuel Cycle Evaluation. *INFCE Summary Volume*. INFCE/PC 2. Vienna: International Atomic Energy Agency, 1980.

Jackson, Robert H., and Carl G. Rosberg. "Why Africa's Weak States Persist: The Empirical and the Juridical in Statehood," *World Politics* 35 (October 1982).

Jacobsen, Harold K., et al. "Revolutionaries or Bargainers? Negotiations for NIEO," *World Politics* 35 (April 1983).

Jekker, Rolf M. "Voting Rights of Less Developed Countries in the IMF," *Journal of World Trade Law* 12 (May–June 1978).

Jervis, Robert. "Security Regimes," *International Organization* 36 (Spring 1982).

Jodice, David. "Sources of Change in Third World Regimes for Foreign Direct Investment, 1968–1976," *International Organization* 34 (Spring 1980).

Jonsson, Christer. "Sphere of Flying: The Politics of International Aviation," *International Organization* 35 (Spring 1981).

Jowitt, Kenneth. *The Leninist Response to National Dependency.* Berkeley, Calif.: Institute of International Studies, 1978.

Joyner, Christopher C. "The Exclusive Economic Zone for Antarctica," *Virginia Journal of International Law* 21 (1981).

Katzenstein, Peter J. "Capitalism in One Country? Switzerland in the International Economy." *International Organization* 34 (Autumn 1980).

————. "The Small European State in the International Economy: Economic Dependence and Corporatist Politics." *In* John G. Ruggie, ed., *The Antinomies of Interdependence.* New York: Columbia University Press, 1983.

Katzenstein, Peter J., ed. *Between Power and Plenty.* Madison: University of Wisconsin Press, 1977.

Keohane, Robert O. *After Hegemony. Cooperation and Discord in the World Political Economy.* Princeton: Princeton University Press, 1984.

————. "The Demand for International Regimes," *International Organization* 36 (Spring 1982).

————. "Lilliputian Dilemmas: Small States in International Politics," *International Organization* 23 (Spring 1969).

————. "The Theory of Hegemonic Stability and Changes in International Economic Regimes, 1967–1977." *In* Ole R. Holsti, Randolph M. Siverson, Alexander L. George, *Change in the International System.* Boulder, Colo.: Westview Press, 1980.

Keohane, Robert O., and Joseph Nye, Jr. *Power and Interdependence.* Boston: Little-Brown, 1977.

————. "Transgovernmental Relations and International Organizations," *World Politics* 27 (October 1974).

Kindleberger, Charles P. *The Great Depression.* Berkeley, Los Angeles, London: University of California Press, 1973.

Klein, Robert A. *Sovereign Equality Among States: The History of an*

Idea. Toronto: University of Toronto Press, 1974.

Knudsen, Odin, and Andrew Parnes. *Trade Instability and Economic Development: An Empirical Study.* Lexington, Mass.: Lexington Books, D. C. Heath, 1975.

Korany, Bahgat. *Social Change, Charisma, and International Behavior: Toward a Theory of Foreign Policymaking in the Third World.* Leiden: A. W. Sijthoff, 1976.

Kotschnig, Walter M. "The United Nations as an Instrument of Economic and Social Development," *International Organization* 22 (Winter 1968).

Krasner, Stephen D. "Business-Government Relations: The Case of the International Coffee Agreement," *International Organization* 27 (Autumn 1973).

———. *"Defending the National Interest: Raw Materials Investments and U.S. Foreign Policy.* Princeton: Princeton University Press, 1978.

———. "Manipulating International Commodity Markets: Brazilian Coffee Policy 1906–1962," *Public Policy* 21 (Fall 1973).

———. "Oil Is the Exception," *Foreign Policy* 13 (Spring 1974).

———. "Power Structures and Regional Development Banks," *International Organization* 35 (Spring 1981).

———. "Regimes and the Limits of Realism: Regimes as Autonomous Variables," *International Organization* 36 (Spring 1982).

———. "State Power and the Structure of International Trade," *World Politics* 28 (April 1976).

———. "Structural Causes and Regime Consequences: Regimes as Intervening Variables," *International Organization* 36 (Spring 1982).

———. "U.S. Commercial and Monetary Policy: Unravelling the Paradox of External Strength and Internal Weakness," *International Organization* (Autumn 1977).

Kravis, Irving B., Alan W. Heston, and Robert Summers. "Real GDP Per Capita for More Than One Hundred Countries," *The Economic Journal* 88 (June 1978).

Krishnamuti, R. "UNCTAD as a Negotiating Institution," *Journal of World Trade Law* 15 (January/February 1981).

Kroloff, George M. "The View from Congress," *Journal of Communication* 29 (Winter 1979).

Krueger, Anne O. *Foreign Trade Regimes and Economic Development: Liberalization Attempts and Consequences.* Cambridge: Ballinger, 1978.

Kuznets, Simon. *National Income and Its Composition.* New York: National Bureau of Economic Research, 1954.

LaFeber, Walter. *America, Russia and the Cold War.* New York: John Wiley, 1976.

Lall, Sanjaya. "The Rise of Multinationals from the Third World," *Third World Quarterly* 5 (July 1983).

Laursen, Finn. "Security versus Access to Resources: Explaining a Decade of U.S. Ocean Policy." *World Politics* 34 (January 1982).

Lawrence, S. A. *International Sea Transport: The Years Ahead.* Lexington, Mass.: Lexington Books, D. C. Heath, 1972.

Leff, Nathaniel. "Multinationals in a Hostile World," *Wharton Magazine* 2 (Spring 1978).

Leontief, Wassily, et al. *The Future of the World Economy: A UN Study.* New York: Oxford University Press, 1977.

Levy, Walter J. "Oil and the Decline of the West," *Foreign Affairs* 58 (Summer 1980).

Lewis, W. Arthur. *The Evolution of the International Economic Order.* Princeton: Princeton University Press, 1978.

Liao, Kuang-Sheng. "Linkage Politics in China: Internal Mobilization and Articulated External Hostility in the Cultural Revolution 1967–1969," *World Politics* 28 (July 1976).

Libby, Ronald T. "External Co-optation of a Less Developed Country's Policy Making: The Case of Ghana, 1969–72," *World Politics* 29 (October 1976).

Lipson, Charles H. "Corporate Preferences and Public Choices: Foreign Aid Sanctions and Investment Protection," *World Politics* 28 (April 1976).

Lloyd's. *Register of Shipping* (1979).

Loehr, William, and John Powelson, *Threat to Development; Pitfalls of the NIEO.* Boulder, Colo.: Westview Press, 1983.

Lowenthal, Abraham. "Dateline Peru," *Foreign Policy* 38 (Spring 1980).

Luard, Evan. "Who Owns the Antarctic?" *Foreign Affairs* 62 (Summer 1984).

Lukes, Steven. *Power: A Radical View.* London: The Macmillan Press, 1974.

Mabry, Ralph T., Jr. "The Present International Nuclear Regime." *In* Joseph A. Yager with the assistance of Ralph T. Mabry, Jr., *International Cooperation in Nuclear Energy.* Washington, D.C.: Brookings Institution, 1981.

McCoy, Terry L. "Linkage Politics and Latin American Population Policies." *In* Terry L. McCoy, ed., *The Dynamics of Population Policy in Latin America.* Cambridge, Mass.: Ballinger, 1974.

McGraw, Marsha M. "The NPT Review Conference," *Arms Control Today* 11 (February 1981).

McLaughlin, Martin M. "The United States in the North-South Dialogue: A Survey." *In* Martin M. McLaughlin, *The United States and World Development, Agenda 1979.* New York: Praeger, for the Overseas Development Council, 1979.

McNamara, Robert S. *Address to the Board of Governors,* International Bank for Reconstruction and Development, October 2, 1979. Washington, D.C.: IBRD.

―――. "The Population Problem," *Foreign Affairs* 62 (Summer 1984).

Maddison, Angus. *Economic Progress and Policy in Developing Countries.* London: George Allen and Unwin, 1970.

Magdalent, Jean-Louis. "The Story of the Life and Death of the CAB Show Cause Order," *Air Law* 5 (1980).

Mahler, Vincent A. *Dependency Approaches to International Political Economy: A Cross-National Study.* New York: Columbia University Press, 1980.

Maier, Charles. "The Politics of Productivity," *In* Peter Kazenstein, ed., *Between Power and Plenty.* Madison: University of Wisconsin Press, 1977.

Marden, Parket G., et al. *Population in the Global Arena.* New York: Holt, Rinehart and Winston, 1982.

Mason, Edward S., and Robert E. Asher. *The World Bank Since Bretton Woods.* Washington, D.C.: Brookings Institution, 1973.

Meltzer, Ronald I. "Restructuring the United Nations System: Institutional Reform Efforts in the Context of North-South Relations," *International Organization* 32 (Autumn 1978).

Mikesell, Raymond F. "The Emergence of the World Bank as a Development Institution." *In* A. L. K. Acheson, J. F. Changt, and M. F. J. Prachowny, eds., *Bretton Woods Revisited.* Toronto: University of Toronto Press, 1972.

Miles, Edward. "Introduction." *Restructuring Ocean Regimes: Implications of the Third United Nations Conference on the Law of the Sea. International Organization* 31 (Spring 1977, Special Issue).

―――. "The Structure and Effects of the Decision Process in the Seabed Committee and the Third United Nations Conference on the Law of the Sea." *In* Edward Miles, ed., *Restructuring Ocean Regimes: Implications of the Third United Nations Conference on the Law of the Sea. International Organization* 31 (Spring 1977, Special Issue).

Miller, Debra L. "An Economic Appraisal of the Proposed Code of Conduct for Technology Transfer," *Aussenwirtschaft* 36 (1981).

Miller, Debra Lynn, and Joel Davidow. "Antitrust at the United Nations: A Tale of Two Codes," *Stanford Journal of International Law* 28 (Summer 1982).

Mitchell, B. R. *European Historical Statistics, 1750–1970.* Abridged Edition. New York: Columbia University Press, 1978.

Mitchell, Barbara. "Antarctica: A Special Case?" *New Scientist* 13 (January 1977).

Mitchell, Barbara, and Lee Kimball. "Conflict Over the Cold Continent," *Foreign Policy* 35 (Summer 1979).

Moore, John C. "The Hamburg Rules," *Journal of Maritime Law and Commerce* 10 (October 1978).

Moran, Theodore H. *Multinational Corporations and the Politics of Dependence: Copper in Chile.* Princeton: Princeton University Press, 1974.

—————. "Transnational Strategies of Protection and Defense by Multinational Corporations: Spreading the Risk and Raising the Cost for Nationalization in Natural Resources," *International Organization* 27 (Spring 1973).

Morawetz, David. *Twenty-five Years of Economic Development: 1950 to 1975.* Washington, D.C.: International Bank for Reconstruction and Development, 1977.

Morris, David. *Measuring the Condition of the World's Poor: The Physical Quality of Life Index.* New York: Pergamon, 1979.

Moulton, Anthony D. "On Concealed Dimensions of Third World Involvement in International Economic Organizations," *International Organization* 32 (Autumn, 1978).

Murphy, Craig N. "The Emergence of the New International Economic Order Ideology." Ph.D. diss. Department of Political Science, University of North Carolina, 1980.

Neff, Stephen C. "The UN Code of Conduct for Liner Conferences," *Journal of World Trade Law* 15 (September/October 1980).

Nettl, J. P. "The State As a Conceptual Variable," *World Politics* 20 (July 1968)

New York Times

Nye, Joseph S. "Maintaining a Nonproliferation Regime," *International Organization* 35 (Winter 1981).

———. *Should We Cut Our Losses? U.S. Foreign Policy and International Regimes.* Seattle: A Washington Sea Grant Publication, 1980.

———. "UNCTAD: Poor Nation's Pressure Group." *In* Robert W. Cox and Harold Jacobsen, eds., *The Anatomy of Influence: Decision Making in International Organizations.* New Haven: Yale University Press, 1973.

OECD. *Development and Cooperation* (various issues).

———. *DAC Review* (various issues).

———. *External Debt of Developing Countries, 1982 Survey.* Paris: OECD, 1982.

———. *The Flow of Financial Resources* (various issues).

———. *Geographic Distribution of Financial Flows to Developing Countries: Data on Disbursements* (various issues).

———. *International Investment and Multinational Enterprises: Recent International Direct Investment Trends.* Paris: OECD, 1981.

O'Flaherty, J. Daniel. "Finding Jamaica's Way," *Foreign Policy* 31 (Summer 1978).

O'Leary, James P. "Controlled Dis-Integration: Toward a Strategy for United States Foreign Economic Policy," *Comparative Strategy* 1 (1979).

Oliver, Robert W. *Early Plans for a World Bank.* Princeton Studies in International Finance, no. 29. International Finance Section, Princeton University. September 1971.

———. *International Economic Cooperation and the World Bank.* London: Macmillan, 1975.

Olson, Mancur. "Rapid Growth as a Destabilizing Force," *Journal of Economic History* 23 (December 1963).

Olson, Mancur, and Richard Zeckhauser. "An Economic Theory of Alliances," *The Review of Economics and Statistics* 48 (1966).

Organski, A. F. K., and Jacek Kugler. *The War Ledger.* Chicago: University of Chicago Press, 1980.

Oribe-Stemmer, Juan E. "Flag Preferences in Latin America," *Journal of Maritime Law and Commerce* 10 (October 1978).

Orton, Keith, and George Modelski. "Dependency Reversal: National Attributes and Systemic Processes." Paper prepared for delivery at the 20th Annual Convention of the International Studies Association in Toronto, Canada, March 21–24, 1979.

Overseas Development Council. *The United States and World Development Agenda for Action.* Washington, D.C. (various years).

Ozawa, Terutomo. *Multinationalism, Japanese Style: The Political Economy of Outward Dependency.* Princeton: Princeton University Press, 1979.

Paarlberg, Robert L. "Domesticating Global Management," *Foreign Affairs* 54 (April 1976).

Packenham, Robert A. *Liberal America and the Third World: Political Development Ideas in Foreign Aid and Social Science.* Princeton: Princeton University Press, 1973.

Pellicer, O. "Tercermundismo del Capitalismo Mexicano: Ideologia y Realidad." *Cuadernos Politicos* 3 (*Enero–Marzo*).

Peterson, M. J. "Antarctica: The Last Great Land Rush on Earth," *International Organization* 34 (Summer 1980).

———. "Antarctica." *In* Donald Puchala, ed., *Issues Before the 39th General Assembly.* New York: UNA-USA, 1984.

Pinto, M. C. W. "The International Community and Antarctica," *University of Miami Law Review* 33 (December 1978).

Plender, Richard. *International Migration Law.* Leiden: A. W. Sijthoff, 1972.

Prebisch, Raul. "Commercial Policy in the Underdeveloped Countries," *American Economic Review* 49 (May 1959).

Purcell, S. K., and J. F. H. Purcell. "State and Society in Mexico," *World Politics* 32 (January 1980).

Quester, George. "Preventing Proliferation: The Impact on International Politics," *International Organization* 35 (Winter 1981).

Quigg, Philip W. *A Pole Apart: The Emerging Issue of Antarctica.* New York: McGraw-Hill, 1983.

Ravenhill, Frederick J. *Asymmetrical Interdependence: The Lome Convention and North-South Relations.* Unpublished Ph.D. diss. University of California, Berkeley, 1981.

Richards, J. H. *International Economic Institutions.* London: Holt, Rinehart & Winston, 1970.

Richardson, Neil R. *Foreign Policy and Economic Dependence.* Austin: University of Texas Press, 1978.

Ringen, Stein. "Fruits of the United Nations: The Distribution of Development Aid," *Journal of Peace Research* (1974).

Roffe, P. "UNCTAD: Code of Conduct for the Transfer of Technology," *Journal of World Trade Law* 14 (March/April, 1980).

Rosenau, James N. "Pre-Theories and Theories of Foreign Policy." *In* R. Barry Farrell, ed., *Approaches to Comparative and International Politics.* Evanston, Ill.: Northwestern University Press, 1976.

Rothstein, Robert I. *Alliances and Small Powers.* New York: Columbia University Press, 1968.

——. *Global Bargaining: UNCTAD and the Quest for a New International Economic Order.* Princeton: Princeton University Press, 1979.

——. *The Third World and U.S. Foreign Policy: Cooperation and Conflict in the 1980s.* Boulder, Colo.: Westview Press, 1981.

——. *The Weak in the World of the Strong: The Developing Countries in the International System.* New York: Columbia University Press, 1977.

Ruggie, John Gerard. "Collective Goods and Future International Collaboration," *American Political Science Review* 66 (September 1972).

——. "International Regimes, Transactions and Change: Embedded Liberalism in the Postwar Economic Order," *International Organization* 36 (Spring 1982).

——. "On the Problem of the 'Global Problematique': What Role for International Organizations?" *Alternatives* V (May 1980).

Russett, Bruce. "The Marginal Utility of Income Transfers to the Third World," *International Organization* 32 (Autumn 1978).

Sabel, Charles. *Work and Politics: The Division of Labor in Industry.* Cambridge: Cambridge University Press, 1982.

Salas, Rafael M. *International Population Assistance: The First Decade.* New York: Pergamon, 1979.

Sauvant, Karl P. "Toward the New International Economic Order." *In* Karl P. Sauvant and Hajo Hasenpflug, *The New International Economic Order: Confrontation or Cooperation Between North and South?* Boulder, Colo.: Westview Press, 1977.

Scully, R. Tucker. "The Marine Living Resources of the Southern Ocean." *University of Miami Law Review* 33 (December 1978).

Selvig, Erling. "The Hamburg Rules, the Hague Rules and Maritime Insurance Practice," *Journal of Maritime Law and Commerce* 12 (April 1981).

Sepulveda, I. "Structural Constraints on Recent Mexican Foreign Economic Policy: Bilateralism or Multilateralism?" Unpublished paper. Department of Political Science, UCLA, Spring 1979.

Sewell, John W. *The United States and World Development: Agenda 1977.* New York: Praeger, 1977.

Shapley, Deborah. "Antarctic Problems: Tiny Krill to Usher in New Resource Era," *Science* 196 (April 1977).

Sheehan, Glen, and Mike Hopkins. *Basic Needs Performance: An Analysis of Some International Data.* Geneva: International Labour Office, 1979.

Shils, Edward. "Ideology: The Concept and Function of Ideology." *International Encyclopedia of the Social Sciences,* vol. 7. New York: Macmillan, 1968.

Singer, Hans W. "The Distribution of Gains Between Investing and Borrowing Countries," *American Economic Review* 40 (May 1950).

Singer, J. David, and Melvin Small. *The Wages of War, 1816–1965.* New York: John Wiley, 1972.

Singer, Marshall R. *Weak States in a World of Powers: The Dynamics of International Relationships.* New York: Free Press, 1972.

Skelton, James W., Jr. "UNCTAD's Draft Code of Conduct on the Transfer of Technology: A Critique," *Vanderbilt Journal of Transnational Law* 14 (Spring 1981).

Smyth, Douglas C. "The Global Economy and the Third World: Coalition or Cleavage?" *World Politics* 29 (July 1977).

Soroos, Marvin S. "The Commons in the Sky: The Radio Spectrum and Geosynchronous Orbits as Issues in Global Policy," *International Organization* 36 (Summer 1982).

Southard, Frank A., Jr. *The Evolution of the International Monetary Fund.* Essays in International Finance, no. 135. Princeton: International Finance Section, Princeton University, 1979.

Stein, Arthur A. "Coordination and Collaboration: Regimes in an Anarchic World," *International Organization* 36 (Spring 1982).

Stein, Arthur A., and Bruce Russett. "Evaluating War: Outcomes and Consequences." *In* Ted Robert Gurr, ed., *Handbook of Conflict Theory and Research.* New York: Free Press, 1980.

Stevenson, John R. "Legal Regulation of Mineral Exploitation of the Deep Seabed," *Department of State Bulletin,* vol. 65, no. 1672 (July 12, 1971).

Stone, Jeffrey E. "International Agreements: Antarctic Resources," *Harvard International Law Journal* 22 (Winter 1981).

Story, Dale. "Trade Politics in the Third World: A Case Study of the Mexican GATT Decision," *International Organization* 36 (Autumn 1982).

Strange, Susan. "Who Runs World Shipping?" *International Affairs*

(London) 52 (July 1976).

Stycos, J. Mayone. "Politics and Population Control in Latin America." *In* Terry L. McCoy, ed., *The Dynamics of Population Policy in Latin America*. Cambridge, Mass: Ballinger, 1974.

Sunkel, Osvaldo. "Big Business and *Dependencia*: A Latin American View," *Foreign Affairs* 50 (April 1972).

Swing, John Temple. "Who Will Own the Oceans?" *Foreign Affairs* 54 (April 1976).

Taubenfeld, Howard J. "A Treaty for Antarctica," *International Conciliation*, no. 531 (January 1961).

Thomas, George M., and John W. Meyer. "Regime Changes and State Power in an Intensifying World-State System, 1980." *In* A. Bergesen, ed., *Studies of the Modern World System*. New York: Academic Press, 1980.

Trakman, Leon E. "The Evolution of the Law Merchant: Our Commercial Heritage," Part I and Part II, *Journal of Maritime Law and Commerce* 12 (October 1980, January 1981).

Tschoegl, Adrian. *The Regulation of Foreign Banks in Countries Other Than the United States*, Working Paper No. 233, Division of Research, Graduate School of Business Administration, University of Michigan (August 1980).

Tucker, Robert W. *The Inequality of Nations*. New York: Basic Books, 1977.

———. "A New International Order?" *Commentary* 59 (February 1975).

Ungar, Sanford J. "Dateline West Africa," *Foreign Policy* 32 (Fall 1978).

United Kingdom, Board of Trade, Committee of Inquiry into Shipping, *Report* (May 1970).

U.N. *Human Rights International Instruments*. New York: 1982.

U.N. *Statistical Yearbook* (various years).

U.N. *A Study of the Capacity of the United Nations Development System (Jackson Report)*. E. 70. I. 10. Geneva, 1969.

U.N. *Transnational Corporations in World Development: A Re-Examination*, E/C.10/38. March 1978.

U.N. *Yearbook* (various years).

UNCTAD. *Monthly Bulletin* (various issues).

UNCTAD. *Report of the Ad Hoc Intergovernmental Working Group on the Economic Consequences of the Existence or Lack of a Genuine Link Between Vessel and Flag of Registry on Its Second Session*. TD/B/784 (February 8, 1980).

—— *Report of the United Nations Conference on a Convention on International Multimodal Transport on Its Resumed Session, 8 to 23 May 1980*, TD/MT/CONF/16/Add. 1 (August 22, 1980).

—— *Report of the United Nations Conference on a Convention on International Multimodal Transport, Part Two, 12 to 30 November 1979* TD/MT/CONF/12/Add. 1 (January 15, 1980).

—— *United Nations Convention on International Multimodal Transport of Goods.* Adopted 24 May 1980. TD/MT/CONF/16 (June 10, 1980).

UNCTAD Trade and Development Board. *Review of Recent Trends and Developments in Trade in Manufactures and Semi-Manufactures.* TD/B/C.2/190 (March 21, 1978).

UNCTAD Trade and Development Board, Committee on Shipping. *Economic Consequences of the Existence of Lack of a Genuine Link Between Vessel and Flag of Registry: Report by the Secretariat.* TD/B/C.4/168 (March 10, 1977).

—— *Merchant Fleet Development: Control by Transnational Corporations Over Dry Bulk Cargo Movements.* Report by the UNCTAD Secretariat. TD/B/C.4/204 (May 20, 1980).

—— *Report of the Ad Hoc Intergovernmental Working Group on the Economic Consequences of the Existence or Lack of a Genuine Link Between Vessel and Flag of Registry.* TD/B/C.4/177 (March 16, 1978).

—— *Review of Maritime Transport, 1979.* TD/B/C.4/198 (May 22, 1980).

U.N. Centre on Transnational Corporations. *Transnational Corporations in World Development, Third Survey.* ST/CTC/46. New York, 1983.

U.N. Development Program. *A Graphic Picture of Its Operations.* Circa 1974.

—— . *Report of the Administrator* (various issues).

—— . *United Nations Capital Development Fund, Annual Report of the Administrator* (various issues).

—— . *The United Nations Development Program: Questions and Answers.* September 1975.

—— . *The United Nations Development Program: Why, What, How, Where.* 1977.

—— . *United Nations Revolving Fund for Natural Resources Exploration: Operational Procedures and Administrative Arrangements.* DP/142 (October 1975).

—— . *United Nations Revolving Fund for Natural Resources Explora-*

tion. DP/368 (April 1979).

U.N. Economic and Social Council, Commission on Transnational Corporations, *Transnational Corporations in World Development: A Re-Examination*, E/C.10/38. New York: March 20, 1978.

U.N. Economic and Social Council, Commission on Transnational Corporations, Sixth Session, Mexico City 23 June–4 July 1980. (1) *Issues Arising from Decisions Taken by the General Assembly and the Economic and Social Council:* (2) *Progress Made Toward the Establishment of the New International Economic Order:* (3) *The Role of Transnational Corporations. Report of the Secretariat.* E/C.10/74 (May 16, 1980).

U.S. Central Intelligence Agency. *Non-OPEC LDCs: External Debt.* Washington, D.C.

U.S. Civil Aeronautics Board. *Report to Congress. Annual Report* (1978). Washington, D.C.: U.S. Government Printing Office.

U.S. Congress, House, Committee on Appropriations, Hearings. *Foreign Assistance and Related Agencies Appropriations for 1978.* 95th Congress, 1st session, 1977.

U.S. Congress, House, Committee on Appropriations, Hearings. *Foreign Assistance and Related Agencies Appropriations for 1979.* 95th Congress, 2d session, 1978.

U.S. Congress, House, Committee on Appropriations, Hearings. *Foreign Assistance and Related Agencies Appropriations for 1979*, Part 5, "An Assessment of the Effectiveness of the World Bank and the Inter-American Development Bank in Aiding the Poor," 95th Congress, 2d session, 1978.

U.S. Congress, House, Committee on Appropriations, Hearings. *Foreign Assistance and Related Programs Appropriations for 1980.* 96th Congress, 1st session, 1979.

U.S. Congress, House, Committee on Foreign Affairs. *The U.S. and Multilateral Development Banks.*

U.S. Congress, House, Committee on Foreign Affairs, Hearings. *U.S. Foreign Policy and the Law of the Sea.* 97th Congress, 2d session, 1982.

U.S. Congress, House, Committee on Governmental Affairs, *Nuclear Proliferation Factbook* (various issues).

U.S. Congress, Senate, Committee on Appropriations. Hearings on HR 12931. *Foreign Assistance and Related Programs Appropriations for Fiscal Year 1979.* 95th Congress, 2d session, 1978.

U.S. Congress, Senate, Committee on Commerce. *The Economic Value of Ocean Resources to the United States.* 93d Congress, 2d session, 1974.

U.S. Congress, Senate, Committee on Foreign Relations, Hearings. *Exploitation of Antarctic Resources.* 95th Congress, 2d session, 1978.

U.S. Congress, Senate, Committee on Government Operations. *U.S. Participation in International Organizations.* 95th Congress, 1st session, 1977.

U.S. National Advisory Council on International Financial and Monetary Policies, *Annual Report* (various years).

U.S. State Department. *Bulletin* (various issues).

U.S. State Department. *Current Policy* (various issues).

U.S. State Department. *U.S. Contributions to International Organizations* (various years).

U.S. State Department. *U.S. Participation in International Organizations* (various years).

U.S. Treasury Department. *Treasury News* (various issues).

U.S. Treasury Department. *United States Participation in the Multilateral Development Banks in the 1980s.* Washington, D.C.: 1982.

Vance, Cyrus R. "America's Commitment to Third World Development," Department of State *Bulletin*, vol 79, no. 2026 (1979).

————. "America's Growing Relationship with the Developing World," Department of State *Bulletin*, vol 79. no. 2030 (1979).

Varon, Bension, and Kenji Takeuchi. "Developing Countries and Non-Fuel Minerals," *Foreign Affairs* 52 (April 1974).

Vernon, Raymond. *Sovereignty at Bay.* New York: Basic Books, 1971.

————. *Storm Over the Multinationals: The Real Issues.* Cambridge: Harvard University Press, 1977.

Viner, Jacob. "Power Versus Plenty as Objectives of Foreign Policy in the Seventeenth and Eighteenth Centuries." *World Politics* 1 (1948).

Vital, David. *The Inequality of States: A Study of the Small Power in International Relations.* Oxford: Oxford University Press, 1967.

Wall Street Journal.

Waltz, Kenneth. *Man, the State, and War.* New York: Columbia University Press, 1964.

————. *Theory of International Relations.* Reading, Mass.: Addison-Wesley, 1979.

Washington Post

Wassermann, Ursula. "Law of the Sea Convention Adopted," *Journal of World Trade Law* 16 (1982).

————. "UNCLOS: 1981 Session," *Journal of World Trade Law* 16 (1982).

Weaver, James H. *The International Development Association: A New Approach to Foreign Aid.* New York: Praeger, 1965.

Weber, Max. *Economy and Society: An Outline of Interpretive Sociology.* Berkeley, Los Angeles, London: University of California Press, 1978.

Wells, Louis T., Jr. *Third World Multinationals: The Rise of Foreign Investment from Developing Countries.* Cambridge: MIT Press, 1983.

Weinstein, Franklin B. *Indonesian Foreign Policy and the Dilemma of Dependence: From Sukarno to Soeharto.* Ithaca: Cornell University Press, 1976.

————. "The Uses of Foreign Policy in Indonesia: An Approach to the Analysis of Foreign Policy in the Less Developed Countries," *World Politics* 24 (April 1972).

Wenig, Michael M. *Structure and Process as Determinants of Oceans Regime Change: Power, Cognition and the Law of the Sea.* Unpublished B.A. Honors Thesis. Department of Political Science, Stanford University, June 1982.

Wenk, Edward, Jr. *The Politics of the Ocean.* Seattle: University of Washington Press, 1972.

Weston, Burns H. "The Charter of Economic Rights and Duties of States and the Deprivation of Foreign-Owned Wealth," *The American Journal of International Law* 75 (1981).

White, John. *Regional Development Banks: The Asian, African, and Inter-American Development Banks.* New York: Praeger, 1972.

Whiting, Van R., Jr. "State Intervention in the Mexican Economy: The Regulation of Foreign Direct Investment and Technology Transfer." Mimeo. Department of Political Science, University of California, Berkeley, 1981.

Wijkman, Per Magnus. "Managing the Global Commons," *International Organization* 36 (Summer 1982).

————. "UNCLOS and the Redistribution of Ocean Wealth," *Journal of World Trade Law* 16 (Jan.–Feb. 1982).

Wilkens, Mira. *The Emergence of Multinational Enterprise: American Business Abroad from the Colonial Era to 1914.* Cambridge: Harvard University Press, 1970.

Wilkie, James W. *The Narrowing Gap: Primary Social Change in the Americas.* Los Angeles: UCLA Latin American Center, forthcoming.

Willard, Matthew R. "Understanding the Landsat Market in Developing

Countries." Report no. 30, Program in Information Policy, Engineering-Economic Systems Department, Stanford University, November 1980.

———. *Political Determinants of Technological Change: Remote Sensing of Earth Resources from Space*. Ph.D. diss. Stanford University, 1983.

Willetts, Peter. *The Non-Aligned Movement: The Origins of a Third World Alliance*. London: Frances Pinter; New York: Nichols Publishing Co., 1978.

Williamson, John. *The Lending Policies of the International Monetary Fund*. Washington, D.C.: Institute for International Economics, August 1982.

———. "SDRs: The Link." *In* Jagdish N. Bhagwati, ed., *The New International Economic Order: The North-South Debate*. Cambridge, Mass.: MIT Press, 1977.

Williamson, John, ed. *IMF Conditionality*. Washington, D.C.: Institute for International Economics, 1983.

Wilson, Gregory P. "Antarctica, the Southern Ocean, and the Law of the Sea," *The JAG Journal* 30 (Summer 1978).

World Bank. See also International Bank for Reconstruction and Development.

World Bank. *Annual Report* (various years).

World Bank. *IDA in Retrospect*. New York: Oxford University Press, 1982.

World Bank. *World Bank Atlas* (various years).

World Bank. *World Development Report* (various years).

World Bank. *World Tables*, 1st ed. (1976); 2d ed. (1980); 3d ed. (1983).

World Business Weekly (various issues).

Woytinsky, W. S., and E. S. Woytinsky. *World Population and Production Trends and Outlook*. New York: Twentieth Century Fund, 1953.

Wriggins, W. Howard. "Third World Strategies for Change: The Political Context of North-South Interdependence." *In* W. Howard Wriggins and Gunnar Adler-Karlsson, *Reducing Global Inequities*. New York: McGraw-Hill, 1978.

Yager, Joseph A., with the assistance of Ralph T. Mabry, Jr. *International Cooperation in Nuclear Energy*. Washington, D.C.: Brookings Institution, 1981.

Yale Law Journal 87 (1978). "Thaw in International Law?"

Yoffie, David B. *Power and Protectionism*. New York: Columbia University Press, 1983.

————. "The Newly Industrializing Countries and the Political Economy of Protectionism," *International Studies Quarterly* 25 (December 1981).

Young, Oran. "International Regimes: Problems of Concept Formation," *World Politics* 32 (April).

Zvobgo, Eddison J. M. "A Third World View." *In* Donald P. Kommers and Gilbert D. Loescher, eds., *Human Rights and American Foreign Policy*. Indiana: University of Notre Dame Press, 1979.

Zysman, John, and Stephen Cohen. "Open Trade and Competitive Industry," *Foreign Affairs* 61 (Summer 1983).

Index

Designer:	UC Press Staff
Compositor:	Prestige Typography
Printer:	Maple-Vail Book Mfg. Group
Binder:	Maple-Vail Book Mfg. Group
Text:	10/13 Stempel Garamond
Display:	Stempel Garamond